# Yearbook of International Humanitarian Law

Volume 16

More information about this series at http://www.springer.com/series/8912

Terry D. Gill
General Editor

# Yearbook of International Humanitarian Law Volume 16, 2013

ASSER PRESS    CAMBRIDGE UNIVERSITY PRESS    Springer

*General Editor*
Terry D. Gill
Professor of Military Law
University of Amsterdam and Netherlands Defence Academy
Amsterdam/Breda
The Netherlands

Cover Photo: © CICR/VII/HAVIV, Ron Haïti—Prison in Port au Prince

ISBN 978-94-6265-037-4 ISBN 978-94-6265-038-1 (eBook)
DOI 10.1007/978-94-6265-038-1


This Volume is also available as a journal product through Cambridge University Press. In addition to the electronic version published on www.springerlink, the Yearbook is also available online through the Cambridge Journals Online service.
Published by T.M.C. ASSER PRESS, The Hague, The Netherlands www.asserpress.nl
Produced and distributed for T.M.C. ASSER PRESS by Springer-Verlag Berlin Heidelberg



Printed on acid-free paper

Springer is part of Springer Science+Business Media (www.springer.com)

# Contents

In order to make the *Correspondents' Reports* immediately and widely accessible, they are now available online at

www.asser.nl/YIHL/correspondentsreports

This brings the added benefit of making them fully searchable, thereby more easily serving the needs of scholars and practitioners.

# Part I
# Detention in Non-International Armed Conflict

# Chapter 1
# The Copenhagen Process: Principles and Guidelines

**Jacques Hartmann**

**Abstract** This article analyses the outcome of the 'Copenhagen Process on the Handling of Detainees in International Military Operations': a five-year multi-stakeholder effort to develop principles and good practices on detention in international military operations. The Process concluded in 2012 when 18 States 'welcomed' a set of non-binding 'Principles and Guidelines.' The Principles and Guidelines address uncertainties surrounding the legal basis for the detention, treatment, and transfer of detainees during international military operations, drawing on both human rights and international humanitarian law. This article comments on the Principles and Guidelines, shedding some light on the context in which they were developed and adopted.

**Keywords** Copenhagen process · Detention · International military operations · International armed conflicts · Non-international armed conflicts · Human rights

## Contents



---

The author is grateful for comments and suggestions provided by the peer and other anonymous reviewers.

---

J. Hartmann (✉)
School of Law, University of Dundee, Dundee DD1 4HN, UK
e-mail: jhartmann@dundee.ac.uk

 
T.D. Gill et al. (eds.), *Yearbook of International Humanitarian Law 2013*,
Yearbook of International Humanitarian Law 16, DOI 10.1007/978-94-6265-038-1_1

## 1.1 Introduction

The changing nature of international military operations has engendered increasing uncertainty on the law applicable to detention when governmental armed forces operate abroad. The 1949 Geneva Conventions[1] contain detailed rules on detention in international armed conflicts.[2] However, many modern military operations are fundamentally different from the armed conflicts that the Geneva Conventions were primarily established to regulate. The past decades have seen a significant change in the character of international military operations, which have:

> […] developed from traditional peacekeeping operations […] through peacemaking operations […] to a new type of operation in which military forces are acting in support of governments that need assistance to stabilise their countries or in support of the international administration of territory.[3]

A common feature of modern military engagement in foreign countries is that they rarely involve the use of force between States. Not only do these new kind of military operations often not satisfy the conditions of an 'international armed conflict',[4] but they may not even reach the threshold of a 'non-international armed conflict', which requires a certain intensity of fighting and organisation of the parties involved.[5] As a result, armed forces on missions abroad are seldom involved in conflicts falling within the general scope of the Geneva Conventions, and they may not even fall within the scope of Common Article 3, which sets forth a minimum core of mandatory rules of international humanitarian law.[6] Armed forces on missions abroad may, in other words, de facto operate outside the scope of the

---

[1] Convention for the Amelioration of the Condition of the Wounded and Sick in Armed Forces in the Field, opened for signature 12 August 1949, 75 UNTS 31 (entered into force 21 October 1950) (hereinafter: GCI), Article 2; Convention for the Amelioration of the Condition of Wounded, Sick and Shipwrecked Members of Armed Forces at Sea, opened for signature 12 August 1949, 75 UNTS 85 (entered into force 21 October 1950) (hereinafter: GCII), Article 2; Convention relative to the Treatment of Prisoners of War, opened for signature 12 August 1949, 75 UNTS 135 (entered into force 21 October 1950) (hereinafter: GCIII), Article 2; Convention relative to the Protection of Civilian Persons in Time of War, opened for signature 12 August 1949, 75 UNTS 287 (entered into force 21 October 1950) (hereinafter: GCIV).

[2] ICRC 2012, p. 3.

[3] Ministry of Foreign Affairs of Denmark 2007, p. 363.

[4] Cf. Common Article 2 of the 1949 Geneva Conventions.

[5] Cf. ICTY, *Prosecutor v. Limaj*, Judgment Trial Chamber (IT-03-66-T), 30 November 2005, para 90; ICTY, *Prosecutor v. Haradinaj* et al., Judgment Trial Chamber (IT-04-84-T), 3 April 2008, paras 39–100.

[6] ICTY, *Prosecutor v. Zejnil Delalic* et al., Judgment Appeals Chamber (IT-96-21-A), 20 February 2001, para 143. On Common Article 3 see generally Pejic 2011b.

legal framework that traditionally regulates the operation of armed forces, viz. international humanitarian law.

While such missions may not always involve the use of force, they often involve detention. In fact, detention is common in contemporary military operations, many of which are 'law and order operations', where governmental armed forces are sent to establish, maintain, or restore the rule of law. In law and order operations, foreign armed forces are often asked to act in support of governments in need of assistance to stabilise their countries, filling a governmental and institutional void. Whilst offering such support, armed forces are frequently required to act as police or conduct tasks normally performed by domestic authorities. These tasks may include arrest and detention.

There is widespread disagreement on the applicable rules on detention in this kind of operations. The right to liberty is widely protected under both domestic and international law. The Geneva Conventions explicitly regulate detention in international armed conflicts, whereas human rights law applies both in times of peace and during armed conflict.[7] But the law applicable to operations such as the Multinational Force in Iraq,[8] the International Security Assistance Force (ISAF) in Afghanistan,[9] and the United Nations Interim Administration Mission in Kosovo (UNMIK)[10] is or was contentious. The contention concerns a range of legal issues, including the legal basis for detention, applicable procedures, and rules for the treatment and transfer of detainees. As a result, the answer to the apparently simple question, 'what rules apply to detention when military forces are operating abroad?' is often complicated, and disagreement may hamper cooperation among troop-contributing States.

To address these legal uncertainties, in 2007 the Danish Government initiated an *ad hoc* diplomatic process, called the 'Copenhagen Conference on the Handling of Detainees in International Military Operations'.[11] The Process was aimed at bringing major troop-contributing States together to discuss uncertainties surrounding the legal basis for detention, and the treatment and transfer of detainees during international military operations not reaching the threshold of an international armed conflict.

---

[7] See for example ICJ, *Legality of the Threat or Use of Nuclear Weapons*, Advisory Opinion, (1996) ICJ Rep 226, para 25; ICJ, *Legal Consequences of the Construction of a Wall in the Occupied Palestinian Territory*, Advisory Opinion, (2004) ICJ Rep 136, paras 134–137; ICJ, *Case Concerning Armed Activities on the Territory of the Congo (Democratic Republic of the Congo v. Uganda)*, Judgment, (2005) ICJ Rep 168, paras 216–219.

[8] The presence of the Multinational Force in Iraq had been mandated by a succession of UNSC Resolutions since 2003. See UNSC Resolutions 1511 (2003), 1546 (2004), 1637 (2005), and 1723 (2006). Annexed to UNSC Res. 1541 (2004) was a letter by the Prime Minister of the Interim Government of Iraq requesting the Security Council to extend the mandate of the multinational force in Iraq.

[9] ISAF was established by UNSC Res. 1386 (2001). Annexed to UNSC Res. 1386 was a letter by the acting Minister of Foreign Affairs of the Interim Afghan Authority consenting to the deployment of the multinational force in Afghanistan.

[10] The mandate for UNMIK was established by UNSC Res. 1244 (1999).

[11] Hereinafter referred to as the 'Copenhagen Process' or 'Process'.

'International military operations' is not a term of art. Neither was the term defined during the Copenhagen Process. Rather, the term was used as a catch-all phrase covering everything from 'peacekeeping' and 'peace enforcement' to a new type of operations where military forces are sent to support foreign governments in need of assistance. These kinds of situations have been described in the literature as 'multinational non-international armed conflicts'.[12] But the term 'international military operation' is even broader, encompassing operations that do not reach the threshold of an armed conflict. The term could, for instance, describe peacekeeping operations authorised by the United Nations, or other military operations where there is only a limited use of force.[13] The Copenhagen Process therefore had a wide scope, including international operations conducted under the authority of the United Nations or regional organisations, as well as military operations by individual or coalitions of States, for example as a result of an invitation from a foreign government.[14]

This article explains how the Copenhagen Process attempted to address uncertainties surrounding detention in international military operations, by analysing its outcome and making some predictions about its impact. The article opens with an overview of legal questions arising with regard to detention in international military operations and their effect on cooperation between troop-contributing States. The Copenhagen Process is then introduced, shedding light on how the Principles and Guidelines were developed and adopted. The subsequent sections comment on the substance of the Principles and Guidelines and their legal status. The conclusions provide some reflections on the overall outcome of the Copenhagen Process, making some predictions on its impact on the law on detention in international military operations.

## 1.2 The Complexity of the Law Applicable to Detention

A non-paper from 2007 presented at the beginning of the Copenhagen Process described the law applicable to international military operations as a 'complex web of international humanitarian law and/or human rights law'.[15] This complexity is largely due to the overlap between these two areas of law, and disagreement on how they interact. There is, in addition, a significant variation in the legal obligations of States. Of the four Geneva Conventions, only the first has been universally ratified.[16]

---

12 Pejic 2011b, pp. 5–9.

13 On detention in peacekeeping missions, see Oswald 2011.

14 Such as the recent French intervention in Mali in January 2013. On the problems of detention, see, e.g., Le Monde, Guerre au Mali: que faire des prisonniers djihadistes? (8 March 2013), available at: http://www.lemonde.fr/afrique/article/2013/03/08/guerre-au-mali-que-faire-des-prisonniers-djihadistes_1845394_3212.html. Accessed 14 April 2014.

15 Ministry of Foreign Affairs of Denmark 2007, p. 371.

16 As of December 2012 GCI had 194 State parties. GCII had 174 parties whereas GCIII and GCIV had 166 parties. For a list of ratifications, see ICRC Annual Report 2012, p. 550.

Similarly, most human rights treaties have not achieved universal ratification.[17] As a result, the human rights obligations of troop-contributing States in international military operations are far from uniform.

Even when States are parties to the same international treaties, their international obligations may vary. Reservations, for example, add an additional element of complexity.[18] Even where there are no reservations and the applicable law is the same, significant differences have emerged in the interpretation of human rights treaties.[19] The outcome is a wide variation in the legal positions held by States participating in international military operations.

As a result, the standards applicable to detention in international military operations may vary greatly, depending on the nationality of the military personnel responsible for a person's detention. Far from being a trivial point, this conundrum may greatly affect cooperation in international military operations, exerting a 'chilling effect' on the willingness of States to participate, and 'on what they are prepared to allow their armed forces to do when they do participate.'[20] Reportedly, coalition forces in Afghanistan not only interpreted their international obligations differently, but also had 'radically different approaches to international law itself'.[21] Former Legal Adviser for the United States (US) Department of State, John B. Bellinger III, has voiced frustration over European States:

> [...] go[ing] to great lengths to avoid detaining anybody because their soldiers carry on their backs with them the International Covenant on Civil and Political Rights or the European Convention on Human Rights.[22]

The 2007 non-paper emphasised how such differences present a practical day-to-day challenge for soldiers in the field, as well as a political challenge for States participating to international military efforts.[23] In turn, these challenges may have a

[17] The 1966 International Covenant on Civil and Political Rights (hereinafter: ICCPR) has 168 parties. Other human rights instruments have even fewer. See United Nations Treaty Series Online Collection, available at: https://treaties.un.org. Accessed 14 April 2014.

[18] One example is the United Kingdom, which has entered reservations to Article 10 ICCPR and to Article 37(c) of the Convention on the 1989 Rights of the Child, provisions that require juveniles to be detained separately from adults. Reservations to human rights treaties are controversial, but far from uncommon. See, e.g., ILC Report 2011, especially, Principles 3.1.5.6 and 3.2.

[19] Wood 2008, p. 143.

[20] Ibid. Many States have grappled with the issue of detention in international armed conflict. Referring to the case studies of Israel in Lebanon (2008), the Second Congo War (1998–2003) and the South Ossetian Conflict (2008), Elizabeth Wilmshurst confirms 'the difficulty which arises from the lack of clear rules in non-international armed conflicts, particular regarding the grounds for detention and procedural safeguards.' Wilmshurst 2012, p. 498. Ministry of Foreign Affairs of Denmark 2007, pp. 363–392.

[21] Hampson 2012, p. 266. See also House of Commons Defence Committee 2014, para 28.

[22] Bellinger 2012.

[23] Ibid, p. 263.

negative impact on the ability of the military force to engage in certain types of operations and on the general efficiency of international military operations.[24]

The intricacies of the legal framework applicable to international military operations[25] may be imputed to three main complicating factors, namely: the classification of armed conflicts, an uncertain interaction between human rights and international human rights law, and differences between States' international obligations. The following sections explain how these elements contribute to create uncertainty in the law. The aim is not to give an exhaustive account of the legal framework applicable to international military operations, but to illustrate the inadequacy and complexity of the legal landscape in which the Copenhagen Process was established, as well as to provide a benchmark against which to measure its outcomes.

### *1.2.1 The Classification of Armed Conflicts*

The first complicating factor in establishing the legal framework applicable to detention in a given international military operation is the distinction between international and non-international armed conflict. As a matter of treaty law, the difference between the two types of conflict is vast.[26]

The Geneva Conventions only apply to armed conflicts between 'two or more' High Contracting Parties, thus limiting their scope to conflicts between States.[27] This means that the bulk of their provisions do not apply in non-international armed conflicts or international military operations, as defined above.

While some have argued that the distinction between international and non-international armed conflict should be discarded,[28] States have been reluctant to do so.[29] The Copenhagen Process provided yet another manifestation of States' resolve to maintain the traditional distinction,[30] with critical implications on the rules of detention.

---

[24] In this regard, see also House of Commons Defence Committee 2013, pp. 14–21.

[25] For a fuller analysis, see Pejic 2005; Bellinger and Padmanabhan 2011; Dörmann 2012; Krieger 2011; ICRC 2011; ICRC 2012.

[26] It should be noted that the ICRC Customary International Humanitarian Law Study identifies 161 rules as part of customary international law, most of which are said to apply both in international and non-international armed conflicts, including Rule 128 that specifically addresses detention as well as several rules prohibiting various forms of ill treatment. Henckaerts and Doswald-Beck 2005a. The study has, however, been subject to criticism and States have not necessarily accepted all of its conclusions.

[27] Cf. Common Article 2 to the 1949 Geneva Conventions.

[28] See, e.g., Crawford 2007.

[29] Akande 2012, p. 37.

[30] While the adopted Principles and Guidelines may blur the line between international and non-international armed conflicts the Parties clearly wished to maintain the traditional distinction. Cf. preambular paras VII and IX.

While the Geneva Conventions address the issue of detention in great detail,[31] the only provision applicable in non-international armed conflict is Common Article 3. This provision establishes minimum rules for human treatment, without specifically addressing detention. The only international humanitarian law provisions addressing detention in non-international armed conflict are Articles 4–6 of Additional Protocol II.[32] The purpose of Article 5 is to ensure that conditions of detention for persons whose liberty has been restricted be reasonable,[33] but none of the provisions provides any explicit legal basis for detention or procedural safeguards. According to the International Committee of the Red Cross (ICRC), these provisions 'do not provide sufficient guidance to detaining authorities on how an adequate detention regime may be created and operated.'[34] Additional Protocol II is, moreover, limited to situations where a State is engaged in an armed conflict on its own territory against an armed group that controls part of that territory.[35]

As is clear from this short overview, the classification of an armed conflict makes a significant difference with regard to the law the applicable to detention in international military operations. However, the classification of armed conflicts is not straightforward, as States do not always agree whether a specific situation reaches the threshold of an international or non-international armed conflict and, as a consequence, they may not agree on the applicable law.

Determining whether an armed conflict exists between two States is essentially a factual question. In most cases this determination is uncomplicated.[36] In contrast, determining when a situation reaches the threshold of a non-international armed conflict is more difficult, partly because of the complex and often highly politicised nature of such conflicts.[37] In addition, different types of conflicts may exist in different parts of a State, resulting in the applicability of distinct rules.[38] As explained in the 2007 non-paper:

> [...] during the same operation in the same country, the soldier may at one time be in an international armed conflict and at another time be in a non-international armed conflict or even outside the scope of an armed conflict [...] Consequently both the soldier and the legal adviser may be unclear as to which rules of international humanitarian law apply, if any.[39]

---

[31] The 1949 Geneva Conventions contain more than 175 provisions on detention. Cf. ICRC 2012, p. 3.

[32] Protocol Additional to the Geneva Conventions of 12 August 1949, and Relating to the Protection of Victims of Non-International Armed Conflicts, opened for signature 12 December 1977, 1125 UNTS 609 (entered into force 7 December 1978) (hereinafter: APII).

[33] Sandoz et al. 1987, p. 1384.

[34] ICRC 2011, p. 9.

[35] For the practical problems related hereto, see, e.g., Hampson 2012, pp. 257–258.

[36] Although the question may be difficult to answer where one party refuses to recognise the other party as a State. Cf. Akande 2012, p. 43.

[37] Ibid, p. 50. See also Cullen 2010.

[38] Hampson 2012, p. 257.

[39] ICRC 2011, p. 9.

Factual circumstances, in other words, have profound implications on the applicable legal framework. In addition, other factors may cause disagreement concerning the classification of an armed conflict. In some cases, States have denied the applicability of international humanitarian law, even though the facts on the ground clearly indicated that an armed conflict was taking place. In other instances, States have applied international humanitarian law to situations that could not be classified as armed conflicts. The non-application or selective application of international humanitarian law has been identified as one of the challenges facing contemporary armed conflicts.[40] For example, States may want to rely on the legal basis for detention applicable in international armed conflict, without applying the full legal framework, as happened in Afghanistan, where the US initially denied the application of the Geneva Conventions, even though it seemed to accept involvement in an international armed conflict.[41] Such differences in application may weaken the protection of the law and hamper cooperation in international military operations.

### *1.2.2 The Interaction Between Human Rights and International Humanitarian Law*

The second complicating factor is the unclear interaction between human rights and international humanitarian law. Unlike international humanitarian law, human rights law does not distinguish between various forms of conflict, although it may allow for derogation in times of conflict.[42] Derogation, however, only implies a lowering of existing standards, and not a complete annulment of a given right or protection.[43] Thus provisions from which derogation is made remain otherwise in force. Some provisions are, moreover, non-derogable.[44]

The 2007 non-paper states that when detention takes place outside the scope of an armed conflict, the 'rules governing detention and the handling of detainees may be found in relevant human rights law, such as the International Covenant on Civil

[40] Ibid.

[41] Cf. Hampson 2012, p. 249.

[42] Article 4(2) ICCPR; Article 15(2) European Convention on Human Rights (hereinafter: ECHR); Article 27(2) American Convention on Human Rights (hereinafter: ACHR). See further HRC 2001.

[43] While most human rights treaties allow for derogation of the right to liberty, the Inter-American Court of Human Rights has noted that even in emergency situations the writ of *habeas corpus* may not be suspended or rendered ineffective. IACtHR, *Habeas Corpus in Emergency Situations*, Advisory Opinion (OC-8/87), 30 January 1987. See also HRC 2001, paras 11, 13(a). The European Court of Human Rights has allowed detention for up to 7 days with derogations, but even with derogation 14 days has been found to violate the right to liberty. Cf. ECtHR, *Brannigan and McBride v. the United Kingdom,* Judgment (App. No. 14553/89), 26 May 1993, paras 61–66; ECtHR, *Aksoy v. Turkey*, Judgment (App. No. 21987/93), 18 December 1996, paras 79–87; IACtHR, Advisory Opinion OC-8/87, IACtHR Series A No. 8, 30 January 1987.

[44] See, e.g., Article 4(2) ICCPR; Article 27(2) ACHR; Article 15(2) ECHR. See further HRC 2001.

and Political Rights.'[45] Some States, however, have consistently rejected the idea that human rights treaties apply to military operations abroad.[46]

The resistance to the application of human rights law to international military operations primarily rests on two arguments. First, some States reject the extraterritorial application of human rights treaties.[47] The US, for example, maintains that the International Covenant on Civil and Political Rights only applies when a person is 'both within the territory of a State Party and within that State Party's jurisdiction.'[48] While the US may be softening its stance,[49] it continues to maintain that the Covenant does not apply with respect to individuals outside its territory.[50] The rejection of the extraterritorial application of human rights treaties may affect cooperation in international military operations. For example, Hampson reports how in Afghanistan ISAF members' differing views on the extraterritorial application of human rights law caused 'significant problems of interoperability in the area of detention.'[51]

The second argument against applying human rights to international military operations concerns the principle of *lex specialis* and only applies when the relevant operation reaches the threshold of an armed conflict, even though it has at times been used indiscriminately. The US, for example, maintains that detention operations in Afghanistan, Iraq and Guantánamo Bay, Cuba, are governed by the law of armed conflict, which they consider as *lex specialis* in those situations.[52] However, the application of the principle of *lex specialis* in these circumstances is problematic as neither Common Article 3 nor Additional Protocol II have been specially designed to regulate detention.[53] The changing nature of military operations has, moreover,

[45] Ministry of Foreign Affairs of Denmark 2007, p. 372.

[46] On the extraterritorial application of human rights treaties, see generally Milanovic 2011.

[47] In regard to extraterritorial application of human rights treaties, see replies to the HRC 2009, issue 4.

[48] See, e.g., HRC 2011, para 505; HRC 2014.

[49] In its latest report to the Human Rights Committee, the US reiterated its previous position, but also took notice of three important legal sources setting forth the contrary view. HRC 2011, para 505.

[50] HRC 2014, para 4.

[51] Hampson 2012, p. 265.

[52] CAT 2006, para 14. The US further emphasised that it had made its position clear at the conclusion of the negotiations of the Torture Convention, when it stated that the Convention was never intended to apply to armed conflicts. The Committee against Torture provided a terse reply, regretting the US opinion that the Convention did not apply in armed conflict. It further stated that the US 'should recognize and ensure that the Convention applies at all times, whether in peace, war or armed conflict, in any territory under its jurisdiction [...]'. CAT 2004, para 14.

[53] Common Article 3 and APII contemplate security detention, but provide no explicit legal basis for detention nor any procedural safeguards. For an opposite view, see Bellinger and Padmanabhan 2011, p. 212. The purpose of 'design' was emphasised in the *Nuclear Weapons* Advisory Opinion, where the Court stated that 'The test of what is an arbitrary deprivation of life, however, then falls to be determined by the applicable *lex specialis*, namely, the law applicable in armed conflict which is *designed* to regulate the conduct of hostilities.' (emphasis added). *Legality of the Threat or Use of Nuclear Weapons*, supra n 7, para 25. The statement was repeated in *Legal Consequences of the Construction of a Wall in the Occupied Palestinian Territory*, supra n 7, para 105.

weakened this traditional argument. The more military operations resemble traditional State peacetime functions, such as ensuring law and order, the greater the need to ensure that these novel powers are exercised within an adequate legal framework. That is the role of human rights law.[54]

Moreover, the *lex specialis* argument does not entail that human rights do not apply, but, quite to the contrary, it merely confirms the applicability of human rights law, even if international humanitarian law supersedes it.[55] The *lex specialis* argument is therefore inconclusive, especially in cases of non-international armed conflicts, where almost no rule on detention exists. The argument is further weakened by the fact that international humanitarian law has been 'sporadically and selectively applied' in places such as Guantánamo Bay.[56] This is yet another area where States' diverging interpretation and approaches to international law may hamper cooperation in international military operations.

### *1.2.3 Differences in International Obligations*

The third and last complicating factor is the variety of legal obligations States are subjected to, which largely depend on the treaties they have ratified. A few States have not, for example, ratified Additional Protocol II and are therefore only bound by Common Article 3 and customary international law.[57] The single most important source of differentiation, however, is the law and practice of the European Convention on Human Rights.[58]

The importance of the Convention in relation to international military operations can hardly be overestimated. The Convention has been incorporated into the domestic law of most European States,[59] in some cases functioning as a '*surrogate* or shadow constitution'.[60] Moreover, unlike many other human rights bodies, the

[54] On this issue, see also Pejic 2005, pp. 377–379.

[55] The principle *lex specialis derogat legi generali* is a principle of conflict resolution. As such it only applies where there is a genuine conflict of norms, that is when two or more norms simultaneously apply to the same subject matter and concurrent application leads to a conflict. Under this principle the more specific rule prevails. See, e.g., *Legality of the Threat or Use of Nuclear Weapons*, supra n 7, para 25; *Legal Consequences of the Construction of a Wall in the Occupied Palestinian Territory*, supra n 7, paras 106, 134–137.

[56] Sliedregt and Gill 2005, p. 53. The application in non-international armed conflicts is likewise problematic as the law in many cases is almost non-existent.

[57] Due to the paucity of treaty rules, customary law plays a more significant role in non-international armed conflict than in international armed conflicts. Dörmann 2012, p. 348.

[58] Afghanistan again provides a useful example. Hampson writes: 'Whilst the US was of the view that detention was not subject to international legal regulation […] its European partners were concerned about detaining anyone, not knowing how intrusive the European Court might be.' Hampson 2012, pp. 265–266.

[59] Cf. Keller and Stone Sweet 2008, pp. 683–686.

[60] Ibid, p. 694.

judgments of its Court are binding.[61] The position of the European Convention on Human Rights means that it is often unlawful for any public authority to act in a way that is incompatible with the Convention, also when acting abroad.

The European Court of Human Rights has heard several cases concerning international military operations and consistently confirmed that the Convention applies to such operations.[62] This is especially important as, unlike other human rights treaties,[63] the European Convention on Human Rights contains an exhaustive list of permissible grounds for detention, which do not include detention for reasons of security.[64] In national emergencies States may derogate from the right to liberty,[65] but no State has ever availed itself of the right to derogate with regard to a situation outside its national borders, and some even question whether this is permissible.[66]

The European Court of Human Rights has consistently insisted on the need for an express legal mandate for detention. In *Al-Jedda*, the Court specifically found that a United Nations Security Council resolution authorising 'all necessary measures to contribute to the maintenance of security and stability' is insufficient to satisfy this requirement.[67] As a consequence, European States may only detain people for reasons of security where there is an express mandate for detention in operations conducted under the authority of the United Nations Security Council.[68] Such mandates are, however, rare.[69] European States are thus precluded from detaining people on security grounds only, unless there is an intention to bring criminal charges within a reasonable time.[70]

In international military operations where foreign forces operate by invitation, the law of the host State will commonly provide a legal mandate for detention. But

---

61 Article 46(1) ECHR.

62 See, e.g., ECtHR, *Cyprus v. Turkey*, Judgment (App. No. 25781/94), 10 May 2001; ECtHR, *Loizidou v. Turkey*, Judgment (App. No. 15318/89), 23 March 1995; ECtHR, *Issa v. Turkey*, Judgment (App. No. 31821/96), 16 November 2004; ECtHR, *Al-Skeini and Others v. The United Kingdom*, Judgment (App. No. 55721/07), 7 July 2001; ECtHR, *Al-Jedda v. The United Kingdom*, Judgment (App. No. 27021/08), 7 July 2011.

63 See HRC 1982, para 4.

64 *Al-Jedda v. The United Kingdom*, supra n 62, para 100.

65 Cf. Naert 2011, p. 319.

66 In *Al-Jedda*, Lord Bingham expressed serious doubts that an overseas peacekeeping operation could ever satisfy the requirements of Article 15 ECHR, referring to 'time of war or other public emergency threatening the life of the nation [...]'*R (Al-Jedda) v. Secretary of State for Defence*, Judgment, (2007) UKHL 58, para 38.

67 *Al-Jedda v. The United Kingdom*, supra n 62, paras 100, 105.

68 In 2008 the UK Court of Appeal held that after the expiry of UNSC Res. 1790 (2007) on 31 December 2008 the UK had no legal power to detain individuals in Iraq. *R (Al-Saadoon and Mufhdi R) v. Secretary of State for Defence*, (2009) EWCA Civ 7.

69 The Security Council provided an explicit mandate for detention in UN Operations in the Congo, UNSC Res. 169 (1961); in Somalia, UNSC Res. 838 (1993); in Iraq, UNSC Resolutions 1546 (2004), 1637 (2005) and 1723 (2006). According to letters annexed to these latter resolutions 'internment' was allowed 'where this is necessary for imperative reasons of security'.

70 In the influence of the *Al-Jedda* judgment in international humanitarian law, see Pejic 2011a.

even where such a mandate exists, variations in States' human rights obligations might impede cooperation. Human rights law generally prohibits transfer where there is a real risk of torture or inhuman and degrading treatment or punishment. The influence of human rights on cooperation was evident when the British Government had to halt the transfer of detainees to Afghan authorities in 2012, following a High Court injunction.[71] Other North Atlantic Treaty Organization (NATO) States followed the British example.[72]

In sum, the wide variation in the legal obligations of States and their interpretation of the law, together with the changing nature of international military operations and the obscure relationship between human rights and international humanitarian law, have created a great of deal of uncertainty on the law applicable to detention, treatment and transfer of detainees in international military operations. Such considerations are especially significant in law and order operations, which must not only comply with the law, but arguably should also set a good example for the host State to follow. It was against this complex legal backdrop that the Danish Government initiated the Copenhagen Process to re-examine the law and identify 'a solution to the challenges' facing troop-contributing States in relation to the rights and treatment of detainees.[73]

## 1.3 The Copenhagen Process

As a troop-contributing State to international military operations, Denmark had first-hand experience with difficulties arising in connection with the detention and transfer of detainees. In 2002 Danish troops in Afghanistan transferred 31 detainees to US custody. While initially 'nobody thought about the [legal] implications of what was taking place on the ground,'[74] it was later alleged that Denmark had ignored the risk of ill-treatment in US custody.[75] These challenges made Danish forces wary of transferring detainees to the custody of other States.

---

[71] This was despite Afghanistan being a party both to the ICCPR and the 1984 Convention against Torture and Other Cruel, Inhuman or Degrading Treatment or Punishment. On 6 June 2013, the UK Government announced that transfers would restart as soon as it had been satisfied that it was 'safe to transfer detainees' to Afghan detention facilities. See http://www.gov.uk/government/news/transfer-of-detainees-to-afghan-custody-to-resume. Accessed 14 April 2014.

[72] See, e.g., ABC News, Australian troops in Afghanistan stop transferring detained prisoners amid torture fears (3 June 2013), available at: http://www.abc.net.au/news/2013-06-03/australia-stops-afghanistan-prisoner-transfers/4728388. Accessed 14 April 2014.

[73] Ministry of Foreign Affairs of Denmark 2007, p. 364.

[74] Winkler 2008, p. 245.

[75] The allegation was made in a documentary 'Den Hemmelige Krig' [The Secret War] (2006), directed by C. Guldbrandsen. The case was decided in 2013, when the Danish Supreme Court found that the Government could not have known of any risks when it decided on the transfer in March 2002. See *Ghousouallah Tarin v. Ministry of Defence*, Judgment (Case No. 180/2011), 27 June 2013.

It was these challenges that spurred the establishment of the Copenhagen Process, initiated in 2007 as a multilateral multi-stakeholder effort to develop principles and good practices on detention, treatment and transfer of detainees in international military operations. The Process consisted of three conferences held in 2007, 2009, and 2012, as well as an expert meeting in 2008. The Conferences were conducted in a closed setting, and only the 2007 non-paper and minutes of the final conference have been made public.[76]

The aim of the Process was to bring major troop-contributing States together to discuss the uncertainties surrounding the legal basis for detention, treatment and transfer of detainees during international military operations. The main challenge was described in the 2007 non-paper as:

> [...] how do troop-contributing States ensure that they act in accordance with their international obligations when handling detainees, including when transferring detainees to local authorities or to other troop-contributing countries?[77]

Initially, some States were reluctant to participate in the Process. The US, for example, was concerned that it would simply become a forum to criticise US practice.[78] But the Danish Government was able to demonstrate that detention, treatment and transfer led to real legal challenges and that the rules in non-international armed conflicts were 'hazy'.[79] Several States shared this belief and the original 15 States that participated in the first conference in 2007 grew to 28 States in 2009.[80] Representatives from the African Union, the European Union, NATO, the United Nations and the ICRC attended as observers, while human rights organisations were consulted on an intermittent basis.[81]

During the first conference a number of issues was identified as key areas for further exploration, namely: the legal basis for detention in international military operations, standards and procedures associated with transfer of detainees, the

---

[76] The then Chief Legal Adviser to the Danish Ministry of Foreign Affairs explained that the Copenhagen Process was closed to 'encourages the openness of the States and organizations involved, enabling them to share their experiences and discuss the best (and worst) practices.' Winkler 2009b.

[77] Ministry of Foreign Affairs of Denmark 2007, p. 368.

[78] Bellinger 2012.

[79] Ibid.

[80] The participants of the first conference in 2007 were Argentina, Australia, Belgium, Canada, Denmark, France, Germany, The Netherlands, New Zealand, Nigeria, Norway, Pakistan, South Africa, Sweden, and the United Kingdom. The ICRC and NATO attended as observers. Cf. Ministry of Foreign Affairs of Denmark 2007, p. 364. The States attending the 2009 conference have not been made public, but the number is mentioned in Winkler 2009a, p. 497.

[81] Some organisations, such as Amnesty International, complained about lack of involvement. Cf. Outcome of Copenhagen Process on Detainees in International Military Operations undermines Respect for Human Rights (23 October 2012), available at: http://www.amnesty.org/en/library/asset/IOR50/003/2012/en/00bb3c11-e2e3-4aab-9c71-e933c56756e8/ior500032012en.html. Accessed 14 April 2014.

interaction and complementarity of human rights norms with international humanitarian law, and a legal definition of detention.[82]

The ambition of the Process was to:

> [...] establish a common platform for the handling of detainees, which all States participating in a given military operation will use regardless of the character of the operation. Such a platform should be based on and respect relevant international law such as Common Article 3 of the Geneva Conventions and Article 75 of Additional Protocol I.[83]

This common platform was to be established partly with reference to existing legal principles and partly from the practice of the participating States. There was no intention to establish new legal rules. Instead, the participants sought to establish 'principles to guide the implementation of existing obligations'.[84] This guidance was to be based on a common understanding of the existing law and shared best practice.

The motivation of the Process was not strictly humanitarian, but also practical, as 'legal ambiguity [...] may hamper the efficiency of [...] military operations'.[85] The concern was that varying legal standards would impede cooperation among troop-contributing States, as those States subject to the highest level of protection would not transfer detainees to other States for fear of violating human rights law. This was, after all, the Danish experience.

In 2008 States met to collect and discuss practice and the meeting was later described as a 'key element in the identification of best practices'.[86] In 2009, it was agreed that the Danish Government should elaborate a draft for a final outcome document, which according to the then Chief Legal Advisor to the Danish Ministry of Foreign Affairs, Thomas Winkler, would provide 'a catalogue of best practice guidelines'.[87]

The *Copenhagen Process: Principles and Guidelines* were completed and published in October 2012.[88] The Principles and Guidelines were 'welcomed' by 18 States,[89] which also 'took note' of the accompanying Chairman's Commendatory, published under the 'sole responsibility of the Chairman of the Process'.[90]

---

[82] Ministry of Foreign Affairs of Denmark 2007, p. 365.

[83] Ibid, pp. 365–366.

[84] Preamble, II.

[85] Winkler 2009a, p. 491. The same is stressed in Ministry of Foreign Affairs of Denmark 2007, p. 363.

[86] Winkler 2009a, p. 497.

[87] Ibid.

[88] Reproduced in Correspondents' Reports 2012.

[89] The relevant States were Argentina, Australia, Canada, China, Denmark, France, Finland, Germany, Malaysia, the Netherlands, Norway, South Africa, Sweden, Turkey, Uganda, United Kingdom, the United States of America and the Russian Federation. See Minutes of the 3rd Copenhagen Conference 2012 (hereinafter: Minutes 2012), available at: http://um.dk/en/~/media/UM/English-site/Documents/Politics-and-diplomacy/Official%20minutes_CP%20ny.pdf. Accessed 14 April 2014.

[90] Preamble, XIII.

## 1.4 The Principles and Guidelines

The outcome document of the Copenhagen Process consists of 13 preambular paragraphs and 16 Principles and Guidelines broadly covering issues relating to the scope and applicable law, the treatment of detainees, and procedural safeguards. As noted by Bellinger, few of the principles are 'new' or 'surprising', but in some cases they are endowed with greater specificity than extant human rights or international humanitarian law.[91]

The Principles and Guidelines are generally vague and carefully avoid the use of words that might imply individual rights.[92] Most Principles reflect rules in the Geneva Conventions, their Additional Protocols or standards that seem to have been derived from human rights law. In other words, the Principles and Guidelines draw freely on both human rights and international humanitarian law. But the Principles and Guidelines do not clarify the interaction between human rights and international humanitarian law, even though this specific issue had been identified as one of the key areas for further exploration at the first conference.[93]

The Principles and Guidelines also do not define 'detention'.[94] This is an important shortcoming, which leaves the scope of application of the Principles and Guidelines undetermined.[95] Nevertheless, the Principles and Guidelines do distinguish situations of 'detention' from those where 'liberty is being restricted', giving the impression that the first is more severe than the second.[96]

The preamble further states that the participants 'recognised that detention is a necessary, lawful and legitimate means of achieving the objectives of international military operations'. This statement could be interpreted as an expression of *opinio juris* that, together with the widespread practice of detention in international military operations, could contribute to the establishment of a customary basis for detention in international military operations.[97] Whether or not this was the intention of the participants, this line of argument seems to have been thwarted by the European Court of Human Rights' in *Al-Jedda*.[98]

---

[91] Bellinger 2012.

[92] Cf. ICJ, *LaGrand* case *(Germany v. United States of America)*, Judgment, (2001) ICJ Rep 446.

[93] Ministry of Foreign Affairs of Denmark 2007, p. 365.

[94] On the issue of definition of detention, see HRC 2012, paras 52–53.

[95] Chairman's Commentary notes that 'States have differing views as to when and under what circumstances a "restriction on liberty" amounts to detention.' Chairman's Commentary to the Copenhagen Process: Principles and Guidelines (hereinafter: Chairman's Commentary), para 1.4.

[96] This seems to be confirmed in the Chairman's Commentary, which notes that 'evidence that a person has been detained may include substantial limitations on the freedom to move, or involuntarily confinement within a bounded or restricted area such as a military camp or detention facility.' Ibid, para 1.1.

[97] It might be argued that this would require some indications of the circumstances in which detention could legitimately take place. It is debatable whether the Principles and Guidelines satisfy this requirement.

[98] *Al-Jedda v. The United Kingdom*, supra n 62.

Despite the above-mentioned omissions, some of the principles arguably clarify or add to the existing legal framework, either by confirming customary rules and their applicability in non-international armed conflicts, or by endorsing the application of human rights-inspired standards to international military operations. At the same time, by not explicitly endorsing the application of human rights, while apparently relying on principles of international humanitarian law, the Principles and Guidelines may also be regarded as a lowering of existing standards. The following provides an assessment of whether the selected Principles and Guidelines are in conformity with, or add anything to, the existing legal framework.[99]

### *1.4.1 The Scope of the Principles and Guidelines*

The Principles and Guidelines are intended to apply to the detention of persons who are deprived of their liberty for reasons related to an international military operation in the 'context of non-international armed conflicts and peace operations.' Instead, the Principles and Guidelines explicitly exclude their application to international armed conflicts.[100]

The Principles and Guidelines do not explicitly state that they apply in situations not reaching the threshold of an armed conflict, but it is nonetheless clear from the text and the overall focus of the Process. First, the drafters deliberately chose not to use the term 'armed conflict' when defining the scope of the Principles and Guidelines. Secondly, the Chairman's Commentary states that the law applicable to detention varies 'depending on whether there is a situation of armed conflict or not.'[101] The Commentary further adds that in:

> [...] situations of detention that are not based in armed conflict justification for detention may be founded in the application of national law principles, such as self-defence and the protection of property.[102]

It is unclear how detention can be based on such principles. There seems, however, to be little doubt that the Principles and Guidelines were intended to apply both to operations that are governed by international humanitarian law and those that are not.[103] Otherwise, the aim of establishing a common platform that could apply regardless of the 'character of the operation' would not have been met.[104]

---

[99] For the sake of convenience, the selected Principles and Guidelines will be referred to simply as 'Principles'.

[100] Preambular para IX and Principle 1.

[101] Chairman's Commentary, para 4.1.

[102] Ibid, para 4.2.

[103] Cf. Ministry of Foreign Affairs of Denmark 2007, pp. 371–372, 374; Winkler 2009a, pp. 490–491.

[104] Ministry of Foreign Affairs of Denmark 2007, pp. 365–366.

The broad scope of the Principles and Guidelines implies that they may apply to situations that are regulated both by human rights and international humanitarian law. In this regard, the Chairman's Commentary asserts that, in cases not governed by international humanitarian law, 'human rights law will be the appropriate body of international law.'[105] However, this assertion is not repeated in the Principles and Guidelines and has therefore not been 'welcomed' by the participating States.[106] Although the Principles and Guidelines do not clarify the relationship between human rights and international humanitarian law, they draw freely on both areas of the law, as discussed in more detail below.

### *1.4.2 Treatment of Detainees*

Four Principles specifically concern the treatment of detainees,[107] drawing heavily on Common Article 3 and occasionally also going beyond international humanitarian law. However these Principles may not be regarded as an unequivocal advancement of the law, especially for States that have already accepted the extraterritorial application of human rights and their applicability in armed conflict.

The first concerning treatment is Principle 2, which states:

> All persons detained or whose liberty is being restricted *will* in all circumstances be treated humanely and with respect for their dignity without any adverse distinction founded on race, colour, religion or faith, political or other opinion, national or social origin, sex, birth, wealth or other similar status. Torture, and other cruel, inhuman, or degrading treatment or punishment is prohibited. [Emphasis added]

The first part of this Principle borrows heavily from Common Article 3, except that the word 'will' replaces the word 'shall'. The list of prohibited acts enumerated in Common Article 3 has, moreover, been compounded and rephrased. Among others, whereas Common Article 3 refers to 'outrages upon personal dignity' mentioning in particular 'humiliating and degrading treatment', Principle 2 refers to 'respect for [...] dignity'. Also the list of grounds prohibiting discrimination is wider than that in Common Article 3.[108]

The provision is further notable because the wording is much stronger than the rest of the text. This is no surprise, as torture is widely abhorred and its prohibition is generally regarded as part of customary international law.[109] Moreover, there is a

105 Chairman's Commentary, para 4.2.

106 Preambular para XII.

107 Principles 2, 6, 9.

108 The list is similar, although not identical, to Rule 88 in ICRC Customary Law Study. Henckaerts and Doswald-Beck 2005a, p. 308.

109 ICJ, *Questions Relating to the Obligation to Prosecute or Extradite (Belgium v. Senegal)*, Judgment (2012) ICJ Rep 422, para 99.

broad similarity between human rights and international humanitarian law on torture.[110]

Common Article 3 has long been considered as part of customary international law,[111] applying both in international and non-international armed conflicts, and Principle 2 therefore seems to add little to the existing legal framework.

Another important Principle relating to the treatment of detainees is Principle 6, which states that '[p]hysical force is not to be used against a detained person except in circumstances where such force is necessary and proportionate.' This high standard does not appear in international humanitarian law, but it is arguably not as high as those embodied in some human rights instruments.

Human rights law provides a strict test for the use of force, especially against people deprived of their liberty. Manfred Nowak, former United Nations Special Rapporteur on torture, has stated that:

> [...] from the moment the person concerned is under the de facto control of the police officer (e.g. hors de combat, otherwise unable to resist or flee [...]) the use of physical or mental coercion is no longer permitted. If such coercion results in severe pain or suffering inflicted to achieve a certain purpose, it must even be considered as torture [...].[112]

This means that the use of force is only permitted as long as a person is at liberty. As soon as a person is under the direct control of a government officer, for example, when a person is shackled or detained in a cell, the use of force is no longer permitted.[113]

It is unclear whether the Principles and Guidelines follow this strict rule. Instead, the Chairman's Commentary explains that physical force against a detainee 'must be proportional to the threat or other legitimate military necessity [...]'[114] How military necessity might justify the use of force against a detainee is not explained. It might refer to force used in self-defence against a dangerous detainee, or force used to prevent an escape, both of which would be permissible under human rights law, but only where this has been made strictly necessary by the detainee's own conduct.[115]

---

[110] Nowak 2014, p. 400. The drafters in each area have drawn from the other when they developed new instruments, as demonstrated for example by APII, several provisions of which were modelled on provisions in the ICCPR. This is true of Article 4, among others. Cf. Sandoz et al. 1987, p. 1368.

[111] Relying on the *Nicaragua* case, this was confirmed by the ICTY Appeals Chamber in *Tadić*. ICTY, *Prosecutor v. Tadić*, Decision on the Defence Motion for Interlocutory Appeal on Jurisdiction, Appeals Chamber (IT-94-1-AR72), para 102.

[112] Nowak 2006, p. 39.

[113] Nowak 2014, p. 395. The ECtHR applies a similar strict test, but only if the mistreatment reaches the specific threshold of severity required by Article 3. See ECtHR, *Bouyid v. Belgium*, Judgment (App. No. 23380/09), 21 November 2013, para 51.

[114] Chairman's Commentary, para 6.2.

[115] See, e.g., ECtHR, *Izci v. Turkey*, Judgment (App. No. 42606/05), 23 July 2013, para 54; ECtHR, *Ivan Vasilev v. Bulgaria*, Judgment (App. No. 48130/99), 12 April 2007, para 63. See, however, ECtHR, *Bouyid v. Belgium*, Judgment (App. No. 23380/09), 21 November 2013.

Principle 9 states that the detaining authorities are responsible for providing detainees with 'adequate conditions of detention,' including 'food and drinking water'. This is in line with conventional and customary international humanitarian law and human rights law.[116] This is therefore another area where there seems to be a broad agreement between human rights and international humanitarian law. As such, Principle 9 adds little to the existing legal framework.[117]

Principle 9 does, however, add some detail, naming 'access to open air' and 'protection against the rigours of the climate and the dangers of military activities'. The text recalls that of Geneva Convention IV,[118] which does not *ex se* apply to situations covered by the Principles and Guidelines, as well as that of Additional Protocol II,[119] which not all the participants of the Copenhagen Process have ratified.[120] Thus, on this specific issue, Principle 9 may be regarded as an addition to the extant legal framework.

Finally, Principle 10 states that detainees should have 'appropriate contact with the outside world' and be held in a 'designated place of detention'. Also here, there was already some agreement between conventional and customary international humanitarian law and human rights law. The text bears similarities with Geneva Convention IV,[121] which regulates the treatment of protected persons in the territory of the parties to an armed conflict and in occupied territory, and does not necessarily apply to international military operations. The ICRC Customary International Humanitarian Law Study argues that a customary rule already exists, according to which 'persons deprived of their liberty must be allowed to correspond with their families, subject to reasonable conditions relating to frequency and the need for censorship by the authorities.'[122]

In contrast, 'general' human rights treaties do not contain specific requirements concerning the designated place of detention or rules on contact, but human rights bodies have at times regarded them as part and parcel of the right to liberty.[123]

---

[116] The Commentary to APII states that 'Although food and water seem the most essential elements, hygiene, health and protection against the rigors of the climate are also important factors for human survival'. Sandoz et al. 1987, p. 1368. Similarly, the ICRC Customary Law Study notes that persons deprived of their liberty must be provided with 'adequate food, water, clothing, shelter and medical attention. This, according to the study, is a long-standing rule of customary international law, applicable both in international and non-international armed conflicts. Henckaerts and Doswald-Beck 2005a, Rule 118, p. 428. The Committee Against Torture has likewise noted that lack of adequate food in prisons may be tantamount to inhuman and degrading treatment. See CAT 2004, para 6(h).

[117] A strengthening of the existing legal framework is in the ICRC's view nevertheless desirable. Cf. Dörmann 2012, p. 351.

[118] Article 85 GIIV.

[119] Article 59(1)(b) APII.

[120] The States that have not ratified APII are Pakistan, Turkey and the United States.

[121] Article 25 GCIV.

[122] Henckaerts and Doswald-Beck 2005a, Rule 125, p. 445.

[123] See, e.g., ECtHR, *El-Masri v. The Former Yugoslav Republic of Macedonia*, Judgment (App. No. 201239630/09), 13 December 2012, paras 230–240.

In addition, 'specialised' human rights treaties, such as the 2006 International Convention for the Protection of All Persons from Enforced Disappearance, contain specific provisions that resemble Principle 10.[124] The Convention only entered into force in 2010 and has so far attracted a modest number of ratifications.[125] This is therefore one area where the Principles and Guidelines may be regarded as an advancement of the existing legal framework for many of the participating States.[126]

### 1.4.3 Procedural Safeguards

The Principles and Guidelines provide important procedural safeguards of general application, as well as specific provisions concerning those detained for reasons of security and on suspicion of having committed a criminal offence. As noted above, extant rules applicable to non-international armed conflicts do not contain procedural safeguards. This is therefore an area where the Principles and Guidelines could make a significant contribution to the existing legal framework.

Principle 5 notes that detaining authorities 'should develop and implement operating procedures regarding the handling of detainees'. Persons detained are to be 'promptly informed of the reasons for their detention in a language that they understand.' A similar provision already exists in relation to international armed conflicts,[127] but no international humanitarian law treaty applicable to non-international armed conflicts contains comparable provisions.[128] In contrast, most human rights treaties contain a right for any person arrested to be informed, at the time of arrest, of the reasons for the arrest, as well as of any charges.[129] Unless one takes the view that human rights law standards also should be applied in situations of armed conflicts, this is another area where the Principles and Guidelines may have added to the existing legal framework.

The remaining Principles distinguish between people detained for reasons of security and those detained on suspicion of having committed a criminal offence. The first group should have their detention reviewed 'periodically by an impartial and objective authority', whereas suspected criminals should be 'transferred to or

[124] See, e.g., Article 17(3) of the 2006 International Convention for the Protection of All Persons from Enforced Disappearance.

[125] As of April 2014 it had 42 Parties. See United Nations Treaty Series Online Collection, supra n 17.

[126] Although there is no provision on vulnerable groups (such as women, children, the disabled and the elderly) which sometimes are allocated special protection in international humanitarian law. Cf. Dörmann 2012, p. 352.

[127] Article 75(3) API. Principle 7 is similar to institutional position on relevant standards for internment in armed conflict and other situations of violence adopted by the ICRC in 2005. The standards were inspired by both human rights and international humanitarian law. See Pejic 2005, p. 384.

[128] Although some see this as part of the obligation of human treatment. Cf. Dörmann 2012, p. 357.

[129] See, e.g., Article 9(2) ICCPR; Article 5(2) ECHR; Article 7(4) ACHR.

have proceedings initiated against him or her by an appropriate authority'.[130] According to Principle 12, the continued detention of those deprived of their liberty for security reasons is to be periodically reviewed by an 'impartial and objective authority that is authorised to determine the lawfulness and appropriateness of continued detention.'[131]

Also here the standards embedded in human rights and international humanitarian law instruments are broadly similar. International humanitarian law requires that internment in international armed conflicts be reviewed by 'appropriate court or administrative board,'[132] and furthermore requires a sufficient element of independence and impartiality.[133] Arguably, the relevant body must also 'have the authority to render final decisions on internment or release.'[134]

A similar requirement is found in human rights law, which contains both substantive and procedural rights against arbitrary deprivation of liberty. These rights inter alia include the right to independent judicial scrutiny of the reasons leading to the deprivation of liberty. Independent scrutiny not only secures against arbitrary detention, but also helps to protect against violations of fundamental guarantees, such as the prohibition against torture or inhuman or degrading treatment.[135]

Thus Principle 12 seems to be in line with both human rights and international humanitarian law, although it provides little detail. The Chairman's Commentary adds that the authority conducting the initial review must be 'objective and impartial but not necessarily outside the military'.[136] This clearly raises concerns of impartiality, but there are no strong rules on this matter in international humanitarian law.[137] Similarly, most human rights instruments merely require that a 'judge or other officer authorised by law to exercise judicial power' review the legality of detention for criminal proceedings.[138] The exact meaning of the expression 'other officer' is unclear, but the European Court of Human Rights has emphasised independence and impartiality,[139] as well as the power of release. The Court, moreover, has not excluded the possibility that military personnel could satisfy the

---

130 Principles 12 and 13, respectively. Principle 13 is the only provision that specifically addresses suspected criminals. However, it is generally accepted that Article 74(4) API reflects customary international law applicable in all types of conflict. This means that fair trial rights in human rights and international humanitarian law are almost identical. Cf. Dörmann 2012, pp. 352–353.

131 Principle 12.

132 Article 43 GCIV.

133 Pictet 1958, p. 261.

134 Pejic 2005, p. 387.

135 See, e.g., *Aksoy v. Turkey*, supra n 43, paras 82–83; *El-Masri v. The Former Yugoslav Republic of Macedonia*, supra n 123, para 233.

136 Chairman's Commentary, para 12.2.

137 Pejic notes that 'judicial supervision would be preferable to an administrative board and should be organized whenever possible'. Pejic 2005, p. 387.

138 The wording is identical in most human rights instruments. See Article 9(3) ICCPR; Article 5 (3) ECHR; Article 7(5) ACHR.

139 ECtHR, *Schiesser v. Switzerland,* Judgment (App. No. 7710/76), 4 December 1979, paras 30–31.

requirements of an officer authorised by law to exercise judicial power.[140] In this regard, Principle 12 seems to conform to existing human rights and international humanitarian law.

The Principles and Guidelines, nonetheless, lack important details, compared to both areas of law in relation to the frequency and the basis for the review of the grounds for detention. The Principles and Guidelines provide no information on this issue, whereas the Chairman's Commentary asserts that reviews should 'occur as often as necessary, as close as practicable to every 6 months.'[141] A similar standard applies to internment in international armed conflicts.[142] It is however unclear why this minimum standard should apply beyond the context of international armed conflicts.[143] Internment in international armed conflict is, moreover, an exceptional measure, which is only allowed when necessary for 'imperative reasons of security'.[144] In contrast, the Principles and Guidelines do not provide any indications on when detention may be legitimate.[145] Principle 4 merely states that detention 'must be conducted in accordance with applicable international law.' But, as already mentioned, the law is often contentious and there are insufficient rules on detention in non-international armed conflicts.[146]

Frequency and basis for review of detention is also a problem in relation to human rights law. As already noted, the European Convention on Human Rights jurisprudence does not generally allow preventive detention. The Human Rights Committee allows preventive detention, provided it is subject to the same guarantees as other forms of detention.[147]

---

[140] The Court has heard at least three cases where detention was considered by a military judge-advocate (auditeurs-militair). ECtHR, *De Jong, Baljet and Van den Brink v. The Netherlands*, Judgment (App. Nos. 8805/79; 8806/79; 9242/81), 22 May 1984, paras 46–50; ECtHR, *Van der Sluijs, Zuiderveld and Klappe v. The Netherlands,* Judgment (App. Nos. 9362/81; 9363/81; 9387/81), 22 May 1984, paras 42–45; ECtHR, *Duinhof and Duijf v. The Netherlands,* Judgment (App. Nos. 9626/81; 9736/82), paras 33–35. In *De Jong*, the Court did find a violation of Article 5(3), because the military judge-advocate could be called upon to perform the function of prosecuting authority after referral of the case to the Military Court.

[141] Chairman's Commentary, para 12.3.

[142] Article 43 GCIV specifies that a periodical review shall take place 'at least twice yearly' whereas Article 78 provides that such review shall take place 'if possible every 6 months'.

[143] Ibid.

[144] Article 78 GCIV. The exceptional nature of internment is further emphasised in Article 42, which states that 'internment [...] may be ordered only if the security of the Detaining Power makes it absolutely necessary'. See further Pejic 2005, pp. 380–381 and Dörmann 2012, pp. 356–357.

[145] The ICRC has suggested that this standard should apply also to non-international armed conflicts. Cf. ICRC 2012, p. 13. See also Pejic 2005, p. 380.

[146] ICRC 2011, p. 9.

[147] See HRC 1982, para 4. See in this regard, also IACtHR, *Coard* et al. *v. United States*, Case No.10.951, Report No.109/99, 29 September 1999, para 45. There are, however, diverging views on the legality of preventive detention. Cf. Dörmann 2012, p. 354.

Generally, human rights law requires that detention be reviewed within a matter of days.[148] Some human rights bodies have, in exceptional circumstances, shown a degree of flexibility, but the requirements are generally strict.[149] Human rights law, moreover, requires individual grounds for detention and not merely a general risk to security.[150]

In sum, both human rights and the law applicable to international armed conflicts have strict rules regarding detention. Procedural safeguards in international humanitarian law have been described as 'rudimentary'[151] yet the Principles and Guidelines do not seem to add anything to the existing legal framework. On the contrary, in some respects the Principles and Guidelines seem to fall below the standards of both human rights and international humanitarian law.

## 1.5 The Legal Status of the Principles and Guidelines

The participants of the Copenhagen Process were 'not seeking to create new legal obligations or authorizations under international law.'[152] Instead, they sought to 'develop principles to guide the implementation of the existing obligations with respect to detention in international military operations'.[153] To further emphasise the point, the preamble of the Principles and Guidelines states that they 'do not affect the applicability of international law to military operations' or the obligations of States to ensure that 'their personnel…respect such law'.

Thus while the participants unequivocally asserted that they would abide by the law, they did not seek to change the existing legal framework. This might seem curious, given the initial aim and the overall lack of rules. The participants were nevertheless in no doubt that the Principles and Guidelines were not to be endowed with normative force. They had no intention to create new laws, but only to establish a 'common platform for the handling of detainees'.[154] This lack of

[148] See, e.g., HRC, *Wilfred Pennant v. Jamaica,* Communication No. 647/1995, UN Doc. CCPR/C/64/D/647/1995 (3 December 1998); ECtHR, *Brogan and Others*, Judgment (App. No. 11209/84), 29 November 1988.

[149] In view of the 'wholly exceptional circumstances', the Court did not find a violation of Article 5(3) in the *Medvedyev* case, where it took 13 days to bring the applicants before an investigating judge. ECtHR, *Medvedyev and Others v. France,* Judgment (App. No. 3394/03), 29 March 2010, para 105.

[150] See, e.g., HRC, *David Alberto Cámpora Schweizer v. Uruguay,* Communication No. 66/1980, UN Doc. CCPR/C/OP/2 (15 March 1980), where the Committee States that 'administrative detention may not be objectionable in circumstances where the person concerned constitutes a clear and serious threat to society which cannot be contained in any other manner […]', para 18.1. This is not unlike international humanitarian law. Cf. Pejic 2005, p. 382.

[151] Pejic 2011b, p. 19.

[152] Preambular para II.

[153] Ibid.

[154] Ministry of Foreign Affairs of Denmark 2007, p. 366.

intention to create a legally binding document does not make the Principles and Guidelines irrelevant. But the question remains whether a non-legally binding text that was only 'welcomed' by the participants can contribute to international law.

The short answer is: yes.[155] First, the adoption of non-binding texts is at times a significant step in the process of negotiating a legally binding agreement.[156] In the case of the Principles and Guidelines, however, this prospect seems unlikely, as no further action has been taken after the conclusion of the Copenhagen Process.

Second, non-binding texts may also represent an agreed understanding of binding law,[157] and, in this specific case, of human rights or international humanitarian law.[158] However, the Principles and Guidelines do not identify any specific rules of international law they represent an agreed understanding of.[159]

Third, the Principles and Guidelines may aid the development of customary international law. In this regard, however, the Chairman's Commentary clearly asserts:

> Since The Copenhagen Process Principles and Guidelines were not written as a restatement of customary international law, the mere inclusion of a practice in The Copenhagen Process Principles and Guidelines should not be taken as evidence that States regard the practice as required out of a sense of legal obligation.[160]

It cannot nevertheless be discounted that the Principles and Guidelines may reflect State practice, and in fact in a few instances they do.[161]

Some support for the customary status of the Principles and Guidelines may be found in statements by the then Danish Minister of Foreign Affairs, Villy Søvndal, who noted that the Principles and Guidelines might play an important role in filling existing gaps in the law.[162] He added that it is 'not inconceivable that this practice

---

[155] As stated by Rosalyn Higgins, 'if international law was just "rules", then international law would [...] be unable to contribute to, and cope with, a changing [...] world '. Higgins 1994, p. 3.

[156] Boyle and Chinkin 2007, p. 216.

[157] Cf. Article 31(3)(a) of the 1969 Vienna Convention on the Law of Treaties.

[158] Boyle and Chinkin 2007, p. 220. The 2007 non-paper states that 'the Copenhagen Conference clearly showed that the solution was not the elaboration of new rules on handling of detainees, but to make the existing legal framework comprehensible and feasible to apply in practice [...]'. Ministry of Foreign Affairs of Denmark 2007, p. 365.

[159] They do not even contain a reference to Common Article 3 or APII, although the 2007 non-paper stated that the common platform should be based on 'relevant international law such as Common Article 3 of the 1949 Geneva Conventions and Article 75 API.' Ministry of Foreign Affairs of Denmark 2007, p. 366.

[160] Chairman's Commentary, para 16.2.

[161] It should be noted that at times it may be difficult to separate State practice from *opinio juris* which may be contained within that practice itself. Cf. Henckaerts and Doswald-Beck 2005a, xlvi.

[162] Briefing to the Parliamentary Committee on Foreign Affairs on the Copenhagen Process, URU Alm.del Bilag 73, UPN Alm.del Bilag 100 (19 December 2012), available at: http:www.ft.dk/samling/20121/almdel/upn/bilag/100/1204215/index.htm. Accessed 14 April 2014. Author's own translation.

may in time become so prevalent in the international community, that certain principles, over time will be reflected as international customary law'.[163]

The Minister also suggested that the Principles and Guidelines could be developed further under the auspices of the United Nations, and indeed the participants to the 2012 conference agreed to promote the Principles and Guidelines 'in relevant regional and international fora, including the United Nations'.[164] It could, for example, be possible to turn the Principles and Guidelines into model provisions to be included in Security Council resolutions authorising international military operations.[165] This would solve legal uncertainties over their legal nature and provide 'a realistic approach'.[166] However, this suggestion has not been officially considered and thus far the Principles and Guidelines have not been discussed by the Security Council.

## 1.6 Conclusions

The then Danish Minister of Foreign Affairs expressed satisfaction that the Copenhagen Process had managed to reach consensus among States with such divergent views.[167] The fact that only 18 States participated in the 2012 conference whereas 28 States had taken part to the 2009 Conference goes some way in illustrating the extent of the disagreement between countries participating to the Process. While it is unclear why several States abandoned the Process, some States openly argued that stronger references to human rights should have been made. The delegation of Sweden indicated that they would have preferred an explicit reference to human rights in Principle 16, which states that nothing in the Principles and Guidelines affects the applicability of international law to international military operations.[168] Russia also indicated a preference for a stronger reference to human rights.[169] Such statements provide a good illustration of the problems facing the participants to the Copenhagen Process. Because of the uncertainties in the law and because of States' widely diverging interpretations of applicable legal systems, it was difficult to advance the law. For some States the outcome document may be regarded as advancement, whereas for others it is clearly a regression.

163 Ibid.

164 Minutes 2012, supra n 89.

165 Wood 2008, p. 144.

166 Ibid. See also House of Commons Defence Committee 2013, para 94.

167 Briefing to the Parliamentary Committee on Foreign Affairs on the Copenhagen Process, supra n 162.

168 Minutes 2012, supra n 89.

169 Russia stated that the Principles and Guidelines 'could contribute more' to the safeguarding of the humane treatment of detainees by placing greater emphasis on 'their inherent rights which derive from the international human rights law and the international humanitarian law'. Ibid.

The Principles and Guidelines have been criticised by human rights organisations. Amnesty International, for instance, expressed concern that they 'can be read as allowing for a lowering of standards to a kind of muddled compromise, in several respects falling well below even the 'lowest common denominator' among participating States.'[170]

The Principles and Guidelines, however, may still be regarded as a positive contribution to the clarification of the law. Firstly, the Copenhagen Process promoted debate on an area in need of further development, and might in some instances help settling uncertainties concerning the application of international humanitarian law to non-international armed conflicts, something scholars have long advocated for.[171] But while they may in some cases provide greater specificity than rules set forth in the Geneva Conventions or human rights instruments, at times the Principles and Guidelines fall short of existing law.[172]

The Principles and Guidelines should also have been clearer on the relationship between human rights and international humanitarian law, which was from the beginning identified as a key area for clarification.[173] While it is 'unrealistic' and 'even counterproductive' to give captured fighters the benefit of *habeas corpus* as defined by human rights law in armed conflict,[174] the current legal framework applicable to non-international armed conflict is insufficient. The Principles and Guidelines have introduced important procedural safeguards, but they may also engender further confusion by justifying the application of international humanitarian law outside the scope of an armed conflict.

The lack of an explicit reference to human rights in the Principles and Guidelines may be regarded as a sign of participating States' continued disagreement on the relationship between human rights and international humanitarian law. A crucial opportunity to influence the development of this important area of the law was

---

[170] Amnesty International 2012. This is not the first time that the Copenhagen Process has been criticised. Several NGOs have complained of their lack of involvement. This criticism has been rejected by the Danish Government. See Winkler 2009b.

[171] For example, Wilmshurst has suggested that 'A unilateral statement by a government, accepting much of the law on international armed conflicts for the purpose of non-international armed conflicts, would make clear what law is being applied, carving out certain areas of the law and modifying others to fit the situation of non-international armed conflict.' Wilmshurst 2012, p. 501. See also Dörmann 2012, p. 351.

[172] For a discussion of the existing gaps, see ICRC 2011, pp. 8–24. For the ICRC initiative on strengthening legal protection for victims of armed conflict, see http://www.icrc.org/eng/what-we-do/other-activities/development-ihl/strengthening-protection-victims-armed-conflict.htm. Accessed 14 April 2014.

[173] Minutes 2012, supra n 89.

[174] The statement was made with reference to Peace Operations, but is equally applicable to many international military operations. Fleck 2014, p. 239.

therefore missed and, as a result, many uncertainties surrounding detention and transfer in international military operations have not been solved.

The Danish experience of a transfer stop in Afghanistan in 2012 well illustrates the dilemma presently facing many States: if they are to remain faithful to their human rights obligations (and national law and international law might ensure that they do) then they might not be able to detain or transfer persons whom they regard as a danger. Prosecution in domestic courts may be difficult or impossible. Human rights and domestic law may equally make it difficult to devise protective mechanisms, such as preventive detention, as an alternative to criminal prosecution. The solution to this conundrum is in theory clear: a State must protect itself and its partners as best as it can in compliance with its human rights obligations. This may mean that dangerous people will have to be set free. Politically, however, this is not easy and existing practice has been much criticised. The conundrum facing States was recently confirmed by the Danish Minister of Defence, who acknowledged that by keeping Afghan detainees in a legal limbo, the Government was deliberately breaching the right to liberty in order not to violate the principle of *non-refoulement*.[175] The adoption of the Principles and Guidelines seem to have been of little effect to address situations such as these.

The most important failing of the Principles and Guidelines, however, is that they seem to be based on a lowest-common-denominator approach. If the aim was to secure better cooperation among troop-contributing States in international military operations, then the existing approach will not suffice. The 2007 non-paper rightly drew attention to the need to adopting a 'multilateral approach,' as bilateral *ad hoc* solutions may lead to 'unacceptable differences in the handling of individual detainees.'[176] These caveats still hold true.

The fact the European Court of Human Rights explicitly confirmed the full application of the right to liberty in international military operations makes it even more pressing that States agree on a common platform of rules on the handling of detainees. But as long as standards are based on the common lowest denominator, some States (and most notably those that adhere to the European Convention on Human Rights) will not be able to cooperate fully. The same is true for States with high domestic legal standards. A more ambitious approach is therefore needed, if human rights are to be respected and cooperation between troop contributing States ensured.

[175] For the statement of the Danish Minister of Defence, see http://www.information.dk/462071. Accessed 14 April 2014. Curiously, the Minister did not mention the possibility of release. The ban on prisoner transfers has meant that some prisoners have been detained in Afghanistan for over a year without being charged with any crime. See BBC, Afghans 'unlawfully held' by UK forces at Camp Bastion (29 May 2013), available at: http://www.bbc.co.uk/news/uk-22691655. Accessed 14 April 2014.

[176] Ministry of Foreign Affairs of Denmark 2007, p. 370.

## References

Akande D (2012) Classification of armed conflicts: relevant legal concepts. In: Wilmshurst E (ed) International Law and the classification of conflicts. Oxford University Press, Oxford, pp 32–79

Bellinger J (2012) Completion of Copenhagen process principles and guidelines on detainees in international military operations. www.lawfareblog.com/2012/12/completion-of-copenhagen-process-principles-and-guidelines-on-detainees-in-international-military-operations/. Accessed 14 Apr 2014

Bellinger J, Padmanabhan V (2011) Detention operations in contemporary conflicts: four challenges for the Geneva conventions and other existing law. Am J Int Law 105:201–243

Boyle A, Chinkin C (2007) The making of International Law. Oxford University Press, Oxford

CAT (2004) Conclusions and recommendations of the committee against torture: Argentina (10 Dec 2004). UN Doc CAT/C/CR/33/1

CAT (2006) Consideration of the second periodic report of the United States of America submitted to the committee against torture (12 May 2006). UN Doc CAT/C/SR.703

Chairman's Commentary (2012) The Copenhagen process on the handling of detainees in international military operations, the Copenhagen process: principles and guidelines. Annexed thereto the Chairman's Commentary (Oct 2012). http://um.dk/en/~/media/UM/English-site/Documents/Politics-and-diplomacy/Copenhangen%20Process%20Principles%20and%20Guidelines.pdf. Accessed 14 Apr 2014

Correspondents' Reports (2012) State practice—completion of the Copenhagen process on the handling of detainees in international military operations. http://www.asser.nl/upload/documents/20130912T030111-Denmark%20YIHL%2015%202012.pdf. Accessed 14 Apr 2014

Crawford E (2007) Unequal before the law: the case for the elimination of the distinction between international and non-international armed conflicts. Leiden J Int Law 20:441–465

Cullen A (2010) The concept of non-international armed conflict in international humanitarian law. Cambridge University Press, Cambridge

Dörmann K (2012) Detention in non-international armed conflicts. In: Watkin K, Norris A (eds) Non-international armed conflict in the twenty first century. Military Bookshop, Newport, pp 347–368

Fleck D (2014) The law applicable to peace operations. In: Clapham A (ed) The Oxford handbook of international law in armed conflict. Oxford University Press, Oxford, pp 206–247

Hampson F (2012) Afghanistan 2001–2010. In: Wilmshurst E (ed) International Law and the classification of conflicts. Oxford University Press, Oxford, pp 242–279

Henckaerts J-M, Doswald-Beck L (eds) (2005a) Customary international humanitarian law (vol I). Cambridge University Press, Cambridge

Henckaerts J-M, Doswald-Beck L (eds) (2005b) Customary international humanitarian law (vol II: practice—part 1). Cambridge University Press, Cambridge

Higgins R (1994) Problems and process: international law and how we use it. Clarendon Press, Oxford

Hill-Cawthorne L (2013) The Copenhagen principles on the handling of detainees: implications for the procedural regulation of internment. J Confl Secur Law 18:481–497

House of Commons Defence Committee (2013) UK armed forces personnel and the legal framework for future operations. Twelfth report of session 2013–14

HRC (1982) General comment no 8, right to liberty and security of persons (Article 9) (30 June 1982)

HRC (2001) General comment no 29, states of emergency (Article 4) (24 July 2001). UN Doc CCPR/C/21/Rev.1/Add.11

HRC (2009) Replies to the list of issues (CCPR/C/AUS/Q/5) to be taken up in connection with the consideration of the fifth periodic report of the government of Australia (CCPR/C/AUS/5) (21 Jan 2009). UN Doc CCPR/C/AUS/Q/5/Add.1

HRC (2011) Fourth periodic report of the United States of America to the United Nations committee on human rights concerning the international covenant on civil and political rights (30 Dec 2011). UN Doc CCPR/C/USA/4

HRC (2012) Report of the working group on arbitrary detention (24 Dec 2012). UN Doc A/HRC/22/44

HRC (2014) Concluding observations on the fourth report of the United States of America, advanced unedited version (26 Mar 2014). www.justsecurity.org/wp-content/uploads/2014/03/UN-ICCPR-Concluding-Observations-USA.pdf. Accessed 14 Apr 2014

ICRC (2011) Report, international humanitarian law and the challenges of contemporary armed conflicts, (28 Nov–1 Dec 2011). http://www.icrc.org/eng/resources/documents/report/31-international-conference-ihl-challenges-report-2011-10-31.htm

ICRC (2012) Strengthening legal protection for persons deprived of their liberty in relation to non-international armed conflict, regional consultations 2012–13, background paper. www.icrc.org/eng/what-we-do/other-activities/development-ihl/strengthening-legal-protection-ihl-detention.htm. Accessed 4 Jun 2014

ICRC (2013) Annual report 2012. www.icrc.org/eng/resources/documents/annual-report/icrc-annual-report-2012.htm. Accessed 14 Apr 2014

International Law Commission (2011) Reservations to treaties. UN Doc A/66/10/Add.1. http://legal.un.org/ilc/reports/2011/2011report.htm. Accessed 14 Apr 2014

Keller H, Stone Sweet A (2008) Assessing the impact of the ECHR on national legal systems. In: Keller H, Stone Sweet A (eds) A Europe of rights: the impact of the ECHR on national legal systems. Oxford University Press, Oxford, pp 678–712

Krieger H (2011) After Al-Jedda: detention, derogation and an enduring dilemma. Mil Law Law War Rev 50:419–441

Milanovic M (2011) Extraterritorial application of human rights treaties: law, principles, and policy. Oxford University Press, Oxford

Ministry of Foreign Affairs of Denmark (2007) The Copenhagen process on the handling of detainees in international military operations. Mil Law Law War Rev 46:363–392

Naert F (2011) The European Court of Human Rights' Al-Jedda and Al-Skeini judgments: an introduction and some reflections. Mil Law Law War Rev 50:315–320

Nowak M (2006) Report of the special rapporteur on civil and political rights, including the questions of torture and detention (23 Dec 2005). UN Doc E/CN. 4/2006/6

Nowak M (2014) Torture and other cruel inhuman or degrading treatment or punishment. In: Clapham A, Gaeta P (eds) The Oxford handbook of international law in armed conflict. Oxford University Press, Oxford, pp 387–409

Oswald B (2011) Detention by United Nations peacekeepers: searching for definition and categorisation. J Int Peacekeep 15:19–151

Pejic J (2005) Procedural principles and safeguards for internment/administrative detention in armed conflict and other situations of violence. Int Rev Red Cross 87:375–391

Pejic J (2011a) The European Court of Human Rights Al-Jedda judgment: the oversight of International Humanitarian Law. Int Rev Red Cross 93:837–851

Pejic J (2011b) The protective scope of common Article 3: more than meets the eye. Int Rev Red Cross 93:189–225

Pejic J (2012) Conflict classification and the law applicable to detention and the use of force. In: Wilmshurst E (ed) International law and the classification of conflicts. Oxford University Press, Oxford, pp 80–116

Pictet J (ed) (1958) Commentary on the Geneva conventions of 12 August 1949 (vol IV). International Committee of the Red Cross, Geneva

Sandoz Y, Swinarski C, Zimmermann B (eds) (1987) Commentary on the additional protocols of 8 June 1977 to the Geneva conventions of 12 August 1949. Martinus Nijhoff, Geneva

Sliedregt E, Gill TD (2005) Guantánamo Bay: a reflection on the legal status and rights of unlawful enemy combatants. Utrecht Law Rev 1:28–54

Wilmshurst E (2012) Conclusions. In: Wilmshurst E (ed) International law and the classification of conflicts. Oxford University Press, Oxford, pp 478–504

Winkler T (2008) The Copenhagen process on the handling of detainees in international military operations, 31st round table on current problems of International Humanitarian Law Sanremo. www.icrc.org/eng/assets/files/other/sanremo-2008_peace_ops.pdf. Accessed 14 April 2014

Winkler T (2009a) The Copenhagen process on detainees: a necessity. Nord J Int Law 78:489–498

Winkler T (2009b) The handling of detainees in international military operations: An update on the Copenhagen process. www.biicl.org/files/4547_copenhagen_process.pdf. Accessed 14 April 2014

Wood M (2008) Detention during international military operations: article 103 of the UN charter and the Al-Jedda case. Mil Law Law War Rev 47:139–166

# Chapter 2
# Beyond Process: The Material Framework for Detention and the Particularities of Non-International Armed Conflict

**Ramin Mahnad**

**Abstract** Deprivation of liberty in non-international armed conflict (NIAC) has suffered no shortage of attention over the last decade with issues surrounding the legal basis and procedural requirements for detention having received the most focused attention. In the course of these debates, international lawyers have looked to rules found in international humanitarian law (IHL) applicable in international armed conflict (IAC) for guidance, and many have argued that as a matter of either law or policy, the procedural aspects of detention in NIAC should be approached in a similar manner. As these discussions have evolved, their focus on grounds and procedure has left another core aspect of IHL relatively unnoticed, along with its potential role in the evolution of NIAC detention law and policy: in addition to providing a procedural framework for detention in armed conflict, IHL also provides material framework for detention that addresses the physical conditions in which detainees are to be held and the way detention and detention facilities are managed. It is often overlooked that in IAC, IHL's accounting for the unique situation of armed conflict does not stop at the right to detain or the grounds and procedures for doing so, but also informs extensive rules on the material aspects of detention. The result is a series of essential and unique protections—often going beyond those found in human rights law—designed to address specific vulnerabilities caused by armed conflict. This article calls attention to this aspect of IHL and asks whether the logic and reasoning that informs the material framework for detention established by the Geneva Conventions should have a role to play in the evolution of law and policy governing the material framework for detention in NIAC.

---

The author is a legal advisor for the International Committee of the Red Cross (ICRC). The views expressed in this article reflect the author's opinions only and not necessarily those of the ICRC.

---

R. Mahnad (✉)
International Committee of the Red Cross, Geneva, Switzerland
e-mail: rammahnad@icrc.org

 
T.D. Gill et al. (eds.), *Yearbook of International Humanitarian Law 2013*,
Yearbook of International Humanitarian Law 16, DOI 10.1007/978-94-6265-038-1_2

**Keywords** Armed conflict · International armed conflict · Non-international armed conflict · Detention · Deprivation of liberty · Humane treatment · Material conditions of detention

## Contents



## 2.1 Introduction

Deprivation of liberty in non-international armed conflict (NIAC) has suffered no shortage of attention from international lawyers over the last decade.[1] States experiencing internal armed conflicts have repeatedly passed counterterrorism laws enabling them to detain outside the ordinary criminal justice system, triggering debate and discussion around the international legality of long-term preventive detention regimes. Meanwhile, extraterritorial detention operations during the conflicts in Iraq and Afghanistan have given rise to challenging questions about the detention policies instituted by multinational forces and their consistency with international law. Over the years, there have been many attempts to bring clarity to these issues. Courts and legislatures have grappled with questions related to jurisdiction, the authority to detain and the procedures for doing so.[2] Multinational forces have revised standard operating procedures, focusing greater attention on ensuring that they are equipped with regulations that contain adequate detention provisions. Diplomatic initiatives such as the Copenhagen Process have aimed to produce concrete principles governing detention in extraterritorial coalition

[1] See, e.g., Webber 2012; Corn and Chickris 2012; Huskey 2012; Pejic 2011; Chesney 2011; Bellinger and Padmanabhan 2011; Goodman 2009.

[2] See ECtHR, *Al-Jedda v. The United Kingdom,* Judgment (App. No. 27021/08), 7 July 2011; *Boumediene v Bush*, 553 U.S. 723 (2008), *Hamdan v. Rumsfeld*, 548 U.S. 557 (2006); National Defense Authorization Act of 2012, Pub. L. No. 112-81, §§ 1021–1034, 125. Stat. 1298, 1562–1573; Military Commissions Act of 2009, Pub. L. No. 111-84, § 948b(a), 123 Stat. 2190 (codified at 10 U.S.C. § 47A (2006)).

operations.[3] And currently, the International Committee of the Red Cross (ICRC) is consulting with States to strengthen the law of armed conflict, or international humanitarian law (IHL), when it comes to detention in all types of NIACs, whether extraterritorial or purely internal.[4]

For many lawyers, it is the issues surrounding the permitted grounds and the required procedural safeguards for detention that have required the most urgent attention.[5] In the simplest terms, the debate centers on the extent to which the particular circumstances generated by NIAC justify departures from how grounds and procedures for detention are ordinarily handled outside armed conflict. Situations of NIAC often prompt implicated States to establish exceptional detention regimes, ones that might allow prolonged administrative detention without criminal charge, prevent access to counsel, or dispense entirely with judicial supervision.[6] The debate quickly converges around the question of who may be detained, on what basis, and subject to what limitations. Policies have varied greatly among States, but the more they have moved away from ordinary prosecutions for criminal offenses, the more these deviations from the norm have given rise to accusations of arbitrary deprivation of liberty and other concerns.[7] These arguments have in turn met with legal and policy arguments justifying the measures as necessary and lawful in the exceptional situation of armed conflict.[8]

When faced with the particularities of armed conflict, one would ordinarily look to IHL to determine whether, in light of the circumstances, a certain course of action is lawful. Inconveniently however, IHL applicable in NIAC does not provide clear guidance on this issue. This reality has given rise to a well-worn debate and discussion on the applicability and adequacy of human rights law and the precise contours of customary IHL.[9] But it has also sparked thinking on the extent to which an analogy can be drawn to the law of international armed conflict (IAC). In IACs,

---

[3] See Ministry of Foreign Affairs of Denmark 2012, Copenhagen Process: Principles and Guidelines. It should be noted that the Copenhagen Principles are not limited to NIAC situations. They apply to international military operations in NIAC as well as peace operations, which may fall below the threshold for armed conflict.

[4] See 31st International Conference of the Red Cross and Red Crescent 2011: Resolution 1—Strengthening legal protection for victims of armed conflicts, available at http://www.icrc.org/eng/resources/documents/resolution/31-international-conference-resolution-1-2011.htm. Accessed 27 April 2014.

[5] See Goodman 2009.

[6] See Corn and Chickris 2012; Huskey 2012 (discussing access to counsel in the context of U.S. detention); Webber 2012 (discussing preventive detention generally).

[7] See, e.g., Human Rights First, Detained and Denied in Afghanistan: How to make U.S. detention comply with the law (May 2011); Human Rights Watch, Israel: End abusive practices: Hunger Striking Detainees Denied Due Process (24 February 2013), available at: www.hrw.org/news/2013/02/23/israel-end-abusive-detention-practices. Accessed 27 April 2014.

[8] Koh, Annual Meeting of the American Society of International Law Speech (25 March 2010), available at: http://www.state.gov/s/l/releases/remarks/139119.htm. Accessed 27 April 2014.

[9] For a comprehensive overview of the debate, see Bellinger and Padmanabhan 2011, pp. 205–213.

the rules of IHL do indeed diverge from the assumptions and requirements of human rights law, permitting and regulating a procedural framework for detention that is specifically designed to take into account the realities of armed conflict. The law applicable in IAC directly confronts the questions of who may be detained and what the outer limits of that detention authority are. And it also provides a procedural regime that serves to protect against arbitrary detention.[10] Looking to IAC rules for guidance, some argue that as a matter of either law or policy, the procedural aspects of detention in NIAC should be approached in a similar manner.

As these arguments have developed, their focus on grounds and procedure has left another core aspect of IHL relatively unnoticed, along with its potential role in the evolution of NIAC detention law and policy: in addition to providing a *procedural* framework for detention in armed conflict, IHL also provides *material* framework for detention that addresses the physical conditions in which detainees are to be held and the way detention and detention facilities are managed. It is often overlooked that in IAC, IHL's accounting for the unique situation of armed conflict does not stop at the right to detain or the grounds and procedures for doing so, but also informs extensive rules on the material aspects of detention.

Approached from the perspective of humane treatment and associated prohibitions against torture and other abuse, one might assume that, unlike the procedural framework, the rules related to the material framework simply mirror the logic and content of human rights law and standards, and indeed, to a large extent they do. Upon closer examination, however, it becomes evident that provisions in the Geneva Conventions that govern the material detention environment in IAC also carry their own logic reflecting the particularities of armed conflict. The result is a series of essential and unique protections—often going beyond those found in human rights law—designed to address specific vulnerabilities caused by armed conflict. These protections ensure, for example, that detainees are kept safe from the dangers of hostilities, that information about their detention is transmitted through mechanisms designed to reach across enemy lines, and that persons detained purely for security reasons are not held in close confinement or treated as criminals.

This article calls attention to this aspect of IHL and asks whether the logic and reasoning that informs the material framework for detention established by the Geneva Conventions should not have a role to play in the evolution of law and policy governing the material framework for detention in NIAC. It will first examine how IHL applicable in IAC takes into account the particularities of armed conflict, demonstrating the ways that the rules governing the material framework for detention are tailored to the specific vulnerabilities and challenges generated by such situations. It will then explain the relative scarcity of current IHL on material aspects of detention in NIAC and explore the extent to which the underlying logic

[10] For example, IAC law permits internment of prisoners of war—essentially members of enemy armed forces—until the end of active hostilities without any periodic review. Articles 21, 118 GCIII. It permits the internment of others only if and so long as it is necessary for imperative reasons of security. Articles 42, 78 GCIV. A system of initial and periodic review ensures that these individuals are not held arbitrarily. Articles 43, 78 GCIV.

of IHL rules applicable in IAC might be relevant to the detention environment in NIAC as well. The point of comparison when identifying the aspects of IHL uniquely tailored for armed conflict will of course be human rights law. However, this article will not try to resolve questions related to the interplay of IHL with human rights treaties and standards. Rather, it will simply highlight unique aspects of IAC law that might be useful to bear in mind as the discussion and debate surrounding detention in NIAC continues.

## 2.2 The Material Framework for Detention in IAC

The material framework for detention in IAC is governed for the most part by the Third and Fourth Geneva Conventions of 1949 (GC III and GC IV). GC III applies to prisoners of war, essentially members of an adversary State's regular armed forces, members of certain irregular armed groups fighting for the adversary, and certain authorized civilians who accompany the armed forces, such as members of military aircraft crews, war correspondents, and supply contractors.[11] GC IV, in turn, applies to those who are not protected by GC III—or the other Geneva Conventions protecting sick, wounded and shipwrecked—and who "at a given moment and in any manner whatsoever, find themselves, in case of a conflict or occupation, in the hands of a Party to the conflict or Occupying Power of which they are not nationals."[12]

The circumstances created by IAC have had a significant bearing on Geneva Convention rules governing the material framework for detention. The types of detainees foreseen by GC III and GC IV are, in simple terms, members of the enemy State's armed forces or other non-nationals of the detaining State determined to be hostile but not charged with a crime. Accordingly, the types of vulnerabilities foreseen are not just those that arise in any deprivation of liberty, but those that flow from detention by one's adversary in an environment of intense, organized violence between two opposing parties. Accordingly, in addition to many of the rules that one expects to see in any instrument regulating material conditions of detention, Geneva Convention rules reflect a number of additional conflict-specific considerations.

IAC-tailored detention provisions appear throughout the GC III and GC IV, but certain areas are particularly illustrative of the extent to which the material framework for detention required by the law has a very specific situation in mind. This section focuses on two such areas of protection. First, it discusses the degree of

---

[11] Article 4(A) GCIII. Other persons who may be entitled to prisoner of war (POW) treatment include members of the merchant marine, crews of civil aircraft, and participants in a *levee en masse*.

[12] Article 4 GCIV. Excluded from the scope of GCIV are all nationals of States not bound by the Convention, as well as nationals of neutral or co-belligerent States, so long as the State in question has normal diplomatic representation in the State in whose territory they are.

confinement permitted in an internment facility, demonstrating how the material detention environment is adapted to the types of detainees and reasons for detention foreseen in IAC. Second, it discusses the rules related to registration and notification of detention, demonstrating IHL's accounting for the heightened vulnerability to disappearance caused by the existence of the conflict and the breakdown in communications between the warring parties. Other areas in which the Geneva Conventions provide armed-conflict-specific protections are also briefly mentioned.

### *2.2.1 Degree of Confinement*

The term "confinement" in this section and in the IHL provisions that it cites refers to the severity of the restrictions placed on the physical movement of a person already deprived of liberty.[13] The physical space to which a person is restricted can range, for example, from a large, fenced-in camp to a solitary cell. For purposes of clarity, it bears noting that the term "confinement" is used to mean different things in different provisions of IHL. For example, "unlawful confinement" in Article 147 of GC IV is synonymous with arbitrary deprivation of liberty, not the unlawful application of overly severe restrictions on an already detained person.[14] As noted, this discussion only deals with the latter notion.

When it comes to criminal detention, Geneva Convention rules on confinement do not differ drastically from what human rights law might require; however, when it comes to internment, IHL's distinctive material framework for detention becomes immediately apparent. Internment is a type of deprivation of liberty for security purposes ordered by the executive without criminal charges being filed.[15] An inherently non-punitive measure of control, the purpose of internment is to limit the movements (and therefore activities) of certain individuals, rather than to charge them with an offense and subsequently punish or rehabilitate them. The occurrence of internment in IAC can stem from a number of conflict-related circumstances. For example, upon capture, most members of the armed forces of an enemy State will enjoy combatant's privilege and be immune from prosecution under domestic law for actions taken that complied with IHL. Nonetheless, the detaining power will be unwilling to allow them to return to combat, giving rise to the need for an alternative framework to govern their deprivation of liberty. Alternatively, the parties to

[13] Human rights law and jurisprudence of course address confinement as well, both in the context of humane conditions generally and in the specific context of solitary confinement as a punishment. See, e.g., Rule 32 of the Standard Minimum Rules for the Treatment of Prisoners (hereinafter: SMR), available at: www.ohchr.org/EN/ProfessionalInterest/Pages/TreatmentOfPrisoners.aspx. Accessed 27 April 2014. See also Rodley and Pollard 2009, pp. 402–406. However, unlike IHL, human rights instruments do not link the degree of confinement to the particular legal framework or grounds on which the deprivation of liberty is based.

[14] See Pictet 1958 (hereinafter: Commentary GCIV), p. 599.

[15] See Pejic 2005, p. 375.

the conflict might encounter civilians—in particular certain nationals of the adversary State or inhabitants of occupied territory—who participate in hostilities or otherwise pose a security threat. If necessary, they will impose various measures of control on these individuals as well, measures up to and including deprivation of liberty.

IHL foresees and regulates these realities. The Third Geneva Convention accepts that prisoners of war (POWs) may be interned until the cessation of active hostilities, but provides them with a host of protections.[16] GC IV foresees the likelihood of internment of civilians but simultaneously limits the circumstances in which it is permitted: for aliens on the territory of a party to the conflict, GC IV ensures that internment is only carried out when "the security of the detaining power makes it absolutely necessary";[17] for inhabitants of occupied territory, it permits internment only when necessary for "imperative reasons of security".[18]

Beyond regulation of whether and in what circumstances internment is permissible, IHL applicable in IAC regulates the conditions of detention and degree of confinement to which internees may be subjected and ensures that the severity of deprivation of liberty is consistent with internment's non-punitive nature. By restricting the degree of confinement to which detaining authorities in IACs may subject internees, IHL at once anticipates the reality that armed conflict will give rise to detention without charge and ensures that such persons are not treated as criminals.

GC III expressly prohibits holding prisoners of war in "close confinement," unless it is in connection with penal or disciplinary sanctions, or unless it is necessary to safeguard their health.[19] Illustrating the relatively lenient detention environment, GC III provides that the Detaining Power "may impose on [POWs] the obligation of not leaving, beyond certain limits, the camp where they are interned, or if the said camp is fenced in, of not going outside its perimeter".[20] The ICRC Commentary to GC III adds that:

> Internment involves the obligation not to leave the town, village, or piece of land, whether or not fenced in, on which the camp installations are situated, but it does not necessarily mean that a prisoner of war may be confined to a cell or a room. Such confinement may only be imposed in execution of penal or disciplinary sanctions, for which express provision is made.[21]

Although GC IV does not explicitly prohibit close confinement of internees in the same manner as GC III, it does contain a number of contextual indications of the degree of confinement that should be applied to internees. First, as noted above, GC IV frames internment as a way of controlling the activities of individuals for

---

[16] Article 21 GCIII.

[17] Article 42 GCIV.

[18] Article 78 GCIV.

[19] Article 21 GCIII.

[20] Article 21(1) GCIII.

[21] Pictet 1960 (hereinafter: Commentary GCIII), p. 178.

security reasons. It specifically provides that protected persons generally may not be subjected to "any other measure of control more severe than that of assigned residence or internment."[22] The grouping of internment with assigned residence, and its framing as the most severe measure that can be taken indicate circumstances that would certainly amount to a deprivation of liberty, but that would stop short of the circumstances one typically associates with criminal detention.

Additionally, provisions within GC IV that do mention "confinement" are limited to cases of judicial proceedings or disciplinary measures. For example, the GC IV addresses the humane treatment of "protected persons who are confined pending proceedings or serving a sentence involving loss of liberty" and it ensures that women who are accused of offences "shall be confined in separate quarters [...]".[23]

GC IV also refers to confinement as something above and beyond what would normally occur in an internment environment. It requires, for example, that "in case of offences against discipline, confinement awaiting trial shall be reduced to an absolute minimum for all internees, and shall not exceed 14 days. Its duration shall in any case be deducted from any sentence of confinement."[24] In other words, internees are presumably deprived of their liberty without being subjected to physical restrictions that would amount to confinement.

Finally, it should be noted that certain provisions in GC IV actually consider the possibility of internees temporarily leaving the place of internment. For example, they are to be permitted, as far as possible, "to visit their homes in urgent cases, particularly in cases of death or serious illness of relatives."[25] Additionally, children who are interned must be allowed to attend schools "either within the place of internment or outside."[26] Although these provisions do not deal with the degree of confinement while in the camp as such, they are indicative of the overall restrictiveness of the detention regime.

The point at which a restriction on physical movement within a place of detention becomes severe enough to amount to confinement is not clear. However, that such a distinction exists is sufficient to illustrate the general notion that the drafters of the Conventions intended conditions of detention for internees to be relatively unrestrictive.

---

[22] Article 41(1) GCIV. See also Article 78(1) GCIV, providing that the detaining authority may "at the most, subject them to assigned residence or internment."

[23] Articles 37(1), 76(3) GCIV.

[24] Article 122(2) GCIV. Similarly, Article 118(4) GCIV provides that "the duration of preventive detention undergone by an internee shall be deducted from any disciplinary or judicial penalty involving confinement to which he may be sentenced."

[25] Article 116(2) GCIV.

[26] Article 94(2) GCIV.

### *2.2.2 Registration and Notification*

Rules governing registration and notification are another area in which IHL is specifically adapted to take into account the particular circumstances of international armed conflict. As a general matter, secret detention and incommunicado detention are universal targets of international legal preventive measures. Rules related to recording the identities and other details about detainees, notifying their families and other individuals and entities, and ensuring ongoing family contact are at the heart of the legal obligations established to prevent disappearance and protect against ill treatment. Registration and notification provisions in human rights law—particularly the Convention on Enforced Disappearances—and provisions in IHL all work toward these ends. However, unlike human rights law, the Geneva Conventions contain several provisions specifically designed to overcome obstacles generated by situations of armed conflict.

With respect to the obligation to register or record the details of detainees, IHL and human rights law contain largely similar provisions. Differences lie primarily in the formal requirements for recording information and in the details regarding the type of information to be recorded. For example, while human rights law focuses on the requirement of maintaining official registers and records that are then to be made available to a number of third parties,[27] GC IV requires each Detaining Power to "establish an official Information Bureau responsible for receiving and transmitting information in respect of the protected persons who are in its power."[28] It then requires that information be supplied to the bureau in a number of different circumstances.[29] Compared to IHL, the Convention against Enforced Disappearances also focuses to a greater extent on recording not only the time and place of the detention, but also the identity of the authority that deprived the person of liberty, the authority that ordered the deprivation of liberty, grounds for the deprivation of liberty, and the authority responsible for supervising the deprivation of liberty.[30]

---

[27] See Article 17(3) of the 2006 International Convention for the Protection of All Persons from Enforced Disappearance (hereinafter: CED) (providing that "the compilation and maintenance of one or more up-to-date official registers and/or records of persons deprived of liberty, which shall be made promptly available, upon request, to any judicial or other competent authority or institution authorized for that purpose by the law of the State Party concerned or any relevant international legal instrument to which the State concerned is a party"); Rule 7(1) SMR (providing that "in every place where persons are imprisoned there shall be kept a bound registration book with numbered pages in which shall be entered in respect of each prisoner received: (a) information concerning his identity; (b) the reasons for his commitment and the authority therefor; (c) the day and hour of his admission and release"); and Principle 12(1) of the Body of Principles for the Protection of All Persons under Any Form of Detention or Imprisonment (requiring that the authorities record the reasons for the arrest; the time of the arrest and the taking of the arrested person to a place of custody as well as that of his first appearance before a judicial or other authority; the identity of the law enforcement officials concerned; and precise information concerning the place of custody).

[28] Article 136(1) GCIV.

[29] Article 136(2) GCIV.

[30] Article 17(3) CED.

Concerning notification requirements, on the other hand, the specificity of IHL in dealing with armed conflict situations becomes increasingly apparent. The particular obstacles to notification presented by IAC, and IHL's role in surmounting them, are particularly evident in a number of areas. First, rules governing notification of national authorities and families of foreign detainees are designed to overcome the breakdown in relationship between the two parties to the conflict. Second, provisions allowing for detainees to directly notify their families and other entities upon capture mitigate delays in the transmission of information caused by high numbers of detainees or other circumstances related to the IAC. And third, the use of a uniform "capture card" ensures that the security concerns of the detaining power do not unduly interfere with the transmission of information regarding detention.

Regarding foreign detainees, human rights law certainly does envisage the possible need for contact to be established with foreign governments. The Convention on Enforced Disappearances requires the detaining State to "[g]uarantee that any person deprived of liberty shall be authorized to communicate with […] his or her consular authorities, in accordance with applicable international law."[31] However, human rights law does not directly tackle the complexities that arise when the detainee's government is an adversary in the armed conflict. IHL, on the other hand, contains provisions designed to address precisely such a situation. For example, once the Information Bureaus are in possession of information related to detainees, GC IV requires that they "immediately forward information concerning protected persons by the most rapid means to the Powers of whom the aforesaid persons are nationals, or to Powers in whose territory they resided."[32] As the addressee of the information is likely to be an enemy and direct contact between the warring parties is unlikely, GC IV provides for the information to be transmitted through the intermediary of the Protecting Powers or through a Central Information Agency established in a neutral State.[33] The agency is empowered to collect information through both official and private channels and to transmit it to the countries of origin or of residence of the persons concerned.[34] GC III contains similar provisions regarding a Central Prisoners of War Agency. The ICRC has historically played the role of the central agencies.

IHL also takes into account the possibility that transmission of certain information to the State of which the detainee is a national might not be in the detainee's interest in all circumstances. This is particularly true in the case of civilian internees, who do not benefit from combatant's privilege and whose involvement in

---

[31] Article 2(d) CED.

[32] Article 137(1) GCIV. It also requires the bureau to reply to all enquiries which may be received regarding protected persons.

[33] Article 140 GCIV.

[34] Ibid.

the conflict might create problems with respect to their own governments.[35] IHL addresses this issue by ensuring that the State concerned would not automatically receive the information, while nonetheless maintaining the requirement that a third party is effectively notified about the detention. The Information Bureau is required to transmit information concerning a protected person "unless its transmission might be detrimental to the person concerned or to his or her relatives."[36] But even in such circumstances, "the information may not be withheld from the Central Agency which, upon being notified of the circumstances, will take the necessary precautions."[37] GC III contains similar provisions applicable to POWs in this regard.[38] Human rights law does provide for international mechanisms that can be informed of and investigate instances of enforced disappearances.[39] However, none of these mechanisms involves a systematic obligation to inform a neutral body of each instance of detention.

Regarding direct notification by detainees to avoid delays, both GC III and GC IV recognize that the Information Bureau will require time to notify captures—perhaps in light of high numbers of detainees or other exigencies related to the conflict. They therefore contain provisions ensuring that detainees can directly notify their own detention as a prompt and effective alternative.[40] Accordingly, GC III provides, for example, that every POW shall be enabled to write direct to his family and to the Central Prisoners of War Agency "immediately upon capture, or not more than 1 week after arrival at a camp, even if it is a transit camp, likewise in case of sickness or transfer to a hospital or another camp."[41] GC IV contains a substantially similar provision. No such mechanism for expedited notifications of large-scale detention exists in human rights law.

Finally, in order to minimize security concerns arising from direct external communication by detainees, GC III and GC IV both provide model, uniform capture cards containing only the most basic information regarding the detainees.[42]

---

[35] See Commentary GCIV, pp. 446–447 ("In general, indeed, their political activities may make the position of civilians in internment more complicated than that of members of the armed forces captured in battle and obstacles which do not exist in the latter case may stand in the way of revealing the situation in which civilian internees may find themselves. It was therefore preferable to leave the Agency the task of judging whether or not to transmit any information received, after consultation, if need be, with those concerned").

[36] Article 137(2) GCIV.

[37] Ibid.

[38] Article 123 GCIII.

[39] See, e.g., Article 30 CED.

[40] See Commentary GCIII, p. 341 ("The International Committee of the Red Cross noticed, however, that the Information Bureaux of Detaining Powers invariably required some time to notify captures and transfers; it therefore suggested to the Detaining Powers the dispatch to the Central Prisoners of War Agency of printed cards, called 'capture cards', in order to expedite receipt by the Agency and subsequently by their families of essential information concerning prisoners of war").

[41] Article 70 GCIII. See also Article 106 GCIV.

[42] See GCIII, Annex IV and GCIV, Annex III.

The simplicity of the capture cards and the minimal but vital information they contain facilitate their transmission by limiting (or even eliminating) the need for censorship and mitigating possible security concerns.[43] The ease with which pre-printed capture cards can be distributed also ensures that information concerning large numbers of detainees can be quickly transmitted after capture, even before they arrive at a place of internment.[44] As with the other aspects of the Geneva Conventions notification regime highlighted here, no equivalent approach is provided for in human rights law.

### *2.2.3 Other IHL Provisions*

The rules governing confinement and notification are just two examples that illustrate how IHL applicable to the material framework for detention in IAC takes into account the particularities of armed conflict. Of course, there are many other provisions of the Geneva Conventions that are indicative of the particular circumstances IHL is designed to regulate and that provide protections of a nature or degree beyond human rights law. For example, GC III and GC IV both contain rules requiring that detention take place away from hostilities and in facilities that provide shelter from bombardment and other conflict-related hazards.[45] They address the fact that detainees are in most cases not nationals of the detaining power through numerous rules regulating the languages in which information is to be distributed, procedures are to be carried out and correspondence to be written, as well as rules on the nationality of persons providing medical care to detainees.[46] And rules ensuring that detainee property is not unduly confiscated, and that it is returned upon release, are crafted in a way that takes into account complex considerations related to the freezing of enemy assets by belligerent States and subsequent reparations.[47]

There are of course a host of other provisions beyond the scope of this article that similarly reflect the fact that IHL is a regime specifically tailored for a specific

---

[43] See Commentary GCIII, p. 343 ("The information on the cards is of a very summary kind and censorship should therefore be a mere formality. Cards addressed to the Central Agency might even perhaps be forwarded without censorship").

[44] See Commentary GCIII, p. 341 ("The introduction of a standard card as provided under the present Convention will enable the Detaining Power to prepare a stock of such cards at the commencement of hostilities, ready for distribution to prisoners of war during the first formalities after capture. These cards, on which the main headings are printed, can be filled in easily and within the required time-limit. Article 70 is not only applicable when a prisoner of war is definitely installed in a camp, since there is an express reference to transit camps").

[45] See Articles 22, 23 GCIII; Articles 83, 85 GCIV.

[46] See, e.g., Articles 17(6), 22(3), 30(3), 35(1), 41(2), 71(3), 105(4), 107(1) GCIII; Articles 50(3), 65(1), 71(2), 82(1), 93(2), 99, 107(3) GCIV.

[47] See Articles 18, 64 GCIII; Article 97 GCIV.

type of situation. The purpose here has been merely to illustrate that this holds true not only for the grounds and procedures for detention, but also for the material aspects.

## 2.3 The Material Framework for Detention in NIAC

Recognizing that the material framework for detention in IAC carries with it a logic that is informed by the realities of armed conflict, the natural question arises as to whether NIACs do not also give rise to a set of special circumstances requiring a tailored material framework. The first place to look for an answer would obviously be IHL applicable in NIAC. However, this set of rules remains relatively limited when it comes to detention in such situations. This section will provide an overview of currently existing NIAC law and explain its shortcomings. It will then pose several questions regarding whether and how IAC law discussed above might be relevant to law and policy developments related to the material framework for detention in NIAC.

### *2.3.1 The Currently Applicable IHL Framework for NIAC*

As the detailed rules from the previous section imply, detention in IAC is heavily regulated. GC III and GC IV both require compliance with more than 100 provisions governing the conditions in which prisoners of war and civilians may be held. They address a vast range of concerns in addition to those already discussed, including the provision of food and water, the adequacy of accommodations, access to medical care, family contact, the specific needs of vulnerable detainees, the severity of disciplinary measures, and much more. Where NIAC is concerned, however, virtually all of the detail contained in the Geneva Conventions disappears, leaving only the very general (though vital) protections of Common Article 3, the additional (though incomplete) protections of Additional Protocol II (AP II), and the general (but always subject to dispute) rules of customary IHL.

Protecting all persons not or no longer directly participating in hostilities—including detainees—Common Article 3 is the sole provision in the four Geneva Conventions that applies to NIAC. It requires humane treatment without any adverse distinction and enumerates specific prohibitions: violence to life and person, in particular murder of all kinds, mutilation, cruel treatment and torture; outrages upon personal dignity, in particular humiliating and degrading treatment; and the specific form of deprivation of liberty that is 'the taking of hostages.' Beyond these general requirements, however, Common Article 3 is silent regarding material aspects of detention specifically.

APII applies to a subset of NIACs and supplements the provisions found in Common Article 3. In order for AP II to apply, the NIAC in question must take place between a State and "dissident armed forces or other organized armed groups which, under responsible command, exercise such control over a part of its territory as to enable them to carry out sustained and concerted military operations and to implement this Protocol."[48] Its application is therefore excluded when an armed group does not exercise sufficient control over territory, or when neither party to the NIAC is a State (i.e., NIACs between two non-State armed groups). Article 4(2) of AP II adds to Common Article 3's list of prohibited acts by specifically outlawing slavery and the slave trade, corporal punishment, pillage, rape, enforced prostitution, indecent assault, and acts of terrorism.[49] Unlike Common Article 3, however, AP II goes on to address the material detention environment. At a general level, it requires the provision of food and water and the safeguarding of health and hygiene to the same extent as the local civilian population.[50] It secures the rights of detainees to receive individual or collective relief and to practice their religion.[51] And it expressly requires that sick and wounded detainees be cared for on the basis of medical need and without adverse distinction.[52] AP II also contains more advanced protections when within the limits of the capabilities of the detaining authorities. These include rules governing the separation of men and women and the placement of the latter under the direct supervision of women, the sending and receiving of correspondence and medical examinations.[53]

In a manner similar to IHL applicable in IAC, AP II does contain a few provisions on material conditions of detention that are clearly tailored to vulnerabilities arising from armed conflict. These include the requirement that detainees be protected against the dangers of armed conflict to the same extent as the local population and the requirement that, where possible, detention facilities be located away from the combat zone.[54] In addition, the proviso that certain protections need only be implemented within the limits of the capabilities of the detaining authority is clearly intended to take into account that NIACs will always include non-state parties with varying degrees of organization and resources.[55]

Beyond these few elements, however, AP II does not provide a great number of protections that deal with NIAC-specific problems in a manner that human rights instruments do not. It acknowledges the possibility of internment, but rules on the degree of confinement like those found in the Geneva Conventions are absent. It provides for correspondence rights, but it does not mirror the Geneva Convention provisions on capture cards to facilitate notification and family contact, or on a neutral intermediary that can share information across enemy lines. Finally, it has to

48 Article 1(1) APII.

49 Article 4(2) APII.

50 Article 5(1) APII.

51 Ibid.

52 Article 5(1), 7 APII.

53 Article 5(2) APII.

54 Articles 5(1), 5(2) APII.

55 See Article 5(2) APII.

be noted that AP II has not been universally ratified and, as mentioned above, only applies to certain types of NIACs.

International criminal law has also played an important role in the understanding and development of rules that apply in NIAC. In the course of their work, the various courts have had occasion to deal with the material framework for detention, including issues highlighted in the previous section. The International Criminal Tribunal for the Former Yugoslavia has, for example, assessed whether certain conditions of detention and confinement amounted to cruel treatment.[56] It has also advanced the law surrounding obligations to notify instances of detention, playing a formative role in the eventual codification of enforced disappearance as a crime against humanity.[57] But as courts tasked with the prosecution of serious violations of existing IHL, the involvement of international criminal tribunals in the clarification or development of law and policy not directly related to the commission of war crimes—such as the degree of confinement appropriate for internment versus criminal detention, or the establishment of specific procedures or mechanisms for notifying detention to third parties across enemy lines—will logically tend to be limited.[58]

### *2.3.2 Using IAC Rules to Inform the Material Framework for Detention in NIAC*

In light of the limitations of current IHL applicable in NIAC, as well as the fact that human rights law was not designed specifically to address armed-conflict-related vulnerabilities, this section asks whether thinking on law and policy in NIAC should not focus on the material framework as much as the procedural one, and in

[56] See, e.g., ICTY, *Prosecutor v. Limaj,* Judgment Trial Chamber (IT-03-66-T), 30 November 2005 (holding that conditions of detention that involved overcrowding, unhygienic conditions, detainees sleeping on floors, irregular and infrequent meals, lack of light or ventilation, and rare access to fresh air, constant application of restraints, and lack of medical care to treat serious injuries amounted to cruel treatment).

[57] ICTY, *Prosecutor v. Zoran Kupreškić* et al., Judgment Trial Chamber (IT-95-16-T), 14 January 2000, para 566 (holding that the expression "other humane acts" found in Article 5(i) of the ICTY Statute "undoubtedly embraces [...] the enforced disappearance of persons."). For more on the development of international law on the issue of enforced disappearance, see Vermeulen 2012.

[58] It should be noted that human rights bodies have also dealt with the material framework for detention in NIAC, with similar limitations. See, e.g., ECtHR, *Kurt v. Turkey,* Judgment (App. No. 24276/94), 25 May 1998, para 125 (holding that failure to record the date, time and location of detention, the name of the detainee as well as the reasons for the detention and the name of the person effecting it is incompatible with Article 5 ECHR); HRC 2001 ("The prohibitions against [...] unacknowledged detention are not subject to derogation."). See also, HRC Draft General Comment on Article 9 ICCPR, available at: www.ohchr.org/EN/HRBodies/CCPR/Pages/DGCArticle9.aspx (accessed 27 April 2014), para 56 (noting that prolonged incommunicado detention violates Article 9 ICCPR and may also amount to ill-treatment or even torture in violation of Article 7 ICCPR).

doing so carefully consider drawing upon IHL applicable to IAC. To illustrate, this section explores the same aspects of detention previously discussed, including the degree of confinement and the process of registration and notification.

Before all else, it must be noted that NIACs differ from IACs in significant ways. IACs predominately involve the regular forces of adversary States. In NIAC, the forces of at least one party to the conflict are non-State armed groups. Captured enemies in IAC are therefore in most cases POWs, bringing with them the internal discipline and command structure of the military they belong to. As they enjoy combatant immunity, they are in most cases interned without charge and benefit from the non-punitive detention context already discussed. In NIAC by contrast, States remain free to criminalize and punish all conflict-related activities committed by their adversaries. IACs also involve parties of different nationalities, and possibly languages and customs. NIACs typically take place within the same State, with the notable exception of extraterritorial NIACs.

Yet there are also some important similarities between IACs and NIACs, and it is with respect to these similarities that parallel approaches might be considered. Beginning with the issue of confinement, for example, even though detained members of non-State forces in NIAC could be prosecuted under domestic law, States often hold them on grounds and according to procedures that do not fall squarely within the criminal justice system. As with internment in IAC, administrative detention in NIAC is often intended to ensure the security of the detaining party, and the detainees are not being punished for having committed a crime. This parallel with IAC raises the question of whether a non-punitive detention environment is equally appropriate for security detainees in NIAC. In other words, to what extent would the reasoning behind the Geneva Convention prohibition of confinement and other rules related to freedom of movement inside and outside the camp in IAC law be of use when it comes to security detention in NIAC?

Certain differences between IAC and NIAC might immediately come to mind in response. For example, one could point out that GC III's prohibition on confinement works because State armed forces bring their internal command structure and order into the detention facility with them—confinement is not required because order will be guaranteed by the detainees themselves. Armed groups, by contrast, generally do not have the discipline of State forces and they therefore cannot constitute a fair analogy to State forces in this regard.

However, the assumption that armed groups are necessarily distinguishable in their discipline from State armed forces might not always hold true. Some armed groups are in fact highly organized and have a leadership and structure that is capable of imposing order on them both on and off the battlefield.[59] Additionally, care should be taken not to assume that the IAC internment regime is intended to apply only to regular, disciplined State armed forces. In addition to the formally regulated, uniformed armed forces of a State, the Geneva Conventions cover the

59 For an analysis of the variation in degree of organization among different armed groups, see Sinno 2011.

internment of other individuals, including irregular forces that meet certain requirements under GC III and individual civilian security threats that meet certain criteria under GC IV.[60] In other words, IAC law already contemplates the internment of irregular forces and individuals who engage in hostile activities, and the material framework for detaining them remains that of either GC III or GC IV.[61] Do these individuals differ so greatly from members of non-State armed groups in NIAC? And, if not, would the degree of confinement and other conditions of detention foreseen by GC IV for members of irregular forces and other direct participants in hostilities perhaps be appropriate for members of armed groups in NIAC as well?

Another potentially relevant difference between IAC and NIAC is the involvement of a non-State armed group in the latter. IHL regulates all sides to a NIAC, meaning that the non-State party to the conflict has obligations as well. But, given the generally limited capabilities and resources of most non-State armed groups relative to States, do they even have a margin to decide the degree to which their detainees will be confined? The question is certainly pertinent, but considering the diversity of armed groups that have existed past and present, the answer necessarily has to be that it depends. At a general level, however, it may be sufficient to draw attention to the underlying principle that security detention in armed conflict must have a non-punitive character and invite further exploration on what this notion might mean for a non-State armed group.

The issue of registration and notification of detention illustrates another similarity between IAC and NIAC: in both situations, a number of factors are likely to impede or delay the collection and transmission of information regarding detainees. Sudden influxes of large numbers of detainees—along with the other destabilizing effects of armed conflict—will likely stress State institutions in both types of armed conflict, creating the need for a system to expedite the collection and communication of detainee information. In addition, the parties to the conflict will almost certainly not have direct contact with one another, creating the need for some sort of neutral intermediary to pass along the information. In light of these exigencies, would an approach similar to the direct notification by detainees via capture card envisaged by the Geneva Conventions be of potential interest as a way of facilitating and ensuring notifications? And how might the model of the central information agency inform thinking about how best to enable messages to be transmitted to areas and individuals when they otherwise could not be?

Here again, the similarities and differences between IAC and NIAC would have to be carefully considered, and much might depend on the intended recipient of the notification. When it comes to notification of family members, the analogy to IAC might not be difficult to draw. In both IAC and NIAC, it is likely that families of detainees will live in areas that the detaining party cannot reach for security reasons.

---

[60] See Article 4(A)(2) GCIII; Article 4 GCIV.

[61] It should be noted that some take the position that GCIV was not intended to apply to unprivileged belligerents. For a detailed discussion of the issue, see Dörmann 2003.

From the perspective of States, a neutral institution can (and the ICRC often does) serve as an intermediary for notifications and other contact with families. From the perspective of armed groups—many of which are often accused of secret and incommunicado detention—the existence of some sort of neutral depository of basic information for purely humanitarian reasons might also have the advantage of stripping away some of the deterrents to transparency. Armed groups that capture State forces would not have to compromise on an unwillingness to communicate with the government they seek to defeat, communicate directly with the families of the service-members they capture, or risk revealing information about the location of their forces through direct communication with the government. However, when it comes to notification of the adversary as such, drawing an analogy to IAC will likely become more fraught. The objectives of notifying a State of which the detainee is a national versus notifying a non-State armed group for which the detainee fought are difficult to compare, and States involved in NIACs are likely to be cautious about the potential legitimizing effect of communicating with non-State armed groups, even through an intermediary.

Finally, in addition to rules on confinement and notification, some of the other protections previously discussed help illustrate similarities between IAC and NIAC. Most obvious, for example, is the risk of harm resulting from exposure to hostilities. Keeping detainees away from the combat zone and in facilities that provide shelter from bombardment and other conflict-related hazards is clearly as relevant in NIAC as it is in IAC, a commonality that is evidenced by the provisions of AP II discussed above. Additionally, although classic NIACs may in most cases take place on the territory of a single State, it is not unusual for them to occur along ethnic or religious lines or to involve extraterritorially operations, making many of the protections in IAC related to language and culture equally relevant. Thus, whatever the differences might be between IAC and NIAC, it seems clear that many of the core concerns that IHL seeks to alleviate are present in both types of conflicts.

## 2.4 Conclusion

The exceptional circumstances generated by armed conflict do not only create a need for clarity on the legal grounds and procedures for detention. They also give rise to unique vulnerabilities among detainees and a corresponding need to ensure that the parties to the conflict effectively safeguard against them through adequate material conditions of detention. The provisions found in IHL applicable in IAC are evidence of this need. IHL rules on confinement and the general detention environment, registration and notification, safety from the dangers of hostilities, and ensuring that detainees are communicated with in a language they understand are all, to some degree, tailored to address the particular vulnerabilities that result from armed conflict. Therefore, while it is true that IAC and NIAC differ in important respects, their similarities should not be overlooked when attempting to determine how best to adapt to the needs arising from the particular situation that is NIAC. The protections found in the Geneva Conventions are a sensible starting point for reflection.

Finally, it should be recalled that the most important similarity between IAC and NIAC is that the inherent vulnerability and the fundamental human needs of persons deprived of liberty remain regardless of the type of conflict that is occurring. What changes is the surrounding context and the actors involved. It is true that the specific dynamics of NIAC might necessitate adaptations in approach. But any conversation about a material framework for detention in NIAC should be driven by an effort to ensure humanitarian protection where the realities of war might tend toward its erosion.

## References


Bellinger J, Padmanabhan V (2011) Detention operations in contemporary conflicts: four challenges for the Geneva conventions and other existing law. Am J Int Law 105:201–243

Chesney R (2011) Who may be held? Military detention through the habeas lens. Boston Coll Law Rev 52:769–870

Corn G, Chickris P (2012) Unprivileged belligerents, preventive detention, and fundamental fairness: rethinking the review tribunal representation model. Santa Clara J Int Law 11:99–168

Dörmann K (2003) The legal situation of unlawful/unprivileged combatants. Int Rev Red Cross 85:45–74

Goodman R (2009) The detention of civilians in armed conflict. Am J Int Law 103:48–74

HRC (2001) General comment no. 29, states of emergency (article 4) (24 July 2001). UN Doc. CCPR/C/21/Rev.1/Add.11

Huskey K (2012) A strategic imperative: legal representation of unprivileged enemy belligerents in status determination proceedings. Santa Clara J Int Law 11:195–208

Ministry of Foreign Affairs of Denmark (2012) The Copenhagen process on the handling of detainees in international military operations: principles and guidelines. www.um.dk/en/~/media/UM/English-site/Documents/Politics-and-diplomacy/Copenhangen%20Process%20Principles%20and%20Guidelines.pdf. Accessed 27 April 2014

Pejic J (2005) Procedural principles and safeguards for internment/administrative detention in armed conflict and other situations of violence. Int Rev Red Cross 87:375–391

Pejic J (2011) The European Court of Human Rights Al-Jedda judgment: the oversight of international humanitarian law. Int Rev Red Cross 93:837–851

Pictet J (ed) (1958) Commentary on the Geneva conventions of 12 August 1949, vol IV. International Committee of the Red Cross, Geneva

Pictet J (ed) (1960) Commentary on the Geneva conventions of 12 August 1949, vol III. International Committee of the Red Cross, Geneva

Rodley N, Pollard M (2009) The treatment of prisoners under International Law, 3rd edn. Oxford University Press, Oxford

Sinno A (2011) Armed groups' organizational structure and their strategic options. Int Rev Red Cross 93:311–332

Vermeulen M (2012) Enforced disappearance: determining state responsibility under the international convention for the protection of all persons from enforced disappearance. Intersentia, Cambridge

Webber D (2012) Preventive detention in the law of armed conflict: throwing away the key? J Nat Secur Law Policy 6:167–205

# Chapter 3
# A Dialogue: Ethics, Law, and the Question of Detention in Non-International Armed Conflicts

**James Turner Johnson**

**Abstract** This chapter begins with the observation that non-international armed conflicts pose serious challenges to the efforts to regulate war in both international law and recent ethical discourse, and argues that neither has responded well to these challenges. Various problems in both are identified. The second part of the chapter examines the historical conception of just war accepted as consensual in the West from the high Middle Ages till early in the modern period, arguing that it provides a helpful frame for thinking ethically about non-international armed conflicts. The third section of the chapter carries this reasoning forward, applying it to non-international armed conflicts generally and to the problem of detention in such conflicts specifically.

**Keywords** Aquinas · Armed conflicts · Detainees · Ethics of war · Grotius · International law · Just war

## Contents



---

James Turner Johnson (Ph.D., Princeton 1968) is Distinguished Professor of Religion and Associate of the Graduate Program in Political Science at Rutgers—The State University of New Jersey, where he has been on the faculty since 1969. His research and teaching have focused principally on the historical development and application of the Western and Islamic moral traditions related to war, peace, and the practice of statecraft. This particular article was not subject to the peer-review process. Used by the YIHL.

---

J.T. Johnson (✉)
State University of New Jersey, New Brunswick, NJ 08901-8525, USA
e-mail: jtj@rci.rutgers.edu



T.D. Gill et al. (eds.), *Yearbook of International Humanitarian Law 2013*,
Yearbook of International Humanitarian Law 16, DOI 10.1007/978-94-6265-038-1_3

## 3.1 Introduction

The majority of armed conflicts in the world since World War II have been non-international. This includes the ongoing conflicts in Iraq, Afghanistan, and Syria, numerous past and present conflicts in various African countries, the various stages of the conflicts in the Caucasus region of Russia, civil wars like the case of Ceylon and those of the breakup of Yugoslavia, and conflicts involving on one side acts of terrorism under the auspices of groups like Al Qaeda and the IRA and on the other various forms of military response, as well as many other examples.[1] This is, for practical purposes, the new face of war, and it poses serious challenges to efforts, both legal and moral, to impose restraints on the conduct of armed conflict.

International law, on armed conflict as well as on everything else it treats, depends finally on agreements among states, and imposing the standards set in such agreements on armed conflicts that do not arise between or among states is hardly straightforward or in any way easy. The states in which such conflicts occur understandably claim precedence for their own domestic standards, including not only domestic laws but more permissive frames for emergency action by government forces against those challenging the government. Measures taken, or proposed to be taken, against non-state threats may controvert rights and liberties guaranteed to a state's own citizens and may even, as an undesired but real effect, impinge on those rights and liberties. At the same time, the asymmetric nature of such conflicts mean that the particular forms of armed force employed will be different for each party to the conflict, the lines of division between combatants and noncombatants will be indistinct,[2] and lines of responsibility and accountability will intentionally be kept obscure on the side of insurgent forces. Existing international mechanisms aiming at limiting the harm done in armed conflict, as well as the specific limits themselves, do not transfer well to non-international conflicts; nor do the means of enforcement, which depend finally on the ability to gather information about the conduct of the parties to a conflict, function evenly or otherwise well when the focus is non-state armed groups whose very existence may hinge on closing off access by outsiders to information about their operational procedures. Finally, the most prominent example of an effort to craft positive international law so as to apply to non-international conflicts, 1977 Geneva Protocol II, has never attracted anything like the same level of state approval as the 1949 Geneva Conventions it intends to supplement. This does not provide an encouraging precedent. It has been suggested to me that customary law has by now closed various gaps left by Protocol

[1] While in legal discussions there may be disagreement as to whether all the examples named properly qualify as "non-international armed conflicts," this listing reflects usage in the fields of ethics, history, and international relations and, I think, also ordinary language. In any case, my broader point is the one made in the following sentence.

[2] I am using "combatant" and "noncombatant" here as these terms are normally used by ethicists to refer to the functional relationship of the denoted classes of people to direct participation in the use of armed force. This usage differs from the legal.

II, and that may be so in certain respects, though I suggest the degree to which it has done so is far from self-evident, and there are importantly different conceptions of what constitutes customary law.

Approaching non-international armed conflicts from the standpoint of ethics has its own difficulties. Contemporary ethical reflection and discourse on armed conflict takes place largely through one or another form of just war thinking, but any review of recent discourse on just war shows widespread disagreement as to what the idea of just war is, what is the proper way of drawing out its meaning, and what its implications may finally be for specific issues in contemporary armed conflict.[3] Much of this thinking, moreover, is rooted in debates about potential and actual uses of armed force by the United States against other states, and it has sometimes been argued that the just war idea has only to do with such state-against-state uses of force. The idea of just war was effectively lost as a basis for ethical reflection through much of the modern period and was only recovered in the context of debates over nuclear weapons and the Vietnam war, efforts that in fact reinvented the just war idea in different ways. Three major streams of recent just war thinking flow out of the work that defined that recovery and reinvention: Paul Ramsey's books *War and the Christian Conscience* and *The Just War*, both from the 1960s,[4] focused on the Christian ethical obligation of love of neighbor and reaching back to Augustine's conception of divinely inspired love, *caritas*, for its foundation, whose influence is exemplified in recent work by Jean Bethke Elshtain, Oliver O'Donovan, and Nigel Biggar[5]; Michael Walzer's 1977 book *Just and Unjust Wars*,[6] whose conception of just war has influenced most recent philosophical thought on just war, though in different ways, as exemplified in the work of David Rodin,[7] who follows Walzer in basing his conception of just war in human rights, and Jeff McMahan,[8] who bases his version of just war in the requirements of individual ethics, developed by utilitarian moral reasoning; and finally, the United States Catholic bishops' 1983 pastoral letter, *The Challenge of Peace*,[9] which as a way of seeking compromise with Catholic pacifists defined their conception of just war as beginning with a general "presumption against war" and described an expanded list of criteria which, if all are satisfied, could overrule this general presumption in a particular case.[10] This last conception of just war, which is functionally a form of modern-war pacifism, has influenced a number of Catholic thinkers, including later spokesmen for the bishops' national conference, who have used it to oppose the use of force in even such cases as the action to reverse the Iraqi takeover of Kuwait in 1990–1991. More

[3] For a fuller analysis of this matter see Johnson 2013.

[4] Ramsey 1961 and 1968.

[5] See Elshtain 2003; O'Donovan 2003; Biggar 2013.

[6] Walzer 1977.

[7] See Rodin 2003.

[8] See McMahan 2009.

[9] National Conference of Catholic Bishops 1983.

[10] See my critical analysis of the bishops' conception of just war in Johnson 2005.

broadly, participants of various stripes in public policy debates have adopted the bishops' list of just war criteria, which focuses heavily on their newly added criteria of last resort, reasonable hope of success, and overall proportionality. Besides these examples, a further new version of just war based on Kantian thinking has been advanced by philosopher Brian Orend.[11] Finally, my own conception of just war is based on what I regard as the classic statement of the just war idea, which originally coalesced in Western canonical and theological thought beginning in the twelfth century and remained stable as a cultural consensus until well into the modern period.[12] I describe this conception and its roots more fully in the following section as a way of defining the frame for my thinking about the matter of detention of enemies in non-international armed conflicts today. The differences among all these various "just war" positions are so substantial that recent just war thinkers are effectively at war with one another, rather than representing an ethical consensus. Much of recent just war thinking, moreover, has focused on limiting international wars and especially on restraining United States use of military force; when the subject has included non-international armed conflict, as is the case particularly for just war thinkers who have addressed terrorism and United States military efforts against it, the focus has remained on how the United States should behave.

The gist of what I have described above is that neither international law nor major forms of contemporary ethical discourse are well positioned to address the particular problems posed to efforts to restrain armed conflict of a non-international character. I would add that the loss of their common historical connection makes it difficult to pursue dialogue between international lawyers and ethicists. In the next section I move to explain further my own approach to contemporary ethical reasoning about armed conflict on the basis of the classic historical understanding of just war, which I will argue by its nature connects ethics and law and provides a useful basis for thinking about what is right and wrong in the context of non-international armed conflicts. In the final section I use the frame of thus established to directly address the matter of detention of enemies in non-international conflicts.

## 3.2 Setting the Frame

For an ethicist to write in a volume devoted to international humanitarian law will no doubt strike some readers as an anomaly: what do ethicists know about law, anyway? The differences in our uses of language noted above illustrate a conceptual divide: how we think about particular matters in armed conflict is not the same, and professionals on each side of the divide may fault those on the other for lack of precision or for simply getting the important issues wrong. For others, though, the

---

[11] See Orend 2006.

[12] For recent summary statements of this conception see Johnson 1999, pp. 41–70; Johnson 2011, pp. 15–20.

recognition of such differences may perhaps serve as a reminder of the need for a dialogue that could be of use to both ethicists and lawyers, when such dialogue tends in fact to occur only sporadically and in limited contexts, without resulting in the creation of continuing personal interaction across the territorial lines of these two professional fields of discourse on the specific topic that brought the parties together for the moment. There are of course exceptions to this rather bleak view, some of the most notable being the continuing efforts exemplified by publications on particular topics that include chapters by both specialists in law and specialists in ethics. But at the end of the day most of the contributors to such interactions return to their own disciplinary frame, where by the nature of things it is difficult to incorporate whatever might have been learned from those working in a different frame, even if it might have seemed valuable to do so while the interaction was going on. I suggest an important reason the links between these two professional fields are in practice so hard to maintain traces to a loss of historical consciousness and knowledge in both. In setting out to explain the historically based conception of just war I work from, I reach back to the common roots of later legal and ethical thinking on the use of armed force on political authority, to a time when ethics and law were not the distinct fields they have since become.[13]

While the deep roots of the just war idea extend into classical Roman and Greek thought and political practice and into the biblical depictions of the wars of the ancient Israelites, and while the late classical Christian theologian Augustine drew on both these influences in a number of brief passages on just war found in various contexts in his writings, the creation of a coherent, systematic conception of just war came only in the Middle Ages. The original statement of such a conception appeared in the canonist Gratian's 1148 compilation of canon law, the *Decretum*. This was debated, clarified, and more tightly focused by the contributions of two generations of his canonical successors, the Decretists and the Decretalists, over the next century. A succinct statement of their resulting position in a theological frame was provided by Thomas Aquinas in his *Summa theologiae* (II/II, Q. 40, "On War") three-quarters of the way through the thirteenth century. The concept for which these writers used the phrase "just war," *bellum justum*, focused on the moral conditions for resort to the use of armed force: who could authorize such resort (a temporal ruler with no temporal superior), a justifying cause (broadly, the vindication of justice when an injustice had been done; more specifically, as Aquinas puts it, quoting Augustine, the recovery of that which had been wrongly taken and the punishment of evildoers), and the governing intention (again understood through language taken from Augustine: negatively, the avoidance of wrong intentions such as those specified by Augustine in his treatise *Contra Faustum* XXII.75, and positively, the end of peace. Just war as thus conceived had directly to do with the exercise of government in the face of challenges to the fundamental purposes of political community. Though Aquinas used Augustine's language to explain the necessary

[13] For full development of this historical conception see, besides the two summary statements referenced in the previous note, Johnson 1981, pp. 121–189.

conditions for *bellum justum*, the three conditions he specified corresponded directly to the three goods of politics as identified in Roman thought—order, justice, and peace. The nature of good order (and thus the ruler's responsibility) and of justice was defined here in terms of natural law, understood through the recovery of Roman legal thought that took place at the same time the just war conception was being pulled together and systematized. *Bellum justum*, thus defined, had to do with use of armed force by the supreme public authority for the public good, and was set off from two other kinds of use of such force by private persons for private reasons: *duellum*, dueling, the use of force between private parties to settle a dispute between them, and *defensio*, self-defense "on the spot" (*incontinenti*) against an immediate threat, understood to be a right given by natural law to everyone. *Bellum justum* sought to limit and even eliminate the former, since private parties could appeal to the highest ruler for adjudication of any dispute, and it supplemented self-defense "on the spot" by providing for repairing any injustice done and punishing those responsible for such injustice. In these functions *bellum justum* functioned juridically. The sovereign ruler, of course, had the responsibility of *defensio* against both internal and external threats to the interlocked order, justice, and peace of the political community, but this required no special notation in the definition of just cause for such a ruler to resort to armed force.

As thus described, *bellum justum* had to do with disturbances of public order, justice, and peace, whether these arose internally or externally. "Just war," as we now translate this Latin term, did not refer specifically to conflicts between and among distinct political communities,[14] as modern usage of the term "war" implies, but rather referred to the fundamental responsibility of the governing authority, given in the natural law, to protect and maintain a just and peaceful order in the community wherever a threat to it might arise. The classical conception of just war thus aimed at brigandage or crime by self-constituted armed bands as well as the unjust actions of subordinate warlords within the political community using the forces in their control for their own personal ends. Indeed, in the twelfth-century context, these were the main threats to the well-being of political communities. Among the three goods of politics order thus had the place of "first among equals," since without right order there was no peace and no justice. Violence was endemic to medieval societies; descent of organized community life into anarchy was a persistent threat. But at the other extreme, a ruler with no superior might use the power at his command to become a tyrant. Thus the responsibility of the ruler was defined in terms of his responsibility for the good of the community as a whole and manifested specifically as the responsibility for vindicating justice. Neither anarchy nor tyranny did this: one was the absence of order, the other a wrongful order, and neither, in their neglect of justice, produced peace. Disputes might occur between sovereign rulers of different political communities which could ultimately be settled

---

[14] I use the term "political community" to render the Latin *res publica/respublica*, literally "public entity"; it is often rendered as "commonwealth." These were not yet states, in the modern sense of that word, but they are what became states.

only by appeal to arms, but *bellum justum* referred centrally to the exercise of the sovereign ruler's responsibility to maintain and protect the good of his own political community against whatever injustices might arise. The use of armed force might be necessary to discharge this responsibility; force itself was good or bad depending on whether it served this overall good. Such was the classical understanding of *bellum justum*, just war.

I suggest this way of thinking transfers rather straightforwardly to the present-day phenomenon of non-international armed conflict, understood broadly as exemplified by the various examples I offered at the beginning of this paper. A present-day terrorist threat is much like the problem of brigandage by well organized, self-constituted bands confronted by the governing authorities in the Middle Ages.[15] A present-day rebellion resulting in control by force of arms over part of a country's territory and populace can look much like the effort of a local medieval nobleman to carve out his own territory for his own benefit. This is simply to say that the classic understanding of just war attempted to address these "non-international" issues, not to say that today we should come to the same conclusions about them. For the classic conception of just war centrally prioritized order. Aquinas categorized "sedition"—which he described as "contrary to the unity of the multitude"—as a mortal sin.[16] Shortly before that, in speaking of "strife," he wrote, "Strife seems to be a kind of private war. [As such,] strife is always sinful."[17] This became the default position in medieval and early modern just war thinking, for which the major threat to the goods of political life was the rampant lawlessness that only public order could check. Luther took the same position: in the German Peasants' Rebellion of 1524–25 he believed many of the peasants' grievances justified, but when they took up arms against the established authorities, he urged the nobility to put them down ruthlessly by force of arms: "Stab, smite, slay."[18] But in perspective this seems extreme, and medieval and Reformation thought also imposed its own correctives. In the present day a just war thinker might well come to judge opposition to an especially harsh and unjust rule more justified than the need to maintain governmental order as such, perhaps citing Aquinas's position on the injustice of tyranny[19] or Calvin's argument for subordinate "magistrates" to depose an unjust superior,[20] and likely moving on to join international lawyers in citing the responsibility to protect doctrine as formalized in the 2005 World Summit

---

[15] Noting this might seem to reinforce the argument that terrorist threats and acts are a problem for domestic law enforcement (that is, a police problem), not properly occasions for military response. In the context of classic just war thinking this is not a distinction that would matter, since the focus was on the responsibility of the ruler to maintain order, and thus peace, by responding to threats and/or acts violating justice. My suggestion is that refocusing present attention similarly may lead to different, and perhaps more useful, thinking about threats, acts, and proper responses.

[16] Aquinas 2006, Q. 42, Article 2.

[17] Ibid., Q. 41, Article 1, *I answer that.*

[18] Lehmann and Schultz 1967, p. 54.

[19] Aquinas 1965, p. 37.

[20] Calvin 1957, pp. 1499–1502.

Outcome document.[21] But the form of the classic understanding of just war also provides a reminder that rebellion and resistance against perceived injustices are not enough: non-state groups engaging in the use of armed force to support their claims must be held to a standard of justice that applies to all, and they have their own obligation to produce an order that vindicates such justice. The ongoing present-day conflict in Syria provides a potent illustration of how hard it is to maintain the balance this way of thinking requires: the government has a record of tyrannical and unjust rule, but the alternative order offered by the al Qaeda-linked "Islamic Emirate" forces opposing it offers its own version of injustice and tyranny, while the loosely linked indigenous Syrian rebels are thus far united only in opposition to the Assad government and do not seem to have enough unity to offer their own alternative order for the society as a whole.

While, in the classic definition of just war, the term *bellum justum* was first applied only to the conditions for resort to armed force, when this definition came together there was already in existence in the canon law two kinds of restraints on conduct in the use of armed force: first, a definition of noncombatant immunity in terms of lists of classes of people not normally involved in the use of arms—women, children, the aged and infirm, clergy and members of religious orders, peasants working their land, townspeople, travelers on a journey, and the property of all of these; and second, efforts to ban certain types of weapons (crossbows, bows and arrows, siege weapons) which, in the context of medieval warfare, posed special kinds of problems: the first two were more deadly in battle, since the penetrating wounds they caused often led to infection and death, while siege machines by their nature tended to cause indiscriminate and disproportionate damage, and all three types of weapons were associated with hired soldiers, who were not subject to the limits imposed by the code of chivalry—the medieval forerunner of today's military codes of conduct and rules of engagement. Over time these canonical rules became closely associated with the code of chivalry or *loi d'armes*, with the combined result rendered in Latin as *jus in bello*. A century after Aquinas, during the latter part of the fourteenth century and in the context of moral reflection related to the 100 Years War, this *jus in bello* was consolidated with the summary conception of just war put in place by Aquinas, so that the idea of just war as understood afterwards had both components commonly cited in defining just war today: one defining the conditions for resort to the use of armed force (the term *jus ad bellum* was invented and applied to this much later) and one defining limits on conduct in the just use of armed force (the *jus in bello*).[22]

[21] UN General Assembly Resolution on the 2005 World Summit, available at: http://www.un.org/womenwatch/ods/A-RES-60-1-E.pdf, paras 138–139.

[22] While most recent just war thinking follows Ramsey in rendering the *jus in bello* in terms of the moral principles of discrimination and proportionality, international law on armed conflict has followed the pattern of lists of specific classes of noncombatants and efforts to limit or outlaw certain weapons and means of war. Each approach has its strengths and weaknesses, and they are best when combined.

This consolidated conception of just war remained in stable form as a broad cultural consensus in the West well into the modern period, with a variety of thinkers commenting on it and drawing out its implications for the changing shape of politics and warfare through the sixteenth and early seventeenth centuries.[23] But during this period also the natural-law basis of this inherited conception of just war was gradually eroding, first for the Spanish thinkers as a result of the Spanish encounter with the diverse cultures of the New World and later throughout European society as a result of the tensions, conflicts, and cultural divisions caused by the Protestant Reformation and the Catholic reaction to it. The Spanish Jesuit Suarez's 1584 treatise *De Bello*, developed as part of a broader work on Aquinas's treatment of the theological virtue of *caritas* (divine love), was the last major specifically ethical discussion of just war for nearly 400 years. Grotius's much better known and more influential *De Jure Belli ac Pacis*, first published in 1625, proceeded importantly from the inherited idea of just war, but this work substantially rethought and refocused this idea. Putting the important changes briefly, for him what could be known from natural law about the justification of using armed force was reduced to the right of self-defense against attack, which was a natural right of every individual. From this Grotius reasoned upwards to the state's right to use armed force as the result of the delegation of their individual right of self-defense against attack from the individuals in the political community to those who ruled in that community. The idea of sovereignty, which on the medieval natural-law conception employed in the classic form of just war thinking referred to the personal moral responsibility of the ruler with no superior to serve the good of the political community as a whole, was redefined by Grotius in terms of the sanctity of the borders of each political community, and thus the inhabitants of this community and their own "laws and privileges," against external threat. On this conception it became the state that is sovereign, and the ruler is reconceived as an agent of the people of the state, acting on their delegated authority. This was the intellectual birth of the modern understanding of sovereignty and the modern conception of justified resort to armed force as defensive only. Where the older just war tradition survived more intact, and indeed received new emphasis, was in Grotius's working out in detail the requirements of the *jus in bello*. This also set the pattern for later modern thinking. Finally, though, a fundamental impact of Grotius's work was his reformulation of thinking about justified warfare in terms of law, placing the rules he drew out and described in terms of the "law of nations," which he connected to the basic kind of natural law he recognized. His title, *De Jure Belli ac Pacis*, *On the Laws of War and Peace*, was no accident; after him a form of just war tradition continued in Western thought, but now it took the form of reflection on war in terms of law, as seen in the work of later theoretical writers like Pufendorf, Wolff, and Vattel, in the late nineteenth-century phrase "the laws and customs of war," and in

---

[23] The broad range of backgrounds, interests, and perspectives of these thinkers is well reflected in the authors included in the Carnegie Institute series *Classics of International Law*, which included volumes covering works by Francisco de Vitoria, Pierino Belli, Alberico Gentili. Francisco Suarez, and Hugo Grotius, among others.

the development of international positive law on armed conflict. Fundamentally, though, this way of thinking drew on the earlier just war tradition, and ethicists and lawyers alike might gain from reflecting back on the history of development of that tradition. In important respects what the "law of nations" theorists were engaged in doing was recovering a sufficient basis of consensus on right use and conduct regarding armed force, rebuilding what had been lost when the older idea of natural law collapsed into a minimal conception of the individual right of self-defense against threat or attack. The same can still be said about the present-day conception of positive international law: the fact of agreement signifies deeper agreement on values, but disagreement signals the opposite. More attention to the underlying traditions of value, I have argued in various contexts especially for the case of Western and Islamic cultures, holds some promise of uncovering further areas of agreement, but also may sharpen areas of difference. It may be particularly useful to explore these underlying traditions in regard to limiting non-state uses of armed forces.[24]

## 3.3 Working from the Frame: Ethical Reflections on Detention in Contemporary Non-International Armed Conflict

My approach to thinking about ethics and armed conflict, based in the classical historical conception of just war, puts me at odds with three themes that have been prominent in recent ethical thought based in reinvented versions of the just war idea: (1) that the idea of just war represents a special possibility of exemption to a general presumption against any use of armed force, a conception that is the official position of the U.S. Catholic bishops; (2) that the very idea of justified war needs to yield to non-forceful means of resolving conflicts, a fundamentally pacifist position argued from a variety of perspectives: and (3) that the just war idea is fundamentally about restraints that must be placed on the use of armed force to protect individual rights in contexts of conflict, a position widespread among contemporary philosophers as well as human rights advocates. All three of these themes agree in beginning with the idea that the use of armed force is always morally tainted and thus to be avoided whenever possible and heavily restrained if any use does occur. Here the use of force is the moral problem. The classical frame of just war thinking instead focuses on the responsibility of government to deal with threats of harm or harm already done to the order, justice, and peace—in brief, to the overall good—of the society governed and the web of connections between and among that society and other societies, whose continuing welfare affects one's own. On this way of thinking the use of armed force is not inherently an evil to be avoided but a tool that may need to be employed to rectify injustice and punish wrongdoing. Just war, on

[24] See for example, Johnson 2011, pp. 49–71.

this reading, is a response to a fault, and those responsible for causing that fault are proper objects of the just use of force.

Because the just use of armed force is to respond to some injustice threatened or already accomplished, the force used is justified only so far as it seeks to restore the justice that has been violated and prevent the violation from happening in the future. For classic just war thinking it is the responsibility of the governing authority to make sure that force is used only this way. Though this conception dates to the Middle Ages, it describes very well the responsibility of good government in any time and place. If the use of force for this purpose oversteps and goes beyond a response to the existing threat or accomplished harm and an effort to protect against its recurrence in the future, then this use of force itself becomes a source of injustice, and the responsible governing authority slides into a form of unjust government, for which medieval and early modern thinkers used the term "tyranny." On the model of classic just war thinking the limits of justified use of force are determined by the level of the threat of harm as well as by harm already done. In armed conflict it is the enemy's threat or use of lethal measures that justifies our own use of such measures: in the simplest form of this model, he is threatening to kill or has already done so, and this justifies our killing him, either to protect ourselves or to punish him for the wrong he has done. Ramsey and other recent theorists would argue, and I think this is right, that morally speaking this is an upper limit, and that if injustice can be averted or righted by less than lethal means, then these should be employed. But the upper limit remains: killing may be morally responded to by killing. Moreover, this is not simply permission in such a case: the wrongdoing threatened or already accomplished imposes a moral obligation to respond, to set the wrong right.

In warfare, whether international or not, it is moral to kill because the enemy has already killed and is threatening to kill some more. Whether one has to kill in response depends on the circumstances, but to respond is a moral obligation, and killing those engaged in activity harmful to the well-being of the community is a moral option. For Ramsey the Christian theologian, choosing not to kill if killing can be avoided follows from Christian love of neighbor, since the enemy, Ramsey reminds his readers, is also a neighbor. But three centuries earlier Hugo Grotius had made a similar argument without drawing on Christian neighbor-love when he commented positively on the practice of the Romans to take their enemies prisoner when they could do so instead of simply killing them all, although they could, by the law of nature, justifiably do the latter.[25] Grotius's argument was that in terms of proportionality as defined in the law of nature, taking someone prisoner who might justifiably be killed satisfies natural justice while staying within the bounds of proportionality.

One might go in a variety of directions from Grotius's reasoning, but to do so for all of them would not be productive here. One of these directions, though, raises an interesting and ultimately troubling question. The Roman army and Roman society

---

[25] Grotius 1949, pp. 71–77.

were well enough organized to have the capacity for accommodating prisoners, even if not very well by present-day standards. Not all military forces or all their parent societies, though, possess this capacity. The requirement that soldiers no longer capable of fighting for whatever reason should be taken prisoner goes back, in the West, at least to the chivalric code, and the obligation to make such persons prisoners of war is a core requirement of the law of war. Granted that states engaged in international armed conflict have this obligation, to what degree does it apply in non-international armed conflicts? If parties to such conflicts have this same obligation, does this imply that if they do not in fact have the capacity to take prisoners and hold them in humane conditions, they should not have taken up arms? Is there a link between not having such a capacity and indiscriminate attacks against any and all members of the enemy population? Conversely, what are the implications for the other party's conduct?[26]

The line of reasoning regarding the taking of prisoners during an armed conflict, offered in different terms by Ramsey and Grotius, bears directly on the morality of detention in non-international armed conflict, including such diverse contexts as the ongoing conflict in Congo, other recent and ongoing African conflicts, and the war against terrorism. But drawing direct conclusions as to how it bears is far from straightforward. In the African conflicts the targeting of noncombatants is a routine means of making war, but so is also the taking of prisoners for the purpose of enslaving them: to provide child soldiers, for example, or to provide women to serve as sex slaves for the fighters. These practices illustrate the difficulty of simply preferring captivity to killing those affected: both are inhumane forms of behavior. For an external force attempting to establish order and end the conflict to adopt a

---

[26] It is also worth recalling in the present context that classic just war reasoning, as noted earlier in references to Aquinas on the evil of "strife" and Luther's denunciation of the German Peasants' Rebellion of 1524–25, generally took the preservation of social order as *prima facie* justified and accordingly opposed "private" taking up of arms even if for the purpose of responding to injustice. Grotius stood at the end of this way of thinking, stressing the rights of the Dutch to fight against the rule of the King of Spain to protect their integrity as a people and their right to control the territory on which they had lived for generations. He also relocated the idea of sovereignty so as to define it, not from the personal moral responsibility of the ruler, but from the right of individuals to protect themselves against injustice, delegating that right upwards to the state but never relinquishing it. Later human rights theory, down to the present, follows this same model. For this reason much modern thought on who possesses justice in armed conflicts turns out to prefer movements challenging state power as having an inherently more just cause, and the very military weakness of a non-state actor compared to that of the state it opposes may provide reason to hold them to different standards as to conduct. A present-day debate among philosophers challenges the idea of the moral equality of combatants, arguing that those persons fighting in an unjust cause are, in effect, murderers. Much of this line of argument appears to be directed against particular uses of military force by certain states: e.g., United States military action in Iraq and Afghanistan. I myself think Grotius was correct to carry the thrust of his argument towards equal obligations of all parties to an armed conflict, and this definitely has implications for how all parties to a present-day armed conflict should conduct themselves—in regard to provision for prisoners as in regard to who may rightly be a target.

practice of internment of fighters in the various local armed movements might be admirable, but the eventual release of these detainees might well lead to a reignition of the conflict. Ethicists have written on the evils of child soldiers and women being taken captive for use as sex slaves, as they have also written against practices such as rape and amputation of limbs as means of war, but I know of no efforts to apply moral analysis to the whole range of evils found in these conflicts, including the relative moral status of detention of captured fighters from the various parties to the conflicts.

The means cited above all qualify as terrorism in the general sense, because they are part of an overall pattern of fighting so as to terrify and demoralize the whole population of those regarded as enemies. In much recent usage, of course, the term "terrorism" is applied more narrowly to the sorts of activity associated with particular groups, and the designation of such groups and any activity associated with them as "terrorist" becomes a way of indicating their illegitimacy. Within the United States there has understandably been much focus on Al Qaeda, with the "long war" against it defined as much by its own declaration of an enduring enmity against "America and the West" as by U.S. policy to eradicate Al Qaeda and its influence. Detention of persons identified as linked in various ways to Al Qaeda for indeterminate periods at Guantánamo continues to be a focus of criticism from a variety of quarters. In line with what I have argued above, where there is someone who may justifiably be killed in such a context, taking that person prisoner and detaining him (or her) until the conflict is over or until that person can be reasonably judged not to pose a threat of future harm is a moral step exemplifying restraint in comparison to what maximally be done (e.g., killing him or her either in a firefight or by a drone strike). In simple moral terms, detention of such persons is directly comparable to taking prisoners of war in a state-on-state armed conflict. But because the just war idea originated not only (or mainly) to address conflicts between political communities or harm threatened or accomplished by actors outside one's own community, but also to address the responsibility of government to deal with criminal behavior within the society, and since there are many in the present day who have argued for dealing with terrorists and other non-state actors involved in armed conflict within the frame of criminal activity, detention of those implicit in the threat or harm already done is also, in simple terms, like locking up criminals to punish them for their crimes and prevent them from future criminal activity.

This way of thinking, as also noted earlier, is at odds with several other themes found in recent moral argument. The last of these, focused on the importance of protecting individual rights in situations of armed conflict, has sometimes been taken to mean that there can be no use of force to correct injustice if it harms such rights, whether the rights of noncombatants or even the rights of those persons responsible for perpetrating the injustice. A version of this argument is that detention of enemies in the conflict with groups engaging in such terrorism (often referred to as against terrorism as a phenomenon) and, implicitly, in other non-international armed conflicts, necessarily violates the rights of those individuals detained, so that their detention is immoral.

Now, there are numerous morally important issues here. One is whether the persons detained in fact deserve to be, and the important test here, following the reasoning offered above, is whether if in the context of the use of armed force they might legitimately have been killed rather than taken prisoner. The fundamental guide for this is the combatant-noncombatant distinction found in both just war reasoning and, translated into legal language, in international law.

A second issue is how long any individual should be detained, and on this the burden of proof falls on the detaining authority. In situations of armed conflict, and especially in non-international kinds of armed conflict involving fighters who live and work in close proximity to noncombatants, discrimination between who is properly treated as a combatant and who is not is often hard to achieve, and it may not be possible at all in specific situations. The moral rule of double effect clarifies when harm to noncombatants may not be morally wrong: when the action in question is not wrong in itself, when the intention of the action and its specific direction are a legitimate target (including combatant persons), and when the indirect, unintentional harm to noncombatants is not so great as to outweigh the good of damage to the legitimate target.[27] Michael Walzer adds a further qualification that has not been generally accepted in moral reasoning: that the actor, foreseeing the unwanted evil effect, "seeks to minimize it, accepting costs to himself." In the ambiguities of non-international armed conflicts people may unavoidably be taken prisoner and detained even when they are not genuinely combatants properly subject to such treatment. Detention, at least ideally, provides an opportunity to verify their status, and unlike the case of indirect, unintended victims of a lethal strike, this opportunity in principle allows detention to avoid the unwanted, unintended "double effect" of a kinetic strike. I say "in principle" because the fog of non-international armed conflict is inherently thicker than that of international war, but the obligation remains to try to avoid the harm that detention does to persons not rightly detained.

Another moral issue is the treatment of detainees. I am among those who believe that humane treatment should be the rule and transparency should be practiced to verify this. This rules out "black sites" and treatment that rises to the level of torture.

Still another issue is how long the detention may properly last. In international war the rule is that it may continue only so long as the war lasts; when peace is agreed, the prisoners must be released to go home. Modifications of this may provide for prisoner exchanges and paroles during the conflict. Non-international conflicts, though, are often long in duration, may never end in a formal "peace," and when prisoners are released, they may not have a "home"—or at least a safe home—to go to. If they are regarded as guilty of violations of domestic law in their own homelands, then they may be at more risk than during their period of detention. How long detention ought to last in a non-international conflict is thus problematic, with no clear answer

[27] Ramsey 1961, pp. 39–49; Walzer 1977, pp. 152–159.

of the sort found in a formal state of international war. This problem forces us back to the reasons for the detention in the first place: that those persons detained represent a reasonable threat of wrongful harm or may have been involved in wrongful harm already done. For the latter, the measure of the length of detention is the appropriate punishment for the wrong done. But even when this is satisfied, there remains the question of the use of detention to remove a likely threat. A serious problem in contemporary non-international conflicts is that they are often rooted in reasons tracing to religious, ethnic, or other such difference. Now, of course, such animosity alone does not suffice to justify the use of armed force against those who bear it, either in ethics or in law; the justification requires acts. But in cases of actual conflicts in which such forms of animosity provide a rationale for action, so long as the animosity remains that is fired by these causes, releasing a detainee may simply be to allow him or her to return to the fight. This may, in effect, mean a life sentence, but if the detainee was subject to being killed in combat already, such a sentence may be the more moral choice, though clearly still one with difficulties.

Another important issue is the problem of persons detained who become known to have been involved in activities prohibited by law, whether domestic or international. Their imprisonment is of a different sort entirely from the detention of other persons in the course of a non-international armed conflict.

I turn now to one last issue, which has already been introduced above in another context: non-international armed conflicts by definition involve non-state groups as actors, and such groups may be inherently unable to take large numbers of their enemies prisoner and detain them as a way of taking them out of the conflict. In my experience opponents of detention in non-international armed conflicts do not take seriously the option which the behavior of many non-state groups makes plain: that their enemies may be treated with no regard for the combatant-noncombatant distinction and those taken prisoner will be held not simply to take them out of the fighting but to serve as hostages or slaves, subject to death, to serve some purpose of the captors. Examples I have in mind include the behavior cited above from conflicts in Africa, the taking of hostages by Al Qaeda-related militant groups, and various forms of behavior by Bosnian Serb forces during the Bosnian war, some of which qualify as forms of genocide. Of course not all non-state actors engage in such practices; the behavior of the indigenous rebel groups in the current Syrian conflict has been notably different from that of the fighters of ISIS (the self-styled Islamic State of Iraq and Syria) and, for that matter, the Syrian government forces. But the option between taking prisoners and engaging in more all-out forms of combat remains. Confronting this thought we are drawn back to the rationale for taking prisoners in warfare in the first place: it avoids killing them. One could take this reflection on the practice of non-state actors in armed conflicts in a variety of directions, I will simply make the observation that detention of enemies who have functioned as combatants is at bottom a humane measure, though it has to be carried out with due regard for the other responsibilities identified above.

## References

Aquinas T (1965) Selected writings of St. Thomas aquinas (trans Goodwin R). Bobbs-Merrill Co., Indianapolis
Aquinas T (2006) Summa Theologica Part II-II (Secunda Secundae) (trans: Fathers of the English Dominican Province). Benziger Brothers, New York
Biggar N (2013) In defence of war. Oxford University Press, Oxford
Calvin J (1957) Institutes of the Christian religion (trans: Beveridge H). Wm. B. Eerdmans Publishing Co., Grand Rapids
Elshtain J (2003) Just war against terror: the burden of American power in a violent world. Basic Books, New York
Grotius H (1949) The law of war and peace (De jure belli ac pacis) (trans: Loomis L). Walter J. Black Inc., Roslyn
Johnson J (1981) Just war tradition and the restraint of war: a moral and historical inquiry. Princeton University Press, Princeton
Johnson J (1999) Morality and contemporary warfare. Yale University Press, New Haven
Johnson J (2005) The war to oust Saddam Hussein: just war and the new face of conflict. Rowman & Littlefield Publishers, Lanham
Johnson J (2011) Ethics and the use of force: just war in historical perspective. Ashgate, Farnham
Johnson J (2013) Contemporary just war thinking: which is worse, to have friends or critics. Ethics Int Aff 27(1):25–45
Lehmann H, Schultz R (1967) Luther's works: the Christian in society III, vol 46. Fortress Press, Philadelphia
McMahan J (2009) Killing in war. Oxford University Press, New York
O'Donovan O (2003) The just war revisited. Cambridge University Press, Cambridge
Orend B (2006) The morality of war. Broadview Press, Peterborough
Ramsey P (1961) War and the Christian conscience: how shall modern war be conducted justly?. Duke University Press, Durham
Ramsey P (1968) The just war. Charles Scribner and Sons, New York
Rodin D (2003) War and self-defense. OUP, New York
Walzer M (1977) Just and unjust wars: a moral argument with historical illustrations. Basic Books, New York

# Part II
# Other Articles

# Chapter 4
# Autonomous Attack—Opportunity or Spectre?

**Bill Boothby**

**Abstract** This article tackles the tricky legal issues associated with autonomy and automation in attack. Having clarified the meanings of these notions, the implications of the rules of weapons law for such technologies are assessed. More challenging issues seem, however, to be raised by the law of targeting, and in particular by the evaluative assessments that are required of attackers, for example in relation to the precautions in attack prescribed by Additional Protocol I. How these rules can sensibly be applied when machines are undertaking such decision-making is therefore addressed. Human Rights Watch has called for a comprehensive ban on autonomous attack technologies and the appropriateness of such a proposal at the present stage of technological development is therefore assessed. The article then seeks to draw conclusions.

**Keywords** Autonomous · Automation · Distinction · Weapons law · Targeting · Precautions

## Contents



William Henry Boothby, Air Commodore (Retired)

B. Boothby (✉)
Woking, Surrey, UK
e-mail: williamboothby@hotmail.com



T.D. Gill et al. (eds.), *Yearbook of International Humanitarian Law 2013*,
Yearbook of International Humanitarian Law 16, DOI 10.1007/978-94-6265-038-1_4

## 4.1 Introduction

The horrors that warfare can impose on soldiers, fighters and on hapless civilians unwillingly caught up in the fight was played out in the 1940s throughout Europe, North Africa, in the Atlantic and Pacific Oceans and Far East, in the 1960s and 1970s in Indo-China, in the 1990s in the former Yugoslavia, in more recent times in Libya and Syria and in all of these years and many more besides in countless other parts of the world. As carefully worded legal rules strive more prescriptively to protect those who try to keep out of the fight, it is those very individuals who form an ever-increasing proportion of the casualties. War in which men use weapons against one another is, truly, a miserable affair.

Against this depressing reality, in this article we consider whether increasing levels of automation in attack and futuristic notions of autonomous attack decision-making represent an opportunity to be grasped with both hands, or yet another unwanted scientific advance that promises even less discrimination in the 'killing game'.

Autonomy and automation are of course discrete notions, but we must be clear as to the meaning to be ascribed to each. Section 4.2 of this article will therefore assess what a clear taxonomy might look like. International law prohibits the use of some weapons, means and methods of warfare in armed conflict and imposes restrictions on the use of other weapons. In Sect. 4.3 we will consider the weapons law rules of most evident relevance to autonomous attack technologies. A distinct branch of the law of armed conflict, the law of targeting, regulates how weapons may be used. In Sect. 4.4, we will discuss what targeting law rules are likely to have the greatest relevance to autonomous attack technologies. The notion of autonomous attack decision-making has provoked controversy, and Human Right Watch has proposed a comprehensive ban on such technologies. In Sect. 4.5 we will ponder whether a comprehensive ban is merited at this stage. In Sect. 4.6 we will conclude by proposing a way ahead.

## 4.2 What Do We Mean?

The 2002 attack in which the US targeted Qaed Senyan al-Harthi in Yemen by means of a Predator remotely piloted aircraft equipped with a Hellfire missile proved the concept of aerial attack in the modern era using remotely piloted aircraft.[1] Applied to this use of the air environment, automation involves the mechanisation of the platform's decisions to a degree falling short of autonomy. It would, however, be wrong to think of these matters exclusively in terms of the air

[1] Dworkin, 'The Yemen Strike', *Crimes of War Project* 14 November 2002, http://www.mafhoum.com/press4/122P7.htm (last accessed on 27 January 2014).

environment, as automation and autonomy are equally applicable in maritime warfare,[2] on land, in outer space and indeed in cyberspace. Nevertheless, elements of the discussion in the present article will be by reference to air platforms. But what do automation and autonomy mean? We start by considering what doctrine has to say.

An automated system has been described as one that, responding to inputs from one or more sensors, is programmed logically to follow a pre-defined set of rules to provide an outcome.[3] If you know the rules under which it operates, you can predict that outcome. An automated system functions in a self-contained manner once deployed, and will independently verify or detect a particular type of target object and then fire or detonate the munitions.[4] Automated weapons are nothing new; consider for example certain kinds of mine or booby-trap.[5]

Autonomous systems, by contrast, take the matter several stages further. They employ an understanding of higher-level intent and direction and an awareness of their environment to take appropriate action and thereby bring about a desired state. Critical to autonomy is the system's ability to decide a course of action from alternatives without depending on human oversight and control. Its overall activity is predictable but individual actions may not be.[6] The system operates independently; the software identifies and engages targets without being programmed to target a specific object. Importantly, the International Committee of the Red Cross (ICRC) has suggested that development of a truly autonomous weapon system that can implement international humanitarian law represents a monumental programming challenge that may well prove impossible.[7]

No doubt the increasing role of automation in everyday life and consequent familiarity with it will influence its perceived acceptability in warfare, and logic suggests that peacetime technologies that are clearly adaptable for use in military

---

[2] The UK Ministry of Defence Joint Doctrine Note 2/11 (JDN 2/11), 'The UK Approach to Unmanned Aircraft Systems', 30 March 2011, issued by the UK Development Concepts and Doctrine Centre (DCDC), para 508. For an assessment of future development of maritime autonomous capabilities, see Mackenzie et al., 'Autonomous Sea Platforms Emerge at Euronaval', 15 October 2012, http://www.aviationweek.com/Article.aspx?id=/article-xml/AW_10_15_2012_p04-500687.xml (last accessed on 27 January 2014), but note currently available autonomous maritime weapons such as the Sting Ray Mod 1 torpedo described at BAE Systems, 'Sting Ray Mod 1 Lightweight Torpedo', http://www.baesystems.com/product/BAES_021507/sting-ray-mod-1-lightweight-torpedo?_afrLoop=876128570457000 (last accessed on 27 January 2014).

[3] Markus Wagner observes that automated systems "do not involve a human operator during the actual deployment but rather the necessary data is fed into the system prior to deployment of the system"; Wagner 2013, pp. 104–105.

[4] Kellenberger 2011, p. 5.

[5] Backstrom and Henderson 2012, pp. 488–490.

[6] JDN 2/11 at para 205. See also Wagner 2012, p. 12.

[7] ICRC Report to the 31st Conference of the Red Cross and Red Crescent, 'International Humanitarian Law and the Challenges of Contemporary Armed Conflicts', EN 31IC/11/5.1.2, October 2011, p. 40.

environments will increasingly be seen on the battlefield.[8] This will be attributable to their appeal, which in turn will be derived, for example, from their convenience of use, from their tendency to limit the dangers faced by friendly force personnel and from their ability to enable timely responses to rapidly appearing, potentially overwhelming threats. The future battlespace will involve threats that require rapid and flexible responses at speeds that presuppose automated decision-making; other advantages claimed for these new technologies include saving lives; fearlessness; remembering orders; absence of emotional responses; suitability for dull, dangerous and dirty tasks; needing no or less rest; having shareable intelligence and computation speed.[9] It follows from this that the weapons discussed in this article are likely to be seen as having such utility that their further development and eventual procurement will likely be regarded as critical to operational success.

Autonomous weapons can loiter, seek, identify and engage targets and can report the point of weapon impact. The Wide Area Search Autonomous Attack Miniature Munition, for example, is a small cruise missile with a loiter capability that can seek a specific target and that, on acquisition, attacks or requests permission to do so. The autonomous element of the weapon is, it seems, posing significant engineering issues, for example because it is likely beyond current technology for the machine to make the complicated assessments required to determine whether or not a particular attack would be lawful if there is an expectation of collateral damage.[10]

Burrowing down a little deeper, "so long as it can be shown that the system logically follows a set of rules or instructions and is not capable of human levels of situational understanding, then they should only be considered automated."[11] If that is doctrine's interpretation, Peter Asaro describes as autonomous "any system that is capable of targeting and initiating the use of potentially lethal force without direct human supervision and direct human involvement in lethal decision-making," a formulation which could include systems current doctrine sees as 'automated'. So working out a widely accepted taxonomy is a clear priority for future work.[12]

For example, under national doctrine, an unmanned aircraft would be part of an automated system if, first, it is pre-programmed either to proceed to a set location and there to fire a weapon or if, second, having reached a pre-set location, it searches a defined area of territory for specified objects which, when detected, it recognises using on-board image recognition technology, and attacks. If, third, a similarly equipped unmanned platform were additionally programmed to make

[8] Anderson and Waxman 2013, pp. 2–3. Consider, perhaps as an example of automation, the data fusion systems that are increasingly to be found in combat aircraft in which data from diverse sensors is fused for presentation to the operating aircrew, with a view to alleviating cockpit workload, for example on such systems as Typhoon/Eurofighter; see for example Eurofighter Technical Guide 2009, http://www.eurofighter.com/fileadmin/web_data/downloads/misc/EFTechGuideENG-1109.pdf.

[9] Singer 2011, pp. 337–340.

[10] Backstrom and Henderson 2012, p. 491 and pp. 493–494.

[11] JDN 2/11, para 206(b).

[12] See Asaro 2012, p. 690.

evaluations or decisions or to undertake certain procedures before it then decides whether and how to undertake the attack, this would seem to render it an autonomous as opposed to an automated system. So the doctrinal distinction seems to lie in genuinely mechanical decision-making processes that go beyond simple recognition resulting in automatic attack.[13]

An apparently different understanding is reflected in a recent United States Department of Defense Directive[14] which describes a weapon system that "can select and engage targets without further intervention by a human operator" as autonomous. It would seem clear that this would characterise the second and third examples discussed in the previous paragraph as autonomous systems.

The US definition would seem to focus the discussion on all technologies that cause the machine to select the target for an attack without human involvement at that moment. It seems to matter little to this definition that recognition technology is used to decide that an observed object or person is a target. The point deserves repeating that if we are to have a sensible debate on these matters, generally accepted terminology is essential. For the purposes of the following discussion, autonomy and automation will be understood in accordance with the JDN 2/11 definitions noted earlier in this Section. Legal issues are likely to arise, however, in relation to both autonomous and certain automated attack technologies, so in the following discussion the reader will frequently see reference to both.

## 4.3 Feasible Limits What Is Expected Regarding Weapons with a Defensive Posture

### *4.3.1 Weapons Law, Automation and Autonomy*

The basic principle is that "[i]n any armed conflict, the right of the parties to the conflict to choose methods or means of warfare is not unlimited."[15] Certain legal principles applying to weaponry flow from this. The first, cardinal principle that is customary and thus binds all states prohibits the employment of "weapons, projectiles and materials and methods of warfare [that are] of a nature to cause superfluous injury or unnecessary suffering."[16] It would, however, seem unlikely that the automated or autonomous nature of the target selection mechanism will directly contribute to the degree of suffering or injury that the weapon system causes. That is most likely to be affected by the munition, the missile, bomb or other

[13] Anderson and Waxman 2013, p. 2: "genuine autonomy in weapons will probably remain rare for the foreseeable future and driven by special factors such as reaction speeds and the tempo of particular kinds of operations".

[14] US Department of Defense Directive 3000.09, 'Autonomy In Weapon Systems 13', 21 November 2012.

[15] API, Article 35(1) and see Oeter 2013, pp. 121–125.

[16] API, Article 35(2).

device, that is actually being delivered to the target. It is not therefore necessary to discuss the principle further.

The second fundamental weapons law principle prohibits weapons, means or methods of warfare that are indiscriminate by nature. The treaty formulation of the rule that is so widely accepted as to be customary and thus universally binding includes as prohibited indiscriminate attacks: "(b) those which employ a method or means of combat which cannot be directed at a specific military objective; or (c) those which employ a method or means of combat the effects of which cannot be limited as required by th[e] Protocol; and [which], consequently, in each such case, are of a nature to strike military objectives and civilians or civilian objects without distinction."[17]

This rule will have great importance where automated and autonomous attack technologies are concerned. The likelihood, however, is that the recognition technology will be specifically designed to try to ensure that the weapon engages the intended kinds of object or the intended persons, which in each case have previously been assessed as constituting lawful targets. If the system reasonably achieves that intended purpose it will not be indiscriminate by nature. If, however, when tested it is found to be just as likely to attack, for example, civilian vehicles as military ones, the rule is likely to be breached by its use. It will therefore be critical to test the technology in realistic conditions of the sort likely to be encountered in the intended circumstances of use, and then to consider that test performance carefully in determining whether the rule has been complied with, that is whether the automated or autonomous technology adequately distinguishes between objects and persons it is lawful to attack and those entitled to protection.

The third composite, but not customary, rule of the law of weaponry protects the environment. It comes in two parts, the first of which prohibits States party to the UN Environmental Modification Convention (ENMOD) to "engage in military or any other hostile use of environmental modification techniques having widespread, long-lasting or severe effects as the means of destruction, damage or injury to any other State party."[18]

'Widespread' encompasses "an area on the scale of several hundred square kilometres", 'long-lasting' suggests "a period of months, or approximately a season" and 'severe' involves "serious or significant disruption or harm to human life, natural and economic resources or other assets."[19] Again, the automated or autonomous nature of the decision processes we are discussing in this article would not seem to have a direct impact on the environment. The rule will have greater relevance for the warhead, munition and associated damage technologies. This will also be the case in relation to the second part of the environmental protection rule

---

[17] API, Article 51(4).

[18] Convention on the Prohibition of Military or any Other Hostile Use of Environmental Modification Techniques, Geneva, 2 September 1976 (ENMOD), Article I.

[19] Conference Understanding relating to Article I, available at the ICRC treaty database at www.icrc.org.

which prohibits the employment of "methods or means of warfare which are intended, or may be expected, to cause widespread, long-term and severe damage to the natural environment"[20]; it is therefore prohibited to "use [...] methods or means of warfare which are intended or may be expected to cause such damage to the natural environment and thereby to prejudice the health or survival of the population."[21] The terms 'widespread, long-term and severe' do not necessarily have the same meaning as in ENMOD, and while in the ENMOD rule breach of any one of the criteria suffices to breach the rule; in the API rule all three features must be established, so the threshold for an API rule breach is that much higher.

There are no rules of international law of armed conflict that specifically address automated or autonomous attack technologies. Such technologies might of course be applied to weapons for which there are specific weapons law rules, such as anti-personnel landmines, cluster munitions, chemical or biological weapons, particular fragmentation weapons, incendiary weapons and so on. The *ad hoc* weapons law rule will tend, however, to address the lawfulness of the munition that is employed as opposed to the lawfulness of the automated or autonomous decision-making process.

States party to API have the obligation, "[i]n the study, development, acquisition or adoption of a new weapon, means or method of warfare [...] to determine whether its employment would, in some or all circumstances, be prohibited by th[e] Protocol or by any other rule of international law applicable to the High Contracting Party."[22] It is therefore important to work out what 'weapons', 'means' and 'methods' of warfare entail. 'Weapons' are offensive capabilities that can be applied to a military object or enemy combatant.[23] The current use of an object,[24] the intention to use it in a particular way[25] and the operational purpose that it is designed to fulfil[26] are all individually capable of characterising an object as a 'weapon,' so the term seems to describe an offensive capability applied, or intended or designed to be applied, to a military object or enemy combatant. The damaging or injurious effect of the weapon does not need to derive from a kinetic impact,[27] which leads to the conclusion that a cyber tool would be a weapon if it has the violent consequences referred to in the present paragraph were it to be used, or intended or designed to be used against a military objective or enemy combatant.[28]

---

20 API, Article 35(3).

21 API, Article 55(1).

22 API, Article 36.

23 Boothby 2009, p. 4 citing McClelland 2003.

24 If a combatant uses an autonomous system to damage an adverse party to an armed conflict, that 'use' converts the system into a weapon.

25 If an autonomous system is intended to be used to cause damage to an adverse party to an armed conflict, the intention to use the system in that way converts it into a weapon.

26 Designing an autonomous system to be used against an adverse party to an armed conflict to cause death, injury or damage would cause the system to constitute a weapon system or part of such a system as the case may be.

27 See Commentary to AMW Manual Rule 1(ff), at para 1.

28 Tallinn Manual, para 2 of the Commentary accompanying Rule 41.

Means of warfare are weapons, weapon systems[29] or platforms employed for the purposes of attack[30] and methods of warfare are activities designed adversely to affect the enemy's military operations or military capacity.[31]

In an Article 36 weapon review of an automated or autonomous weapon system, the generic circumstances in which it will be used are considered. The question for the reviewing state is whether the legal rules that apply to it prohibit or restrict those intended circumstances of use. If they do, the weapon review should draw attention to those prohibitions or restrictions. States that are not party to API are, arguably, bound by a customary rule requiring that they review new weapons before fielding them.[32] Neither the treaty nor the customary rule prescribes the form or procedures associated with such reviews. Depending on the circumstances, advice to a commander or full, reasoned and written advice to ministerial authorities may be called for.[33]

## 4.4 Targeting Law and Autonomy

One of the core, customary rules of the law of armed conflict requires that a distinction be constantly maintained between civilians and combatants and between civilian objects and military objectives.[34] Whether autonomous attack technologies can be employed consistently with this principle will depend on the technical performance of the recognition technology. Where there is doubt as to certain matters, an attack must not proceed.[35] In the case of attacks against objects, the decisive question is whether a weapon system can differentiate sufficiently between, for example, the military objects[36] it is designed to recognise and civilian objects that are protected by the law. An automated or autonomous system may, for example, be programmed to examine an object it observes by reference to the

---

[29] Dinstein 2010, p. 1.

[30] AMW Manual, Rule 1(t).

[31] AMW Manual, Rule 1(v).

[32] See St. Petersburg Declaration, 1868, final paragraph, Article 1 of Hague Convention II of 1899 and Article 1 of Hague Convention IV of 1907. The Regulations referred to include Article 23(e), which prohibits the employment of weapons of a nature to cause superfluous injury or unnecessary suffering. Hays Parks, applying the maxim *pacta sunt servanda,* concludes that states have a general duty to engage in good faith performance of their treaty obligations and that "[t]his would have included a duty to ensure military weapons and munitions complied with the Hague Convention IV and obligations contained in other treaties: Hays Parks 2005, pp. 55–57. See also Lawand 2006, p. 4.

[33] Tallinn Manual, commentary accompanying Rule 48, para 3.

[34] API, Articles 48, 51(1) and (2) and 52(1).

[35] Wagner 2013, p. 113.

[36] The technology is likely to seek to distinguish, in the case of objects, between those that are military in nature and those that are not, so the reference to military object, as opposed to objective, is deliberate.

particular characteristics of, say, a tank, artillery piece or armoured personnel carrier. If sufficient points of similarity are achieved, the controlling software may determine that the observed object is a military object that it is lawful for the weapon system to attack. Testing will, however, be important to evaluate the reliability with which the weapon system conducts this recognition process and, thus, its ability to comply acceptably with the distinction principle. Such testing may prove challenging and it seems likely that computer modelling will also be required.[37]

Even greater technical challenges confront the development of technology for the automated or autonomous attack of individuals. The principle of distinction, when applied to attacks that target persons, requires that combatants and civilians directly participating in hostilities be differentiated from civilians taking no part in the hostilities.[38] Some research may focus on the mechanical observation of characteristics peculiar to combatants, such as their metallic footprint or, perhaps, aspects of their behaviour and movement.[39] In relation to metallic footprint, however, nanotechnological developments in military equipment such as the manufacture of rifles using plastics and other substances may challenge the appropriateness of such an approach.

Article 41(1) of API requires that a "person who is recognized, or who in the circumstances, should be recognized to be hors de combat shall not be made the object of attack." This will require that an automated or autonomous weapon system be capable of determining whether the person is in the power of an adverse party to the conflict, for example by virtue of capture, whether he has clearly expressed an intention to surrender or whether he is incapacitated by wounds or sickness and thus unable to defend himself.[40] An argument that the automated or autonomous character of the attacking platform means that the 'should be recognized' element of Article 41(1) does not apply would seem to raise complex issues. If, say, the pilot of a manned aircraft might be expected to recognise hors de combat status, there will be those who will suggest that the test in Article 41(1) is made out. If, however, an autonomous or automated technology that is unable to recognise hors de combat status is employed because it is the only viable method of countering a relevant enemy capability, the argument becomes more tenable that the circumstances were such that no recognition of hors de combat status could reasonably be expected.

Developing software to identify when a potential human target is manifesting an intent to surrender, is incapacitated by wounds or sickness or is in the power of an adversary is likely to prove challenging. It follows that if automated or autonomous

37 Asaro 2012, pp. 692–693.

38 API, Article 48.

39 For approaches based on behaviour modelling, see Schachtman, 'Army Tracking Plan: Drones that Never Forget a Face', 28 September 2011, www.wired.com/dangerroom/2011/09/drones-never-forget-a-face/ (last accessed on 27 January 2014).

40 API, Article 41(2).

attack systems are to be procured that are incapable of making such determinations, a human operator should, where practicable, be 'on the loop', that is in a position to observe and countermand the system's attack decisions. If it is not practicable for the human operator to countermand decisions, say because of the rapidity of required decision-making, the 'should be recognised' criterion in Article 41(1) would, arguably, not apply and the use of the automated or autonomous technology in such circumstances without a human operator 'on the loop' would seem to be justifiable.

However compliance with the distinction principle is achieved, the software must also be able to determine whether the targeted individual is otherwise protected from attack[41] and must comply with the precautions that the law requires to be taken in attack. Article 57 requires that constant care be taken to spare the civilian population, civilians and civilian objects.[42] The use of the passive mood in this formulation makes it clear that all persons who are involved in automated or autonomous attack operations must take care and that there is no time when they are excused from the obligation.[43] In the context of automated and autonomous attack technology, this means that designers of the software, those who load the relevant data into the mission control systems, those who plan the mission, those who authorise the mission, platform operators who monitor the mission and all those processing information on which mission-relevant decisions, whether mechanically-made or human, are based are obliged to do all they can to ensure that civilians and civilian objects remain protected.

Having set forth this somewhat general precautionary obligation, Article 57 specifically requires those who plan or decide upon attacks to do everything feasible[44] to verify that the objective of the attack is neither civilians nor civilian objects but is a military objective.[45] Two aspects of this rule require elucidation, namely who is implicated and what verification will involve. In the context of automated or autonomous attacks, the notion of 'those who plan' would clearly extend to those who plan the particular sortie. Common sense suggests that those who develop the target recognition software also have a responsibility to do all that they can to ensure that only lawful targets are recognised. It would seem to be

41 Numerous classes of individual are specifically protected from attack, including medical and religious personnel, journalists, certain persons involved in cultural property protection duties, parlementaires, and civil defence personnel. By the same token, numerous classes of object are entitled to specific protection, including hospitals and other medical facilities and transports, cultural objects, objects indispensable to the survival of the civilian population and certain works and installations containing dangerous forces.

42 API, Article 57(1).

43 AMW Manual, rule 34 and associated Commentary.

44 The word 'feasible' has been interpreted by the UK as referring to that which is practicable or practically possible taking into account both military and humanitarian considerations; see UK statement (b) made on ratification of API on 28 January 1998.

45 Military objectives are defined in Article 52(2) of API. Article 57(2)(a)(i) does not refer explicitly to combatants, but it is clear that the precautionary rule involves verifying, in the case of an attack targeting persons, that the objectives are either combatants or civilians taking a direct part in hostilities.

unsatisfactory to adopt too narrow a definition of 'planning' for these purposes. In any case, this obligation to do all they can is really only a development of the earlier general obligation to take constant care. Developing recognition systems that differentiate well between civilians and combatants/directly participating civilians, testing the reliability of these systems carefully before use, ensuring that systems that do not perform satisfactorily during realistic tests are not fielded, ensuring that those who initiate the sorties are properly trained in the employment of the relevant technology, ensuring that the workloads of persons tasked with countermanding inappropriate automated/autonomous attack decisions are commensurate with the proper performance of that function are among the duties that this rule would seem to impose on planners of such sorties and on those in command of units that undertake them.

The reference in Article 57(2)(a)(i) to persons who 'decide upon' attacks may require clarification where by virtue of automated or autonomous technology, the weapon system is making the individual targeting decision. Who, in such circumstances, is deciding on the attack? The answer must be that those who decide that a sortie involving automated/autonomous attack technology shall be initiated have, for these purposes, 'decided upon' the attacks that the weapon system undertakes in accordance with the instructions that are fed into the mission control system at the commencement of the sortie. Those decision-makers therefore have a responsibility to satisfy themselves before the sortie commences that the scope of possible decisions that the weapon system is being permitted to make properly reflects the Article 57(2)(a)(i) obligations.

Article 57(2)(a)(i) also requires everything feasible to be done to verify that the objectives to be attacked are not entitled to special protection and that it is not otherwise prohibited to attack them. This immediately means that the target recognition software must be able to recognise, for example, items of cultural property, medical facilities, personnel, and transports, dams, dykes and nuclear electrical generating stations. Where the locations of such items are fixed, allocating a no-strike categorisation to their co-ordinates should be achievable, and thus would be feasible for the purposes of the obligation. If it would be feasible for alternative, manned platforms to implement these precautions in relation to movable objects and persons entitled to special protection, an automated or autonomous weapon system will be required to comply with similar precautions. Achieving that will likely involve the mission control software recognising features that are specific to the relevant movable object or class of objects or person or class of persons and, having made that recognition, the system will need to refrain from directing an attack at the relevant object(s) or person(s).

In practice, it will be for the lawyer to specify to the engineer developing the autonomous or automated capability the precautionary obligations that the system must comply with, the level of probability of correct target identification that is required and the probability of incorrect identification that cannot be tolerated.[46]

---

[46] See further Backstrom and Henderson 2012, pp. 510–513.

The final element in Article 57(2)(a)(i) is the more general obligation to do everything feasible to verify that it is not prohibited by the Protocol to attack the persons or objects that are the objective of the attack. This means, among other duties, that planners and decision-makers must do everything practically possible to ensure that the attack will not breach the discrimination rule in Article 51(4). Thus, while the focus in the Article 57(2)(a)(iii) precautionary rule that we will consider next is explicitly on compliance with the proportionality rule, this last element of Article 57(2)(a)(i) would, for example, require those planning or deciding to undertake automated or autonomous missions to do everything feasible to ensure that Article 51(5)(a) of API is complied with. This implies that the mission control software must be capable of determining whether the military objective that it is planned for the weapon system to attack, or that the weapon system itself decides to attack, in fact comprises separate and distinct military objectives. If the software determines that the target does in fact comprise separate and distinct military objectives, the software will need to assess whether those discrete military objectives are located within a similar concentration of civilians or civilian objects. This would likely have to be broken down into determining whether there are any civilians or civilian objects at all in the relevant vicinity. If there are, once the mission control software has determined that fact, it would then have to determine their quantity and would be required to assess whether their concentration can be described as 'similar' to that of the military objectives. This may of course involve comparing unlike phenomena, such as tanks with civilian persons. Finally, there would need to be a facility built into the software whereby the attack will be called off if these criteria, set forth in Article 51(5)(a), apply.

Those who plan or decide upon automated or autonomous missions must also refrain from deciding to launch an attack which may be expected to cause incidental loss of civilian life, injury to civilians or damage to civilian objects, or a combination of these things, that would be excessive in relation to the concrete and direct military advantage anticipated from the attack considered as a whole.[47] This is the proportionality rule, reflected in API, Articles 51(5)(a) and 57(2)(a)(iii). Such decision-making will in practice be based on an assessment of all the relevant information that is available at the relevant time, including 'pattern of life' data, information drawn from satellites, data derived from manned information-gathering aircraft and from unmanned information-gathering aircraft, information from human intelligence and other sources.

When planning an autonomous or automated mission, activities in the area of search may be seen to be so predictable that an expectation can be developed as to the civilians/civilian objects that will be present in a particular location at a specified time. Thus, it may be possible to undertake an unmanned autonomous attack mission in accordance with the rule if the area of search allocated to the platform is either remote desert, open ocean, some other depopulated area in which there is no

[47] API, Article 57(2)(a)(iii) and see statement (i) made by the UK on ratification of API on 28 January 1998.

prospect of civilians or civilian objects being present or where, perhaps for some other reason, the civilian injury or damage to be expected can be determined with acceptable reliability in advance of the mission. The generic military advantage to be anticipated from the attack of an object, say, that the algorithm software is designed to identify may, but will not necessarily, be known in advance. If it is known, this, coupled with the apparent reliability of the collateral damage forecast, may give a basis on which a proportionality evaluation can properly be undertaken.

However, an attack must be cancelled if it becomes clear that the objective of the attack is not a lawful target or that the attack will breach the proportionality rule.[48] This would seem to require that the mission control software of an automated or autonomous mission be programmed before the mission begins with information as to the situation that it should expect to observe in the vicinity of the target at the time when an attack is about to occur. If, as seems likely, it will not be feasible for the foreseeable future for software to conduct proportionality assessments because of the inherently evaluative nature of such assessments, perhaps an approach to this precautionary requirement would be to require the platform to refrain from undertaking any attack if the image that it observes of the vicinity of the target differs in any respect from that which it has been programmed to expect. One would have to accept that this may in practice imply the machine refraining from attack in circumstances where the changed situation in the vicinity of the target would either not affect the lawfulness of an attack, or even in circumstances where the altered circumstances imply increased military advantage or reduced danger of incidental injury or damage to civilians or civilian objects. Until the evaluative aspect of the proportionality test can be appropriately mechanised, there seems little alternative to such an approach.

The limited space available for this discussion dictates that other precautions that the law requires shall be considered somewhat more briefly. Thus, when a choice of targets exists for a similar military advantage, the target the attack of which involves least danger to civilians or civilian objects must be chosen.[49] This would imply that the weapon control software must be able to determine the similarity of the military advantage to be anticipated from the attack of competing objectives, to assess whether a choice is realistically available between particular targets and to assess which of these involves the least civilian danger.

If an attack may affect the civilian population, an effective advance warning must be given unless circumstances do not permit.[50] In relation to the matters discussed in the present article, circumstances might not permit the giving of a warning if, for example, a warning would improve the ability of the enemy to attack the automated or autonomous platform, or to remove the objective that the sortie is intended to attack, or to conceal it or in any other manner effectively to frustrate the purpose of the sortie.

---

[48] API, Article 57(2)(b).

[49] API, Article 57(3).

[50] API, Article 57(2)(c) and AMW Manual, Rule 37.

It will be for the development engineers to find ways of fulfilling the obligations identified in the present article. If target recognition equipment fulfils the military task of identifying and engaging the objects it was developed to attack, in doing so it will likely also fulfil the legal obligation to distinguish military objectives from civilian objects. As we have seen, however, the precautionary rules are more complex, and it is not at present clear that autonomous and highly automated attack technology is capable of ensuring that all of the persons and objects entitled at law to protection from attack are not in fact made the object of attack. If, however, the automated or autonomous platform is only permitted to search for targets within, say, an isolated and uninhabited area and at a time when it is known that civilians and civilian objects will be absent, the use of such technology to seek and prosecute targets within such narrow constraints may well be lawful, because evaluative precautions, such as consideration of the proportionality of foreseeable attacks, can be undertaken by human decision-makers before the mission starts.

If, however, there are civilians and civilian objects in the area where the search is to take place, or they are expected to enter that area during the period when the autonomous platform is operating, it will no longer be possible for human planners and those deciding whether to launch the automated or autonomous mission to know in advance the civilian injury or damage (or both) that are to be expected. This and the difficulty of knowing in a dynamic military campaign the military advantage that a target represents at a specific time may make it very difficult to mechanise the proportionality assessments required by API and discussed above.

It will also be challenging for an automated or autonomous weapon system to comply with the precautionary obligation to compare alternative, including non-automated, non-autonomous, ways of undertaking an attack with a view to assessing which available method minimises civilian damage and injury.[51] It may be that planners will consider the targets that the autonomous mission is intended to engage, will assess whether an autonomous mission is indeed the method that will minimise civilian dangers given what is known of the target area and will then cause the platform to call for the intervention of an operator if what it observes in the target area suggests that an alternative method should be considered. Ensuring that the automated or autonomous system is able to detect that an alternative method or means of attack should be considered, and that where such consideration is required it is given and an appropriate decision is made and implemented, may prove challenging.

Let us imagine an autonomous unmanned aircraft that is employing its sensors to search for targets. If incoming information leads, for example, to the conclusion that the object or person being searched for is no longer a military objective, combatant or directly participating civilian or that the attack would breach the discrimination rule, the mission should be called off and the search should be stopped. Similarly, if

[51] API, Article 57(2)(a)(ii) requires those who plan or decide upon attacks to "take all feasible precautions in the choice of means and methods of attack with a view to avoiding, and in any event to minimizing, incidental loss of civilian life, injury to civilians and damage to civilian objects".

for example new information reveals that a column of refugees is moving across the area of search, the assessment that was performed before the autonomous mission was planned should be reassessed and, if it is now concluded that the attack would no longer comply with the proportionality rule, the search and any decision to attack should be cancelled.

It follows from the discussion in this Section that for the foreseeable future a person will always need to be in a position to cancel automated or autonomous attack operations if the need should arise; so while the technology may be capable of operating autonomously or automatically, it will for legal reasons be necessary to keep a human being sufficiently in or on the loop to be able to observe what is taking place and, if necessary, to over-ride autonomously or automatically reached attack decisions. Foreseeable workloads of those monitoring such platforms must enable them to take proper decisions taking all available information into account.[52]

Automated and autonomous attack technologies are likely to raise complex issues concerning responsibility for the resulting attack decisions. An argument that it was the automated or autonomous weapon system that was at fault may lie if indeed the machine was not operating correctly in the technical sense, but if the machine was performing in accordance with the technical specification, an unacceptable outcome is likely to be the responsibility of those whose task it is to plan and initiate the mission or perhaps of those who were responsible for testing and/or procuring the weapon system. The mere fact that the platform has automated or autonomous decision making facilities does not shield the numerous human scientists, procurement personnel, engineers, technicians, computer experts, planners, commanders and others from the obligation to take constant care when undertaking their roles in the operation of the autonomous technology, and it seems likely that unacceptable automated or autonomous attacks will be due to human failure by one or more such individuals.

## 4.5 Is a Comprehensive Ban Appropriate?

Human Rights Watch has called for a global ban on autonomous weapons,[53] an outcome which would seem to be neither appropriate nor sensible.[54] The two preceding sections of this article have identified the vital legal rules that will

---

[52] This may have implications, as Peter Singer suggests, for plans that a single operator should control multiple platforms; Singer 2011, p. 342. Mike Schmitt and Jeffrey Thurnher take the view that at least for the foreseeable future, autonomous weapon systems will only attack targets meeting pre-determined criteria and will function within an area of operations set by human operators; Schmitt and Thurnher 2013, p. 241.

[53] See Human Rights Watch, 'Arms: New Campaign to Stop Killer Robots', 23 April 2013, http://www.hrw.org/news/2013/04/23/arms-new-campaign-stop-killer-robots.

[54] Following a comprehensive analysis of the subject, Mike Schmitt and Jeffrey Thurnher reach a similar conclusion; see Schmitt and Thurnher 2013.

determine the lawfulness of any weapon system employing such technology and the targeting rules with which any operation employing it must comply. We have noted that a state is legally obliged to review all new weapons in order to determine whether their employment would breach current law. We have seen that under particular carefully formulated and implemented constraints, autonomous attack technology is capable of being used in a manner that complies with existing targeting law rules. The discourse as to the legitimacy of using remotely piloted aircraft to undertake attacks has applied existing rules of the law of targeting. There is no doubt that those existing rules will also be applied in determining whether evolving autonomous attack technologies are legally compliant. So states must legally review new autonomous weapons and those that conflict with existing legal norms must not be fielded.

Mike Schmitt and Jeffrey Thurnher reach four critical, and correct, conclusions. First, autonomous weapons are not unlawful per se as a weapons category, in the sense that autonomy does not bear on their compliance with the superfluous injury and indiscriminate weapons rules. Second, their use in certain circumstances would be lawful and in other circumstances would not; the existing targeting rules are sufficiently robust to safeguard human values and such new technologies must abide by existing law. Third, though humans will be making the subjective proportionality and precautions decisions somewhat earlier than is normally the case, this does not impact on lawfulness and humans are not therefore really 'out of the loop'. Finally, humans remain accountable, including criminally, for the appropriate use of such systems, for orders to deploy them and for judgments as to their programming.[55]

While it is clear that those seeking to develop highly automated and autonomous weapons technologies have as an ultimate objective their use in more complex, urban environments in which protected persons and objects are present in considerable numbers, technical and legal challenges remain at the time of writing and it may well be that the ICRC's scepticism noted earlier in the present article is well-placed. However, in advance of the development of the technology to maturity, it is not appropriate to conclude that it will necessarily not be capable of satisfying the applicable legal norms, and it is difficult to see why the possibility of developing a technology that does satisfy all current relevant rules should be prevented simply because a human is not involved at a certain stage in the attack decision-making process. Such a logic would have been strengthened were it to be the case that human attack decision-making is always perfectly lawful. Regrettably, experience teaches us otherwise. It remains possible that the use of machines to make such decisions will remove the emotions that so often trigger mistaken attacks or, worse still, atrocities.

Perhaps the most important point is that it would be unbalanced to seek to prohibit automated and autonomous attack technologies without also considering the threats that the technologies are seeking to address. Threats that cannot be

55 Schmitt and Thurnher 2013, pp. 279–280.

countered by human decision-making because of their number, speed, scope or other factors may well necessitate automated or autonomous countermeasures. So, for example, if rockets and other munitions are being fired against a state in quantities that more conventional, manned defensive measures have some difficulty in countering, it is understandable that the authorities of a state confronted with such attacks will choose to develop an automated weapon to counter them.[56] Confronted with threats that conventional, manned defensive measures have difficulty in addressing, states may be expected to acquire the technologies that are required to establish and maintain security. It therefore seems unlikely that, at this relatively early stage in the evolution of these technologies, such states will be persuaded by the Human Rights Watch call for a blanket ban.

## 4.6 Concluding Remarks

Developmental work on highly automated and autonomous attack technologies and the fielding of weapon systems employing such techniques is likely to continue and even accelerate. Ken Anderson and Matthew Waxman are probably right that these developments are likely to be incremental, with each element of technical progress tending to build on what went before.[57] Undoubtedly, some complex autonomous technologies will emerge that raise complex legal issues. It will be for legal reviewers to resolve these issues by applying extant international law principles in accordance with Article 36 of API or the corresponding customary rule. It would seem sensible for states to discuss these matters, so far as national classification issues permit, with a view to achieving common legal understandings. Certainly, progress in the international discourse seems to require internationally agreed definitions of the relevant terms used. Furthermore, there would be merit in a more general discourse among states in which all new and emerging weapons technologies are considered with a view to taking timely international action where this is required.

---

[56] See Bumiller and Sanger, 'Israel Unveils Iron Dome Missile Defense System', New York Times 23 May 2011, http://atwar.blogs.nytimes.com/2011/05/23/israel-unveils-iron-dome-missile-defense-system/?_r=0, but consider for example Barry, 'Iron Dome: A Double-Edged Shield?', 23 November 2012, http://www.iiss.org/en/iiss%20voices/blogsections/2012-6d11/november-2012-f24f/iron-dome-4690 (last accessed on 27 January 2014) where the point is made that the Iron Dome weapon system, deployed by Israel as part of a comprehensive suite of measures to address e.g., rockets and certain other threats fired by Hamas against Israel from Gaza, does not appear to have 100 % success and can be overwhelmed if rockets are fired in greater numbers than the Iron Dome system has the capacity to address.

[57] See the explanation at Anderson and Waxman 2013, pp. 5–8. Mike Schmitt and Jeffrey Thurnher take the view that at least for the foreseeable future, autonomous weapon systems will only attack targets meeting pre-determined criteria and will function within an area of operations set by human operators; Schmitt and Thurnher 2013, p. 241.

## References

Anderson K, Waxman M (2013) Law and ethics for autonomous weapon systems: why a ban won't work and how the laws of war can. Hoover Institution, Stanford University. http://media.hoover.org/sites/default/files/documents/Anderson-Waxman_LawAndEthics_r2_FINAL.pdf. Accessed 27 Jan 2014

Asaro P (2012) On banning autonomous weapon systems: human rights, automation, and the dehumanization of lethal decision-making. IRRC 94:687–709

Backstrom A, Henderson I (2012) New capabilities in warfare: an overview of contemporary technological developments and the associated legal and engineering issues in article 36 weapons reviews. IRRC 94:488–490

Boothby WH (2009) Weapons and the law of armed conflict. Oxford University Press, Oxford

Dinstein Y (2010) The conduct of hostilities under the law of international armed conflict. Cambridge University Press, Cambridge

Hays Parks W (2005) Conventional weapons and weapons reviews. Yearb Int Humanitarian Law 8:55–142

Kellenberger J (2011) International humanitarian law and new weapon technologies. In: 34th round table on current issues of international humanitarian law. San Remo, 8–10 Sept 2011

Lawand K (2006) A guide to the legal review of new weapons, means and methods of warfare: measures to implement article 36 of additional protocol I of 1977. ICRC, Geneva

McClelland J (2003) The review of weapons in accordance with article 36 of additional protocol I. IRRC 850:397–415

Oeter S (2013) Methods and means of combat. In: Fleck D (ed) The handbook of international humanitarian law, 3rd edn. Oxford University Press, New York, pp 115–230

Schmitt MN, Thurnher J (2013) 'Out of the loop': autonomous weapon systems and the law of armed conflict. Harvard Natl Secur J 4:231–281

Singer PW (2011) Robots at war: the new battlefield. In: Strachan H, Scheipers S (eds) The changing character of war. Oxford University Press, Oxford, pp 333–355

Wagner M (2012) The dehumanization of international humanitarian law: legal, ethical and political implications of autonomous weapon systems. http://robots.law.miami.edu/wp-content/uploads/2012/01/Wagner_Dehumanization_of_international_humanitarian_law.pdf. Accessed 27 Jan 2014

Wagner M (2013) Autonomy in the battlespace: independently operating weapon systems and the law of armed conflict. In: Saxon D (ed) International humanitarian law and the changing technology of war, pp 99–122

# Chapter 5
# The Practices of Apartheid as a War Crime: A Critical Analysis

**Paul Eden**

**Abstract** The human suffering caused by the political ideology of apartheid in South Africa during the Apartheid era (1948–1994) prompted worldwide condemnation and a variety of diplomatic and legal responses. Amongst these responses was the attempt to have apartheid recognised both as a crime against humanity in the 1973 Apartheid Convention as well as a war crime in Article 85(4)(c) of Additional Protocol I. This article examin'es the origins, nature and current status of the practices of apartheid as a war crime and its possible application to the Israeli-Palestinian conflict.

**Keywords** Apartheid · War crimes · Crimes against humanity · International criminal law · Additional Protocol I (AP I) · The Statute of the International Criminal Court (the ICC Statute) · The ICRC customary international humanitarian law project · The Israeli-Palestinian conflict · The principle of legality (*nullum crimen, nulla poena sine lege*)

## Contents



---

Paul Eden Lecturer in Law, University of Sussex. I would like to acknowledge the support and encouragement that I received from a number of friends and colleagues including Craig Barker, Jo Bridgeman, Christine Byron, Rob Cryer, John Dugard, Charles Garraway, Matthew Happold, Michael Kearney, Christophe Paulussen and Yael Ronen. Their support should not, however, be understood as agreement with the views expressed in this article.

---

P. Eden (✉)
University of Sussex, Brighton BN1 9QE, UK
e-mail: p.a.eden@sussex.ac.uk



T.D. Gill et al. (eds.), *Yearbook of International Humanitarian Law 2013*,
Yearbook of International Humanitarian Law 16, DOI 10.1007/978-94-6265-038-1_5

## 5.1 Introduction

The term "apartheid" is derived from the Afrikaans word for apartness or separation. It is most commonly used to denote the policy of racial classification and segregation practised in South Africa between 1948 and 1994.[1] The denial of basic human and political rights that the South African policy of apartheid entailed prompted worldwide condemnation as well as a variety of diplomatic and legal responses. Amongst these responses were the drafting of an international convention declaring that "apartheid is a crime against humanity" in 1973[2] and the inclusion of the "practices of *apartheid*" in the list of grave breaches contained in Article 85 of Additional Protocol I (AP I) in 1977.[3]

[1] See generally Guelke 2005; Dubow 2014.

[2] Article I of the International Convention on the Suppression and Punishment of the Crime of Apartheid, opened for signature 30 November 1973, 1015 UNTS 243 (entered into force 18 July 1976) (Apartheid Convention).

[3] Article 85(4)(c) of the Protocol Additional to the Geneva Conventions of 12 August 1949, and Relating to the Protection of Victims of International Armed Conflicts, opened for signature 12 December 1977, 1125 UNTS 3 (entered into force 7 December 1978) (hereinafter: API).

The focus of this chapter is a critical examination of the origins, nature and current status of the practices of apartheid as a war crime. The current status of apartheid as a crime against humanity will also be considered but more briefly and largely only in so far as it is relevant to the question of its possible application to the Israeli-Palestinian conflict.[4] Although the ending of apartheid in South Africa in 1994 might be thought to have consigned both the concept and the attempts to criminalise it to history, apartheid was included as a crime against humanity in the 1998 Statute of the International Criminal Court (ICC Statute).[5] Further, the obligation, contained in Article 86(1) of AP I, requiring parties to repress grave breaches of the Protocol has ensured that the war crime of the "practices of *apartheid*" has been incorporated into the domestic criminal law of many countries[6] and the demise of apartheid in South Africa has not changed this. Finally, the increasing (but contested) application of the term apartheid to Israeli law and practice in the Occupied Palestinian Territories (OPT) raises the possibility of individual criminal prosecutions in this context.

Section 5.2 examines the inclusion of the "practices of *apartheid*" in the list of grave breaches of AP I. It details the criticism levelled against the inclusion of the "practices of *apartheid*" in the list of grave breaches of AP I. Section 5.3 addresses the process of inclusion of apartheid in the ICC Statute with particular emphasis on the failure to include the practices of apartheid in the list of war crimes. Section 5.4 criticises the inclusion of "[t]he practice of apartheid" in the list of customary international humanitarian law crimes by the International Committee of the Red Cross (ICRC) on the basis that the evidence relied upon relates almost exclusively to state practice declaring apartheid to be a crime against humanity. Section 5.5 asserts that the possible liability of individual Israeli citizens for carrying out policies that fall within the agreed definition of apartheid will depend on the customary status of the various international attempts to criminalise apartheid. The importance of distinguishing between the civil obligations of states and the potential criminal liability of individuals is also stressed. Section 5.6 assesses the customary status of the crime of apartheid as both a crime against humanity and as a war crime paying special attention to the principle of legality (*nullum crimen, nulla poena sine lege*). Section 5.7 concludes by stating that, even if the customary status of the crime of apartheid remains in doubt, the customary status of persecution on racial grounds and the other inhumane acts required to enforce any policy of systematic racial discrimination (whether characterised as apartheid or not) does not.

[4] For detailed consideration of the origins and current status of apartheid as a crime against humanity see, e.g., Clark 2008; Dugard 2012; Bultz 2013; Eden 2014.

[5] Article 7(1)(j) of the Statute of the International Criminal Court, opened for signature 17 July 1998, 2178 UNTS 3 (entered into force 1 July 2002) (hereinafter: ICC Statute).

[6] The "practices of *apartheid*" have been a war crime in the United Kingdom since 20 July 1998, the date of the coming into force of the UK Geneva Conventions (Amendment) Act 1995, section 1(3) amending the UK Geneva Conventions Act 1957.

## 5.2 The Inclusion of the "Practices of *Apartheid*" in the List of Grave Breaches of AP I

### *5.2.1 Introduction*

The debate over the inclusion of the "practices of *apartheid*" in the list of grave breaches of AP I is indicative of the longstanding tensions between the diplomatic and legal agendas of First World countries and Third World and Eastern Bloc states. These tensions compromised some aspects of the drafting of AP I and the inclusion of the "practices of *apartheid*" in the list of grave breaches has been singled out for criticism in this regard. Equally problematic is that the clash between the deep-rooted ideological convictions of the negotiating parties has resulted in what Professor Yoram Dinstein has referred to as a "'Great Schism' separating the Contracting Parties of Additional Protocol I from some key players in the international arena led by the US".[7] This section examines the process by which the "practices of *apartheid*" were included in the list of grave breaches in AP I and the criticism levelled against this inclusion of the "practices of *apartheid*".

### *5.2.2 The Pressure to Include the "Practices of* Apartheid*" in the List of Grave Breaches*

The initial ICRC draft (Article 74) merely extended the application of the provisions of the 1949 Geneva Conventions relating to the repression of breaches to the persons and objects falling within the protection of AP I. As early as the First Session of the Diplomatic Conference in March 1974, the Democratic Republic of Vietnam proposed a number of draft amendments to the ICRC's draft AP I including a proposal to add "[t]he continued existence of colonial regimes, the practice of apartheid and all forms of racial discrimination" to the list of international crimes defined in international law since the Judgment of the Nuremberg International Military Tribunal.[8]

On 23 April 1976, during the debate on the discussion of the repression of breaches of the proposed AP I, the representative of the Byelorussian Soviet Socialist Republic made reference to the Apartheid Convention as an example of a crime against humanity that had been developed since the adoption of the Geneva Conventions of 1949.[9] The representatives of the Union of Soviet Socialist

[7] Dinstein 2010, p. 295.

[8] Official Records of the Diplomatic Conference on the Reaffirmation and Development of International Humanitarian Law Applicable in Armed Conflicts, Geneva (1974–1977) (hereinafter: Official Records), Vol IV, CDDH/41, p. 182.

[9] Official Records, Vol IX, CDDH/I/SR.43, p. 17: summary record of the 43rd meeting, 23 April 1976, para 12.

Republics[10] and the Ukrainian Soviet Socialist Republic[11] made similar observations. The representative of the Syrian Arab Republic also deplored the failure to include apartheid among the list of grave breaches in draft AP I.[12] On 29 April 1976, after the conclusion of the debate on the relevant article, Mongolia, Uganda and the United Republic of Tanzania introduced an amendment to the draft list of grave breaches that had been submitted by Australia to include:

> Outrages upon personal dignity especially inhuman acts such as the practices of apartheid and other humiliating and degrading treatment.[13]

The amendment's sponsors stated that they were particularly concerned (i) with the need to reaffirm and develop international humanitarian law applicable in armed conflicts, (ii) with the need to take into account developments in the years since 1949, and (iii) with the need to prevent human suffering.[14] "The sponsors' aim was to make it clear that the practices of apartheid were serious war crimes as well as dangerous crimes against humanity".[15]

### 5.2.3 *Criticism of the Inclusion of the "Practices of* **Apartheid**" *in the List of Grave Breaches During the Drafting Process*

The list of grave breaches (that ultimately became Article 85 of AP I) was adopted by consensus but several delegations questioned the feasibility of some of the provisions due to the vagueness of the drafting. The inclusion of the "practices of *apartheid*" was singled out for criticism in this regard. Both the Austrian[16] and the Finnish[17] representatives doubted whether the "practices of *apartheid*" could be easily transposed into national criminal laws.

The Australian representative complained that some of the proposed grave breaches "did not embody the degree of specificity essential if abuse and injustice were to be avoided".[18] He confirmed his delegation's condemnation of apartheid but stated:

---

[10] Ibid, p. 23, para 34.

[11] Official Records, Vol IX, CDDH/I/SR.44, p. 34: summary record of the 44th meeting, 26 April 1976, para 37.

[12] Ibid, p. 38, para 58.

[13] Official Records, Vol III, CDDH/I/313 and Add.1, p. 321.

[14] Official Records, Vol IX, CDDH/I/SR.47, p. 68: summary record of the 47th meeting, 29 April 1976, para 5.

[15] Ibid, p. 69, para 10.

[16] Official Records, Vol IX, CDDH/I/SR.64, p. 307: summary record of the 64th meeting, 7 June 1976, para 9.

[17] Ibid, p. 316, para 64.

[18] Ibid, p. 310, para 28.

> the introduction of political ideologies, hateful as they might be, into the system of grave breaches was not to reaffirm and develop humanitarian law but to distort it.

He also stated that his delegation would not have been able to support the inclusion of the "practices of *apartheid*" into the list of grave breaches if a separate vote had been taken.[19] The French representative also expressed his delegation's doubts about the wisdom of including the "practices of *apartheid*" in the list of grave breaches and stated that, although not opposed to consensus as a whole, if a vote had been taken on this point, France would have abstained.[20]

By contrast, the representative of Yugoslavia strongly supported regarding discriminatory practices against protected persons, such as apartheid, as grave breaches.[21] The Polish representative also expressed satisfaction at the inclusion of apartheid and inhuman and degrading practices based on racial discrimination in the list of grave breaches.[22] The Argentinean representative considered the list of grave breaches less than perfect but stated that, given the diversity of legal concepts and political opinions, it appeared to be acceptable.[23]

### *5.2.4 Article 85(4)(c) of AP I—Commentary and Criticism*

Article 85(4)(c) of AP I states that the "[p]ractices of *apartheid* and other inhuman and degrading practices involving outrages upon personal dignity, based on racial discrimination" are grave breaches of AP I when committed wilfully and in violation of AP I. The commentary notes that sub-paragraph (4) is concerned with "off the battlefield" grave breaches and that, outside the scope of application of AP I, the crime of apartheid remains exclusively within the domain of crimes against humanity.[24]

In 1976, while the negotiations were still ongoing, Professor Gerald Draper[25] criticised the creation of a war crime aimed at one State and entirely racial in content, noting that Article 27 of the Fourth Geneva Convention[26] already required respect for protected persons "without any adverse distinction based, in particular, on race, religion or political opinion". In Draper's view, the deletion of the words "practices of *apartheid* and other" would not have altered the substantive nature of the grave breach that ultimately became Article 85(4)(c) of AP I. During the

---

[19] Ibid, p. 310, para 29.

[20] Ibid, p. 317, para 68.

[21] Ibid, p. 313, para 49.

[22] Ibid, p. 317, para 69.

[23] Ibid, p. 314, para 53.

[24] Sandoz et al. 1987, p. 1002, para 3512.

[25] Draper 1976, p. 42.

[26] Geneva Convention Relative to the Protection of Civilian Persons in Times of War, opened for signature 12 August 1949, 75 UNTS 287 (entered into force 21 October 1950) (GCIV).

drafting process, the Ugandan representative pointed out "that all United Nations bodies, and the Security Council in particular, had always drawn a clear-cut distinction between racial discrimination and apartheid".[27] Draper also noted that "[t]he practices of *apartheid*, however morally defective, are not acts in any way linked with armed conflict. Placing them in the Protocol will not make them so".[28] This point had been partially conceded by the Ugandan representative during the drafting process who stated that apartheid, although not arising in a situation of armed conflict, had brought about a combat situation and that recognising apartheid as a grave breach would serve as a preventative measure likely to decrease the risk of war.[29] Draper's counter-argument was that such reasoning constituted an example of "that confusion between *jus ad bellum* and *jus in bello*, now based on racial considerations which nearly wrecked the Conference at its first session in 1974".[30]

### *5.2.5 Conclusion*

There are currently 174 parties to AP I but the drafting of Article 85 remains controversial and although the Netherlands has stated that it regards the offences contained in Article 85 as equivalent to the war crimes specified in the 1949 Geneva Conventions,[31] this assertion of the customary status of the grave breaches regime in AP I is the exception rather than the rule.[32] The fact that the crime of apartheid was not included in the statute of the International Criminal Tribunal for the former Yugoslavia (ICTY) (or the International Criminal Tribunal for Rwanda (ICTR)) despite a request for it to be included from the ICRC[33] is indicative of the controversy over the customary status of this war crime.

---

[27] Official Records, Vol IX, CDDH/I/SR.60, p. 266: summary record of the 60th meeting, 3 June 1976, para 82.

[28] Draper 1976, p. 43.

[29] Official Records, supra n 14, para 16.

[30] Draper 1976, p. 43.

[31] Declaration contained in the instrument of acceptance to the European Convention on the Non-Applicability of Statutory Limitation to Crimes against Humanity and War Crimes (25 January 1974, 2245 UNTS 307) by the Kingdom of the Netherlands, 25 November 1981, available at: www.conventions.coe.int. Accessed 12 May 2014.

[32] See, e.g., Dinstein 2010, p. 266, n 1730 ("Some of the grave breaches listed in the Protocol (pre-eminently, practices of apartheid under Article 85(4)(c) are patently not war crimes per se".).

[33] Some Preliminary Remarks by the ICRC on the Setting-Up of an International Tribunal for the Prosecution of Persons Responsible for Serious Violations of International Humanitarian Law Committed on the Territory of the Former Yugoslavia (UNSC Res. 808 (1993), adopted on 22 February 1993), DDM/JUR/422b (25 March 1993). Reproduced in Morris and Scharf 1995, pp. 391–398. See also Hall 2008, p. 228, n 332.

## 5.3 The ICC Statute and the Crime of Apartheid

### *5.3.1 Introduction*

The crime of apartheid was not included in the list of crimes against humanity in the Draft Statute of the ICC produced by the Preparatory Committee on the Establishment of an International Criminal Court although the core concept undoubtedly falls within the concept of persecution on 'political, racial, national, ethnic, cultural or religious' grounds that was included in subparagraph (h) of proposed article Y (defining crimes against humanity).[34] During the preliminary discussions, some delegations expressed a preference for including apartheid and other forms of racial discrimination as defined in the relevant conventions.[35]

Apartheid was, however, initially included in the possible options for the proposed definition of war crimes as an example of an outrage upon personal dignity.[36] The records of the preliminary discussions reveal a clear disagreement on the customary status of AP I.[37] While a clear majority of states considered AP I to be part of customary international law in the light of the number of ratifications of AP I, other key states (including some who have subsequently become parties to AP I) did not accept this assertion at the time that the ICC Statute was being drafted.[38]

### *5.3.2 The Inclusion of the Crime of Apartheid as a Crime Against Humanity*

The absence of apartheid from the list of crimes against humanity was noted during the discussion of the draft Article 5—Crimes within the jurisdiction of the Court—in the context of the debate about whether crimes against humanity could be

---

[34] See Report of the Preparatory Committee on the Establishment of an International Criminal Court, UN Doc. A/CONF.183/2/Add.1 (14 April 1998), p. 26.

[35] See Report of the Preparatory Committee on the Establishment of an International Criminal Court, Vol I (Proceedings of the Preparatory Committee during March-April and August 1996), UNGA Official Records, Fifty-first Session, Supplement No 22, UN Doc. A/51/22 (13 September 1996), p. 26, para 108.

[36] See Report of the Preparatory Committee on the Establishment of an International Criminal Court, supra n 34, reproduced in UN Diplomatic Conference of Plenipotentiaries on the Establishment of an International Criminal Court (Rome 15 June–17 July 1998), Official Records, Vol III: Reports and other documents, p. 18.

[37] See, e.g., Report of the Ad Hoc Committee on the Establishment of an International Criminal Court, UNGA Official Records, Fiftieth Session, Supplement No 22, UN Doc. A/50/22 (6 September 1995), pp. 15–16, para 73; Report of the Preparatory Committee on the Establishment of an International Criminal Court, Vol I, supra n 35, p. 21, para 81.

[38] See Von Hebel and Robinson 1999, pp. 103–107 for an account of the heated preliminary discussions.

committed in times of peace as well as war. The Mexican representative indicated that apartheid should have been included in the list of crimes within the jurisdiction of the Court[39] and the Irish representative noted that apartheid was the subject of a convention that did not require a link with times of armed conflict.[40] The Chairman, summing up the discussion, observed that it had been suggested that the crime of apartheid should be added to the list of crimes against humanity within the jurisdiction of the Court.[41] Support for the inclusion of apartheid into the list of crimes against humanity was also forthcoming from Bangladesh and Niger.[42] Once the question of the inclusion of apartheid in the list of crimes against humanity had been raised, the South African delegation intervened to lead a coalition of primarily sub-Saharan African countries[43] in ensuring its inclusion into the final draft. Notwithstanding South Africa's unassailable moral authority due to its own painful national experience, the process of negotiating a consensus definition of the crime of apartheid was relatively protracted.[44]

The sub-group of delegates that worked on the consensus language did not consider themselves bound by the definition in the Apartheid Convention. At one level, the existence of the overarching threshold elements for a crime against humanity contained in the *chapeau* rendered much of the Apartheid Convention's definition of the *actus reus* of the crime redundant. At another level, some states (particularly the United States) were anxious that the racist opinions and policies of private individuals or non-state bodies should not fall within the scope of the crime of apartheid due to concerns about freedom of expression. In deference to this, the crime of apartheid as defined in article 7(2)(h) of the ICC Statute requires the inhumane acts to be "committed in the context of an institutionalized regime of systematic oppression and domination by one racial group over any other racial group or groups and committed with the intention of maintaining that regime". As Professor Robert Cryer notes, "it is difficult to envisage any crime covered under this definition that would not be caught under the customary definition of 'persecution-type' crimes against humanity or 'other inhumane acts' in Article 7(1)(k)".[45]

---

39 Third Meeting of the Committee of the Whole, UN Doc. A/CONF.183/C.1/SR3 (17 June 1998), UN Diplomatic Conference of Plenipotentiaries on the Establishment of an International Criminal Court (Rome 15 June–17 July 1998), Official Records, Vol II: summary records of the plenary meetings and of the meetings of the Committee of the Whole, p. 152, para 125.

40 Ibid, p. 153, para 167.

41 Ibid, p. 154, para 178.

42 Fourth Meeting of the Committee of the Whole, UN Doc. A/CONF.183/C.1/SR4 (17 June 1998), UN Diplomatic Conference of Plenipotentiaries on the Establishment of an International Criminal Court (Rome 15 June–17 July 1998), Official Records, Vol II: summary records of the plenary meetings and of the meetings of the Committee of the Whole, p. 156, paras 18–19.

43 Bangladesh, India, Lesotho, Malawi, Mexico, Namibia, Swaziland, Trinidad and Tobago and Tanzania.

44 McCormack 2004, pp. 198–199.

45 Cryer 2005, p. 259. See also Bultz 2013, pp. 225–228 arguing that Article 7(1)(j) of the ICC Statute—the crime of apartheid—is subsumed by Article 7(1)(h) of the ICC Statute—persecution.

### *5.3.3 Apartheid as a War Crime and the ICC Statute*

During the discussions on the provisions concerning war crimes in the draft ICC Statute, 21 states expressed support for the draft version (option 2 under (*p*)) that included a reference to the practices of apartheid.[46] Nine states expressly rejected the reference to "practices of apartheid and other inhuman and degrading practices involving outrages on personal dignity based on racial discrimination" in the list of war crimes.[47] Costa Rica's representative expressed a preference for "the broader formulation under option 1" (excluding the reference to the "practices of apartheid" in option 2) but, confusingly, also indicated that the specific elements of option 2 should possibly be considered separately.[48] The proposal to include apartheid within the list of war crimes made by a group of six African states[49] was not proceeded with and, consequently, there is no reference to the policies of apartheid in the list of war crimes in Article 8 of the ICC Statute.

In the absence of full *travaux préparatoires* for the ICC Statute (particularly the absence of the records of the separate working groups that drafted the definitions of war crimes and crimes against humanity), the reasons for failure to include apartheid within the list of war crimes in the ICC Statute will remain a matter of conjecture. Anecdotal evidence suggests two reasons for the absence. First, the hostility by some states to anything that might strengthen the argument that AP I constituted customary law should not be underestimated. Second, the inclusion of apartheid as a crime against humanity ensured that the agenda of those states that had always supported the criminalisation of apartheid was appropriately acknowledged.

Commentators who draw attention to the discrepancies between the war crimes listed in AP I and the war crimes contained in Article 8 of the ICC Statute tend to focus on the failure to include the wilful and unjustifiable delay in the repatriation of prisoners of war and civilian internees as the key omission in the ICC Statute.[50]

[46] Fourth Meeting of the Committee of the Whole, supra n 42, p. 158, para 44 (Syria); p. 158, para 48 (Lebanon); p. 160, para 63 (Libya); p. 160, para 65 (China); p. 160, para 66 (United Arab Emirates); p. 160, para 67 (Greece); p. 161, para 69 (Vietnam); p. 161, para 70 (Bahrain); p. 161, para 73 (Denmark). Fifth Meeting of the Committee of the Whole, UN Doc. A/CONF.183/C.1/SR5 (18 June 1998), UN Diplomatic Conference of Plenipotentiaries on the Establishment of an International Criminal Court (Rome 15 June–17 July 1998), Official Records, Vol II: summary records of the plenary meetings and of the meetings of the Committee of the Whole, p. 162, para 9 (Kuwait); p. 163, para 18 (Republic of Korea); p. 163, para 23 (Tunisia); p. 163, para 26 (Thailand); p. 164, para 33 (Egypt); p. 165, para 46 (Brazil); p. 165, para 48 (Algeria); p. 165, para 56 (Japan); p. 166, para 62 (Morocco); p. 166, para 69 (Cuba); p. 166, para 70 (Turkey); p. 166, para 72 (Iran); p. 168, para 97 (South Africa).

[47] Belgium, Chile, Italy, Macedonia, the Russian Federation, Senegal, Sweden, Switzerland and the United Kingdom. See further Schabas 2010, p. 183, n 373.

[48] Fourth Meeting of the Committee of the Whole, supra n 42, p. 160, para 61.

[49] UN Doc. A./CONF.183/C.1/L.13 (22 June 1998), reproduced in UN Diplomatic Conference of Plenipotentiaries on the Establishment of an International Criminal Court (Rome 15 June–17 July 1998) Official Records, Vol III: Reports and other documents, p. 239.

[50] See, e.g., Graditzky 1999, p. 204; Dörmann 2003, p. 345; Sandoz 2008, p. 310.

Sandoz submits that the inclusion of the crime of apartheid as a crime against humanity in the ICC Statute changes the language, but not the content, of the equivalent violation of AP I.[51] Sandoz further submits that the "[p]ractices of *apartheid* and other inhuman and degrading practices involving outrages upon personal dignity, based on racial discrimination" (Article 85(4)(c) of AP I) are probably covered by the general terminology used in Article 8(2), Part B (xxi) "Committing outrages upon personal dignity, in particular humiliating and degrading treatment".[52]

### 5.3.4 Conclusion

The inclusion of apartheid as a crime against humanity in Article 7(1)(j) of the ICC Statute is significant for two reasons. First, it represents the first time that apartheid has been criminalised in a manner that is consistent with penal legality and certainty.[53] Second, while Article 7(1)(j) almost certainly represents progressive development, "it could be argued that the ICC Statute has, however, contributed to recent formation of a customary rule on the matter".[54] By contrast, the failure to proceed with the proposal to include apartheid in the list of war crimes in the ICC Statute could be seen as weakening the argument that the practices of apartheid constitute a customary international war crime unless Article 10 of the ICC Statute can be invoked.[55] Article 10 of the ICC Statute states:

> Nothing in this Part shall be interpreted as limiting or prejudicing in any way existing or developing rules of international law for purposes other than this Statute.

As Schabas observes, Article 10 has been "largely ignored by the very bodies to which it is directed, namely specialised tribunals engaged in the interpretation of international law".[56] The current customary status of the crime of apartheid both as a war crime and as a crime against humanity is considered below in Sect. 5.6.

---

[51] Sandoz 2008, p. 311.

[52] Ibid. See also Dörmann 2002, p. 315.

[53] But see also Bultz 2013 who argues that Article 7(1)(j) of the ICC Statute is ambiguous and inoperable.

[54] Cassese 2013, p. 107. See further infra Sect. 5.5.4. But see also Eden 2014, pp. 189–191 for a more cautious assessment of the customary status of Article 7(1)(j) of the ICC Statute.

[55] See further infra Sect. 5.5.3. See also Henckaerts 2009, p. 692. Noting that all war crimes in the ICC Statute are part of customary international law but that "this does not mean that the Statute exhaustively codified all war crimes under customary international law. In other words, there may still be war crimes under customary international law outside the Statute of the ICC".

[56] Schabas 2010, p. 271. See also ICTY, *Prosecutor v. Furundžija*, Judgment Trial Chamber (IT-95-17/1-T), 10 December 1998, para 227; ICTY, *Prosecutor v. Galić*, Judgment Appeals Chamber (IT-98-29-A), 30 November 2006, separate and partially dissenting opinion of Judge Schomburg, para 20. For the views of the ICC in this regard see ICC, *Prosecutor v. Al Bashir*, Decision on the

## 5.4 The ICRC's Customary International Humanitarian Law Project

In 1996, the ICRC embarked on a major international study into current practice in international humanitarian law in order to identify the relevant customary law in the area. The ICRC's Study on International Customary Law (the ICRC Study), published in three volumes in 2005, has been welcomed as a valuable contribution to the development of customary international humanitarian law but concerns have been expressed about its methodology.[57] It is beyond the scope of this article to do justice to the vigorous debate over the methodological concerns beyond assessing the validity of the assertion that "[t]he practice of apartheid or other inhuman and degrading practices involving outrages on personal dignity based on racial discrimination" constitutes a war crime under customary international humanitarian law.[58]

The ICRC Study cites as authority the fact that "[t]his war crime is listed as a grave breach in Additional Protocol I".[59] The ICRC Study acknowledges the omission of the crime of apartheid from the list of war crimes in the ICC Statute but argues "such conduct would amount to a war crime as an outrage on personal dignity, as well as humiliating and degrading treatment".[60] The ICRC Study also states, in the application of international humanitarian law, apartheid is a crime under the legislation of numerous States. With a few notable exceptions,[61] all the examples of national legislation cited involve the incorporation of either AP I or the ICC Statute into domestic law and the rather limited exceptions are all parties to the Apartheid Convention who were formerly members of the Eastern (Soviet) Bloc.

The ICRC Study notes that no practice was found in national case law[62] or international judicial or quasi-judicial bodies[63] to support the existence of the customary war crime of the "practices of *apartheid*". The remaining practice cited relates to debates before the UN General Assembly (UNGA), various UNGA resolutions, UN Security Council resolutions and two resolutions adopted by the UN Commission on Human Rights in 1992 and 1993 declaring apartheid to be a

(Footnote 56 continued)
Prosecution's Application for a Warrant of Arrest, Pre-Trial Chamber I (ICC-02/05-01/09), 4 March 2009, para 127.

[57] See, e.g., Cryer 2006; Dinstein 2006; McCormack 2006; Bellinger and Hayes 2007; Wilmshurst and Breau 2011. But see also Henckaerts 2007.

[58] Henckaerts and Doswald-Beck 2005a, p. 588.

[59] Ibid.

[60] Ibid, p. 589.

[61] Article 418 of the Bulgarian Penal Code as amended (1968); Article 263(a)(1) of the Czech Republic Criminal Code as amended (1961); Section 157 of the Hungarian Criminal Code as amended (1978); Article 263(a)(1) of the Slovakian Criminal Code as amended (1961), as quoted in Henckaerts and Doswald-Beck 2005b, pp. 2055–2058.

[62] Ibid, p. 2058, para 636.

[63] Ibid, p. 2060, para 650.

crime against humanity.[64] The ICRC Study also notes that section 5(i)(j) of UN Transitional Administration in East Timor Regulation No. 2000/15 includes "the crime of apartheid" in the list of crimes against humanity over which the panels established by the Regulation have exclusive universal jurisdiction.[65]

Although, there is a case for arguing that apartheid as defined in Article 7(1)(j) of the ICC Statute is evolving into a customary crime against humanity, it is more difficult to argue that the practices of apartheid constitute a customary international war crime given failure to include a reference to the crime of apartheid within the list of war crimes contained in the ICC Statute and the controversy over the drafting of the grave breaches regime in AP I. Given the clear distinction between the categories of war crimes and crimes against humanity,[66] it is disappointing that the ICRC Study's evidence for the existence of a war crime of the practices of apartheid under customary international humanitarian law is primarily related to state practice declaring apartheid to be a crime against humanity.

## 5.5 Israel and the Crime of Apartheid

### *5.5.1 Introduction*

The term apartheid is used loosely in a number of non-legal contexts to emphasise the seriousness of various inequalities. Increasingly, the paradigm of apartheid has also been applied in relation to Israel.[67] Since 2005 an annual "Israeli Apartheid Week" has been held on university campuses (and in other civic spaces) to raise awareness about Israel's policies, although these events have occasionally drawn accusations of anti-Semitism. The application of the apartheid paradigm in relation to Israel's policies and practices towards Palestinians in the Occupied Territories has recently crossed the divide between rhetorical device and legal analysis.

---

[64] Ibid, pp. 2058–2060, paras 637–647.

[65] See United Nations Transitional Administration in East Timor, UNTAET Reg. 2000/15 (6 June 2000), on the establishment of panels with exclusive jurisdiction over serious criminal offences.

[66] The need for a nexus between an armed conflict and the criminal act in question for a war crime and the contextual threshold for crimes against humanity, i.e. the commission of a listed prohibited act in the context of a widespread or systematic attack directed against a civilian population.

[67] See, e.g., Tutu 2002; Davis 2003; Carter 2006; Tilley 2009; White 2009; Díaz Polanco 2010; Tilley 2012; Dugard and Reynolds 2013a; Falk 2013; Lebrun 2013. But see also Goldstone 2011; Zilbershats 2013.

### 5.5.2 *Israel and the Apartheid Paradigm—The Legal Dimensions*

In 2007 Professor John Dugard, in his capacity as UN Special Rapporteur on the situation of human rights in the Palestinian territories occupied since 1967, concluded that elements of the Israeli occupation constituted forms of colonialism and apartheid, which are contrary to international law.[68] Dugard also noted:

> the 1973 International Convention on the Suppression and Punishment of the Crime of Apartheid appears to be violated by many practices, particularly those denying freedom of movement to Palestinians.[69]

In 2010 Professor Richard Falk, Dugard's successor as UN Special Rapporteur, likewise concluded that Israeli policies in the West Bank and East Jerusalem exhibited "features of colonialism and apartheid, as well as transforming a de jure condition of occupation into a circumstance of de facto annexation".[70] Falk, with reference to Article 7 of the ICC Statute, also noted that "apartheid has come to be formally treated as a crime against humanity"[71] To support the factual basis for his assertions, Falk made reference to a 300-page report from the Human Sciences Research Council (HSRC) of South Africa released in May 2009 (written by an international team of scholars and practitioners of international law) concluding that Israel is practising both colonialism and apartheid in the Occupied Palestinian Territories (OPT).[72] In his final presentation to the Human Rights Council in January 2014, Falk analysed in greater depth whether the continuing occupation of Palestine by Israel constituted apartheid.[73]

In their recent article in the *European Journal of International Law*, Dugard and Reynolds are careful to limit their analysis of the applicability of the international legal prohibition of apartheid in the context of Israeli law and practice in the Occupied Palestinian Territories to "the responsibility of the Israeli state under norms of public international law, as opposed the responsibility of its individual agents under international criminal law".[74] Dugard and Reynolds do acknowledge that individual criminal responsibility *could* arise if state responsibility for a breach of apartheid is *prima facie* established,[75] but their reliance on the definition of apartheid in the 1973 Apartheid Convention and the ICC Statute is premised on the absence of a definition of apartheid in the 1966 International Convention on the Elimination of All Forms of Racial Discrimination (ICERD).

---

[68] Dugard 2007, p. 3.

[69] Ibid, p. 2.

[70] Falk 2010, p. 2.

[71] Ibid, p. 4.

[72] Tilley 2009. See also Tilley 2012; Dugard and Reynolds 2013a.

[73] Falk 2014, pp. 14-20, paras 51–76.

[74] Dugard and Reynolds 2013a, p. 880. See also Tilley 2009, p. 26; Tilley 2012, pp. 3, 223.

[75] Dugard and Reynolds 2013a, p. 880, n 81 (emphasis added).

### 5.5.3 *The Importance of Distinguishing Between Civil and Criminal Obligations*

When discussing the concept of apartheid in relation to Israel's policies towards the Palestinians, it is important to distinguish between a general (civil) obligation owed by the *State* of Israel not to engage in systematic racial discrimination and potential criminal liability for *individual* Israeli citizens as a result of enforcing any Israeli policies towards the Palestinians that can fairly be characterised as apartheid. With regard to the former, Israel—not least because it is a party to ICERD[76]—is obliged to "condemn racial segregation and apartheid and undertake to prevent, prohibit and eradicate all practices of this nature in territories under [its] jurisdiction".[77] In May 2012, the Committee on the Elimination of Racial Discrimination (CERD) urged Israel to prohibit and eradicate all policies of racial segregation and apartheid which severely and disproportionally affected the Palestinian population in the Occupied Palestinian Territories and which violated the provisions of Article 3 of ICERD.[78]

### 5.5.4 *Conclusion*

Israel is not a party to either the Apartheid Convention, AP I or the ICC Statute and consequently is not under an obligation to incorporate the conventional crimes of apartheid into its domestic law. Criminal liability for individual Israeli citizens for carrying out the policies condemned by the CERD in 2012—in the absence of a successful Palestinian ratification of the ICC Statute[79] or AP I[80]—will depend, in

[76] Israel ratified ICERD on 3 January 1979 (excluding Article 22—ICJ jurisdiction over disputes).

[77] Article 3 of the International Convention on the Elimination of All Forms of Racial Discrimination, opened for signature on 7 March 1966, 660 UNTS 195 (entered into force 4 January 1969) (ICERD). See also Committee on the Elimination of Racial Discrimination, General Recommendation XIX, adopted on 17 August 1995, reprinted in UN Doc. A/50/18, p. 140, para 1 ("The reference to apartheid may have been directed exclusively to South Africa, but the article as adopted prohibits all forms of racial segregation in all countries".).

[78] Report of the Committee on the Elimination of Racial Discrimination, Eightieth session (13 February–9 March 2012), UN Doc. A/67/18, p. 20.

[79] The attempt to lodge a declaration pursuant to Article 12(3) of the ICC Statute on 22 January 2009 recognizing the jurisdiction of the ICC was rejected by the ICC's Office of the Prosecutor (OTP) on 3 April 2012 on the grounds that only a "State" could make such a declaration.

[80] The attempt by the Executive Committee of the Palestinian Liberation Organization, entrusted with the functions of the Government of Palestine, to ratify the four 1949 Geneva Conventions and the two Additional Protocols on 21 June 1989 failed due to the uncertainty within the international community as to the existence or non-existence of a State of Palestine at that time. See Palestine and the Geneva Conventions, 30 International Review of the Red Cross (1990), pp. 64–65, or La Palestine et les Conventions de Genève, 72 Review Internationale de la Croix-Rouge (1990), pp. 69–70. For the current situation see infra n 131.

the first instance, on the current customary status of the various international attempts to criminalise apartheid.

To the extent that apartheid constitutes either a customary international crime against humanity and/or a war crime under customary international humanitarian law, it does not appear that Israel can be regarded as a persistent objector to the international criminalisation of apartheid particularly as a crime against humanity. Israel voted in favour of the adoption of the draft 1968 Convention on the Non-Applicability of Statutory Limitations to War Crimes and Crimes Against Humanity (the 1968 Convention) that refers to apartheid as a crime against humanity[81] and Judge Eli Nathan, Head of the Israeli delegation at the drafting of the ICC Statute, in his statement explaining Israel's negative vote in relation to the adoption of the ICC Statute, made it clear that but for the inclusion of Article 8(2)(b)(viii)—the transfer of the population of an occupying power into the territory it occupies or deporting the existing population from the occupied territory—his delegation "would have been proudly able to vote in favour of adopting the Statute".[82] Although Nathan also indicated that Israel had other problems with the ICC Statute which they would address at the appropriate time, given Israel's positive vote for the adoption of the 1968 Convention, it seems inconceivable that this would include the crime of apartheid.[83]

## 5.6 Assessing the Customary Status of the Crime of Apartheid

### *5.6.1 Introduction*

Given the generally non-binding nature of UNGA resolutions, there are three possible origins of a customary international crime of apartheid, namely, the 1973 Apartheid Convention, Article 85(4)(c) of AP I and Article 7(1)(j) of the ICC Statute.

---

[81] Israel also voted in favour of the last part of paragraph 1 of the Preamble containing the reference to apartheid as a crime against humanity during the separate vote requested by the United States during the drafting process. See UN Doc. A/C.3/SR.1573 (15 October 1968), p. 1, para 5. See also Lerner 1969, p. 518.

[82] Nathan 1998. See also 9th Plenary Meeting, UN Doc. A/CONF.183/SR9 (17 July 1998), UN Diplomatic Conference of Plenipotentiaries on the Establishment of an International Criminal Court (Rome 15 June-17 July 1998), Official Records, Vol II: summary records of the plenary meetings and of the meetings of the Committee of the Whole, p. 123, paras 33–34.

[83] Israel signed the ICC Statute on 31 December 2000 stating that it was an active supporter of the concept of an International Criminal Court, and its realisation in the form of the ICC Statute but it rejected any attempt to interpret its provisions "in a politically motivated manner against Israel and its citizens".

### *5.6.2 The Customary Status of the 1973 Apartheid Convention*

Whilst there is some academic support for the existence of a general customary crime of apartheid based on the 1973 Apartheid Convention,[84] there are two key problems with this assertion. First, Article II of the Apartheid Convention limits the geographical scope of the Apartheid Convention to "policies and practices of racial segregation and discrimination as practised in southern Africa". Supporters of the contention that the Apartheid Convention applies beyond the geographical limits of southern Africa,[85] tend to rely on statements made by the representatives of Australia, Cyprus and the United States during the drafting process.[86]

The original draft convention did not contain the phrase "as practised in southern Africa".[87] During the discussion of the draft convention on 22 October 1973, the United States' representative complained:

> Article I would be open to very broad interpretations going beyond both the intentions of its drafters and the geographical limits of southern Africa. The Convention could be applied to situations which currently were entirely unforeseeable.[88]

At the same meeting, the Cypriot representative too expressed concerns about the drafting of the convention "mainly from the legal point of view" and noted that "it must be remembered that it would become part of the body of international law and might last beyond the time when apartheid was being practised in South Africa".[89] The following day, the Australian representative also expressed concerns that "the concept of apartheid was being widened to such an extent that it could be applicable to areas other than South Africa".[90]

In response to these criticisms, the Moroccan representative agreed that Article II should be made clearer and she proposed that the phrase "as practised in southern

84 See, e.g., McCormack and Simpson 1994, p. 42.

85 See UN Economic and Social Council, Implementation of the International Convention on the Suppression and Punishment of the Crime of Apartheid, Report of the Group of Three Established under the Convention, UN Doc. E.CN.4/1995/76 (25 January 1995), para 17 ("While recognizing that the International Convention on the Suppression and Punishment of the Crime of Apartheid applied to any country that might practise racial segregation under an institutionalized apartheid system, the Group noted that thus far there is no claim by any State party that apartheid, as defined by the Convention, exists anywhere else than in southern Africa".). See also Clark 2008, p. 603 (Article II "is drafted so as to 'include' the cases of southern Africa, but not exclusive to them".).

86 See, e.g., Du Plessis 2011, p. 423; Reynolds 2012, p. 211, n 66; Tilley 2012, p. 124; Dugard and Reynolds 2013a, pp. 884–885.

87 See Draft Convention on the Suppression and Punishment of the Crime of Apartheid, UN Doc. A/9095 (28 August 1973), Annex.

88 UN Doc. A/C.3/SR.2003 (22 October 1973), p. 142, para 36.

89 Ibid, pp. 142–143, para 39.

90 UN Doc. A/C.3/SR.2004 (23 October 1973), p. 143, para 4.

Africa" should be added to draft Article II.[91] The Algerian representative supported the Moroccan proposal and stated that "[w]ith regard to the amendment to Article II proposed orally by the representative of Morocco, it would be highly desirable to specify the geographical area".[92] The Tunisian representative also spoke in favour of the Moroccan proposal clarifying and precisely defining the sphere of application of the Convention and she expressed the hope that the amendment would help to dispel certain misgivings expressed by some delegations.[93] The proposed Moroccan amendment was adopted by 89 votes to three with 19 abstentions.[94] It should also be noted that during the drafting of the Draft Code of Offences Against the Peace and Security of Mankind, the International Law Commission (ILC) also expressed the view that the Apartheid Convention was limited in its geographical scope to southern Africa.[95]

The second problem with asserting the customary status of a crime of apartheid based on the Apartheid Convention is the lack of a universal *opinio iuris*.[96] Not only was the Apartheid Convention rejected by the vast majority of Western states, an overwhelming majority of the states that actually ratified the Apartheid Convention conspicuously failed to incorporate the crime into their domestic law prior to the drafting of the ICC Statute.[97]

Even if the Apartheid Convention could be regarded as the basis of a general customary crime of apartheid, the ambit of this crime could not be wider than the conventional crime on which it was based and thus any such customary international crime against humanity would be restricted to the geographical limits of southern Africa and would consequently be inapplicable to the Israeli-Palestinian conflict. Further, given the express limitations on the geographical scope of the Apartheid Convention, it also cannot apply *qua* treaty to the Israeli-Palestinian conflict notwithstanding the fact that the United Nations Treaty Database records the accession of the State of Palestine to the Apartheid Convention on 2 April 2014.

---

[91] See UN Doc. A/C.3/SR.2005 (24 October 1973), p. 150, para 12. The wording of the amendment was as follows: In the third line of article II, after the words "segregation and apartheid", add the words "as practised in southern Africa". UN Doc. A/C.3/L.2020 (24 October 1973) (original French).

[92] UN Doc. A/C.3/SR.2005 (24 October 1973), p. 151, para 26. See also the remarks of the representatives of Ghana and Pakistan supporting the Moroccan amendment, UN Doc. A/C.3/SR.2006 (25 October 1973), p. 152, para 2 (Ghana); p. 153, para 15 (Pakistan).

[93] UN Doc. A/C.3/SR.2008 (26 October 1973), p. 162, para 5.

[94] See ibid, p. 162.

[95] Draft Code of Crimes Against the Peace and Security of Mankind, reprinted in [1991] Yearbook of the ILC, Vol II(2), 79–107, p. 103, para 4.

[96] Cassese 2008, p. 13; Hannum 1997, p. 144; Tomuschat 1995, p. 54.

[97] See Amnesty International 2011 and note the frequent statements that "*apartheid* is not defined/included in the Penal Code [of state X]..., so prosecutions would have to be for ordinary crimes" in relation to states that are parties to the Apartheid Convention. See also Carrillo and Nelson 2013, p. 13 (noting that 10 out of 34 States (29 %) surveyed in 2013 excluded apartheid from the list of prohibited acts in their CAH (crimes against humanity) legislation and that "seven of these 10 States have ratified or acceded to the Convention on Apartheid".).

### 5.6.3 The Customary Status of Article 85(4)(c) of AP I

There are two key factors in the assertion of the existence of a customary war crime of apartheid with potential application to the Israeli-Palestinian conflict. First, unlike the Apartheid Convention, there are no express geographical limits to the operation of Article 85(4)(c) of AP I and, second, the extensive ratification of AP I (174 states are currently party to AP I) raises at least a rebuttable presumption with regard to the customary status of its main provisions.

With regard to the first factor, whilst there are no express geographical limits vis-à-vis Article 85(4)(c) of AP I, an examination of the *travaux préparatoires* of AP I reveals that the racist regimes in southern Africa were the sole targets. In the context of treaty interpretation, the principle of contemporaneity provides:

> The terms of a treaty must be interpreted according to the meaning which they possessed, or which would have been attributed to them, and in the light of the current linguistic usage, at the time when the treaty was originally concluded.[98]

If, at the time that AP I was originally concluded, the current linguistic usage of the term apartheid was limited to South Africa, then Article 85(4)(c) of AP I could only be applied to the Israeli-Palestinian conflict by analogy. However, as early as 1961, the "architect of apartheid", South African Prime Minister Hendrik Verwoerd, criticised what he saw as Israeli hypocrisy in voting in favour of a UNGA resolution deploring South Africa's policies based on racial discrimination as reprehensible and repugnant to human dignity[99] on the grounds that Israel, like South Africa, was an apartheid state.[100]

In the early 1970s, some Palestinian authors also compared Israeli proposals for limited Palestinian autonomy with the Bantustan strategy in South Africa.[101] In an infamous 1975 UNGA resolution (revoked in 1991) declaring Zionism to be a form of racism and racial discrimination, the UNGA took note of an Organisation of African Unity resolution which considered that the racist regimes in occupied Palestine and in Rhodesia (now Zimbabwe) and South Africa had a common imperialist origin and the same racist structure.[102]

In its 1975 resolution on the inter-temporal problem, *L'Institut de Droit International* noted:

> Lorsqu'une disposition conventionnelle se réfère à une notion juridique ou autre sans la définir, il convient de recourir aux méthodes habituelles d'interprétation pour déterminer si

98 Fitzmaurice 1957, p. 212. See also Kotzur 2012.

99 UNGA Res. 1598 (XV) (13 April 1961).

100 The Rand Daily Mail, "Premier Lashes Israel" (23 November 1961), as quoted in Clarno 2009, p. 66.

101 Clarno 2009, p. 67.

102 UNGA Res. 3379 (XXX) (10 November 1975). Revoked by UNGA Res. 64/86 (16 December 1991).

> cette notion doit être comprise dans son acception au moment de l'établissement de la disposition ou dans son acception au moment de l'application.[103]

Thus, even if the current linguistic usage of the term "apartheid" was limited to southern Africa in 1977, a dynamic (evolutive) interpretation might still be appropriate, and the principle of contemporaneity is increasingly honoured only in the breach.[104] Although it is an accepted principle that criminal law provisions must not be extensively construed to the accused's detriment, in *S.W. v. United Kingdom,*[105] the European Court of Human Rights held that an evolutive interpretation of a common law principle (that a husband could not be found guilty of rape upon his wife) was not incompatible with the principle of legality contained in Article 7 of the European Convention on Human Rights.[106]

With regard to the second factor (the customary status of the grave breaches regime in AP I due to the number of ratifications), the inclusion of the "practices of *apartheid*" in the list of grave breaches of AP I was controversial[107] and the ambivalence towards the grave breaches regime in AP I was evident during the drafting of the ICC Statute. The New Zealand representative, for example, argued:

> the definition of war crimes must not fall short of existing, widely accepted standards of international humanitarian law as reflected in the Geneva Conventions and Additional Protocols, which, given the large number of State parties thereto, constituted customary international law.[108]

Views hostile to the customary status of the definitions of war crimes in AP I were also expressed (particularly from Israel)[109] and the absence of the practices of apartheid from the list of war crimes in the ICC Statute suggests continuing unease

[103] Institut de Droit International 1975, p. 538, para 4. The official translation of the authentic French text reads as follows: "Wherever a provision of a treaty refers to a legal or other concept without defining it, it is appropriate to have recourse to the usual methods of interpretation in order to determine whether the concept is to be interpreted as understood at the time when the provision was drawn up or at the time of its application".

[104] See, e.g., ICJ, *Case Concerning the Dispute Regarding Navigational and Related Rights (Costa Rica v Nicaragua)*, Merits Judgment, (2009) ICJ Rep 213, pp. 241–244, paras 62–71; *Arbitration regarding the Iron Rhine ("IJzeren Rijn") Railway (Belgium v. the Netherlands)*, Award of the Arbitral Tribunal (24 May 2005), 27 Reports of International Arbitral Awards (2008), 35–125, pp. 72–75, paras 79–84, noting "a general support among the leading writers today for evolutive interpretation of treaties" (para 81). See also Higgins 1996 (reprinted in Higgins 2009); Jennings and Watts 1996, pp. 1281–1282, para 633.

[105] ECtHR, *S.W. v. The United Kingdom*, Judgment (App. No. 20166/92), 22 November 1995.

[106] Convention for the Protection of Human Rights and Fundamental Freedoms, opened for signature 4 November 1950, 213 UNTS 222 (entered into force 3 September 1953) (European Convention on Human Rights).

[107] See supra Sects. 5.2.3, 5.2.4.

[108] Fourth Meeting of the Committee of the Whole, supra n 42, p. 160, para 64. See also p. 161, para 72 (Denmark); p. 161, para 74 (Sweden). Fifth Meeting of the Committee of the Whole, supra n 46, p. 162, para 9 (Kuwait); p. 163, para 20 (Saudi Arabia); p. 168, para 91 (Chile); p. 168, para 94 (South Africa).

[109] Fifth Meeting of the Committee of the Whole, supra n 46, p. 167, para 79.

over the drafting of Article 85(4)(c) of AP I (notably the problem of category error; i.e., there is no necessary link between the practices of apartheid and armed conflicts).[110]

### 5.6.4 *The Customary Status of the Crime of Apartheid as a Crime Against Humanity in the ICC Statute*

Darryl Robinson has argued that the delegations participating in the Rome Conference were keen to limit the definitions of crimes against humanity to existing customary law and that, with regard to enforced disappearances and the crime of apartheid, both could be regarded as examples of other inhuman acts that now deserved express recognition due to the special concern of the international community.[111] However, in the case of enforced disappearances, the ICC's Elements of Crimes makes it clear that it is to be regarded as a progressive development.[112] No such restriction is included in the elements of the crime against humanity of apartheid but, as Professor Kai Ambos acknowledges, the customary law character of the crime is controversial.[113]

With regard to the customary status of apartheid as a crime against humanity, two possible dates should be considered. First, if the definition of the crime in Article 7(1)(j) of the ICC Statute can be regarded as crystallisation of earlier state practice, then the date of adoption of the ICC Statute (17 July 1998) would be the critical date. However, and second, if the ICC Statute is to be regarded as a new beginning for the worldwide application of the crime of apartheid (progressive development), then only subsequent state practice will suffice. It might be possible to regard the date of the coming into force of the ICC Statute (1 July 2002) as the critical date, but various studies of the ambit of universal criminal jurisdiction made after the adoption and coming into force of the ICC Statute have failed to include the crime of apartheid in their list of customary crimes against humanity although the uncertainty surrounding the status of the crime of apartheid was noted.

The 2001 Princeton Principles on Universal Jurisdiction observed that "*Apartheid*, terrorism, and drug crimes were raised as candidates for inclusion"[114] and the 2002 preamble to the *Cairo-Arusha Principles on Universal Jurisdiction in Respect*

---

[110] Contrary to some assertions (see, e.g., Levie 1993, p. 470, n 4; Solis 2010, p. 134, n 67), there is nothing in the so-called Matheson statement that can be read as an acceptance of the customary status of Article 85(4)(c) of API by the United States. See Matheson 1987, p. 428. "Certain of the principles contained in [the final part of Protocol I] also merit acceptance as customary law", but Article 85(4)(c) of API is not specified as belonging to this category.

[111] Robinson 1999, p. 55.

[112] See ICC 2011, p. 11, n 24.

[113] Ambos 2014, p. 113. See also Zahar 2009; Cassese et al. 2011, p. 11; Gebhard 2012, p. 467; Eden 2014.

[114] Macedo 2001, p. 48.

*of Gross Human Rights Offences: An African Perspective* similarly expresses concern at the fact that "certain offences which have particular resonance in Africa, such as the crime of *apartheid*, have so far not attracted prosecution under the principle of universal jurisdiction".[115] The 2005 *Institut de Droit International* report on universal criminal jurisdiction also failed to include apartheid in the list of crimes to which universal jurisdiction applied.[116] I have argued elsewhere that the use of the "copy out" technique (i.e., the incorporation of the ICC Statute's definition of crimes against humanity into domestic law) by states not party to the ICC Statute will end this uncertainty once and for all.[117]

### 5.6.5 The Crime of Apartheid and the Problem of Legality

Prior to the drafting of the ICC Statute, all the international instruments criminalising apartheid were created with a specific target in mind and, thus, it can be argued that the crimes that they contain could only be applied to the Israeli-Palestinian conflict by analogy. The prohibition against analogy is a generally accepted component of the *nullum crimen* principle,[118] and this may make the application of international instruments criminalising apartheid drafted before the end of the Apartheid era difficult to apply to the Israeli-Palestinian conflict in spite of the absence of any express geographical limitations in Article 85(4)(c) of AP I (unless the principle of dynamic (evolutive) interpretation can be applied to this grave breach).[119]

The interdiction of analogy as part of the principle of legality is particularly important here because the fact that Israel is a party to ICERD has surprising ramifications for the applicability of a customary law crime of apartheid to the Israeli-Palestinian conflict. In various German Border Guards cases, both the European Court of Human Rights[120] and the UN Human Rights Committee[121] have

115 See Kwakwa 2002, pp. 419–420. See also Bultz 2013, p. 218. Asserting that the lack of judicial application of the Apartheid Convention weakens the customary status of the crime of apartheid.

116 Tomuschat 2005, p. 246. But see also Institut de Droit International 2005, pp. 212 ("Disagreement was also expressed with regard to Mr Tomuschat's comments on apartheid".), 236 ("[Mr Koroma] expressed his irritation with the lengthy treatment of the crime of apartheid, because it was included in the Rome Statute and therefore such ruminations were unnecessary".).

117 See Eden 2014, pp. 189–191.

118 See generally Kreß 2012, p. 897, para 28. See also PCIJ, *Consistency of Certain Danzig Legislative Decrees with the Constitution of the Free City*, Advisory Opinion (4 December 1935), 1953 PCIJ, Series A/B No. 65, p. 51 ("In other words, criminal laws may not be applied by analogy".).

119 See supra text accompanying n. 97–105.

120 ECtHR, *Streletz, Kessler and Krenz v. Germany*, Grand Chamber Judgment (App. Nos. 34044/96, 33532/97, 44801/98), 22 March 2001.

121 Human Rights Committee, *Baumgarten v. Germany*, Communication No. 960/2000, UN Doc. CCPR/C/960/2000 (31 July 2003), para 9.5.

held that where an individual's conduct (albeit in furtherance of an official policy) breaches a binding obligation under international human rights law, a subsequent criminal conviction will not breach the principle of legality; i.e., the rules of international law on the protection of human rights ensured that the offences were sufficiently accessible and foreseeable.

Although, as noted above, few states provided for jurisdiction over the crime of apartheid prior to their ratification of AP I and the ICC Statute, the principle of non-retroactivity or *nullum crimen, nulla poena sine lege praevia* is not breached by the failure to incorporate an international crime into domestic law as the *Eichmann* case demonstrates.[122] Although Eichmann was convicted of both war crimes and crimes against humanity, recent state practice suggests that retrospective legislation is more easily applied to war crimes than crimes against humanity.[123]

### *5.6.6 Conclusion*

If doubt remains over the customary status of the crime of apartheid as a crime against humanity, a much stronger case can be made for the customary status of the "practices of *apartheid*" as a war crime. Although Article 85(4)(c) of AP I was both a progressive development and specifically targeted at South Africa, a provision representing progressive development in one multilateral treaty may be regarded as a codification if repeated in a later multilateral treaty. Had apartheid been included in the list of war crimes in Article 8 of the ICC Statute, this would certainly have entailed the codification of the "practices of *apartheid*" as a war crime. However, its absence from the list of war crimes in the ICC Statute weakens but does not necessarily destroy the argument for the customary status of Article 85(4)(c) of AP I for several reasons. First, Article 7(1)(j) ICC Statute confirms the status of apartheid as an international crime albeit as a crime against humanity. Second, the fact that the ICC Statute recognises that crimes against humanity can be committed outside the context of an armed conflict entails that the war crime of the "practices of *apartheid*" is, in effect, a lesser-included offence rendering its inclusion in the ICC Statute as a war crime redundant.[124] Third, the inclusion of the crime of apartheid in

[122] District Court of Jerusalem, *Attorney-General of the Government of Israel v. Eichmann*, Judgment (11 December 1961), 36 ILR 5-276. Although it should be noted that the Israeli Supreme Court held that "the principle *nullum crimen sine lege, nulla poena sine lege*, in so far as it negates penal legislation with retrospective effect, has not yet become a rule of customary international law", see Israeli Supreme Court, *Attorney-General of the Government of Israel v. Eichmann*, Judgment (29 May 1962), 36 ILR 5-277-342, p. 281, para 8.

[123] See, e.g., High Court of Australia, *Polyukhovich v. Commonwealth of Australia* (1991), 172 CLR 501; Supreme Court of Canada, *R v. Finta* [1994] 1 SCR 701 (both recognising that retrospective legislation can be applied to war crimes) and the UK War Crimes Act 1991. See also Gallant 2009, pp. 370–371.

[124] Although war crimes can consist of a single isolated act, apartheid by its very nature will always require widespread and systematic commission against a civilian population.

the ICC Statute can be regarded as acceptance that the concept of apartheid has a worldwide application. Finally, Article 10 of the ICC Statute expressly stipulates that the failure to include a crime cannot be interpreted as limiting or prejudicing existing or developing rules of international law "for purposes other than this Statute".

In her reply to Dugard and Reynolds' recent article in the *European Journal of International Law*, Professor Yaffa Zilbershats accepted the premise that apartheid as practised in the former South Africa "remains today a crime against the law of nations applicable to states practising a similar regime",[125] but asserted that the fundamental error underlying the authors' analysis is that apartheid "both in wider usage and specifically in the South African experience, is characterized by the institutionalized racism of a government against citizens and residents under its sovereign regime".[126] While this might potentially be true of the underlying conceptualisation of crimes against humanity generally, it is certainly not true of the underlying conceptualisation of war crimes, and Article 85(4)(c) of AP I is fully applicable to occupied territories.[127] Further, as Dugard and Reynolds noted in their rejoinder to Zilbershats,[128] her assertion fails to appreciate the imposition of apartheid policies in the Mandated Territory of South West Africa (now Namibia), which led to the first reference to apartheid as a crime against humanity by the UNGA in 1965.[129]

## 5.7 Conclusion

Although all the international instruments criminalising apartheid prior to the drafting of the ICC Statute were produced as part of the international campaign against South Africa, universally applicable norms of international law can emerge in response to a specific historical experience. The prohibition of genocide is an obvious case-in-point. However, in the relation to the prohibition of genocide, the international crime that resulted was not limited by reference to the specific historical experience that prompted its creation. By contrast, the criminalisation of apartheid prior to the drafting of the ICC Statute needed to be expressly linked to the specific political ideology that motivated its creation in order to avoid any claims of exceptionalism that might have been made in response to a less explicit criminalisation.

If the factual basis exists, the application of the apartheid paradigm to the Israeli-Palestinian conflict can serve an important rhetorical function but—in the absence

[125] Zilbershats 2013, p. 916.

[126] Ibid.

[127] See Gasser and Dörmann 2013, p. 277.

[128] Dugard and Reynolds 2013b.

[129] Question of South West Africa, UNGA Res. 2074 (XX) (17 December 1965).

of a successful Palestinian ratification of the ICC Statute[130]—the question of individual criminal responsibility will be beset by the problem of the principle of legality, specifically the prohibition of analogy, until the question of the customary status of the crime of apartheid is settled. The recent ratification of AP I by the Palestinian Authority[131] may not alter the applicability of the war crime of the "practices of *apartheid*" to the Israel-Palestine conflict unless an evolutive interpretation can be applied to Article 85(4)(c) of AP I. However, even if the customary status of the crime of apartheid (as well as the applicability of Article 85(4)(c) of AP I *qua* treaty) remains in doubt, there can be no doubt that the acts required to enforce any policy of systematic racial discrimination would fall squarely within the definition of clearly established customary law crimes against humanity such as persecution and other inhumane acts. Where applicable, such policies would also breach the obligation contained in Article 27 of the Fourth Geneva Convention to treat protected persons "without any adverse distinction based, in particular on race, religion or political opinion" and the war crime codified in Article 8(2)(b)(viii) of the ICC Statute—"[t]he transfer, directly or indirectly, by the Occupying Power of parts of its own civilian population into the territory it occupies, or the deportation or transfer of all or parts of the population of the occupied territory within or outside this territory"—may be relevant too.[132]

## References

Ambos K (2014) Treatise on international criminal law (vol II: the crimes and sentencing). Oxford University Press, Oxford

Amnesty International (2011) Universal jurisdiction: a preliminary survey of legislation around the world. Amnesty International Publications, London

Bellinger J, Hayes W (2007) A US government response to the International Committee of the Red Cross study customary international humanitarian law. Int Rev Red Cross 89:443–471

Bultz A (2013) Redefining apartheid in international criminal law. Crim Law Forum 24:205–233

---

[130] In its Report on Preliminary Examination Activities 2013, the ICC's Office of the Prosecutor (OTP) noted that UNGA Resolution 67/19 (29 November 2012) according Palestine non-member observer State status in the United Nations did not cure the invalidity of Palestine's 2009 declaration and, although the OTP considered that Palestine's status at the UNGA was of direct relevance to the ICC's jurisdiction, "at this stage, the Office has no legal basis to open a new preliminary examination".

[131] The Palestinian Authority declared itself to be a party to the four 1949 Geneva Conventions of 12 August 1949 and API (but not APII) on 2 April 2014. Switzerland formally registered this accession on 10 April 2014. See L'Agence France-Presse (AFP), "Confirmation que la Palestine est partie aux Conventions de Genève", available at: http://www.afp.com/fr/node/2278155. Accessed 30 April 2014.

[132] See, e.g., Report of the independent international fact-finding mission to investigate the implications of the Israeli settlements on the civil, political, economic, social and cultural rights of the Palestinian people throughout the Occupied Palestinian Territory, including East Jerusalem, UN Doc. A/HRE/22/63 (7 February 2013).

Carrillo A, Nelson A (2013) Comparative law study and analysis of national legislation relating to crimes against humanity and extraterritorial jurisdiction. www.law.gwu.edu/Academics/EL/clinics/IHRC/Documents/CAH_Final_Web.pdf. Accessed 12 May 2014

Carter J (2006) Palestine: peace not apartheid. Simon & Schuster Inc., New York

Cassese A (2008) International criminal law, 2nd edn. Oxford University Press, Oxford

Cassese A (2013) Cassese's international criminal law. In: Cassese A, Gaeta P (eds), 3rd edn. Oxford University Press, Oxford

Cassese A, Acquaviva G, Fan M, Whiting A (2011) International criminal law: cases and commentary. Oxford University Press, Oxford

Clark R (2008) Apartheid. In: Bassiouni M (ed) International criminal law (vol I: sources, subjects and contents), 3rd edn. Martinus Nijhoff, Leiden, pp 599–620

Clarno A (2009) The empire's new walls: sovereignty, neo-liberalism and the production of space in post-apartheid South Africa and post-Oslo Palestine/Israel. A dissertation submitted in partial fulfilment of the requirements for the degree of doctor of philosophy (sociology) in the University of Michigan. UMI No. 3354120

Cryer R (2005) Prosecuting international crimes: selectivity and the international criminal law regime. Cambridge University Press, Cambridge

Cryer R (2006) Of custom, treaties, scholars and the gavel: the influence of the international criminal tribunals on the ICRC customary study. J Conflict Secur Law 11:239–263

Davis U (2003) Apartheid Israel: possibilities for the struggle within. Zed Books, London

Díaz Polanco P (2010) Israel y la discriminación de la minoría palestino israelí: la institucionalización del "Apartheid". In: Requena y Díez de Revenga M (ed) Luces y sombras de la seguridad internacional en los albores del siglo XX1 (vol II), Instituto Universitario General Gutiérrez Mellado, Madrid, pp 543–562

Dinstein Y (2006) The ICRC customary international humanitarian law study. Israel Yearb Human Rights 36:1–15

Dinstein Y (2010) The conduct of hostilities under the law of international armed conflict, 2nd edn. Cambridge University Press, Cambridge

Dörmann K (2002) Elements of war crimes under the Rome statute of the International Criminal Court: sources and commentary. Cambridge University Press, Cambridge

Dörmann K (2003) war crimes under the Rome statute of the International Criminal Court, with a special focus on the negotiations on the elements of crimes. Max Planck Yearb United Nations Law 7:341–407

Draper G (1976) The modern pattern of war criminality. Israel Yearb Human Rights 6:9–48

Du Plessis M (2011) International criminal law: the crime of apartheid revisited. S Afr J Crim Justice 24:417–428

Dubow S (2014) Apartheid, 1948–1994. Oxford University Press, Oxford

Dugard J (2007) Report of the special rapporteur on the situation of human rights in the Palestinian territories occupied since 1967 (29 January 2007). UN Doc. A/HRC/4/17

Dugard J (2012) L'Apartheid. In: Ascensio H, Decaux E, Pellet A (eds) Droit international pénal, 2nd edn. Pedone, Paris, pp 197–207

Dugard J, Reynolds J (2013a) Apartheid, international law and the occupied Palestinian territory. Eur J Int Law 24:867–913

Dugard J, Reynolds J (2013b) Apartheid in occupied Palestine: a rejoinder to Yaffa Zilbershats. www.ejiltalk.org/apartheid-in-occupied-palestine-a-rejoinder-to-yaffa-zilbershats/. Accessed 12 May 2014

Eden P (2014) The role of the Rome statute in the criminalization of apartheid. J Int Crim Justice 12:171–191

Falk R (2010) Report of the special rapporteur on the situation of human rights in the Palestinian territories occupied since 1967 (30 August 2010). UN Doc. A/65/331

Falk R (2013) International law, apartheid and Israeli responses to BDS. In: Wiles R (ed) Generation Palestine: voices from the boycott, divestment and sanctions movement. Pluto Press, London, pp 85–99

Falk R (2014) Report of the special rapporteur on the situation of human rights in the Palestinian territories occupied since 1967 (13 January 2014). UN Doc. A/HRC/25/67

Fitzmaurice G (1957) The law and procedure of the International Court of Justice 1951–1954: treaty interpretation and other treaty points. Br Yearb Int Law 33:203–293

Gallant K (2009) The principle of legality in international and comparative criminal law. Cambridge University Press, Cambridge

Gasser H-P, Dörmann K (2013) Protection of the civilian population. In: Fleck D (ed) The handbook of international humanitarian law, 3rd edn. Oxford University Press, Oxford, pp 231–320

Gebhard J (2012) Apartheid. In: Wolfrum R (ed) The Max Planck encyclopedia of public international law (vol I: AA to AC). Oxford University Press, Oxford, pp 461–468

Goldstone R (2011) Israel and the apartheid slander. The New York Times A27, New York

Graditzky T (1999) War crime issues before the rome diplomatic conference on the establishment of an international criminal court, vol 5. University of California Davis Journal of International Law and Policy, pp 199–217

Guelke A (2005) Rethinking the rise and fall of apartheid. Palgrave Macmillan, Basingstoke

Hall C (2008) Article 7 (2)(j)(h): The crime of apartheid. In: Triffterer O (ed) Commentary on the Rome statute of the International Criminal Court: observers' notes, article by article, 2nd edn. C. H. Beck/Hart/Nomos, Munich, pp 263–266

Hannum H (1997) Human rights. In: Joyner C (ed) The United Nations and international law. Cambridge University Press, Cambridge, pp 131–154

Henckaerts J-M (2007) Customary international humanitarian law: a response to US comments. Int Rev Red Cross 89:473–488

Henckaerts J-M (2009) The grave breaches regime as customary international law. J Int Crim Justice 7:683–701

Henckaerts J-M, Doswald-Beck L (2005a) Customary international humanitarian law (vol I: Rules). Cambridge University Press, Cambridge

Henckaerts J-M, Doswald-Beck L (2005b) Customary international humanitarian law (vol II: Practice). Cambridge University Press, Cambridge

Higgins R (1996) Some observations on the inter-temporal rule in international law. In: Makarczy J (ed) Theory of international law at the threshold of the 21st century: essays in honour of Krzysztof Skubiszewski. Kluwer, The Hague, pp 173–181

Higgins R (2009) Some observations on the inter-temporal rule in international law. In: Higgins R (ed) Themes and theories: selected essays, speeches, and writings in international law (vol II). Oxford University Press, Oxford, pp 867–874

Institut de Droit International (1975) Le problème intertemporel en droit international public. 56 Annuaire de l'Institut de Droit International, pp 536–541

Institut de Droit International (2005) Third question: universal criminal jurisdiction with respect to the crime of genocide, crimes against humanity and war crimes. 71(II) Annuaire de l'Institut de Droit International, 199–284

International Criminal Court (2011) Elements of crimes. ICC-PIDS-LT-03-002/11_Eng. http://www.icc-cpi.int. Accessed 12 May 2014

Jennings R, Watts A (1996) Oppenheim's international law (Vol I), 9th edn. Longman, London

Kotzur M (2012) Intertemporal law. In: Wolfrum R (ed) The Max Planck encyclopedia of public international law (vol VI: INto MA). Oxford University Press, Oxford, pp 278–282

Kreß C (2012) Nulla poena nullum crimen sine lege. In: Wolfrum R (ed) The Max Planck encyclopedia of public international law (vol VII: MA to OZ). Oxford University Press, Oxford, pp 889–899

Kwakwa E (2002) The Cairo-Arusha principles on universal jurisdiction in respect of gross human rights offences: developing the frontiers of the principle of universal jurisdiction. Afr Yearb Int Law 10:407–430

Lebrun C (ed) (2013) Israel, un état d'apartheid? Enjeux juridiques et politiques. L'Harmattan, Paris

Lerner N (1969) The convention on the non-applicability of statutory limitations to war crimes. Israel Law Rev 4:512–533
Levie H (1993) The 1977 protocol I and the United States. Saint Louis Univ Law J 38:469–484
Macedo S (ed) (2001) The Princeton principles on universal jurisdiction. http://lapa.princeton.edu/hosteddocs/unive_jur.pdf. Accessed 12 May 2014
Matheson M (1987) Remarks on the United States' position on the relation of customary international law to the 1977 protocols additional to the 1949 Geneva conventions. Am Univ J Int Law Policy 2:419–431
McCormack T (2004) Crimes against humanity. In: McGoldrick D, Rowe P, Donnelly E (eds) The permanent International Criminal Court: legal and policy issues. Hart, Oxford, pp 179–202
McCormack T (2006) An Australian perspective on the ICRC customary international humanitarian law study. Int Law Stud 82:81–97
McCormack T, Simpson G (1994) The international law commission's draft code of crimes against the peace and security of mankind: an appraisal of the substantive provisions. Crim Law Forum 5:1–55
Morris V, Scharf M (1995) An insider's guide to the international criminal tribunal for the former Yugoslavia: a documentary history and analysis (vol II). Transnational Publishers Inc., Irvington-on-Hudson (NY)
Nathan E (17 July 1998) Statement by judge Eli Nathan, head of the delegation of Israel, United Nations diplomatic conference of plenipotentiaries on the establishment of an international criminal court, 9th Plenary Meeting
Reynolds J (2012) Third world approaches to international law and the ghosts of apartheid. In: Kean D, McDermott Y (eds) The challenge of human rights past. Edward Elgar Publishing, Cheltenham, Present and Future, pp 194–218
Robinson D (1999) Defining "crimes against humanity" at the Rome conference. Am J Int Law 93:43–57
Sandoz Y (2008) Penal aspects of international humanitarian law. In: Bassiouni M (ed) International criminal law (vol I: sources, subjects and contents), 3rd edn. Martinus Nijhoff, Leiden, pp 293–321
Sandoz Y, Swinarski C, Zimmermann B (eds) (1987) Commentary on the additional protocols of 8 June 1977 to the Geneva conventions of 12 August 1949. Martinus Nijhoff, Geneva
Schabas W (2010) The International Criminal Court: a commentary on the Rome statute. Oxford University Press, Oxford
Solis G (2010) The law of armed conflict: international humanitarian law in war. Cambridge University Press, New York
Tilley V (ed) (2009) Occupation, colonialism, apartheid?: a re-assessment of Israel's practices in the occupied Palestinian territories under international law. Human Sciences Research Council of South Africa, Cape Town
Tilley V (ed) (2012) Beyond occupation: apartheid, colonialism and international law in the occupied Palestinian territories. Pluto Press, London
Tomuschat C (1995) Crimes against the peace and security of mankind and the recalcitrant third state. Israel Yearb Human Rights 24:41–62
Tomuschat C (2005) Universal criminal jurisdiction with respect to the crime of genocide, crimes against humanity and war crimes. Annuaire de l'Institut de Droit Internationa 71:213–388
Tutu D (2002) Apartheid in the holy land. www.theguardian.com/world/2002/apr/29/comment. Accessed 12 May 2014
Von Hebel H, Robinson D (1999) Crimes within the jurisdiction of the court. In: Lee R (ed) The International Criminal Court. The making of the Rome statute: issues, negotiations, results. Kluwer, The Hague, pp 79–126
White B (2009) Israeli apartheid: a beginner's guide. Pluto Press, London

Wilmshurst E, Breau S (2011) Perspectives on the ICRC study on customary international humanitarian law. Cambridge University Press, Cambridge

Zahar A (2009) Apartheid as an international crime. In: Cassese A (ed) The Oxford companion to international criminal justice. Oxford University Press, Oxford, pp 245–246

Zilbershats Y (2013) Apartheid, international law and the occupied Palestinian territory: a reply to John Dugard and John Reynolds. Eur J Int Law 24:915–928

# Chapter 6
# A Critical Discussion of the Second Turkel Report and How It Engages with the Duty to Investigate Under International Law

**Michelle Lesh**

**Abstract** The aim of this article is to reflect upon accountability under international law through the framework of a specific example. The Turkel Commission is a public commission of inquiry appointed by the Government of Israel. It issued its second and final report, which addresses Israel's mechanisms for investigating violations of international law according to the laws of war, in February 2013. The Report primarily focuses on International Humanitarian Law (IHL) but also attends to International Human Rights Law (IHRL). The duty to investigate under international law is an evolving process because treaty law lacks detail, particularly regarding the manner of conducting an investigation. Under IHRL that duty has been enriched by the jurisprudence of regional human rights courts and soft law. Under IHL duty (which is even sparser in detail) it has been aided by state practice and the jurisprudence of international tribunals. The Turkel Report is the first major study on the duty to investigate and it informs much of the analysis of this article. The article provides a descriptive review of the Report and a critical discussion of the way this current national development offers a meaningful contribution to the development of the obligation imposed by international law to investigate alleged violations.

**Keywords** Turkel commission · Israel · Obligation to investigate · Accountability · War crimes · International law · International humanitarian law · International human rights law

---

Dr. Michelle Lesh is a Golda Meir Post-Doctoral Fellow at the Hebrew University of Jerusalem. She worked as a legal assistant to the Turkel Commission during its second phase. She also provided an experts' paper on the Second Turkel Report to the UN Special Rapporteur on counterterrorism and human rights drones inquiry (A/68/389; A/HRC/25/29). The views expressed in this article are those of the author and do not reflect the views of any other institution or body. All errors remain those of the author.

---

M. Lesh (✉)
Hebrew University of Jerusalem, Jerusalem, Israel
e-mail: michellelesh@gmail.com

 
T.D. Gill et al. (eds.), *Yearbook of International Humanitarian Law 2013*,
Yearbook of International Humanitarian Law 16, DOI 10.1007/978-94-6265-038-1_6

## Contents



## 6.1 Introduction

The aim of this article is to reflect upon accountability under international law through the framework of a specific example. It will provide a descriptive review of the Second Report of Turkel Commission, a commission of inquiry appointed by the government of Israel to examine Israel's mechanisms for investigating violations of international law. The article also provides a critical discussion of the way this current national development offers a meaningful contribution to the development of the obligation imposed by international law to investigate alleged violations. To help the reader to understand the nature of that obligation, the article will begin, in Sect. 6.2, by briefly explaining the mandate of the Turkel Commission and setting out the content and structure of the Second Report. Sections 6.3 and 6.4 will outline different aspects of the obligations under international law, based on the analysis of the Turkel Report, which predominantly focuses on International Humanitarian Law (IHL), but it also attends to International Human Rights Law (IHRL). This will be followed by Sect. 6.5, which will comment on the Commission's approach to international law. Section 6.6 will set out some conclusions.

## 6.2 The Turkel Commission: The Second Report's Structure and Content

In June 2010, the Turkel Commission—a public commission of inquiry—was appointed by the Government of Israel, following the maritime incident in which the Israel Defense Forces (IDF) intercepted the Mavi Marmara, a flotilla sailing from Turkey for Gaza. Supreme Court Justice (Ret.) Jacob Turkel chaired the Commission and its members were Professor Shabtai Rosenne (until his death in September 2010), IDF General (Ret.) Amos Horev, Ambassador Reuven Merhav, and Professor Miguel Deutch. In addition, international observers were appointed to the Commission: Lord David Trimble, Brigadier-General (Ret.) Kenneth Watkin (until May 2011) and Professor Tim McCormack (from June 2011). The Commission was asked to examine the legality of the blockade on Gaza and whether the actions carried out by Israel to enforce the blockade on board the Mavi Marmara were legal. These questions were addressed by the Commission in its First Report, submitted to the government in January 2011.[1]

The Commission's mandate also included assessing Israel's mechanisms for examining and investigating violations of international law according to the laws of war.[2] The Commission reviewed Israeli military and civilian mechanisms for investigating behavior by the IDF, the Israel Police, the Israel Security Agency (ISA), the Israel Prison Service and the civilian echelon, and the compatibility of those accountability structures with Israel's obligations under international law.[3] This part of the mandate formed its Second Report, submitted to the Government of Israel in February 2013, and it is this Report that informs the analysis of this article. The Second Turkel Report is concerned with accountability and, therefore, with a topic of much broader scope than the First Turkel Report. The final (brief) chapter of the Second Report does in fact assess the investigation into the maritime incident; however, this investigation was not the focus of the Report, but rather a case study that was considered against the backdrop of the legal analysis and recommendations made by the Commission in the previous chapters of the Report. Although the government attached the subject of Israel's mechanisms for investigating violations of the laws of war to the Commission's mandate on the maritime incident, the broader political and legal context cannot be ignored, especially given the Commission's decision to divide these two aspects of its mandate into separate reports. In recent years Israel has come under criticism internationally and domestically in its handling of investigations into military operations, most notably

---

[1] Turkel Commission Report Part One 2011a, b.

[2] Resolution No. 1796 of the 32nd Government, Appointment of an Independent Public Commission, Chaired by Supreme Court Justice (ret.) Jacob Turkel, to Examine the Maritime Incident of 31 May 2010 (6 June 2010), para 5.

[3] Turkel Commission Second Report 2013, pp. 432–463.

in the Goldstone Report.[4] Therefore, in discussing the Second Turkel Report, sensitivity to the political and legal setting, far beyond the Gaza Flotilla, is important in understanding the nature of this Report and its place in the larger debate on the international law requirements to conduct investigations.

Mapping the structure and purpose of the Report is helpful in navigating through the content and relevance of its nine hundred pages. This chapter will dedicate much of its attention to the first chapter of the Report (Chapter A), which outlines the Commission's understanding of the duty to investigate under international law. As will be discussed in detail below, it sets the context for the following chapters of the Report, which cover: a survey of state practice (Chapter B), a description of the current Israeli investigative mechanisms (Chapter C), the Commission's recommendations (Chapter D) and, as mentioned above, a final chapter on the investigation into the Marmara incident (Chapter E). In addition to its in-depth analysis of the obligations under international law in Chapter A, one of the contributions of the Turkel Report is its comparative survey. It dedicates a chapter (as well as a hefty annex) to the practice of six countries in the field of investigations.[5] Although it is beyond the scope of this article to discuss specific national investigative processes, it is worth noting that Chapter B of the Report demonstrates how references to the practice of states can help to elucidate some of the key processes involved in adhering to a vague international law obligation. The Commission's recommendations in Chapter D refer to Chapter B. This is done by way of comparison, offering some practical details to aid in conceptualizing an obligation lacking specificity, rather than as a prescriptive way of stating that these are the processes that must be implemented in order to fulfill the international obligation.[6]

Significantly, in terms of the practical impact of the recommendations concerning changes to the Israeli mechanisms for conducting investigations, the final recommendation of the Report calls on the Prime Minister to appoint an implementation team to monitor the implementation of the recommendations. In January 2014, the government appointed an implementation team that has until September 2014 to submit its recommendations to the Prime Minister.[7] The focus of this article

[4] Goldstone Report 2009. See also, Tomuschat Report 2010; McGowan Davis Report 2011; B'Tselem 2010.

[5] The Commission examined the military justice system of six countries and outlined the various mechanisms within those systems. Other reports on accountability have focused on different kinds of state practice. For example, the Report of the Secretary-General's Panel of Experts on Accountability in Sri Lanka interprets relevant state practice to be transitional justice mechanisms in a post-conflict society. See Darusman Report 2011, paras 269, 327, 396.

[6] For example, Chapter B highlights the importance of comprehensive reporting systems. In addition, the Commission further clarifies what it means by a 'fact-finding assessment' (discussed in Sect. 6.3.3 of this chapter) by drawing a comparison to preliminary stages of investigations that exist in some of the countries surveyed. Turkel Commission Second Report 2013, pp. 253–254, para 76; p. 257, para 78; p. 259, para 79; p. 261, para 81; p. 263, para 81.

[7] Turkel Commission Second Report 2013, p. 422, para 101; Decision number 1143 of the government, 5 January 2014, available at: http://www.pmo.gov.il/SECRETARY/GOVDECISIONS/pages/default.aspx?PN=1 (Hebrew).

will be on the way in which the duty to investigate, as outlined in Chapter A of the Report, shaped the Commission's recommendations presented in Chapter D of the Report, which mainly relate to Israel's military justice system. The Report is the first major study on the duty to investigate under international law and therefore in addition to its potential significance for the future face of Israel's military justice system, it contributes to the direction of international legal debate on the scope of the international law obligation to investigate.

## 6.3 The Commission's Analysis of the Obligation to Investigate under International Law

There are various normative frameworks under international law that comprise the obligation to investigate, one of which is IHL. Chapter A of the Turkel Report found IHL to be the primary body of law relevant to the question under consideration for the obvious reason that the mandate required it to assess the obligation to investigate violations deriving from that body of law.[8] Treaty provisions on the duty to investigate under IHL are sparse and therefore the analysis of the Turkel Commission is a welcome contribution to understanding the contours of the duty to investigate according to IHL. Other bodies of law that are discussed in the Report insofar as they are relevant to the duty to investigate in situations of armed conflict are IHRL, international criminal law (ICL) and the law on state responsibility. The way in which the chapter structures its analysis is by dividing it into four questions: Why investigate? What to investigate? When to investigate? and How to investigate? This structure is repeated in the subsequent chapters of the Report. This section of the article will focus on the first three questions posed by the Commission: why investigate (i.e., sources of the duty to examine and investigate complaints and claims of violations of IHL); what to investigate (i.e., violations of IHL that require examination or investigations) and when to investigate (i.e., the grounds for carrying out the obligation to examine and investigate).

### *6.3.1 Examine*

The Turkel Commission distinguished a 'general duty to broadly *examine* all suspected violations of IHL … [from a] duty to *investigate* certain types of alleged violations known as "war crimes".'[9] The Commission saw no difference between the law of international armed conflict (IAC) and non-international armed conflict

[8] Turkel Commission Second Report 2013, pp. 55–59, paras 4–5.

[9] Ibid, pp. 73–74, para 22.

(NIAC) with regard to the obligation to examine and investigate, which is in keeping with the growing trend that the rules of IAC can be applied by analogy to NIAC.[10]

The Commission equates the duty to examine with the general obligation of 'compliance' in IHL.[11] Examples that facilitate compliance include training, reporting duties and disciplinary measures.[12] Furthermore, it connects the duty to examine to the concept of 'suppression', which is found in the relevant treaty law. Article 146 of the Fourth Geneva Convention ('GCIV') states: 'Each High Contracting Party shall take measures necessary for the suppression of all acts contrary to the provisions of the present Convention other than the grave breaches defined in the following Article'.[13] The Commission equates the notion of 'suppress' with 'a general duty to prevent all violations of international humanitarian law'.[14] The focus on *all* violations is consistent with a strict reading of this provision and the corresponding Commentary, which explains this paragraph to cover 'breaches other than the graves breaches listed'.[15] The Commission takes 'suppress' to mean 'examine' and interprets the concept to cover 'prevent'. An examination—according to the Commission's analysis—does not need to abide by the more strict standards for conducting an investigation. The only guidance for its format is that it 'must be conducted in a fashion that guarantees the suppression of violations and ensures future compliance with international humanitarian law'.[16] Therefore, the Commission's conception of the obligation to examine all violations is derived from compliance and prevention, two underlying themes in IHL treaty law.

### 6.3.2 *Investigate*

In addition to the duty to examine, the Commission views the treaty law to place an obligation to 'search and bring to trial those allegedly responsible for certain types

[10] Ibid, pp. 79–81, para 27. The same approach was taken in the Darusman Report 2011, para 268. See, more generally, ICTY, *Prosecutor v. Dusko Tadić*, Decision on the Defence Motion for Interlocutory Appeal on Jurisdiction, Appeals Chamber (IT-94-I-AR72), 2 October 1995, paras 109–127; Henckaerts and Doswald-Beck 2005, p. xxxv.

[11] Turkel Commission Second Report 2013, p. 74, para 23. The primary treaty provision referred to by the Commission is Protocol Additional to the Geneva Conventions of 12 August 1949, and Relating to the Protection of Victims of International Armed Conflicts (Protocol 1), opened for signature 8 June 1977, 1125 UNTS 3 (entered into force 7 December 1978) (hereinafter: API), Article 87; Sandoz et al. 1987, paras 1017–1023.

[12] Turkel Commission Second Report 2013, p. 74, para 23.

[13] Geneva Convention Relative to the Protection of Civilian Persons in Time of War, opened for signature 12 August 1949, 75 UNTS 287 (entered into force 21 October 1950) (hereinafter: GCIV), Article 146(3).

[14] Turkel Commission Second Report 2013, p. 74, para 23.

[15] Pictet 1956, p. 594.

[16] Turkel Commission Second Report 2013, p. 112, para 61.

of violations of the Convention'.[17] It defines and distinguishes this duty in its account of the concept 'repress'. Thus, the Commission has interpreted the first two paragraphs of Article 146 of GCIV as an obligation to 'repress', which requires an investigation (encompassing all stages of the process from searching and bringing to trial to enacting legislation) into certain types of violations.[18]

The distinction made by the Commission between 'suppress' and 'repress' is further developed in its discussion of another source for the obligation to investigate and examine: the obligations imposed on military commanders and other superiors.[19] The Commission interprets the obligation on commanders and other superiors, set out in Articles 86 and 87 of Additional Protocol I to the Geneva Conventions as 'obligating superiors to prevent and punish'. The two Articles and the corresponding Commentary are not consistent in their use of the terms 'suppress', 'repress' 'prevent' and 'punish'. At some points they are used interchangeably (Article 87) while at other points (Article 86) they are used differently.[20] Given this vagueness, the Commission's decision to define 'suppress' to mean 'prevent' and 'repress' to mean 'punish' and to make those definitions correspond to its distinction between 'examine' and 'investigate' is refreshing in its clarity though it may be vulnerable to criticism concerning its legal accuracy.

#### 6.3.2.1 Threshold for Opening an Investigation

The distinction between the duty to 'examine' and the duty to 'investigate' is not limited to the nature of the violations: it also extends to the grounds for carrying out such inquires.

[17] Ibid, p. 75, para 24; Article 146 GCIV.

[18] Ibid, pp. 75–76, para 24; Article 146 GCIV and Article 85 API.

[19] Ibid, pp. 77–79, para 26; Articles 86–87 API. The Commission emphasizes that tribunals, statutes and commentators have recognized this obligation: See, e.g., Statute of the International Criminal Tribunal for the Former Yugoslavia, UN Doc. S/RES/827 (1993), 25 May 1993 (hereinafter: ICTY Statute), Article 7(3); Statute for the International Criminal Tribunal for Rwanda, UN Doc. S/RES/955 (1994), 8 November 1994, (hereinafter: ICTR Statute), Article 6(3); Rome Statute of the International Criminal Court, opened for signature 17 July 1998, 2178 UNTS 3 (entered into force 1 July 2002) (hereinafter: Rome Statute), Article 38(a); ICTY, *Prosecutor v. Blaškić*, Judgment Appeals Chamber (IT-95-14-A), 29 July 2004, para 69; ICTY, *Prosecutor v. Halilović*, Judgment Trial Chamber (IT-01-48-T), 16 November 2005, para 39; ICC, *Prosecutor v. Jean Pierre Bemba*, Decision Pursuant to Article 61(7)(a) and (b) of the Rome Statute on the Charges of the Prosecutor Against Jean-Pierre Bemba Gombo, Pre-Trial Chamber II (ICC-01/05-01/08-424), 15 June 2009, paras 402–443; Henckaerts and Doswald-Beck 2005, rule 152.

[20] See Articles 86–87 API; Sandoz et al. 1987, paras 1007, 1010–1011, 1015, 1019, 1022–1023.

### 6.3.2.2 War Crimes

Allegations of war crimes are the types of violations under IHL that require investigation. The Commission takes the concept of a war crime to be broader in scope than the grave breaches enumerated in the treaty law and sees it to encompass 'serious violations'.[21] This approach is supported by the jurisprudence of the international tribunals.[22] In setting out the threshold for an investigation the Commission found that an investigation is triggered when 'a credible accusation is made or a reasonable suspicion arises that a war crime has been committed'.[23]

The first recommendation made by the Commission in Chapter D of the Report concerns the type of violations that require investigation. Israel does not have comprehensive legislation addressing war crimes.[24] The Commission found it satisfactory to 'translate' the behavior amounting to war crimes into an existing offense into domestic law (for example, murder) as long as such offenses reflect the severity of war crimes, and where there are gaps between the regular penal offenses and the international prohibitions, they must be filled.[25] Nonetheless, the recommendation emphasized the normative value in adopting international norms relating to war crimes into Israeli domestic legislation.[26] It is noteworthy, particularly in the context of its recommendation about the ISA,[27] that the example the Commission provides for the kind of international prohibitions requiring translation into domestic legislation is that of torture and inhuman and degrading treatment.[28] Political willingness to adopt all war crimes into domestic legislation will be predictably weak, particularly in the context of Israel's settlement policy.[29]

---

[21] Turkel Commission Second Report 2013, pp. 94–99, paras 39–45.

[22] Ibid, pp. 96–97, paras 41–42; Article 1 ICTY Statute; *Tadić,* supra n 10; Article 8 Rome Statute.

[23] Turkel Commission Second Report 2013, p. 100, para 46. For an insightful explanation of what makes an allegation credible see Darusman Report 2011, para 52.

[24] See Turkel Commission Second Report 2013, pp. 273–274, para 9; p. 363, para 7.

[25] Ibid, pp. 364–365, paras 8–10.

[26] Ibid, pp. 362–366, paras 5–12.

[27] One of the harshest recommendations of the Report is a response to the criticism of the ISA. Based on the material submitted to the Commission it found that over 700 complaints by individuals interrogated by the ISA were submitted the Interrogatee Complaints Comptroller (Mavtan) who is a senior ISA employee. The Mavtan's supervisor never initiated a criminal investigation on the basis of the complaints. The Commission recommended moving the Mavtan to the Ministry of Justice. The Commission recommended moving the Interrogatee Complaints Comptroller (Mavtan) who is a senior ISA employee the Ministry of Justice. In June 2013 it was reported in the press that this recommendation was implemented. Ibid, pp. 413–416, paras 86–90. See, also, the recommendation that ISA interrogations must be videotaped. Ibid, p. 417, para 97; Ravid 2013.

[28] Ibid, p. 365, para 10.

[29] Article 49(6) GCIV. See also Henckaerts and Doswald-Beck 2005, rule 130; Human Rights Council Report 2013, para 104.

### 6.3.2.3 The Right to Life

The Report is not concerned only with situations of active combat, but also situations of internal disturbances, thus making the duty to investigate relevant under IHRL. Until this point, the discussion in this article has focused on the duty to investigate according to IHL. The Commission does, however, also address the duty to investigate under IHRL. The most significant difference between the duties under the different frameworks is the grounds for triggering an investigation. As stated above, under IHL, a reasonable suspicion of a war crime requires an investigation to be opened. Under IHRL, the range of activities requiring an investigation is much wider, thus making the threshold lower than under IHL. The obligation to investigate violations of IHRL derives from the general obligation 'to uphold and guarantee' human rights and from the right for 'effective remedy' by a competent authority.[30] Various human rights sources have interpreted the substantive rights and the general obligation to ensure the realization of human rights to include the obligation to investigate human rights violations. In particular, the right to life has been interpreted to require an investigation immediately following the use of lethal force in a law enforcement context. This is based on the assumption that in law enforcement situations, non-lethal measures, such as arrest, are available to the relevant authorities due to their level of control over the situation and, as such, it is rare that the nature of the threat is so imminent that lethal force is considered necessary and proportionate.[31]

### 6.3.2.4 Understanding the Commission's Approach to Thresholds

The Commission develops the threshold for opening an investigation by explaining that the obligation to investigate the death of an individual will depend on the legal regime governing the specific activity, for example IHL or IHRL. This is because the context dictates the criminality.[32] For example, in the context of armed conflict,

[30] Turkel Commission Second Report 2013, pp. 82–84, paras 29–31. See, e.g., International Covenant on Civil and Political Rights, opened for signature 20 November 1989, 1577 UNTS 3 (entered into force 2 September 1990) (hereinafter: ICCPR), Article 2; Convention against Torture and Other Cruel, Inhuman or Degrading Treatment or Punishment, opened for signature 10 December 1984, 1465 UNTS 85 (entered into force 26 June 1987), Articles 6–8; Human Rights Committee, General Comment No. 31: The Nature of the General Legal Obligation Imposed on States Parties to the Covenant, UN Doc. CCPR/C/21/Rev.1/Add.13, 26 May 2004, paras 15, 18; ECtHR, *McCann v. The United Kingdom*, Judgment (Appl. No. 18984/91), 27 September 1995, para 42; Articles 6, 11(f), 22–23 of the Basic Principles on the Use of Force and Firearms by Law Enforcement Officials, GA Res. 45/166 (18 December 1999); Articles 9–11 of the Principles on the Effective Prevention and Investigation of Extra-Legal, Arbitrary and Summary Executions, Recommended by ECOSOC Res. 1989/65 (24 May 1989), UN Doc. E/1989/89.

[31] Basic Principles, supra n. 30; Principles on the Effective Prevention, supra n 30, Article 1; *McCann*, supra n 30, paras 203–214.

[32] Turkel Commission Second Report 2013, pp. 100–101, para 46.

the death of an uninvolved civilian during hostilities does not of itself give rise to an immediate duty to investigate, primarily because the principle of proportionality may permit collateral damage (and therefore there may be no reasonable suspicion of a war crime). However, a situation of law enforcement the killing (or serious injury) of an individual by security forces automatically requires an immediate duty to investigate because of the suspicion of criminality inherent in such a situation.[33] Attention is also drawn to the trickier context of law enforcement activity that occurs during armed conflict. When force is used against civilians in operations that are not of a combat nature, the death or serious injury to an individual 'during operations of *this* kind may, *prima facie*, give rise to greater suspicion of criminality than collateral damage during a combat action and, in certain circumstances, will also require the immediate commencement of an investigation'.[34] Therefore, the grounds for triggering an investigation depend very much on the applicable normative framework.

The significance of the Commission's approach to the question of when an investigation is required is demonstrated by the breadth of situations the Commission saw relevant to its analysis. The Report is not only concerned with situations of active combat (akin to Operation Cast Lead or Pillar of Defense in Gaza[35]) but also to situations of internal disturbances during a situation of law enforcement (for example, during a protest in Bil'in in the West Bank[36]). It highlights the importance of understanding and applying this duty not only to situations of 'war' but also to a situation of relative calm. The Commission's well-considered approach should be applauded because it reflects an attempt to assess the legal duty in a way that is sensitive to the realities on the ground. This deliberately expansive approach of the Report must be kept in mind when critics (particularly those familiar with the operational realities) question the practical relevance of the Commission's recommendations in the light of the constraints that occur during active combat. The approach is also pertinent for other reasons, which relate to criticisms raised since the publication of the Turkel Report that note the IDF's ongoing failure to

[33] Ibid, pp. 101, 103, paras 47, 51.

[34] Ibid, pp. 105–106, para 53. The example the Commission provides of such a situation is forcefully clearing a residence because it is usually an act of traditional law enforcement.

[35] 'Operation Cast Lead' occurred between December 2008 and January 2009. The IDF launched the 22-day operation and it is estimated that over 1,300 Palestinians were killed and over 5,320 were wounded. Three Israeli civilians and one soldier were killed and more than 84 injured by rockets fired into Israel. Nine Israeli soldiers were killed in combat within the Gaza Strip (four by IDF fire) and 113 were wounded. 'Pillar of Defense' was an operation launched on 14 November 2012 by the IDF and it lasted 8 days, until a ceasefire was reached between Israel and Hamas. Five Israeli civilians were killed from rocket fire, 167 Palestinians were killed, including at least 87 that did not take part in hostilities, 32 of whom were minors.

[36] See *Abu Rahma* case, which dealt with the investigative file into a death that occurred during a protest in Bi'lin. HCJ 6547/11, *Abu Rahma* et al. *v. the MAG,* available at: http://elyon1.court.gov.il/files/13/470/016/t13/13016470.t13.pdf. See also http://elyon1.court.gov.il/files/11/470/065/c14/11065470.c14.htm. http://www.btselem.org/download/20130903_abu_rahmeh_file_closure_statement.pdf (Hebrew); Turkel Commission Second Report 2013, p. 31.

investigate incidents involving the use of lethal force during civilian protests in the West Bank.[37] Time will reveal whether the Report's efforts to be sensitive to the realities on the ground in fact alter current practice.

### *6.3.3 Fact-Finding Assessment*

In the context of its discussion of the grounds for opening an examination and an investigation, the Commission introduces the concept 'fact-finding assessment'. This lives in the world of examination, where the threshold of reasonable suspicion of war crime has not been met in order to trigger an investigation. However, what distinguishes a fact-finding assessment from an examination is that the former relates to those incidents where further information is required in order to determine if there has been a credible allegation of a violation that may subsequently trigger an investigation if the assessment reveals a reasonable suspicion of a war crime.[38]

One of the motivations behind the fact-finding assessment is to ensure that potential violations that do not quite meet the threshold of reasonable suspicion are still looked into. According to the Commission, a fact-finding assessment is needed when an 'exceptional' incident has occurred that points to facts or circumstances that might subsequently reveal the need for an investigation. The example the Commission provides of such an incident is 'civilian casualties that were not anticipated when the attack was planned'.[39]

The Commission relies on the fact-finding assessment in its recommendation about the operational debriefing, the current mechanism used by the IDF for deciding whether to open an investigation. An operational debriefing is a key 'organizational learning tool' of the IDF, which is aimed at improving the function

[37] See Amnesty International 2014, which focuses on the right to protest and claims that Israeli forces frequently respond to stone-throwing protests using excessive force, including the use of live fire against protesters, causing unlawful deaths and injuries. The report further claims there are deficiencies in the Israeli system for investigating alleged violations by the IDF. The report dedicated particular attention to the case of Samir Awad, a 16-year-old Palestinian who was shot and killed by an Israeli soldier in January 2013 when he was protesting against the construction of a section of separation barrier that cuts across the village of Bodrus, where he lived. Awad's father, together with B'Tselem, petitioned to the High Court of Justice over the delay concerning the investigation into Awad's death and the MAG's failure to decide whether to prosecute those responsible. See http://www.btselem.org/press_releases/20140327_samir_awad_investigation_petition.

[38] Turkel Commission Second Report 2013, pp. 102–103, para 49; p. 106, para 54; p. 378, para 30.

[39] Ibid, p. 103, para 49. See, also, Margalit 2012 for an insightful analysis on the circumstances that give rise to a duty to investigate civilian casualties caused by a suspected failure to take precautions in attack, and more generally on the circumstances that give rise to a duty to investigate civilian casualties, which indicate an IHL violation that does not trigger individual criminal responsibility.

of the military units.[40] Generally, a person in the chain of command of the unit involved in the operation conducts the debriefing. It is classified and the standard rules of evidence do not apply.[41] The Commission found that in its current form, the debriefing fails to adhere to international law and suggests the fact-finding assessment as the alternative mechanism to be established in its place. The Commission recommends that where more information is required to establish whether there is a reasonable suspicion of criminal activity, the Military Advocate General (MAG) can decide to order a special 'fact-finding assessment team' to examine the circumstances of the incident within a specified time frame.[42]

### 6.3.4 Relevant Normative Frameworks

In outlining the sources for the duty to examine and investigate, the violations that require examination or investigations, and the grounds for carrying out the obligation to examine and investigate, the Commission primarily focused on aspects of the duty to investigate according the IHL. Other bodies of law are also relevant to the task of making the content of the obligation more visible, the most notable of which is IHRL. This is reflected in the relevant thresholds for opening an investigation and the significance of IHRL to the Commission's interpretation of the duty to investigate will be further explored in Sect. 6.4. In identifying ICL as a relevant source, the Commission discusses the principle of complementarity, which emphasizes the primacy of investigations by the national justice system over international courts, through the application of the 'unwilling and unable' test.[43] The discussion highlights the close relationship between IHL and ICL, the latter viewed as the natural extension of the former. This is reflected most obviously in the overlap in the content of the crimes; for our purposes, the prosecution of war crimes. Though it is cursory, the discussion on the law of state responsibility adds to the discussion in terms of comprehensiveness in order to illustrate that individual acts can be attributed to the relevant state, making it responsible for dealing with violations of the law.[44] The Report's methodical approach of systematically laying out the relevant normative frameworks contributes to the thoroughness of its analysis, which demonstrates that the meaning of the obligation varies under the different bodies of law and that there is not one 'single' obligation according to international law.

---

[40] Position Paper of the Military Advocate General 2011, pp. 15–16.

[41] Military Justice Law 5715 (1955), Article 539A (Hebrew).

[42] Turkel Commission Second Report 2013, p. 383, para 35. For further discussion of this recommendation see pp. 15–16.

[43] Ibid, pp. 85–92, paras 32–36; Article 17 Rome Statute.

[44] Ibid, p. 92, para 37; Articles and Commentaries on Responsibility of States for Internationally Wrongful Acts, Annex GA Res. 56/83 (21 December 2001). For a discussion of the relationship between state responsibility and accountability see Darusman Report 2011, para 191.

### 6.3.5 *Concluding Comments on the Commission's Legal Analysis of Duty to Investigate International Law Violations*

Section 6.3 has outlined the kinds of inquiries and the types of violations that require investigation according to the Turkel Commission's analysis. In summary, the Report interprets the obligation to investigate to entail a duty to examine all IHL violations and a duty to investigate reasonable suspicions of serious violations under IHL and violations under IHRL. Furthermore, the Report explains the distinct thresholds for opening an investigation through the example of a death of an individual in various contexts. In addition to an examination and an investigation, the Turkel Commission also introduces a fact-finding assessment, which is a type of examination relevant for exceptional incidents where information is only partial and which may lead to an investigation if further evidence determines there is a reasonable suspicion that a war crime has been committed. The detail the Report provides on the kind of inquiries relevant and the potential normative regimes applicable contributes to a rich account of the duty to investigate which is further elaborated in its analysis on the manner of conducting such inquiries, discussed below.

## 6.4 How to Investigate: Principles for an 'Effective Investigation'

Section 6.4 will address the last question addressed by the Commission in its legal analysis: how to investigate (i.e., the method of conducting an examination and an investigation). This goes to the core of the duty to investigate because it provides guidance on how to conduct such inquires. Regrettably, IHL has very little *lex scripta* on the processes for fulfilling the duty to investigate. Fortunately, IHRL jurisprudence, on the other hand, provides detail on the manner of conducting an investigation. The Commission perceives the purpose of this aspect of the obligation as being 'capable of identifying those responsible and committing them to justice'.[45] This is encompassed under the framework 'effective investigation'.[46] The general principles that comprise an 'effective investigation' are independence, impartiality, thoroughness and effectiveness and promptness. These principles have been recognized and accepted in UN documents as well as by scholars.[47]

---

[45] Turkel Commission Second Report 2013, p. 114, para 62.

[46] Ibid, pp. 112–118, paras 62–66; *Halilović*, supra n 19, paras 97–98.

[47] See, e.g., The Basic Principles and Guidelines on the Right to Remedy and Reparations for Victims of Violations of International Human Rights and Serious Violations of International Humanitarian Law, adopted by GA Res. 60/147 (16 December 2005), UN Doc. A/RES/60/147, 21 March 2006; Goldstone Report 2009, para 1814; Tomuschat Report 2010, para 30; Darusman Report 2011, paras 262–264; Schmitt 2011, p. 83; Cohen and Shany 2011, p. 60.

The Commission also identifies a fifth—transparency. Fundamental to understanding the Commission's interpretation of the duty to investigate is that with regard to the four principles the Commission sees 'no fundamental difference' between the principles for conducting an effective investigation in a law enforcement context and an armed conflict context except that the 'precise content' of the principles may differ in their application due to sensitivity to the surrounding context and circumstances.[48] The remainder of Chapter A of the Report is arguably the most important because it is devoted to explaining each of the general principles (based on IHL, ICL and IHRL, and more importantly, the jurisprudence of the European Court of Human Rights jurisprudence) and then how the principles translate to a situation of armed conflict. The Commission's careful approach of applying IHRL principles to armed conflict is demonstrated by the specific modifications of the principles in the context of hostilities. This is one of the real contributions of the Turkel Report.

In order to understand what the Commission envisioned by requiring an 'effective investigation,' each principle, and how it is modified in a situation of armed conflict, will be explained in brief, in addition to the way the Commission drew on this legal analysis in many of its recommendations in Chapter D. In setting out Israel's international law obligations to investigate, the Commission provides recommendations on how the current system can better meet those obligations.

### *6.4.1 Independence*

The requirement of independence is one of the most fundamental and obvious tenants of a credible investigation. On this matter it is generally believed to be a truism that investigators cannot investigate themselves.[49] The principle broadly relates to the requirement that the investigation be both institutionally and practically independent from the event under investigation.[50] Importantly, the Commission found that a military justice system can be sufficiently independent to undertake an investigation.[51] The way the Commission modified the application of the principle in the context of an armed conflict is by explaining that independence (and impartiality) is reflected in the investigation being outside the chain of command, while at the same time ensuring that the investigator has adequate operational knowledge in order to perform an effective investigation.[52]

---

[48] Turkel Commission Second Report 2013, p. 115, para 63.

[49] See, e.g., Benvenisti 2009; B'Tselem 2010.

[50] Turkel Commission Second Report 2013, pp. 118–125, paras 67–74.

[51] Ibid, pp. 123–125, para 73.

[52] Ibid, pp. 140–141, paras 98–100.

The Commission attempted to protect independence within the military justice system by addressing safeguards for the MAG's position, the head of this system.[53] Other relevant recommendations include replacing the function of the operational debriefing with a fact-finding assessment, in part to ensure that the initial information about an alleged violation is gathered by a special team outside the chain of command rather than by the commander of the unit whose activity is under consideration.[54] The internal nature of the debriefing renders it inconsistent with the principle of independence, even in times of armed conflict.[55] It is unclear whether the government will implement the proposal to limit the debriefing—one of the most significant recommendations made by the Commission; however, publicly available information suggests that the operational debriefing was not relied on by the MAG Corps to make the decision whether to open investigations into incidents that occurred in Operation Pillar of Defense. Rather, some kind of 'preliminary examination' was carried out by 'a Special General Staff Commission'. This seems to resemble to concept of the 'fact-finding assessment' and 'fact-finding assessment team' articulated by the Commission.[56] This is a welcomed development if in fact it achieves the purpose of strengthening accountability. The extremely low number of preliminary investigations that resulted in the opening of investigations into incidents that occurred during Pillar of Defense (i.e., the decision that the *threshold of reasonable suspicion of criminality* had not been met) has provoked skeptical response in the MAG Corps approach, notably from the UN Secretary-General.[57]

The Commission found that civilian involvement through oversight and review mechanisms is another way of securing independence. This trend was identified in the countries surveyed in Chapter B.[58] The Commission attempts to promote the

---

[53] It recommended: (i) the MAG's professional subordination to the Attorney General should be institutionalized through legislation and organizational arrangements; (ii) the MAG should be appointed by the Minister of Defense based on the recommendation of a professional committee to which the Attorney-General is a member or chair; (iii) the MAG's tenure and rank should be fixed. See ibid, pp. 391–392, paras 50–52.

[54] Ibid, pp. 382–383, paras 34–35. Other relevant recommendations include recommendation 6 (the decision to open an investigation), which suggests that the MAG provide reasoning for every decision not to open an investigation p. 386, para 41. See also p. 421, para 99: recommendation 17 (commissions of inquiry) where the Commission emphasized the importance of safeguards in the commission's mandate to ensure its independence.

[55] For criticism of the debriefing see Cohen and Shany 2011, pp. 70–71; Yesh Din 2011, p. 9; FIDH 2011, p. 9. For a defense of the debriefing see Position Paper of the Military Advocate General 2011, p. 16.

[56] Israel Defense Forces 2013.

[57] Ibid. In April 2013, the MAG publicly issued an update on the investigative process. The document stated that in relation to the 87 incidents that were cited as having occurred during Operation Pillar of Defense, it found no basis to open criminal investigations into approximately 65 incidents. Moreover, with respect to 15 incidents, additional information was required in order to make a decision whether to open an investigation. See also Report of the Secretary General 2013, para 31.

[58] Turkel Commission Second Report 2013, pp. 184–185, para 23; p. 191, para 25; pp. 192–193, para 27; p. 260, para 80.

independence of the MAG and the MAG Corps primarily by strengthening the oversight authority and involvement of the Attorney General.[59] In Israel, the role of the Attorney General combines prosecutorial and advisory functions.[60] It can be expected, therefore, that the Commission's approach will not be seen as a satisfactory remedy to those who believe that the Attorney General's position is already too powerful for a single unelected individual.

### 6.4.2 Impartiality

The principle of impartiality, according to the Commission, is concerned with the objectivity of the investigator to ensure the investigation is conducted (and is perceived to be conducted) in an unbiased fashion.[61] The Commission addresses the principle of impartiality in its discussion of the 'dual-hat' of the MAG as head of the military prosecution system and legal advisor to the military authorities. The Commission's approach to remedying the perceived conflict of interest was not to dissolve the dual role of the MAG, but to put safeguards in place.[62] It recommended strengthening the status and independence of the Chief Military Prosecutor (CMP), which reduces the MAG's prosecutorial role, and suggested an appeal process to the MAG's decisions to the Attorney General.[63] Considering the Commission saw no problem in strengthening the (dual) role of the Attorney General in its recommendations relating to independence, it is not surprising that it did not find the need to dissolve the dual-hat of the MAG in its recommendations concerning impartiality. This reveals the limitations of relying on (and being confined to) the Attorney General model. That model, it could be argued, does not adequately remedy the fundamental problem relating to independence and impartiality, namely that the person involved in the action cannot be involved in reviewing it.[64]

---

[59] Ibid, p. 401, para 71; pp. 402–403, para 74; p. 408, para 79.

[60] It should be noted that the role of the Attorney General is different in Israel than in common law countries such as the United Kingdom or Australia, where the individual is an elected member of the Cabinet. In Israel the Attorney General is appointed independently by the government. The Attorney General provides the main legal advice to the Government and also represents the government and state authorities before the courts.

[61] Turkel Commission Second Report 2013, p. 125, para 75.

[62] Ibid, p. 393, para 54.

[63] Ibid, pp. 392–396, paras 53–58.

[64] For criticism that the MAG's joint prosecutorial and advisory responsibilities have created the perception of partiality see Tomuschat Report 2010, para 91. For a response to this criticism see Position Paper of the Military Advocate General 2011, Annex I.

### 6.4.3 Effectiveness and Thoroughness

This principle addresses the means for carrying out an investigation in order to achieve the intended purpose of uncovering the truth, while also doing justice to the conditions of armed conflict, which may limit the means available. For example, evidentiary constraints may exist, such as the ability to interview witnesses or conduct an autopsy. While acknowledging the limited resources available during armed conflict, the Commission emphasized that reasonable measures must nonetheless be taken to secure accurate and reliable findings.[65] There are various ways in which the Commission's recommendations attempted to improve the effectiveness and thoroughness of the investigative process. The Commission found that, in practice, the requirement to fill out a Preliminary Report Form within 48 h of the incident and submit it to the MAG is not adhered to.[66] It recommended that the Reporting Procedure be incorporated into Orders and adopted in all IDF units. The Commission also emphasized that adequately documenting the scene of an incident is an important part of the reporting duty.[67] Another relevant recommendation called for establishing a special department for Operational Matters within the Military Police Criminal Investigation Division (CID) consisting of police officers trained in IHL, investigators fluent in Arabic and locating military bases in the areas where the incidents under investigation took place.[68] These recommendations aim at facilitating the ability to collect and secure reliable evidence in order to achieve accurate and credible findings to alleged violations that occur both during armed conflict and relative calm.

### 6.4.4 Promptness

Promptness relates to the need to avoid unreasonable delays both in the commencement and duration of investigations.[69] During a situation of armed conflict, the reasonableness of the delay must be determined by the surrounding circumstances and the intensity of violence. The Commission did note, however, that adhering to the principle of promptness is important during armed conflict because

---

[65] Turkel Commission Second Report 2013, pp. 127–131, paras 80–84; pp. 141–143, paras 101–102.

[66] Ibid, pp. 374–375, para 23; pp. 372–373, para 21.

[67] Ibid, pp. 374–375, paras 22–24.

[68] Ibid, p. 397, para 62. The importance with the Commission saw the need for training in relevant areas of international law in order to achieve effectiveness and thoroughness is also reflected in its recommendation for the Prison Service and the National Unit for International Investigations that investigates complaints against wardens: pp. 417–418, paras 93–95 and in the recommendation to create an International Law Department in the Ministry of Justice: pp. 402–403, para 74.

[69] Turkel Commission Second Report 2013, pp. 132–134, paras 85–89.

it may be helpful in ensuring the availability of evidence and hence contributes to fulfilling the principle of effectiveness and thoroughness.[70] The Commission is critical of the fact that often the decision on whether to open an investigation is not always immediate. It recommended that time frames be set in procedures both for the MAG's decision on whether to open an investigation and the duration of an investigation.[71]

### 6.4.5 Transparency

The Commission divides this principle into two aspects: the duty to inform victims (and their family members) of their rights, in order to give them information concerning proceedings; and a duty to publish the findings of the investigation.[72] The Commission came to the conclusion that although there is no explicit recognition of transparency in IHL, it is desirable that the latter (accountability via public scrutiny) applies during armed conflict because of the way it can contribute to the realization of central aspects of the duty to investigate under IHL: compliance and deterrence.[73] It recommended a strict documentation procedure of the relevant files.[74] In relation to victims' rights, it recommended that the law regulating the rights of victims to access information about a criminal proceeding apply to all investigative mechanisms covering law enforcement incidents only.[75] The emphasis the Turkel Report places on transparency is consistent with (though it does not go as far as) a number of UN reports submitted to the UN General Assembly only months after the Turkel Commission published its report.[76] Although the Commission relied on the UN Tomuschat Report to support its claim that the principle of transparency is not required for IHL investigations (though the public scrutiny aspect is desirable) more recent UN reports seem to indicate a broader application of the principle of transparency in times of armed conflict.[77] It was therefore not

[70] Ibid, pp. 143–144, paras 103–105.

[71] Ibid, p. 385, para 39; p. 386, para 40; p. 399, para 66.

[72] Ibid, pp. 134–137, paras 90–94.

[73] Ibid, p. 145, para 106.

[74] Ibid, p. 400, para 70.

[75] Ibid, p. 399, para 68; p. 400, para 69. This recommendation also applies to recommendation 14. See pp. 408–413, paras 81–85.

[76] Emmerson 2013, paras 44–45; Heyns 2013, para 97.

[77] Also worth noting in this context is that the previous Special Rapporteur on extrajudicial killings, Philip Alston, has (in his academic writing) emphasised the importance of transparency to the concept of accountability and has lamented the lack of it in the context of the US practice of targeted killing conducted by the CIA. See Alston 2011, p. 314. See also Bovens 2007, p. 453 for an interesting discussion on the relationship between transparency and accountability. He argues that transparency is an instrumental dimension of accountability but it is not constitutive of accountability because transparency does not necessarily involve scrutiny by a specific forum.

surprising that the UN Special Rapporteur on Extrajudicial, Summary or Arbitrary Executions took a different approach to that of the Turkel Commission when he extended the right of victims to access information during armed conflict.[78]

Disagreement over the content of transparency in understanding the duty to investigate is further revealed in the Commission's brief explanation of how to conduct a fact-finding assessment effectively during armed conflict and reactions to that explanation. The Report does not provide the detail that it does for how to conduct an investigation. It does, however, raise some of the general principles by way of example to indicate that the purpose of this preliminary form of inquiry is to collect relevant information about the alleged incident that facilitates—rather than hinders—a subsequent investigation.[79] Notably, transparency is not one of the general principles listed in describing how to conduct a fact-finding assessment during armed conflict. It is worth noting that the UN Special Rapporteur on the Promotion and Protection of Human Rights and Fundamental Freedoms While Countering Terrorism and Human Rights welcomed the Turkel Commission's fact-finding assessment and expanded the Commission's approach to include the application of the principle of transparency to this preliminary investigation.[80] Moreover, in the UN Secretary-General's criticism of the MAG's investigative approach into incidents that occurred during Operation Pillar of Defense, (which, as noted above on page 16 of this article, resemble a fact-finding assessment), the Secretary-General claimed that the MAG failed to provide sufficient reason for why criminal investigations into incidents were not opened even though the UN's fieldwork led it to conclude that violations had occurred.[81] If the MAG investigative process can be compared to the Turkel Commission's fact-finding assessment, then the principle of transparency would not in fact apply.

### *6.4.6 Concluding Comment on Applying the General Principles*

The explanation of each principle and corresponding recommendations demonstrates the way in which the Commission interpreted the interaction between the normative frameworks in different contexts (armed conflict and law enforcement), both of which are relevant scenarios in the case of Israel. Most notable are the careful modifications to the principles during armed conflict. The Commission's approach of applying the general principles should be commended, in part because it cannot be expected that the law be a sensitive enough instrument to deal with the specificities of the investigation mechanisms of every state. The principle of

[78] Heyns 2013, para 100.

[79] Turkel Commission Second Report 2013, pp. 147–148, paras 109–112.

[80] Emmerson 2013, para 45.

[81] Report of the Secretary General 2013, para 31.

independence (and impartiality) is one of the most fundamental principles when dealing with a military justice system. The Commission did suggest a number of recommendations to promote the independence of the investigations, the most striking of which is reflected in its recommendation to limit the debriefing to an operational function. Moreover, the recommendations, particularly those concerning effectiveness and transparency, will reduce anxieties over independence in the conduction of investigations. Provided it is done in good faith and true to the spirit of accountability in which they are formulated, the implementation of all of the recommendations would lead to dramatic improvements to the way investigations are conducted in Israel.[82]

## 6.5 The Commission's Approach to International Law

The Commission's interpretation of the duty to investigate and the application of that interpretation to the recommendations it formulated for the Israeli military justice system expresses the Commission's approach to international law. Observations about the Commission's approach can be loosely divided into two, though they remain interconnected. The first relates to the tension between the Commission's general conclusions on whether Israel meets its obligations and the 18 recommendations presented in the Report. The second observation relates to the way in which the Commission viewed the interaction between the two most relevant normative frameworks—IHL and IHRL.

### *6.5.1 Conclusions on Whether Israel Complies with Its International Obligations*

The Commission attempts to seriously engage international law. This is reflected in its efforts towards comprehensiveness in its legal analysis and the explicit connection it draws between its recommendations and the legal requirements it articulates. This approach is sensible because it would be very difficult for a state to satisfy its obligations under international law to ensure accountability (both under IHL and IHRL) without meaningful domestic mechanisms for accountability.[83] Moreover, it is in keeping with UN Policy, which recognizes the need for accountability processes to be defined on national assessments, rather a 'one-size-fits-all' formula, as long as the national model meets international standards.[84] It is interesting, therefore, that the Commission felt the need to state at the outset that

82 Cf. Amnesty International 2014, supra n 37, p. 64.
83 Alston 2011, p. 446.
84 Report of the Secretary General 2004, executive summary.

'the examination and investigation mechanisms in Israel for complaints and claims of violations of IHL and the methods they practice, generally comply with the obligations of the state of Israel under the rules of international law'.[85]

At first glance, this general conclusion appears inconsistent with some of the seriously critical recommendations that the Commission proposes. The general conclusion is followed by what the Report labels 'amendments or changes' that do 'not necessarily indicate essential flaws, but rather […] a blueprint for optimal improvement'.[86] This is a reference to the 18 recommendations that are set out in Chapter D of the Report.[87] A charitable reading would take this as a comment by the Commission on its perception of international law and on the obligation to investigate. The Commission emphasizes at numerous points in the Report that international law leaves a relatively wide margin of appreciation for states to interpret and implement their international obligations because of the need to take into account particular internal and domestic considerations.[88] On the charitable reading, therefore, Israel views the international law obligation to investigate broadly, allowing states considerable latitude on their interpretations of that obligation. A more skeptical reading would interpret the general conclusion that Israel complies with international law as politically motivated—an attempt to soften critical recommendations in order to make them more palatable.

### *6.5.2 Interface Between Normative Frameworks*

In relation to the Commission's approach to the interface between IHL and IHRL, there are two noteworthy aspects. The first relates to the Commission's interpretation of the extent to which IHRL applies in armed conflict and the second relates more specifically to the way in which the Commission injects an IHRL reading into the IHL duty to investigate.

In the introductory section to Chapter A, the Report flags the debate concerning the relationship between IHL and IHRL. The Commission acknowledges the disagreement that exists, which it interprets broadly to cover both the interface between the laws and the extraterritorial application of IHRL.[89] The Commission goes beyond the conservative position of the government of Israel[90] when it states

---

85 Turkel Commission Second Report 2013, p. 49, para 29.

86 Ibid.

87 Ibid, p. 377, para 28.

88 Ibid, p. 49, para 29; p. 153, para 2; p. 361, para 3.

89 Ibid, pp. 64–65, paras 10–11.

90 For example, Israel takes the position that its obligations under the ICCPR do not extend to the Occupied Palestinian Territories (OPT). See, e.g., Consideration of reports submitted by States parties under Article 40 of the Covenant: Addendum to the second periodic report, UN Doc. CCPR/C/ISR/2001/2 (4 December 2001). See also Implementation of the International Covenant on Economic, Social and Cultural Rights: Addendum to the second periodic reports submitted by

that: 'the extent to which this body of law applies extraterritorially is not universally accepted. Nonetheless, the Commission is of the view that in certain circumstances human rights law applies extraterritorially.'[91] This approach is consistent with the theoretical approach of the First Report, but its significance is greater in the Second Report because of the consequences that arise from its application to the question at hand. The Commission should be applauded for extending IHRL to areas to which it had not previously been applied. Notably, the Commission's approach could potentially be read as going as far as narrowing the armed conflict context to the situations of actual combat because it describes the modification of the IHRL general principles to apply to situations governed by the rules regulating the conduct of hostilities. This appears to imply that IHRL applies to all other situations during an armed conflict.[92]

The prominence of IHRL in the Commission's analysis is also partly informed by its finding that the relationship between the military administration and the inhabitants of occupied territory is closer to the relations between a state and its citizens than it is to a Party to an armed conflict and the citizens of the opposing side.[93] The Commission expressed its position on the law governing occupation: '[t]he Commission is satisfied that in occupied territory, and especially in a prolonged occupation, the default position is that the norms regulating the use of force are those of law enforcement'.[94] At first glance this finding of the Commission seems rather progressive. However, the fact that in the remainder of the Report the West Bank is not referred to as occupied territory makes this finding less bold than it appears. Of course, implicitly the Commission's analysis of the law of occupation demonstrates that it thought this to be of relevance to the Israeli situation: it was not just done for the sake of comprehensive legal analysis. Nonetheless, a more explicit connection between the legal analysis and the realities on the ground would have made for a more courageous document.

The Report's heavy reliance on IHRL, in particular concerning the question of 'how' to investigate, confirms that IHRL should come into play when lack of clarity exists in IHL. In its short theoretical discussion, the Commission adopts the traditional approach of explaining the interaction between IHL and IHRL, which is by way of the International Court of Justice's (ICJ) *Nuclear Weapons Advisory*

(Footnote 90 continued)
States parties under Articles 16 and 17 of the Covenant, Israel, UN Doc. E/1990/6/Add.32 (3 August 2001), para 3. For criticism of this position see, e.g., Consideration of reports submitted by States parties under Articles 16 and 17 of the Covenant: Concluding Observations of the Committee on Economic, Social and Cultural Rights, Israel, UN Doc. E/C.12/1/Add.69 (31 August 2001), para12; General Comment No 18: Non-Discrimination, 10 November 1989, para 2.

91 Turkel Commission Second Report 2013, p. 65, para 11.

92 Ibid, pp. 138–139, paras 96–97; p. 146, para 108.

93 Ibid, p. 67, para 13.

94 Ibid, p. 109, para 58.

*Opinion* and its application of the interpretive maxim *lex specialis*.[95] Generally speaking, the ICJ found that in the parallel applicability of IHL and IHRL in armed conflict, the latter (*lex specialis*) supplants the former (*lex generalis*). A strong case could be made that the Report cleverly sidestepped the *lex specialis* debate because the complementary nature of the two regimes on the topic of accountability rendered a detailed discussion on this doctrine unnecessary.[96] A more sophisticated contribution to the nature of the interaction between the two frameworks can be found in academic writings on the duty to investigate; nonetheless, tensions remain in those writings.[97] 'It is hoped that those charged with appraising investigations conducted during an armed conflict will exhibit both sensitivity to the nature of the conflict in question and fidelity to the governing law as it is, not as they might have it to be. Failure to do so will only undercut respect for IHL, as well as the human rights norms that incorporate it, on the part of States conducting investigations.' In contrast, Cohen and Shany 2011, p. 50, argue that:

> 'The upshot of this analysis is that IHRL provides an independent basis for a duty to investigate harms to individuals occurring during armed conflicts. Given the breadth of the scope of rights covered by human rights treaties, which exceed in some important areas the protections afforded by IHL (for example, with respect to freedom of movement), some harmful conduct not covered by the IHL duty to investigate would nonetheless be covered by the parallel duty under IHRL. It therefore appears that, to the extent that they also compromise IHRL norms, violations of IHL norms other than grave breaches should be investigated also by virtue of IHRL; it is also clear that some violations not covered at all by IHL should nonetheless be investigated under IHRL'.

It is therefore worth asking: would it have assisted future applications of IHL and IHRL in an area where there is yet to be a consensus and where there is much that remains unclear, if the Report had provided detailed legal reasoning or a methodology to justify its approach or indicated how that approach might be developed.[98]

Instead, what emerges is a common sense approach to navigating the two legal regimes. The Commission seems to be infusing an IHRL reading into the IHL duty to investigate. In explaining the way the IHRL general principles are modified during armed conflict, the Report explains that 'certain IHRL norms apply to supplement

---

[95] ICJ *Legality of the Threat or Use of Nuclear Weapons*, Advisory Opinion (1996) ICJ Rep 226, para 25.

[96] It should be noted that the ICJ has progressed beyond the *lex specialis* framework in its discussion of the interplay between IHL and IHRL. See ICJ *Legal Consequences of the Construction of a Wall in the Occupied Palestinian Territory*, Advisory Opinion (2004) ICJ Rep 136, para 178; *Case Concerning Armed Activities on the Territory of the Congo (Democratic Republic of the Congo v. Uganda)*, Judgment, (2005) ICJ Rep 168, paras 243–244.

[97] Some of the seminal works on this topic take diverging approaches on the interaction between IHL and IHRL. For example, according to Schmitt 2011, p. 84:

[98] The nuances of the debate over the interaction of IHL and IHRL and the relevance of the *lex specialis* doctrine to that debate are beyond the scope of this article. See more generally Milanovic 2011; Lubell 2010.

IHL'.[99] The Report defined the interaction as complementary.[100] Section 6.3 of this article discussed the way the Commission distinguished between the thresholds for opening an investigation under IHL and IHRL and this distinction between the substantive law on the use of lethal force is important because their content is in conflict. However, on the question of gathering information for conducting an investigation, there is not necessarily any contradiction between them: 'Humanitarian law does not provide for a duty to investigate in such detail, but there is no reason to understand this as a qualified silence in the sense that it would preclude application of the duty under human rights law.'[101] IHRL standards are more specific and therefore fill a lacuna in IHL. The detail and depth of the Turkel Report confirms and extends previous interpretations in the field that have applied the two regimes in a complementary manner on the question of how to conduct an investigation.[102]

Therefore, by creating a degree of convergence between the two legal regimes (because an IHRL reading is injected into an IHL duty), the Turkel Report clarifies the content of the standards that apply to an investigation (the general principles). The standards reflect an adequate concept of accountability because they are faithful to the idea that there is an obligation to explain and justify conduct.[103] This contributes to preventing impunity from the constraints of international law.[104]

If we now return to a concern expressed earlier (in the previous section) about how this relates to the apparent inconsistency between the Commission's general conclusions on international law and the recommendations it presented, further consideration reinforces the impression of inconsistency: the recommendations are, after all, based on the Commission's understanding of the general principles. The Commission's conclusions about international law imply that the standards by which the relevant actors are judged in order to determine whether they have fulfilled their responsibilities are very broad (i.e., there is a wide margin of appreciation).[105] This is hard to square with the Commission's interpretation of the specific standards, which have the effect of strengthening the requirements under IHL because of the detail imported from IHRL.

Two interpretations can be offered to help elucidate this apparent inconsistency in the Commission's approach. The first is that the Commission has exploited the permission to interpret standards of accountability according to national circumstances in order to conclude that there are no 'essential' flaws in Israel's practices, and that therefore its 18 recommendations are merely 'a blueprint for optimal improvement'. This interpretation reads 'broad' standards to mean 'vague' standards, or

---

99 Turkel Commission Second Report 2013, p 69, para 14.

100 Ibid.

101 Droege 2008, pp. 541–542.

102 Goldstone Report 2009; Schmitt 2011; Cohen and Shany 2011.

103 See more generally Bovens 2007, pp. 447–453; Mulgan 2003.

104 See, e.g., Set of Principles for the Protection and Promotion of Human Rights Through Action to Combat Impunity 2005, UN Doc. E/CN.4/2005/102/Add.1 (8 February 2005).

105 See more generally Grant and Keohane 2005, p 29.

standards so general as to be no threat because they permit practices that would be prohibited (proscribed) under a serious concept of accountability. The second interpretation is that the Commission hopes to use its 'general conclusion' to soften the impact of the relatively radical practical implications of the recommendations on those who set up the Commission and on whom the task falls to implement its recommendations. The first interpretation could lead one to conclude that the behavior it describes is the behavior that one would expect from states when they are permitted to interpret the standards under which they are accountable—that is to say, they can be expected to interpret standards of accountability in such a way as to justify minimal change. The second interpretation allows one to say that though it was appointed by the state, the Commission nonetheless interpreted the law in a way that seriously holds the state to account. In order to encourage the state to implement its recommendations, however, it disguised the nature of those recommendations as merely 'optimal developments' that would leave existing practices that it described as having no 'essential' flaws basically untouched.

## 6.6 Concluding Remarks

The Turkel Report is the first major in-depth study on the duty (or duties) to investigate under international law according to three normative frameworks (IHL, IHRL and ICL). It attempted to assess the obligation to investigate under international law comprehensively and articulated the different triggers for the duty to investigate according to the different normative frameworks. The duty to investigate under international law is an evolving process because treaty law lacks detail, particularly regarding the manner of conducting an investigation. The IHRL duty has largely been enriched by the jurisprudence of regional human rights courts and soft law, and the IHL duty (which is even sparser in detail) has been aided by state practice and the jurisprudence of international tribunals. Its evolutionary stage is also reflected in the literature on accountability under international law where the focus has generally been on the prosecutorial and reconciliatory stages of accountability, especially with the growing fields of international criminal law and transitional justice. It is only in recent years that attention has been given to understanding and interpreting the content of the obligation as it applies to the preliminary investigative stages of accountability for alleged violations of IHL and IHRL.

It can be anticipated that the Turkel Commission's work will shape a new legal standard on the topic and, in doing so, the Commission rightly set the bar high. Its approach was expansive in that it found that the standards for conducting an effective investigation (independence, impartiality, effectiveness and thoroughness, promptness and transparency) should apply across the board, to a variety of legal and factual contexts and most significantly, the Report articulated the way in which those standards are modified during armed conflict. The standards for conducting an effective investigation are essential for the integrity of the obligation to investigate which is an important aspect of accountability under international law.

The Second Turkel Report is a national development that potentially has significant implications internationally. It offers a meaningful contribution to the duty to investigate under international law. It will foreseeably be used as a reference point for domestic military justice systems, international tribunals, courts and UN mechanisms faced with determining accountability for international crimes, and domestic legal systems considering the prosecution stage of the investigative process. The legal analysis of the Turkel Report may also be referred to more generally in future analyses of Israel's obligations, particularly its IHL and IHRL obligations toward the Palestinians and the occupied territories. The contribution of the Turkel Report is significant because, as noted in the UN Secretary-General experts' report on Sri Lanka, 'accountability for serious violations of international humanitarian or human rights law is not a matter of choice or policy; it is a duty under domestic and international law'.[106]

## References

Alston P (2011) The CIA and targeted killings beyond borders. Harv Nat Sec J 2(2):283–446

Amnesty International (2014) Trigger-happy: Israel's use of excessive force in the West Bank report. www.amnesty.org/en/library/info/MDE15/002/2014/en. Accessed 1 Apr 2014

B'Tselem (2010) Israel's report to the UN misstates the truth. www.btselem.org/gaza_strip/20100204_israels_report_to_un. Accessed 1 Apr 2014

Benvenisti E (2009) An obligation to investigate—Haaretz (28 Jan 2009). www.haaretz.com/print-edition/opinion/an-obligation-to-investigate-1.269026. Accessed 1 Apr 2014

Bovens M (2007) Analysing and assessing accountability: a conceptual framework. Eur Law J 13 (4):447–468

Cohen A, Shany Y (2011) Beyond the grave breaches regime: the duty to investigate alleged violations of international law governing armed conflict. YIHL 14:37–84

Darusman Report (2011) Report of the secretary-general's panel of experts on accountability in Sri Lanka (31 Mar 2011). www.un.org/News/dh/infocus/Sri_Lanka/POE_Report_Full.pdf. Accessed 1 April 2014

Droege C (2008) Elective affinities? Human rights and humanitarian law. IRRC 90:501–548

Emmerson B (2013) Report of the Special Rapporteur on the promotion and protection of human rights and fundamental freedoms while countering terrorism (interim report) (18 Sept 2013). UN Doc. A/68/389

FIDH (2011) 'Shielded from accountability: Israel's unwillingness to investigate and prosecute international crimes' (23 Sept 2011). www.fidh.org/en/north-africa-middle-east/israel-occupied-palestinian-territories/Shielded-from-accountability. Accessed 1 Apr 2014

Goldstone Report (2009) UN fact-finding mission on the Gaza conflict (25 Sept 2009). UN Doc. A/HRC/12/48

Grant R, Keohane R (2005) Accountability and abuses of power in world politics. Am Pol Sci Rev 99:29-43

Henckaerts J-M, Doswald-Beck L (2005) Customary international humanitarian law, vol 1. Cambridge University Press, Cambridge

Heyns C (2013) Report of the special rapporteur on extrajudicial, summary or arbitrary executions (13 Sept 2013). UN Doc A/68/382

[106] Darusman Report 2005, para 425.

Human Rights Council (2013) Report of the independent international fact-finding mission to investigate the implications of the Israeli settlements on the civil, political, economic, social and cultural rights of the Palestinian people throughout the occupied Palestinian territory, including east Jerusalem, advanced unedited version (Jan 2013). www.ohchr.org/Documents/HRBodies/HRCouncil/RegularSession/Session19/FFM/FFMSettlements.pdf. Accessed 1 Apr 2014

Israel Defense Forces (2013) 'The examination of alleged misconduct during operation pillar of defence—an update' (11 Apr 2013). www.law.idf.il/SIP_STORAGE/files/4/1364.pdf. Accessed 1 April 2014

Lubell N (2010) Extraterritorial use of force against non-state actors. Oxford University Press, Oxford

Margalit A (2012) The duty to investigate civilian casualties during armed conflict and its implementation in practice. YIHL 15:155–186

McGowan Davis Report (2011) Report of the committee of independent experts in international humanitarian and human rights law (18 Mar 2011). UN Doc. A/HRC/16/24

Milanovic M (2011) Extraterritorial application of human rights treaties: law, principles and policy. Oxford University Press, Oxford

Mulgan R (2003) Holding power to account: accountability in modern democracies. Palgrave MacMillan, London

Pictet J (ed) (1956) Commentary of the Geneva convention of 12 August 1949 for the amelioration of the condition of the wounded and sick in armed forces in the field. ICRC, Geneva

Ravid B (2013) Former shin bet head: all interrogations should be videotaped—*Haaretz* (8 Feb 2013). www.haaretz.com/news/national/former-shin-bet-head-all-interrogations-should-be-videotaped.premium-1.502205. Accessed 1 Apr 2014

Sandoz Y, Swinarski C, Zimmermann B (eds) (1987) Commentary on the additional protocols of 8 June 1977 to the Geneva conventions of 12 August 1949. ICRC, Geneva

Schmitt MN (2011) Investigating violations of international law in armed conflicts. Harv Natl Secur J 2(1):31–84

Secretary General (2004) Report on the rule of law and transitional justice in conflict and post-conflict societies (23 Aug 2004). UN Doc. S/2004/616

Secretary General (2013) Report on Israeli practices affecting the human rights of the Palestinian people in the occupied Palestinian territory, including east Jerusalem (4 Oct 2013). UN Doc. A/68/502

Tomuschat Report (2010) Report of the committee of independent experts in international humanitarian and human rights laws to monitor and assess any domestic, legal or other proceedings undertaken by both the government of Israel and the Palestinian side, in the light of general assembly resolution 64/254, including the independence, effectiveness, genuineness of these investigations and their conformity with international standards (23 Sept 2010). UN Doc. A/HRC/15/50. http://unispal.un.org/UNISPAL.NSF/0/B07AE44EC3B4F211852577A5004C709B. Accessed 1 Apr 2014

Turkel Commission (2011a) The public commission to examine the maritime incident of 31 May 2010: report part one (Jan 2011). www.turkel-committee.com/files/wordocs//8707200211english.pdf. Accessed 1 April 2014

Turkel Commission (2011b) Position paper of the military advocate general. www.turkel-committee.com/files/wordocs/niar_emda_eng.pdf. Accessed 1 Apr 2014

Turkel Commission (2013) The public commission to examine the maritime incident of 31 May 2010: second report: Israeli's mechanisms for examining and investigating complaints and claims of violations of the laws of armed conflict according to international law (Feb 2013). www.turkel-committee.gov.il/files/newDoc3/The%20Turkel%20Report%20for%20website.pdf. Accessed 1 Apr 2014

Yesh Din (2011) Alleged investigation: the failure of investigations into offenses committed by IDF soldiers against Palestinians. www.yesh-din.org/userfiles/file/Reports-English/Alleged%20Investigation%20%5BEnglish%5D.pdf. Accessed 1 Apr 2014

# Chapter 7
# Year in Review 2013

**Christophe Paulussen, Jessica Dorsey and Sarah-Jane Koulen**

**Abstract** 2013 was marked with several noteworthy events with particular relevance to international humanitarian law, such as the continuation of the conflict in Syria and the incidents related to the use of chemical weapons in that conflict; several key decisions in international, hybrid and national courts related to the adjudication of war crimes, crimes against humanity and genocide; the passage of an Arms Trade Treaty text; the 150th anniversary of the International Committee of the Red Cross; and the release of the second part of the Turkel Commission Report. This chapter addresses a number of these issues among other events of note.

**Keywords** International humanitarian law · International criminal law · Armed conflict · Chemical weapons · Arms control · Disarmament · Arms trade treaty · Turkel commission report

---

Dr. Christophe Paulussen, LL.M., M.Phil., is a senior researcher international humanitarian law/international criminal law at the T.M.C. Asser Instituut. Jessica Dorsey, J.D., LL.M., is a researcher in international humanitarian, human rights and criminal law at the T.M.C. Asser Instituut and is a Ph.D. candidate at the University of Amsterdam. Sarah-Jane Koulen, LL.M. is a researcher in international human rights and criminal law at the T.M.C. Asser Instituut and a Ph.D. candidate at Leiden University. The Year in Review is not intended to be a comprehensive summary of all events that occurred in 2013, but rather a sampling of events of note with particular relevance to international humanitarian law. We would like to thank our colleagues from the Asser Public International Law Cluster, in particular Fréderique van Oijen, LL.M., and Alejo Martirosjan, LL.M., for their invaluable assistance in the preparation of this article and volume.

---

C. Paulussen · J. Dorsey · S.-J. Koulen (✉)
T.M.C. Asser Instituut, The Hague, The Netherlands
e-mail: s.koulen@gmail.com

C. Paulussen
e-mail: c.paulussen@asser.nl

J. Dorsey
e-mail: j.dorsey@asser.nl

 
T.D. Gill et al. (eds.), *Yearbook of International Humanitarian Law 2013*,
Yearbook of International Humanitarian Law 16, DOI 10.1007/978-94-6265-038-1_7

# Contents



## 7.1 Situations and Phenomena

### *7.1.1 Afghanistan*

The conflict in Afghanistan, in existence since October 2001 (begun as a response to the attacks on the United States on 11 September 2001),[1] was still ongoing in 2013. The Security Council extended the United Nations Assistance Mission in Afghanistan (UNAMA) mandate until 19 March 2014,[2] and the NATO-led International

[1] See 'Afghanistan Profile', *BBC News* (31 March 2013), http://www.bbc.co.uk/news/world-south-asia-12024253 (accessed 26 May 2014).

[2] See UN Security Council Resolution 2096 (19 March 2013), http://www.securitycouncilreport.org/atf/cf/%7B65BFCF9B-6D27-4E9C-8CD3-CF6E4FF96FF9%7D/s_res_2096.pdf (accessed 8 June 2014).

Security Assistance Force (ISAF) authorization until the end of 2014,[3] with an eye toward transitioning the situation into a more "secure and stable Afghanistan."[4] The plan laid out in Resolution 2120 is to "transfer full security responsibility in Afghanistan to the Afghan Government country-wide by the end of 2014."[5] One concrete step toward this was the full transfer of the Parwan Detention Facility (also known as the Bagram Military Prison)—the last prison under U.S. control—from the United States to the Afghan government in March.[6] Additionally, NATO announced jointly with the Afghan government the fifth and final transition phase in June, in which leading combat operations will be carried out by the Afghanis, with ISAF still retaining a training, advising and assistance role.[7]

### *7.1.2 Central African Republic*

The ongoing conflict in the Central African Republic between the Séléka rebels and the governmental forces began at the end of 2012 due to accusations of the Séléka rebels against President François Bozizé of failure to follow peace agreements from 2007 and 2011.[8] Rebel forces began seizing towns at the end of 2012 but a ceasefire was signed at Libreville on 11 January.[9] A few weeks later, the Security Council extended the mandate of the UN Integrated Peacebuilding Office in the Central African Republic until the end of January 2014.[10] A UNICEF report from January called on all sides of the conflict to terminate child soldier recruitment, alleged to be happening in the conflict.[11] Over the next several months, attacks continued to

---

3 See UN Security Council Resolution 2120 (10 October 2013), http://www.securitycouncilreport.org/atf/cf/%7B65BFCF9B-6D27-4E9C-8CD3-CF6E4FF96FF9%7D/s_res_2120.pdf (accessed 8 June 2014).

4 Ibid., p. 3.

5 Ibid., p. 8.

6 See S. Posner, 'US transfers full control of Bagram prison to Afghanistan', *Jurist* (25 March 2013), http://jurist.org/paperchase/2013/03/us-transfers-full-control-of-bagram-prison-to-afghanistan.php (accessed 9 June 2014).

7 See North American Treaty Organization (NATO): 'Inteqal: Transition to Afghan Lead', http://www.nato.int/cps/en/natolive/topics_87183.htm (accessed 10 June 2014).

8 See Uppsala University UCDP Conflict Encyclopedia 'Central African Republic', http://www.ucdp.uu.se/gpdatabase/gpcountry.php?id=31&regionSelect=2-Southern_Africa# (accessed 10 June 2014).

9 See UN Security Council, Press Release, 'Agreements Signed Today in Libreville to Halt Recent Rebellion in Central African Republic, Provide Map for Political Transition, Security Council Told' (11 January 2013), http://www.un.org/News/Press/docs/2013/sc10879.doc.htm (accessed 9 June 2014).

10 See UN Security Council Resolution 2088 (24 January 2013), http://www.securitycouncilreport.org/atf/cf/%7B65BFCF9B-6D27-4E9C-8CD3-CF6E4FF96FF9%7D/s_res_2088.pdf (accessed 9 June 2014).

11 See UNICEF, Press Release, 'UNICEF calls for cessation of child recruitment in Central African Republic' (4 January 2013), http://www.unicef.org/media/media_67117.html (accessed 4 June 2014).

occur—subsequently condemned by the Security Council,[12] which also called for a cessation of all hostilities.[13]

In March, the Séléka rebels marched into the capital of Bangui, overthrew the government causing President Bozizé to flee, and subsequently dissolved the constitution.[14] In the following months, a chorus of rights groups, UN officials and the International Criminal Court voiced concern about various allegations of abuses taking place within the country as well as warnings about continued and escalating violence.[15] In November, the UN Deputy Secretary General Jan Eliasson urged Security Council action to curb the ongoing violence[16] and in December, the UN authorized a peacekeeping force (MISCA) for 1 year.[17] The UN has warned of an impending food crisis, due to a drastic decline in crop production given the situation of armed conflict within the country.[18] At the time of publication, the situation is still ongoing.

---

[12] See UN Security Council, Press Release, 'Security Council Press Statement on Central African Republic' (20 March 2013), http://www.un.org/News/Press/docs/2013/sc10948.doc.htm (accessed 9 June 2014).

[13] See UN Security Council, Press Release, 'Security Council Press Statement on Central African Republic' (22 March 2013), http://www.un.org/News/Press/docs/2013/sc10955.doc.htm (accessed 9 June 2014).

[14] See 'Central African Republic Profile', *BBC News* (19 March 2014), http://www.bbc.co.uk/news/world-africa-13150040 (accessed 1 June 2014). See also, P. Snyder, 'Central African Republic rebels dissolve constitution', *Jurist* (26 March 2013), http://jurist.org/paperchase/2013/03/central-african-republic-rebels-dissolve-constitution.php (accessed 1 June 2014).

[15] See D. Mullen, 'UN rights chief condemns abuses in Central African Republic', *Jurist* (18 April 2013), http://jurist.org/paperchase/2013/04/un-rights-chief-condemns-abuses-in-central-african-republic.php (accessed 2 June 2014); D. Mullen, 'HRW: Central African Republic rebels have committed rights violations', *Jurist* (10 May 2013), http://jurist.org/paperchase/2013/05/hrw-centrial-african-republic-rebels-have-committed-rights-violations.php (accessed 2 June 2014); C. Miley, 'UN rights experts concerned over situation in Central African Republic', *Jurist* (8 June 2013), http://jurist.org/paperchase/2013/08/un-rights-experts-concerned-over-situation-in-central-african-republic.php (accessed 2 June 2014); D. Mullen, 'ICC prosecutor voices concern over situation in Central African Republic', *Jurist* (8 August 2013), http://jurist.org/paperchase/2013/08/icc-prosecutor-voices-concern-over-situation-in-central-african-republic.php (accessed 2 June 2014); E. LaForgia, 'UN rights experts urge Central African Republic authorities to protect population', *Jurist* (2 October 2013), http://jurist.org/paperchase/2013/10/un-rights-experts-urge-central-african-republic-authorities-to-protect-population.php (accessed 2 June 2014); P. Snyder, 'UN rights expert warns of escalating violence in Central African Republic', *Jurist* (8 November 2013), http://jurist.org/paperchase/2013/11/un-rights-expert-warns-of-escalating-violence-in-the-central-african-republic.php (accessed 2 June 2014).

[16] See UN Deputy Secretary General, Press Statement, 'Deputy Secretary-General's Briefing to the Security Council on the Situation in the Central African Republic' (25 November 2013), http://www.un.org/sg/dsg/statements/index.asp?nid=471 (accessed 10 June 2014).

[17] See UN Security Council Resolution 2127 (5 December 2013), http://www.un.org/en/ga/search/view_doc.asp?symbol=S/RES/2127(2013) (accessed 8 June 2014).

[18] See 'Strife-torn Central African Republic faces looming food crisis, UN warns', *UN News Centre* (16 December 2013), http://www.un.org/apps/news/story.asp?NewsID=46746#.U4Rk562Sy_J (accessed 2 June 2014).

## *7.1.3 Colombia*

The conflict in Colombia, categorized by most as a non-international armed conflict,[19] continued between government forces and Fuerzas Armadas Revolucionarias de Colombia (FARC) rebels. As a result of this conflict, ongoing since 1964, figures cited by Human Rights Watch show more than four million Colombians have been displaced and more than 100,000 are displaced each year that the conflict continues.[20] In November of 2012, the first peace talks in approximately a decade between the FARC and Colombian government officials began in Norway.[21] They subsequently moved to Cuba in 2013.[22] In May, a deal was reached regarding land reform, the first of six major areas of discussion.[23] Despite this progress, fighting still continued and 19 Colombian soldiers were killed in clashes with the FARC in July.[24] Additionally, dozens of civilians were killed or injured and hundreds more were forced to flee from their homes.[25] Amnesty International reports that:

> In July, Colombia ratified the International Convention for the Protection of All Persons from Enforced Disappearance. However, it did not recognize the competence of the UN Committee on Enforced Disappearances, thereby denying victims and their families an important recourse to justice. Although accurate numbers were hard to establish, at least 30,000 people were thought to have been forcibly disappeared during the conflict.[26]

In August, FARC threatened to delay peace negotiations after President Juan Manuel Santos proposed legislation to put any agreements reached in negotiations

[19] See 'Colombia: the challenges of a continuing armed conflict', Interview with Christophe Beney, Head of the ICRC Delegation in Colombia (29 September 2011), http://www.icrc.org/eng/resources/documents/interview/2011/colombia-interview-2011-09-29.htm (accessed 28 May 2014). See also Sivakumaran 2012, p. 230: "Despite their very real cross-border elements, the non-international character of the Colombia/FARC armed conflict […] is not seriously challenged."

[20] See Human Rights Watch 2013, p. 214. Amnesty International said that figures were very difficult to verify, but at least tens of thousands of people per year are displaced due to the conflict, See Amnesty International 2013, p. 65.

[21] See 'Colombia's FARC peace talks resume in Cuba', *BBC News* (5 December 2012), http://www.bbc.co.uk/news/world-latin-america-20618131 (accessed 28 May 2014).

[22] See 'Q and A: Colombia peace talks', *BBC News* (2 September 2013), http://www.bbc.co.uk/news/world-latin-america-19875363 (accessed 9 June 2014).

[23] Ibid.

[24] See 'Colombian Rebels Kill 19 Soldiers', *New York Times* (21 July 2013), http://www.nytimes.com/2013/07/22/world/americas/colombian-rebels-kill-19-soldiers.html (accessed 3 June 2014).

[25] See Amnesty International, Report 2013: Colombia, http://www.amnesty.org/en/region/colombia/report-2013 (accessed 22 May 2014).

[26] Ibid.

to a nationwide referendum.[27] In November, the government and FARC rebels reached an agreement on political participation in the case that a peace agreement is signed.[28] At the time of publication, the situation is still ongoing.

### *7.1.4 Democratic Republic of the Congo*

In 2013 in the Democratic Republic of the Congo (DRC), the conflict continued between the various rebel factions and the Congolese government in a continuation of fighting since 2003 (the formal end of the second Congo War), though 2013 did see the end of hostilities after several developments.[29] Human Rights Watch released findings in February outlining war crimes and crimes against humanity committed by both the M23 rebels and the Congolese Army (reporting at least 36 women and girls were reported as being raped, at least 24 allegations of summary executions recorded, children allegedly forcefully recruited and hundreds of homes, offices and vehicles were reportedly looted).[30] In May, a UN report[31] also contained allegations of more than 135 rapes committed by Congolese troops and M23 rebels at the end of 2012.[32]

Also in February, ahead of talks amongst representatives of 11 African countries signing an accord in Ethiopia pledging to end the conflict in the DRC,[33] the M23

---

[27] See S. Romero, 'Rebels Delay Peace Talks in Colombia', *New York Times* (23 August 2013), http://www.nytimes.com/2013/08/24/world/americas/colombian-rebels-put-talks-with-government-on-pause.html (accessed 22 May 2014).

[28] See 'Colombia, FARC agree on rebels' future if peace signed', *Reuters* (6 November 2013), http://www.reuters.com/article/2013/11/07/us-colombia-rebels-idUSBRE9A50JM20131107?feedType=RSS&feedName=worldNews&rpc=69 (accessed 22 May 2014).

[29] See 'Democratic Republic of Congo profile', *BBC News* (11 March 2014), http://www.bbc.co.uk/news/world-africa-13286306 (accessed 24 May 2014).

[30] See 'DR Congo: War Crimes by M23, Congolese Army', *Human Rights Watch* (5 February 2013), http://www.hrw.org/news/2013/02/05/dr-congo-war-crimes-m23-congolese-army (accessed 24 May 2014).

[31] See 'Report of the United Nations Joint Human Rights Office on human rights violations perpetrated by soldiers of the Congolese armed forces and combatants of the M23 in Goma and Sake, North Kivu Province, and in and around Minova, South Kivu Province, from 15 November to 2 December 2012' (May 2013), http://reliefweb.int/sites/reliefweb.int/files/resources/UNJHRO%20-%20HRVs%20Goma%20and%20Minova%20-%20May%202013.pdf (accessed 24 May 2014).

[32] See 'UN report slams rape rampage by DR Congo troops', *Star Africa* (8 May 2013), http://en.starafrica.com/news/un-report-slams-rape-rampage-by-dr-congo-troops.html (accessed 24 May 2014).

[33] See 'Update 4-African leaders sign deal aimed at peace in eastern Congo', *Reuters* (24 February 2013), http://www.reuters.com/article/2013/02/25/congo-democratic-un-idUSL6N0BO16X20130225 (accessed 24 May 2014).

rebels declared a ceasefire.[34] In March, former Congolese General Bosco Ntaganda, who was indicted by the International Criminal Court (ICC) in 2006 for war crimes and crimes against humanity, voluntarily surrendered himself at the US Embassy in Rwanda.[35] He was then extradited to The Hague to face charges at the ICC.[36] The charges from the ICC read as follows: "the Chamber finds that there are reasonable grounds to believe that Mr. Ntaganda is criminally responsible as an indirect co-perpetrator (Article 25(3)(a) of the Statute) for the crimes against humanity of murder (Article 7(1)(a) of the Statute), rape and sexual violence (Article 7(1)(g) of the Statute) and persecution (Article 7(1)(h) of the Statute) and the war crimes of murder (Article 8(2)(e)(i) of the Statute), pillaging (Article 8(2)(e)(v) of the Statute) and rape and sexual violence (Article 8(2)(e)(vi) of the Statute."[37]

Fighting continued in August, with shelling hitting the city of Goma, and a 3,000-member UN Intervention Brigade was deployed in order to fight and disarm rebels in the country's east.[38] Allegations of abuse continued through November,[39] though after suffering defeats in strongholds in the east at the hands of the government as well as UN-backed forces, M23 signed a peace deal.[40] Despite this peace accord, reports allege that M23 forces were recruiting and regrouping in neighboring Rwanda in December.[41]

### *7.1.5 Drones (Unmanned Aerial Vehicles) and Targeted Killing*

In January, UN Special Rapporteur on the Promotion and Protection of Human Rights and Fundamental Freedoms while Countering Terrorism, Ben Emmerson,

---

34 See 'DR Congo: War crimes by M23, Congolese army', supra n 30.

35 See 'Fugitive M23 leader Ntaganda surrenders', *Al Jazeera* (19 March 2013), http://www.aljazeera.com/news/africa/2013/03/2013318163159939611.html (accessed 24 May 2014).

36 See also Sect. 7.2.1.4.

37 See D. Taglioli, 'Congo war crimes suspect surrenders at US embassy in Rwanda', *Jurist* (19 March 2013), http://jurist.org/paperchase/2013/03/fugitive-congo-warlord-surrenders-at-us-embassy-in-rwanda.php (accessed 24 May 2014).

38 See K. Katombe, 'U.N.'s peacekeepers in Congo ordered to protect civilians after city shelled', *Reuters* (22 August 2013), http://www.reuters.com/article/2013/08/22/us-congo-democratic-fighting-idUSBRE97L0WB20130822 (accessed 24 May 2014).

39 See 'Report of the UN High Commissioner for Human Rights on the situation of human rights and the activities of her office in the Democratic Republic of the Congo', A/HRC/24/33 (12 July 2013), http://monusco.unmissions.org/LinkClick.aspx?fileticket=jCGZWLzQqR0%3d&tabid=11243&mid=14383&language=en-US (accessed 24 May 2014).

40 See 'DRC government and M23 sign a peace deal', *Al Jazeera* (12 December 2013), http://www.aljazeera.com/news/africa/2013/12/drc-government-m23-sign-peace-deal-201312121721467981l0.html (accessed 24 May 2014).

41 See 'Exclusive: Congo's army accused of abuse as rebels regroup in Rwanda—UN experts', *Reuters* (16 December 2013), http://www.reuters.com/article/2013/12/16/us-congo-demomcratic-un-idUSBRE9BF1GJ20131216 (accessed 24 May 2014).

QC, announced an official investigation into the civilian impact of drone strikes.[42] This investigation was

> To look at the evidence that drone strikes and other forms of remote targeted killing have caused disproportionate civilian casualties in some instances, and to make recommendations concerning the duty of States to conduct thorough independent and impartial investigations into such allegations, with a view to securing accountability and reparation where things can be shown to have gone badly wrong with potentially grave consequences for civilians.[43]

The United States also continued to make statements about its interpretation of the legality of drone strikes.[44] In May, a drone strike memo was leaked to NBC, containing information about the legality of such strikes against US citizens abroad under domestic legal authority as well as the US interpretation of its international legal authority.[45] Additionally in May, President Obama gave a speech at the National Defense University about the legality and future of the war against Al-Qaeda. He stated:

> America's actions are legal. We were attacked on 9/11. Within a week, Congress overwhelmingly authorized the use of force. Under domestic law, and international law, the United States is at war with al Qaeda, the Taliban, and their associated forces. We are at war with an organization that right now would kill as many Americans as they could if we did not stop them first. So this is a just war—a war waged proportionally, in last resort, and in self-defense

---

[42] See R. DiLeonardo, 'UN rights expert announces investigation into use of drone strikes', *Jurist* (24 January 2013), http://jurist.org/paperchase/2013/01/un-rights-expert-announces-investigation-into-use-of-drone-strikes-by-us-and-other-nations.php (accessed 25 May 2014).

[43] See 'Statement by Ben Emmerson, UN Special Rapporteur on Counterterrorism and Human Rights concerning the launch of an inquiry into the civilian impact and human rights implications on the use of drones and other forms of targeted killing for the purpose of counterterrorism and counter-insurgency' (24 January 2013), http://www.aclu.org/files/assets/emmerson_statement_on_un_tk_inquiry_24.01.12.pdf (accessed 25 May 2014). Disclosure: author Dorsey was involved in a legal research capacity for Special Rapporteur Emmerson's investigation.

[44] See Dorsey and Paulussen, 2012 Year in Review YIHL, pp. 197–198 for previous speeches by US government officials (e.g., 'Attorney General Eric Holder Speaks at Northwestern University School of Law', United States Department of Justice (5 March 2012), http://www.justice.gov/iso/opa/ag/speeches/2012/ag-speech-1203051.html (accessed 25 May 2014); J. Johnson, General Counsel of the US Department of Defense, 'The Conflict Against Al Qaeda and its Affiliates: How Will It End?', Oxford Union, Oxford University (30 November 2012), http://www.lawfareblog.com/2012/11/jeh-johnson-speech-at-the-oxford-union (accessed 25 May 2014); 'Remarks of CIA General Counsel Stephen W. Preston at Harvard Law School' (10 April 2012), http://www.cia.gov/news-information/speeches-testimony/2012-speeches-testimony/cia-general-counsel-harvard.html (accessed 25 May 2014); H. Koh, Legal Adviser, US Department of State, 'The Obama Administration and International Law' (25 March 2010), http://www.state.gov/s/l/releases/remarks/139119.htm (accessed 25 May 2014); 'Remarks of J. Brennan, "Strengthening our Security by Adhering to our Values and Laws"' (16 September 2011), http://www.whitehouse.gov/the-press-office/2011/09/16/remarks-john-o-brennan-strengthening-our-security-adhering-our-values-an (accessed 25 May 2014)).

[45] See D. Taglioli, 'DOJ drone strike publicly released in NBC exclusive', *Jurist* (5 February 2013), DOJ drone strike memo publicly released in NBC exclusive (accessed 25 May 2014).

before going on to say that

> America's legitimate claim of self-defense cannot be the end of the discussion. To say a military tactic is legal, or even effective, is not to say it is wise or moral in every instance. For the same human progress that gives us the technology to strike half a world away also demands the discipline to constrain that power—or risk abusing it.[46]

Attorney General Eric Holder followed in a speech in June specifying the "extraordinary circumstances" under which drone strikes would be legal on US soil.[47] In August, UN Secretary General Ban Ki-Moon stated that US drone strikes must comply with international law.[48]

In October, along with a complementary report by UN Special Rapporteur on Extrajudicial Executions, Christof Heyns, Emmerson presented his preliminary report outlining the legal framework and remaining questions to the General Assembly.[49] Emmerson's report presented the relevant legal framework with respect to the use of drones and targeted killing and concluded that international law demands more transparency in order to ensure compliance with the various applicable legal frameworks (e.g., international humanitarian law and international human rights law). One piece of evidence offered by the report leading to the recommendations on transparency was that many more civilians were killed than were reported by the US Government.[50] The report from Heyns was complementary to that of Emmerson and stated:

> Although drones are not illegal weapons, they can make it easier for States to deploy deadly and targeted force on the territories of other States. As such, they risk undermining the protection of life in the immediate and longer terms. If the right to life is to be secured, it is imperative that the limitations posed by international law on the use of force are not weakened by broad justifications of drone strikes.[51]

---

[46] See 'Remarks by the President at the National Defense University' (23 May 2013), http://www.whitehouse.gov/the-press-office/2013/05/23/remarks-president-national-defense-university (accessed 25 May 2014).

[47] See K. Herting, 'Holder: drone strikes on US soil legal in "extraordinary circumstances"', *Jurist* (6 March 2013), http://jurist.org/paperchase/2013/03/holder-drone-strikes-on-us-soil-legal-in-extraordinary-circumstances.php (accessed 25 May 2014).

[48] See E. Vereen, 'UN SG: US drone strikes must comply with international law', *Jurist* (14 August 2013), http://jurist.org/paperchase/2013/08/un-sg-us-drone-strikes-must-comply-with-international-law.php (accessed 25 May 2014).

[49] See UN General Assembly Report, 'Promotion and protection of human rights and fundamental freedoms while countering terrorism', A/68/39 (18 September 2013), http://www.lawfareblog.com/wp-content/uploads/2013/10/Emmerson-Report.pdf (accessed 25 May 2014).

[50] See K. Hall, 'UN report claims US drone strikes have killed more than publicly stated', *Jurist* (18 October 2013), http://jurist.org/paperchase/2013/10/un-report-claims-us-drone-strikes-have-killed-more-than-publicly-stated.php (accessed 25 May 2014).

[51] See UN General Assembly Report, 'Extrajudicial, summary or arbitrary executions' (13 September 2013), http://justsecurity.org/wp-content/uploads/2013/10/UN-Special-Rapporteur-Extrajudicial-Christof-Heyns-Report-Drones.pdf (accessed 25 May 2014), p. 1.

In the same week as the UN Special Rapporteurs filed their findings, Amnesty International[52] and Human Rights Watch[53] published research reports about the use of drones and civilian casualties in Pakistan and Yemen, respectively. In response, the US subsequently defended the legality of its use of drones, discounting the reports by the human rights organizations, stating that

> [t]o the extent these reports claim that the US has acted contrary to international law, we would strongly disagree…[t]he administration has repeatedly emphasized the extraordinary care that we take to make sure counter-terrorism actions are in accordance with all applicable law.[54]

Following the collection of reports, on December 18, the UN General Assembly adopted a Resolution wherein Para 6(s) of the resolution urges States "to ensure that any measures taken or means employed to counter terrorism, including the use of remotely piloted aircraft, comply with their obligations under international law, including the Charter of the United Nations, human rights law and international humanitarian law, in particular the principles of distinction and proportionality".[55] Eleven days later, a US drone strike targeting a Yemeni wedding party killed 21 civilians and wounded 30 more, a situation that was later condemned by the UN Office of the High Commissioner for Human Rights.[56]

### *7.1.6 Israel/Palestine*

The conflict in Israel/Palestine continued throughout 2013. In January, the UN Humanitarian Coordinator, James W. Rawley, called for an end to the use of live ammunition against civilians in the West Bank by the Israeli armed forces,[57] stating that such use may constitute "excessive use of force" and should be investigated in

---

[52] See 'Will I Be Next? UN Drone Strikes in Pakistan', *Amnesty International* (October 2013), http://www.amnestyusa.org/sites/default/files/asa330132013en.pdf (accessed 25 May 2014).

[53] See 'Between a Drone and Al-Qaeda: The Civilian Cost of US Targeted Killings in Yemen', *Human Rights Watch* (22 October 2013), http://www.hrw.org/reports/2013/10/22/between-drone-and-al-qaeda-0 (accessed 25 May 2014).

[54] See 'White House defends legality of drone attacks', *Al Jazeera* (22 October 2013), http://www.aljazeera.com/news/americas/2013/10/white-house-defends-legality-drone-attacks-20131022173945304421.html (accessed 25 May 2014).

[55] See UN General Assembly Resolution 68/178 (18 December 2013), http://www.un.org/en/ga/search/view_doc.asp?symbol=A/68/PV.70 (accessed 25 May 2014).

[56] See 'Press briefing notes on Cambodia and Yemen', Spokesperson for the High Commissioner on Human Rights (7 January 2014), http://www.ohchr.org/EN/NewsEvents/Pages/DisplayNews.aspx?NewsID=14152&LangID=E (accessed 25 May 2014).

[57] See S.U. Kim, 'Israel to cease use of live ammunition against civilians', *Jurist* (31 January 2013), http://jurist.org/paperchase/2013/01/israel-to-cease-use-of-live-ammunition-against-civilians-un.php (accessed 26 May 2014).

order to hold those responsible accountable.[58] In February, UNHCHR Commissioner Navi Pillay, expressed concern regarding Palestinian prisoners on hunger strike[59] regarding their deteriorating health conditions.[60] This came two weeks before an investigation into the death of a Palestine prisoner, Arafat Jaradat, was urged by the UN Special Rapporteur for human rights in the Occupied Palestinian Territories, Richard Falk.[61] Jaradat died while undergoing interrogation in an Israeli detention facility. Israeli authorities reported that he died of a heart attack, but that was not indicated on the initial autopsy report. Palestinian medical officials reportedly found clear signs of torture on the "previously healthy 30-year-old Jaradat".[62]

UNICEF also reported mistreatment at detention facilities, but this time of children.[63] The UNICEF report outlines that more than 700 Palestinian children are detained at Israeli military facilities per year, and these practices may violate international legal standards.[64]

In March, another report came out in criticism of Israeli practice under the auspices of the Human Rights Council.[65] The International Fact-Finding Mission on Israeli Settlements in the Occupied Palestinian Territory concluded in its report that under the requirements of the Fourth Geneva Convention (Article 49), "cease all settlement activities without precondition…[and] initiate a process of withdrawal of all settlers from the Occupied Palestinian Territory".[66] Additionally, it called on

---

[58] See J. Rawley, 'Statement by the UN Humanitarian Coordinator James W. Rawley on the IDF use of live fire in the West Bank' (30 January 2013), http://reliefweb.int/sites/reliefweb.int/files/resources/Statement%20by%20the%20UN%20Humanitarian%20Coordinator%20James%20W.%20Rawley.pdf (accessed 26 May 2014).

[59] See M. Haggerson, 'UN rights experts concerned over Israel prisoners on hunger strike', *Jurist* (13 February 2013), http://jurist.org/paperchase/2013/02/un-rights-experts-concerned-over-israel-prisoners-on-hunger-strike.php (accessed 26 May 2014).

[60] See UN Office of the High Commissioner for Human Rights, Press Release, 'Pillay concerned about health of Palestinian detainees' (13 February 2013), http://www.ohchr.org/en/NewsEvents/Pages/DisplayNews.aspx?NewsID=12987&LangID=E (accessed 26 May 2014).

[61] See UN Office of the High Commissioner for Human Rights, Press Release, 'The death of a Palestinian prisoner while undergoing interrogation in an Israeli facility must be investigated' (27 February 2013), http://www.ohchr.org/EN/NewsEvents/Pages/DisplayNews.aspx?NewsID=13053&LangID=E (accessed 26 May 2014).

[62] Ibid.

[63] See M. Pomy, 'Israel mistreating detained Palestinian children: report', *Jurist* (6 March 2013), http://jurist.org/paperchase/2013/03/israel-mistreating-detained-palestinian-children-report.php (accessed 26 May 2014).

[64] See UNICEF, 'Children in Israeli Military Detention: Observations and Recommendations' (6 March 2013), http://www.unicef.org/oPt/UNICEF_oPt_Children_in_Israeli_Military_Detention_Observations_and_Recommendations_-_6_March_2013.pdf (accessed 26 May 2014).

[65] See P. Snyder, 'UN rights expert calls on Israel to withdraw settlers from Palestinian territories', *Jurist* (18 March 2013), http://jurist.org/paperchase/2013/03/un-rights-expert-calls-on-israel-to-withdraw-settlers-from-palestinian-territories.php (accessed 26 May 2014).

[66] See UN Human Rights Council, 'Report of the international fact finding mission to investigate the implications of the Israeli settlements on the civil, political, economic, social and cultural rights of the Palestinian people throughout the Occupied Palestinian Territory, including East Jerusalem',

Israel to "put an end to the human rights violations that are linked to the presence of settlements".[67] The European Union also added its voice to the concern about the legality of future settlement plans of over 1,500 homes in Jewish Settlements in East Jerusalem and the West Bank in a statement in October.[68] EU High Representative Catherine Ashton stated: "[t]he EU has repeatedly stated that settlements are illegal under international law. It has also called on Israel to end all settlement activity, including natural growth, and to dismantle outposts erected since March 2001," while deploring the new settlement plans.[69]

Special Rapporteur Richard Falk also presented evidence that approximately 20 % of all Palestinians (75,000) have been detained over the course of the 46-year-long occupation and additionally other human rights violations have occurred.[70] In line with the reports on human rights violations, he called for an end of the Gaza Blockade in June because "the human suffering of the land, sea and air blockade imposed on the 1.75 million Palestinians living in one of the most densely populated and impoverished areas of the world has been devastating…[and] 6 years of Israel's calculated strangulation of the Gaza Strip has stunted the economy and has kept most Gazans in a state of perpetual poverty and aid dependency".[71]

In July, peace talks resumed at the behest of US Secretary of State, John Kerry, between the Israelis and Palestinians,[72] though they would later break down for failure of both sides of upholding pre-arranged concessions and agreements.[73]

---

(Footnote 66 continued)
A/HRC/22/63 (7 February 2013), http://www.ohchr.org/Documents/HRBodies/HRCouncil/RegularSession/Session22/A-HRC-22-63_en.pdf (accessed 26 May 2014), p. 12, para 112.

[67] Ibid., para 113.

[68] See L. Laing, 'Israel settlement plans criticized as unlawful', *Jurist* (31 October 2013), http://jurist.org/paperchase/2013/10/israel-settlement-plans-criticized-as-unlawful.php (accessed 26 May 2014).

[69] See 'European Union Statement by High Representative Catherine Ashton on the latest Israeli announcement of settlement plans' (31 October 2013), http://www.eeas.europa.eu/statements/docs/2013/131031_01_en.pdf (accessed 26 May 2014).

[70] See UN Office of the High Commissioner for Human Rights, Press Release, 'Collective punishment in Gaza must end: Israel's blockade enters its 7th year—UN Special Rapporteur' (14 June 2013), http://www.ohchr.org/EN/NewsEvents/Pages/DisplayNews.aspx?NewsID=13455&LangID=E (accessed 26 May 2014).

[71] Ibid.

[72] See E. McClam, 'A Guide to the 2013 Israeli-Palestinian Peace Talks', *NBC News* (30 July 2013), http://www.nbcnews.com/news/other/guide-2013-israeli-palestinian-peace-talks-f6C10791311 (accessed 26 May 2014).

[73] See M. Landler, 'Mideast Peace Effort Pauses to Let Failure Sink In', *New York Times* (15 May 2013), http://www.nytimes.com/2014/05/16/world/mideast-peace-effort-pauses-to-let-failure-sink-in.html (accessed 26 May 2014).

### 7.1.7 Mali

Beginning in January 2012, several insurgent groups started a campaign for independence or autonomy for northern Mali in the Azawad area against the Malian government.[74] The National Movement for the Liberation of Azawad (MNLA), initially backed by the Ansar Dine Islamist group, led the campaign with the aim of creating an independent homeland for the Tuareg people. Fighting continued throughout 2012, and despite a ceasefire agreement being drawn up, Ansar Dine accused Malian government officials of not meeting the terms of the agreement and suspended the ceasefire in January.[75] In response, the Security Council expressed grave concern at the attacks.[76] As fighting continued, the French and British militaries intervened at the request of the Malian government.[77] January also saw the ICC open an investigation into allegations of war crimes.[78] After another period of fighting, a ceasefire agreement was signed by Malian officials and Tuareg rebels in June in order to pave a way toward national elections in August.[79] However, due to the Tuareg rebels' allegations of Malian forces not upholding commitments agreed to in the peace accord, the ceasefire was again suspended in September.[80] At the time of publication, this conflict was still ongoing.

---

[74] See ICC, Office of the Prosecutor, Report on Preliminary Examination Activities 2012 (November 2012), http://www.icc-cpi.int/NR/rdonlyres/C433C462-7C4E-4358-8A72-8D99FD00E8CD/285209/OTP2012ReportonPreliminaryExaminations22Nov2012.pdf (accessed 27 May 2014), para 168: "Since 17 January 2012, there is an ongoing non-international armed conflict in the territory of Mali between the government forces and different organized armed groups particularly Mouvement National de Libération de l'Azawad (MNLA), Al-Qaeda in the Islamic Maghreb (AQIM), Ansar Dine and Mouvement pour l'Unicité et le Jihad en Afrique de l'Ouest (MUJAO) and 'Arab militias,' as well as between these armed groups without the involvement of government forces".

[75] See 'Mali Islamist group says ends ceasefire with government', *Reuters* (4 January 2013), http://www.reuters.com/article/2013/01/04/us-mali-crisis-ansardine-idUSBRE9030CY20130104 (accessed 27 May 2014).

[76] See 'Security Council Press Statement on Mali' (10 January 2013), http://www.un.org/News/Press/docs/2013/sc10878.doc.htm (accessed 27 May 2014).

[77] See A. Hirsch, 'French troops arrive in Mali to stem rebel advance', *The Guardian* (11 January 2013), http://www.theguardian.com/world/2013/jan/11/france-intervene-mali-conflict (accessed 27 May 2014); on British involvement, see P. Beaumont et al., 'Britain to send aircraft to Mali to assist French fight against rebels', *The Guardian* (13 January 2013), http://www.theguardian.com/world/2013/jan/12/mali-somalia-france-rebels-islamist-francois-hollande (accessed 27 May 2014).

[78] See ICC, Press Statement, 'ICC Prosecutor opens investigation into war crimes in Mali: "The legal requirements have been met—we will investigate"' (16 January 2013), http://www.icc-cpi.int/en_menus/icc/press%20and%20media/press%20releases/news%20and%20highlights/Pages/pr869.aspx (accessed 27 May 2014).

[79] See 'Mali and Tuareg rebels sign peace deal', *BBC News* (18 June 2013), http://www.bbc.co.uk/news/world-africa-22961519 (accessed 27 May 2014).

[80] See 'Mali Tuareg separatists suspend participation in peace process', *Reuters* (26 September 2013), http://www.trust.org/item/20130927071806-0qx16/?source=dpagehead (accessed 27 May 2014).

### *7.1.8 Nigeria/Boko Haram*

Boko Haram is a Salafi-Islamist group based in northern Nigeria that seeks to establish "pure" Sharia law in the country.[81] Boko Haram, which forbids Western influence including education, began in 2001 by Mohammed Yusuf and in its quest to implement Sharia law, schools, mosques, and churches as well as bars and beer gardens have been bombed or attacked. This situation has been ongoing since 2009 and has killed more than 5,000. Since 2012, Human Rights Watch reports that more than 300 schools have been burned and over 10,000 students have been deprived of an education.[82] In May, despite President Jonathan's imposition of a state of emergency in the states where Boko Haram is the most active, attacks continued to occur.[83] Regarding atrocities that occurred, the Prosecutor of the International Criminal Court found reason to believe that crimes against humanity of murder and persecution had been committed by Boko Haram and vowed to continue her investigation.[84] In addition to allegations against Boko Haram, Nigerian security forces were also suspected of committing human rights abuses.[85] One such example is the death of hundreds of Boko Haram suspects in custody in Nigeria's detention system.[86]

### *7.1.9 Somalia*

The armed conflict in Somalia, between Al-Shabaab and Somali government security forces, African Union Mission in Somalia (AMISOM) troops, Ethiopian government troops and other allied militias since 2009, included ongoing attacks and allegations of war crimes and crimes against humanity in 2013. Al-Shabaab

---

[81] See Walker 2012.

[82] Human Rights Watch 2014, p. 148.

[83] Ibid.

[84] ICC, Office of the Prosecutor, 'Situation in Nigeria' (5 August 2013), http://www.icc-cpi.int/iccdocs/PIDS/docs/SAS%20-%20NGA%20-%20Public%20version%20Article%205%20Report%20-%2005%20August%202013.PDF (para 128). The text of the following paragraphs: At the time of writing, the situation in the context of which the alleged crimes are committed by Boko Haram does not seem to qualify as an armed conflict; hence the contextual elements of war crimes are not met. The Office will seek additional information in order to fine-tune its assessment (para 130). Accordingly, the Prosecutor has decided to move the situation in Nigeria to phase 3 of the preliminary examination with a view to assessing whether the Nigerian authorities are conducting genuine proceedings in relation to the crimes committed by Boko Haram (para 131).

[85] Human Rights Watch 2014, pp. 150–151.

[86] See 'Nigeria: Deaths of hundreds of Boko Haram suspects in custody requires investigation', *Amnesty International* (15 October 2013), http://www.amnesty.org/en/news/nigeria-deaths-hundreds-boko-haram-suspects-custody-requires-investigation-2013-10-15 (accessed 28 May 2014).

continues to carry out targeted killings and attacks against civilians. In March, the Security Council extended AMISOM's mandate until the end of February 2014 and partially lifted the arms embargo by stating that the embargo: "shall not apply to deliveries of weapons or military equipment or the provision of advice, assistance or training, intended solely for the development of the Security Forces of the Federal Government of Somalia, and to provide security for the Somali people…"[87] In June, the Security Council also authorized the creation of the UN Assistance Mission in Somalia (UNSOM) and deployed it for an initial phase of 12 months,[88] and in November, increased the number of troops deployed under UNSOM from 17,731 to 22,126.[89]

Throughout the duration of 2013, several attacks were carried out by Al-Shabaab, such as the March attack on the Supreme Court,[90] a June attack on the UNDP compound in Mogadishu,[91] the Turkish embassy in Mogadishu in July,[92] and the September attacks on a village restaurant[93] and on a shopping center in Nairobi, Kenya.[94] Human Rights Watch denounced many of the attacks as war crimes in April.[95] The estimated death toll from 2013 fell from previous years to a total of 3,150 people.[96] At the time of publication, the conflict is still ongoing.

---

87 UN Security Council Resolution 2093 (6 March 2013), http://www.securitycouncilreport.org/atf/cf/%7B65BFCF9B-6D27-4E9C-8CD3-CF6E4FF96FF9%7D/s_res_2093.pdf (accessed 2 June 2014).

88 UN Security Council Resolution 2102 (2 May 2013), http://www.securitycouncilreport.org/atf/cf/%7B65BFCF9B-6D27-4E9C-8CD3-CF6E4FF96FF9%7D/s_res_2102.pdf (accessed 2 June 2014).

89 UN Security Council Resolution 2124 (12 November 2013), http://www.securitycouncilreport.org/atf/cf/%7B65BFCF9B-6D27-4E9C-8CD3-CF6E4FF96FF9%7D/s_res_2124.pdf (accessed 2 June 2014).

90 See A. Guled, 'Death toll rises to 35 in Somalia court attack', *Yahoo! News* (15 April 2013), http://news.yahoo.com/death-toll-rises-35-somalia-court-attack-091204255.html (accessed 2 June 2014).

91 See 'Security Council Press Statement on Somalia' (19 June 2013), http://www.un.org/News/Press/docs/2013/sc11039.doc.htm (accessed 2 June 2014).

92 See F. Omar and A. Sheikh, 'Al Shabaab claim attack on Turkish mission in Somalia, three dead', *Reuters* (27 July 2013), http://www.reuters.com/article/2013/07/27/us-somalia-conflict-idUSBRE96Q0A420130727 (accessed 2 June 2014).

93 See 'UN envoy strongly condemns terrorist attack in Somali capital', *UN News Centre* (7 September 2013), http://www.un.org/apps/news/story.asp?NewsID=45793&Cr=Somalia&Cr1=#.U4xe462Sy_J (accessed 2 June 2014).

94 See D. Howden, 'Terror in Nairobi: the full story behind Al-Shabaab's mall attack', *The Guardian* (4 October 2013), http://www.theguardian.com/world/2013/oct/04/westgate-mall-attacks-kenya (accessed 2 June 2014).

95 See 'Somalia: New Al-Shabaab Attacks are War Crimes', *Human Rights Watch* (16 April 2013), http://www.hrw.org/news/2013/04/16/somalia-new-al-shabaab-attacks-are-war-crimes (accessed 2 June 2014).

96 See Armed Conflict Location and Event Dataset, 'Conflict Trends No. 23: Real-Time Analysis of African Violence' (February 2014), http://www.acleddata.com/wp-content/uploads/2014/02/ACLED-Conflict-Trends-Report-No-23-February-2014.pdf (accessed 2 June 2014), p. 3.

### *7.1.10 Sudan and South Sudan*

The current situation between Sudan and South Sudan can be traced back many years through two separate civil wars. Much of the current conflict stems from the disputed region of Abyei as well as the disagreement regarding the Greater Nile Oil Pipeline.[97] Throughout the duration of the conflict, reports from organizations such as Amnesty International[98] and Human Rights Watch[99] have detailed alleged crimes against humanity and war crimes that have been committed by both sides in the conflict. The Enough Project, a human rights initiative, released a report in April alleging war crimes, instances of torture, and crimes against humanity carried out by the Sudanese government in South Kordofan and Blue Nile States.[100] In August, the UN Security Council also expressed grave concern with the attacks on civilians and looting of UN and other international organizations in South Sudan's Jonglei State.[101] Shortly thereafter, Human Rights Watch reported on unlawful killing of civilians in the Jonglei State by the South Sudanese Army.[102]

The fighting escalated throughout the last three months of 2013, and by December 15, a coup was attempted against President Salva Kiir, led by opposition leader Riek Machar.[103] Reports of ethnically targeted violence and more than 1,000 civilian deaths came from Human Rights Watch in the wake of the attempted coup.[104] The African Union has strongly condemned the killing of UN personnel in South Sudan.[105] At the time of publication, the conflict in South Sudan is ongoing.

---

[97] See 'Sudan and South Sudan in fierce border clashes', *BBC News* (27 March 2012), http://www.bbc.co.uk/news/world-africa-17515209 (accessed 6 May 2014).

[98] See 'Human rights situation in Sudan: Amnesty International's joint written statement to the 24th session of the UN Human Rights Council', *Amnesty International* (29 August 2013), http://www.amnesty.org/en/library/info/AFR54/015/2013/en (accessed 2 June 2014).

[99] See Human Rights Watch, World Report 2013: Sudan, http://www.hrw.org/world-report/2014/country-chapters/sudan (accessed 2 June 2014).

[100] See 'Architects of Atrocity: The Sudanese Government's War Crimes, Crimes against Humanity, and Torture in South Kordofan and Blue Nile States', *The Enough Project and the Satellite Sentinel Project Teams* (3 April 2013), http://www.enoughproject.org/reports/architects-atrocity-sudanese-governments-war-crimes-crimes-against-humanity-and-torture (accessed 5 June 2014).

[101] See 'Security Council Press Statement on Jonglei, South Sudan' (23 August 2013), http://www.un.org/News/Press/docs/2013/sc11103.doc.htm (accessed 5 June 2014).

[102] See 'South Sudan: Army Unlawfully Killed Civilians,' *Human Rights Watch* (13 September 2013), http://www.hrw.org/news/2013/09/12/south-sudan-army-unlawfully-killed-civilians (accessed 5 June 2014).

[103] See 'South Sudan quashes coup attempt, says President Kiir', *BBC News* (16 December 2013), http://www.bbc.co.uk/news/world-africa-25396853 (accessed 5 June 2014).

[104] See 'South Sudan: Ethnic Targeting, Widespread Killings', *Human Rights Watch* (16 January 2014), http://www.hrw.org/news/2014/01/16/south-sudan-ethnic-targeting-widespread-killings (accessed 5 June 2014).

[105] See 'African Union Strongly Condemns Killing of United Nations Personnel in South Sudan', *African Union* (10 April 2013), http://www.au.int/en/content/african-union-strongly-condemns-killing-united-nations-personnel-south-sudan (accessed 5 June 2014).

### 7.1.11 Syria

The armed conflict in Syria—which began as protests from those opposed to the Syrian's Ba'athist regime in response to the Syrian government's attempts to quell an uprising in 2010's Arab Spring and has now developed into an armed rebellion —has taken a massive civilian casualty toll. The death toll as of July 2013, when the UN halted its efforts in trying to keep track of casualties due to inherent difficulties in doing so, was over 100,000.[106] In January, more than 50 nations called for the referral of the situation to the International Criminal Court (ICC).[107] In February, the UN Independent Commission of Inquiry on Syria published a report alleging instances of war crimes committed by both sides of the conflict,[108] in which it stated: "The depth of the Syrian tragedy is poignantly reflected in the accounts of its victims. Their harrowing experiences of survival detail grave human rights violations, war crimes and crimes against humanity. The destructive dynamics of the civil war not only have an impact on the civilian population but are also tearing apart the country's complex social fabric, jeopardizing future generations and undermining peace and security in the entire region".[109] Human Rights Watch documented 156 instances of cluster bomb usage throughout the country, leading to several civilian casualties.[110]

In March, the United Nations Secretary General Ban Ki-Moon announced a probe into the possible use of chemical weapons in the conflict.[111] (For more, please see the Chemical Weapons Sect. 7.3.3). Human Rights Watch published its report in April entitled: "Death From the Skies" outlining indiscriminate and deliberate air strikes on civilians, including attacks on bakeries, hospitals, various instances of cluster bomb attacks, the use of incendiary weapons and other allegations of unlawful air strikes.[112] The UN High Commissioner for Human Rights, Navi Pillay, condemned the atrocities and renewed a call for the situation to be

---

[106] See 'United Nations Literally Gives Up Trying to Count Syrian War Casualties', *The Tower* (8 January 2013), http://www.thetower.org/united-nations-literally-gives-trying-count-syrian-war-casualties (accessed 5 June 2014).

[107] See Letter from Permanent Mission of Switzerland to United Nations (14 January 2014), http://www.news.admin.ch/NSBSubscriber/message/attachments/29293.pdf (accessed 5 June 2014).

[108] See UN General Assembly, 'Report of the independent international commission of inquiry on the Syrian Arab Republic' (5 February 2013), http://www.ohchr.org/Documents/HRBodies/HRCouncil/CoISyria/A.HRC.22.59_en.pdf (accessed 5 June 2014).

[109] Ibid at p 1.

[110] See 'Syria: Mounting Casualties from Cluster Munitions', *Human Rights Watch* (16 March 2013), http://www.hrw.org/news/2013/03/16/syria-mounting-casualties-cluster-munitions (accessed 5 June 2014).

[111] See 'Off-the-Cuff: Secretary-General's Press Encounter on Syrian Government Request' (21 March 2013), http://www.un.org/sg/offthecuff/index.asp?nid=2745 (accessed 5 June 2014).

[112] See 'Death from The Skies', *Human Rights Watch* (11 April 2013), http://www.hrw.org/reports/2013/04/11/death-skies (accessed 5 June 2014).

referred to the International Criminal Court in May. In a press release, she stated: "I believe that serious human rights violations and other acts amounting to war crimes and/or crimes against humanity have been committed. We must make it clear to both the government and the armed opposition groups that there will be clear consequences for the people responsible for these crimes".[113]

The UN International Independent Commission of Inquiry also documented a number of abuses amounting to war crimes and crimes against humanity from both sides of the fighting and echoed a call for referral to justice. In its May report to the Human Rights Council, it found reasonable grounds to believe that chemical agents had been employed as weapons, though exact perpetrators could not be identified. The report concluded with a call for inclusive negotiations for peace.[114] The Human Rights Council also condemned foreign military involvement in Syria, as this phenomenon was on the rise, though it did not call for a cessation of arms flow into the country.[115]

In August, Pillay condemned the allegations of chemical weapons use and urged a prompt investigation, calling on both sides to allow a team of experts to investigate the allegations.[116] The Security Council passed Resolution 2118, approximately one month later, requiring verification and destruction of Syria's chemical weapons stockpiles, calling for convening of Geneva II peace talks and endorsing the establishment of a transitional governing body.[117] Several countries, including the US[118] France,[119] and the UK,[120] had weighed and outlined legal justifications

---

[113] See UN Office of the High Commissioner for Human Rights, Press Release, 'Pillay urges greater attention to atrocities in Syria, warns of threat to Qusayr' (10 May 2013), http://www.ohchr.org/EN/NewsEvents/Pages/DisplayNews.aspx?NewsID=13314&LangID=E (accessed 5 June 2014).

[114] See UN Human Rights Council, 'Report of the independent international commission of inquiry on the Syrian Arab Republic' (4 June 2013), http://www.ohchr.org/Documents/HRBodies/HRCouncil/CoISyria/A-HRC-23-58_en.pdf (accessed 6 June 2014).

[115] See S. Franklin, 'UN rights council condemns foreign military involvement in Syria', *Jurist* (15 June 2013), http://jurist.org/paperchase/2013/06/un-rights-council-condemns-foreign-military-involvement-in-syria.php (accessed 6 June 2014).

[116] See UN Office of the High Commissioner for Human Rights, Press Release, 'Pillay says Syrian chemical weapons allegations "exceptionally grave," investigation essential' (22 August 2013), http://www.ohchr.org/EN/NewsEvents/Pages/DisplayNews.aspx?NewsID=13652&LangID=E (accessed 6 June 2014).

[117] See UN Security Council Resolution 2118 (27 September 2013), http://www.securitycouncilreport.org/atf/cf/%7B65BFCF9B-6D27-4E9C-8CD3-CF6E4FF96FF9%7D/s_res_2118.pdf (accessed 6 June 2014).

[118] See D. Martin and H. Williams, 'U.S. preps for possible cruise missile attack on Syrian gov't forces', *CBS News* (23 August 2013), http://www.cbsnews.com/news/us-preps-for-possible-cruise-missile-attack-on-syrian-govt-forces/ (accessed 6 June 2014).

[119] See 'France says would be hard to bypass U.N. in action against Syria', *Reuters* (26 August 2013), http://www.reuters.com/article/2013/08/26/us-syria-crisis-france-idUSBRE97P04B20130826 (accessed 6 June 2014).

[120] See S. Franklin, 'UK government outlines legal justification for possible strike on Syria', *Jurist* (29 August 2013), http://jurist.org/paperchase/2013/08/uk-government-outlines-legal-justification-for-possible-strike-on-syria.php (accessed 6 June 2014).

and ramifications of possible strikes in Syria, given the use of chemical weapons.[121] This course of action was questioned on the basis of legality by many, including the UN Secretary General Ban Ki-Moon, and ultimately, no strike took place.[122] In November, estimates from the UN signaled that approximately 9.3 million people (or 40 % of the population) were in need of humanitarian assistance.[123]

The conflict had also had spillover effects into neighboring Israel and Lebanon. In March, the Security Council had expressed grave concern about the cross-border fire affecting Lebanese civilians.[124] In July, the President of the Security Council expressed growing concern regarding spillover effects of the conflict on the Lebanese political, security and humanitarian situations.[125] With regard to Israeli involvement, Israeli Defense Forces fired into Syria in December after troops were shot at in the occupied Golan Heights.[126]

### *7.1.12 United States* **versus** *Al-Qaeda and Associated Forces*

The United States has continued to engage in targeted killings via the use of unmanned aerial vehicles (UAVs or drones) against suspected terrorists in its fight against Al-Qaeda and affiliated forces in Pakistan, Afghanistan, Somalia and Yemen.[127] Drone attacks in Pakistan were condemned by the Pakistani Foreign Minister in January,[128] and in May, a Pakistani court (High Court of Peshawar)

---

[121] For more academic discussion on the lead up to potential strikes in August and September, see, 'Syria Insta-Symposium', *Opinio Juris* (31 August 2013), http://opiniojuris.org/2013/08/31/syria-insta-symposium/ (accessed 6 June 2014).

[122] See L. Charbonneau, 'U.N.'s Ban casts doubt on legality of U.S. plans to punish Syria', *Reuters* (3 September 2013), http://www.reuters.com/article/2013/09/03/us-syria-crisis-un-idUSBRE9820VX20130903 (accessed 6 June 2014).

[123] See 'UN estimates 9.3 million Syrians need aid', *Al Jazeera* (5 November 2013), http://www.aljazeera.com/news/middleeast/2013/11/un-estimates-40-percent-syrians-need-aid-201311543349947959.html (accessed 6 June 2014).

[124] See 'UN Security Council Press Release on Lebanon' (14 March 2013), http://www.un.org/News/Press/docs/2013/sc10941.doc.htm (accessed 6 June 2014).

[125] See UN Security Council, 'Statement by the President of the Security Council'(10 July 2013), http://www.securitycouncilreport.org/atf/cf/%7B65BFCF9B-6D27-4E9C-8CD3-CF6E4FF96FF9%7D/s_prst_2013_9.pdf (accessed 6 July 2014).

[126] See 'Israel says returns fire into Syria on occupied Golan Heights', *Reuters* (2 December 2013), http://www.reuters.com/article/2013/12/02/us-israel-syria-idUSBRE9B108P20131202?feedType=RSS&feedName=worldNews&rpc=69 (accessed 6 June 2014).

[127] See C. Woods, J. Serle and A. Ross, 'Emerging from the shadows: US covert drone strikes in 2012', *The Bureau of Investigative Journalism* (3 January 2013), http://www.thebureauinvestigates.com/2013/01/03/emerging-from-the-shadows-us-covert-drone-strikes-in-2012-2 (accessed 6 June 2014).

[128] See T. Whittle, 'Pakistani FM says world shows concerns on U.S. drone strikes', *NZ Week* (23 January 2013), http://www.nzweek.com/world/pakistani-fm-says-world-shows-concerns-on-u-s-drone-strikes-44145/ (accessed 6 June 2014).

declared the strikes to be illegal.[129] In December, the Yemini Parliament carried out a symbolic vote and banned US drone strikes.[130] Around the same time, evidence surfaced that relationships between the United States and Afghanistan and Pakistan had become strained because of the use of drone strikes.[131] (For more on the discussion about drones and targeted killings, see Sect. 7.1.5).

In other news related to the US' fight against Al-Qaeda and affiliated forces, in January, Guantánamo detainee Abu Zubaydah sought a ruling from the European Court of Human Rights (ECHR) on the role of Poland in the CIA's secret prisons based on allegations that Zubaydah was transferred to a secret site in Poland and subject to torture.[132] The Court accepted the case in July,[133] and the first hearing took place in December. This is the first time that the CIA's "extraordinary rendition" program had reached the ECHR.[134] At the time of writing, this case was still pending before the Court. Human Rights Watch urged Lithuania to reopen its investigation into its role and complicity in the CIA secret prison program in June, prior to taking over the EU rotating presidency.[135] In October, the European Parliament, in light of the leaked information surrounding the US' National Security Agency PRISM program, called on the immediate end of complicity and impunity of European nations with the United States' secret prison program as it has led to

---

129 See D. Mullen, 'Pakistan court declares US drone strikes illegal', *Jurist* (9 May 2013), http://jurist.org/paperchase/2013/05/pakistan-court-declares-drone-strikes-illegal-directs-foreign-ministry-to-introduce-resolution-in-un.php (accessed 6 June 2014).

130 See 'Yemeni parliament bans US terror drone strikes', *Press TV* (15 December 2013), http://www.presstv.com/detail/2013/12/15/340201/yemen-votes-motion-on-us-drone-strikes/ (accessed 6 June 2014).

131 See R. Nordland and S. Masood, 'Recent Drone Strikes Strain U.S. Ties With Afghanistan and Pakistan', *New York Times* (29 November 2013), http://www.nytimes.com/2013/11/30/world/asia/drone-strike-pakistan.html?_r=1& (accessed 7 June 2014).

132 See ECtHR, *Zayn Al-Abidin Muhammad Husayn (Abu Zubaydah) against Poland*, App. No. 7511/13, lodged on 28 January 2013, http://hudoc.echr.coe.int/sites/eng/pages/search.aspx?i=001-123768 (accessed 7 June 2014).

133 See G. Redd, 'Europe rights court to hear case against Poland over secret CIA prisons', *Jurist* (30 July 2013), http://jurist.org/paperchase/2013/07/poland-under-scrutiny-for-us-detainment-camps.php (accessed 7 June 2014).

134 See 'Two Gitmo detainees accuse Poland of human rights abuses', *Al Jazeera America* (3 December 2013), http://america.aljazeera.com/articles/2013/12/3/europe-rights-courthearingonsecretciaprisons.html (accessed 7 June 2014).

135 See 'Lithuania: Reopen Investigation into Secret CIA Prisons', *Human Rights Watch* (25 June 2013), http://www.hrw.org/news/2013/06/25/lithuania-reopen-investigation-secret-cia-prisons (accessed 7 June 2014).

violations of fundamental rights.[136] The Council of Europe's Commissioner for Human Rights, Nils Muižnieks, also called for accountability regarding European complicity in torture.[137]

At the end of April, President Obama declared a new attempt at closing the detention facilities at Guantánamo Bay, but at the time of writing, the detention facilities remain open.[138] He did, however, lift the ban on transferring detainees to Yemen at the end of May in his speech at the National Defense University.[139] In related news to Guantánamo Bay, five detainees implicated in the 9/11 attacks pursued charges under the Convention Against Torture (CAT) in October, alleging that the restrictive rules for classifying evidence violated the CAT, in that they disallowed lawyers for the defense to investigate charges that are based on their clients' allegations of torture.[140] With regard to allegations of torture, a court in the Netherlands blocked the extradition of a suspected terrorist (dual Pakistani-Dutch citizen Samir K.) to the United States based on evidence that Samir K. may have been tortured at the hands of American forces during his detention in Pakistan.[141] On the other side of the coin, a court in Nigeria ordered the extradition of another suspected terrorist, Lawal Olaniyi Babafemi, a month after the Dutch court blocked Samir K.'s extradition.[142]

---

[136] See 'US-led CIA rendition and secret detention programmes: impunity must end', *European Parliament/News* (10 October 2013), http://www.europarl.europa.eu/news/en/news-room/content/20131004IPR21520/html/US-led-CIA-rendition-and-secret-detention-programmes-impunity-must-end (accessed 7 June 2014).

[137] See Council of Europe, Commissioner for Human Rights, 'Time for accountability in CIA torture cases' (9 November 2013), http://hub.coe.int/en/web/coe-portal/press/newsroom?p_p_id=newsroom&_newsroom_articleId=1584627&_newsroom_groupId=10226&_newsroom_tabs=newsroom-topnews&pager.offset=90 (accessed 7 June 2014).

[138] See S. Wilson and Z. Goldfarb, 'Obama vows a new effort to close Guantanamo Bay prison', *Washington Post* (30 April 2013), 'http://www.washingtonpost.com/politics/2013/04/30/60eca3a6-b1a0-11e2-9a98-4be1688d7d84_story.html (accessed 7 June 2014).

[139] See White House, Office of the Press Secretary, 'Fact Sheet: The President's May 23 Speech on Counterterrorism' (23 May 2013), http://www.whitehouse.gov/the-press-office/2013/05/23/fact-sheet-president-s-may-23-speech-counterterrorism (accessed 8 June 2014).

[140] See M. Slater, 'Guantanamo inmates pursuing claims under global torture treaty', *Jurist* (23 October 2013), http://jurist.org/paperchase/2013/10/guantanamo-inmates-pursuing-claims-under-global-torture-treaty.php (accessed 8 June 2014).

[141] See S. Normil, 'Dutch judge blocks extradition of terror suspect to US', *Jurist* (24 July 2014), http://jurist.org/paperchase/2013/07/dutch-judge-blocks-extradition-of-terror-suspect-to-us.php (accessed 8 June 2014); *and* See Press Release Hague District Court (23 July 2013): http://www.rechtspraak.nl/Organisatie/Gerechtshoven/Den-Haag/Nieuws/Pages/GerechtshofDenHaagSabirKmagnietwordenuitgeleverd.aspx(inDutch) (accessed 8 June 2014).

[142] See M. Pomy, 'Nigeria court orders extradition of Al Qaeda suspect to U.S.', *Jurist* (28 August 2013), http://jurist.org/paperchase/2013/08/nigeria-court-orders-extradition-of-al-qaeda-suspect-to-us.php (accessed 8 June 2014).

## 7.2 Tribunals and Courts

### 7.2.1 International

#### 7.2.1.1 International Criminal Tribunal for the Former Yugoslavia

At the International Criminal Tribunal for the former Yugoslavia (ICTY), a number of interesting developments transpired in 2013. One of those was the acquittal and release of Momčilo Perišić, the former Chief of the Yugoslav Army (VJ) General Staff. On 6 September 2011, Trial Chamber I found Perišić guilty of aiding and abetting crimes against humanity and violations of the laws or customs of war in Sarajevo and Srebrenica (Bosnia and Herzegovina) between 1993 and 1995 and as a superior for failing to punish crimes against humanity and violations of the laws or customs of war in Zagreb (Croatia) in 1995. Perišić was sentenced to 27 years' imprisonment.[143] However, on 28 February 2013, the Appeals Chamber reversed by majority, Judge Liu partially dissenting, Perišić's convictions.[144] The judges found that although Perišić implemented the Yugoslav Supreme Defence Council's policy of providing support to the Army of the Republika Srpska (VRS) through the VJ, it was not proven that this policy was directed at criminal activities as opposed to legitimate war efforts. It was also not proven that Perišić specifically directed assistance towards crimes committed by the VRS in Sarajevo and Srebrenica. As a result, Perišić could not be held liable as an aider and abettor to the crimes in Bosnia and Herzegovina.[145] As to the crimes in Croatia, which took place during the shelling of Zagreb and which were committed by soldiers from the Serbian Army of the Krajina (SVK), the judges held that Perišić did not possess effective control over these SVK soldiers. In fact, it was noted that Perišić instructed that the shelling of Zagreb cease (but that this instruction was not followed). As a consequence, Perišić could not be held liable as a superior.[146]

One month later, on 27 March 2013, Trial Chamber II found Mićo Stanišić and Stojan Župljanin guilty of crimes against humanity and war crimes committed in Bosnia and Herzegovina in 1992 and sentenced them each to 22 years' imprisonment.[147] Stanišić, Minister of the Interior of Republika Srpska, and Župljanin,

---

143 See ICTY, Trial Chamber I, *Prosecutor v. Momčilo Perišić*, 'Judgement', Case No. IT-04-81-T (6 September 2011), http://www.icty.org/x/cases/perisic/tjug/en/110906_judgement.pdf (accessed 7 March 2014).

144 See ICTY, Appeals Chamber, *Prosecutor v. Momčilo Perišić*, 'Judgement', Case No. IT-04-81-A (28 February 2013), http://www.icty.org/x/cases/perisic/acjug/en/130228_judgement.pdf (accessed 7 March 2014).

145 Ibid., para 73.

146 Ibid., para 119.

147 See ICTY, Trial Chamber II, *Prosecutor v. Mićo Stanišić and Stojan Župljanin*, 'Judgement', Case No. IT-08-91-T (27 March 2013), http://www.icty.org/x/cases/zupljanin_stanisicm/tjug/en/130327-1.pdf, (Volume 1 of 3) http://www.icty.org/x/cases/zupljanin_stanisicm/tjug/en/130327-2.pdf, (Volume 2 of 3) http://www.icty.org/x/cases/zupljanin_stanisicm/tjug/en/130327-3.pdf (Volume 3 of 3) (accessed 7 March 2014).

former Chief of the Regional Security Services Centre of Banja Luka and member of the Crisis Staff of the Autonomous Region of Krajina, were convicted of serious crimes committed in several municipalities. Many of the crimes were committed in infamous detention facilities in Prijedor, including Omarska, Keraterm and Trnopolje. The judges held that both men participated in a joint criminal enterprise (JCE), "the objective of which was to permanently remove Bosnian Muslims and Bosnian Croats from the territory of the planned Serbian state through the commission of crimes on a massive scale".[148]

A JCE was also established in the *Prlić et al.* case, one of the ICTY's largest and most complex cases (the judgement contained 2,629 pages, divided into six volumes).[149] On 29 May 2013, Trial Chamber III convicted six senior officials from the wartime Croat entity of Herceg-Bosna for crimes against humanity, violations of the laws or customs of war, and grave breaches of the Geneva Conventions committed between 1992 and 1994. All six men were found guilty, (Presiding) Judge Antonetti dissenting as to the form of responsibility, for their participation in a JCE, which had the objective to permanently remove the Muslim population from Herceg-Bosna. Jadranko Prlić, former president of the Croatian Defence Council (HVO), and later of the government of the Croatian Republic of Herceg-Bosna, was sentenced to 25 years' imprisonment; Bruno Stojić, former head of the HVO Department of Defence to 20 years; Milivoj Petković, chief of the HVO Main Staff and later deputy commander of the HVO forces to 20 years; and Valentin Ćorić, chief of the Military Police Administration and later on Minister of the Interior to 16 years.[150] Slobodan Praljak, former Assistant Minister of Defence of Croatia and later commander of the Main Staff of the HVO, was convicted of 20 counts and was sentenced to 20 years' imprisonment and finally, Berislav Pušić, former president of the HVO commission in charge of the exchange of prisoners and other persons and head of the HVO Commission in charge of detention facilities, was convicted of 18 counts and received 10 years' imprisonment.[151] The siege and shelling of Mostar and the infamous destruction of the Old Bridge was also addressed by the Trial Chamber. About this, President Antonetti, reading the summary of the judgment, stated:

> On 8 November 1993, as part of the offensive, an HVO tank fired throughout the day at the Old Bridge until it was unusable and on the verge of collapse. The Bridge then collapsed on the morning of 9 November 1993. The Chamber finds, by a majority, with the Presiding Judge dissenting, that although the Bridge was used by the Army of Bosnia-Herzegovina (ABiH) and thus constituted a legitimate military target for the HVO, its destruction caused disproportionate damage to the Muslim civilian population of Mostar.[152]

---

[148] *Prosecutor v. Mićo Stanišić and Stojan Župljanin*, supra n 147, (Volume 2 of 3), paras 929 (Stanišić) and 948 (Župljanin).

[149] For the six volumes (in French), see http://www.icty.org/case/prlic/4 (accessed 2 May 2014).

[150] See ICTY, Press Release, 'Six Senior Herceg-Bosna Officials Convicted' (29 May 2013), http://icty.org/sid/11324 (accessed 2 May 2014).

[151] Ibid.

[152] See ICTY, Trial Chamber, 'Judgement Summary for Jadranko Prlić and others' (29 May 2013), http://www.icty.org/x/cases/prlic/tjug/en/130529_summary_en.pdf (accessed 2 May 2014), p. 3.

Only one day later, on 30 May 2013, the majority of Trial Chamber I, Judge Picard dissenting, acquitted of all charges Jovica Stanišić, former Chief of the Serbian State Security Service and Franko Simatović, former employee of the Serbian State Security Service.[153] According to the Prosecution, the two men had participated in a JCE, the purpose of which was the forcible and permanent removal of the majority of non-Serbs from large areas of Croatia and Bosnia-Herzegovina, and had directed, organized, equipped, trained, armed, financed, planned, ordered, and otherwise aided and abetted the crimes that were committed by the Serbian Security Service units.[154] The judges found that these units had indeed committed serious crimes (persecution as a crime against humanity) against non-Serb civilians from Bosnia-Herzegovina and Croatia between 1991 and 1995, but they held, Judge Picard dissenting, that the two men could not be held criminally responsible for these crimes as they lacked the intent to further the JCE's common criminal purpose.[155] In addition, the majority found that Stanišić and Simatović had not planned or ordered the crimes and that in the instances that the two had assisted the units, this assistance was not specifically directed towards the commission of crimes.[156]

In the *Karadžić* case, the Appeals Chamber unanimously reversed, on 11 July 2013, Karadžić's acquittal for genocide in municipalities of Bosnia-Herzegovina, which was entered at the close of the Prosecution case on 28 June 2012 by Trial Chamber III pursuant to Rule 98*bis* ICTY RPE, which states that "[a]t the close of the Prosecutor's case, the Trial Chamber shall, by oral decision and after hearing the oral submissions of the parties, enter a judgement of acquittal on any count if there is no evidence capable of supporting a conviction".[157] According to Trial Chamber III, there was "no evidence, even taken at its highest, which could be capable of supporting a conviction for genocide", through Karadžić's participation in a JCE, the purpose of which was to permanently remove Bosnian Muslims and Bosnian Croats from municipalities in Bosnia and Herzegovina between 31 March 1992 and 31 December 1992.[158] Conversely, the Appeals Chamber was of the opinion that the Trial Chamber erred by finding that evidence adduced by the Prosecution was incapable of proving certain types of genocidal acts.[159] It held that certain evidence, taken at its highest, could prove that the underlying genocidal acts

---

[153] See ICTY, Press Release, 'Jovica Stanišić and Franko Simatović acquitted of all charges' (30 May 2013), http://icty.org/sid/11329 (accessed 4 May 2014). For the judgment itself, see http://icty.org/x/cases/stanisic_simatovic/tjug/en/130530_judgement_p1.pdf (Volume 1) and http://icty.org/x/cases/stanisic_simatovic/tjug/en/130530_judgement_p2.pdf (Volume 2).

[154] Ibid.

[155] Ibid.

[156] Ibid.

[157] See ICTY, Press Release, 'Appeals Chamber reverses Radovan Karadžić's acquittal for genocide in municipalities of Bosnia and Herzegovina' (11 July 2013), http://icty.org/sid/11345 (accessed 4 May 2014).

[158] Ibid.

[159] Ibid.

of causing serious bodily or mental harm[160] and the underlying genocidal act of deliberately inflicting conditions of life calculated to bring about the physical destruction of victims[161] in fact occurred. In addition, the Appeals Chamber was of the opinion that the Trial Chamber's conclusion that the evidence adduced by the Prosecution was incapable of proving that Karadžić (and other members of the JCE) possessed relevant genocidal intent was incorrect.[162] To illustrate this point, the Appeals Chamber noted for instance that Karadžić allegedly stated that his goal was "to get rid of the enemies in our house, the Croats and Muslims, and not to be in the same state with them [anymore]"[163] and that Muslims would disappear and be annihilated if war started in Bosnia.[164] The Appeals Chamber consequently sent the matter back to the Trial Chamber for further action, taking into account its judgment.

In the summer of 2013, something peculiar happened at the ICTY, which sparked a lot of discussion in the media. On 6 June 2013, the Danish Judge Frederik Harhoff circulated a private e-mail to 56 recipients,[165] in which he criticized the Appeals Chamber's acquittals in the *Gotovina* (see last year's *Year in Review*) and *Perišić* (see above) cases and the Trial Chamber's acquittal in the *Stanišić/Simatović* (see above) case. In his letter, he referred, among other things, to "a more or less set practice at the court [until the autumn of 2012] that military commanders were held responsible for war crimes that their subordinates committed during the war in the former Yugoslavia from 1992 to 1995"[166] and wondered whether the military establishment in leading states, such as the US and Israel, felt that the judges were getting too close to the military commanders' responsibilities, whether, as a result of this, ICTY President Meron was put under pressure by US or Israeli officials to ensure a change of direction and finally, whether Meron himself had exerted pressure on his colleagues in deliberations.[167] Harhoff concluded his e-mail, stating:

> The latest judgements here have brought me before a deep professional and moral dilemma, not previously faced. The worst of it is the suspicion that some of my colleagues have been behind a short-sighted political pressure that completely changes the premises of my work in my service to wisdom and the law.

---

160 See ICTY, Appeals Chamber, *Prosecutor v. Radovan Karadžić*, 'Judgement', Case No. IT-95-5/18-AR98bis.1 (11 July 2013), http://www.icty.org/x/cases/karadzic/acjug/en/130711_judgement_rule98bis.pdf (accessed 4 May 2014), paras 37–38.

161 Ibid., paras 49–50.

162 Ibid., paras 97–102.

163 Ibid., para 98.

164 Ibid.

165 See http://www.bt.dk/sites/default/files-dk/node-files/511/6/6511917-letter-english.pdf (accessed 4 May 2014).

166 Ibid.

167 Ibid.

As Harhoff was also on the bench in the *Šešelj* case, the Defence in that case argued that the 6 June e-mail showed the Judge's bias in the *Šešelj* proceedings. As a result, on 9 July 2013, a motion was filed seeking the disqualification of Harhoff from the *Šešelj* case and on 28 August 2013, Judge Harfhoff was indeed disqualified.[168] The Chamber reasoned:

> By referring to a "set practice" of convicting accused persons without reference to an evaluation of the evidence in each individual case, the Majority, Judge Liu dissenting, considers that there are grounds for concluding that a reasonable observer, properly informed, would reasonably apprehend bias on the part of Judge Harhoff in favor of conviction. This includes for the purposes of the present case. This appearance of bias is further compounded by Judge Harhoff's statement that he is confronted by a professional and moral dilemma, which in the view of the Majority, is a clear reference to his difficulty in applying the current jurisprudence of the Tribunal.[169]

#### 7.2.1.2 International Criminal Tribunal for Rwanda

On 4 February 2013, the Appeals Chamber of the International Criminal Tribunal for Rwanda (ICTR) acquitted and released Justin Mugenzi and Prosper Mugiraneza.[170] Mugenzi was Minister of Trade and Industry and Mugiraneza was Minister of Civil Service in the Interim Government in April 1994,[171] when Jean-Baptiste Habyalimana was removed as prefect of the Butare Prefecture and was replaced by Sylvain Nsabimana.[172] On this day, 19 April 1994, Interim President Théodore Sindikubwabo delivered an infamous speech calling for the killing of Tutsis.[173] In 2011, Trial Chamber II of the ICTR found Mugenzi and Mugiraneza guilty of conspiracy to commit genocide (based on their roles in removing Habyalimana) and guilty of direct and public incitement to commit genocide (based on their roles in the installation of Nsabimana) and sentenced them each to 30 years' imprisonment.[174]

---

[168] See ICTY, Press Release, 'Judge Harhoff disqualified from Šešelj case' (29 August 2013) http://icty.org/sid/11357 (accessed 4 May 2014).

[169] See ICTY, Chamber Convened by Order of the Vice-President, *Prosecutor v. Vojislav Šešelj*, 'Decision on Defence Motion for Disqualification of Judge Frederik Harhoff and Report to the Vice-President', Case No. IT-03-67-T (28 August 2013), http://www.icty.org/x/cases/seselj/tdec/en/130828.pdf (accessed 4 May 2014), para 13.

[170] See ICTR, Appeals Chamber, *Justin Mugenzi and Prosper Mugiraneza v. The Prosecutor*, 'Judgement', Case No. ICTR-99-50-A (4 February 2013), http://www.unictr.org/Portals/0/Case%5CEnglish%5CMugenzi%5CJudgment%5C130204-Appeal%20Judgment.pdf (accessed 4 May 2014).

[171] Ibid., paras 2–3.

[172] Ibid., para 4.

[173] Ibid.

[174] Ibid.

However, the Appeals Chamber reversed these convictions due to errors in the Trial Chamber's assessment of circumstantial evidence, with Judge Liu dissenting on the reversal with regard to the convictions for conspiracy to commit genocide.[175] For instance, it noted

> that the Trial Chamber erred in concluding that the only reasonable inference that could be drawn from the evidence on the record is that Mugenzi and Mugiraneza knew that Sindikubwabo's speech at the ceremony would be aimed at sparking the killing of Tutsis and that, therefore, their presence at the ceremony demonstrates their shared genocidal intent.[176]

#### 7.2.1.3 Mechanism for International Criminal Tribunals

On 1 July 2013, The Hague Branch of the Mechanism for International Criminal Tribunals (MICT) was launched,[177] following the Arusha Branch that already commenced on 1 July 2012 (see last year's *Year in Review*). The MICT was established in the context of the Completion Strategies of the *ad hoc* tribunals and is mandated to continue a number of functions from the ICTY and ICTR after they have completed their mandate and to preserve their legacy.

On 17 July 2013, officials of the ICTR/MICT handed over the case file of Bernard Munyagishari, charged with conspiracy to commit genocide, genocide, complicity in genocide and crimes against humanity for murder and rape, to a representative of the Rwandan Prosecutor General's Office, hereby marking the last of such transfers pursuant to Rule 11*bis* of the ICTR RPE ('Referral of the Indictment to another Court') and concluding an important phase in the ICTR's Completion Strategy.[178]

Finally, on 14 October 2013, MICT President Meron presented the first Annual Report of the MICT[179] to the UN General Assembly.[180] Meron addressed, among

---

175 See ICTR, Press Release, 'Appeals Chamber Acquits and Releases Justin Mugenzi and Prosper Mugiraneza', ICTR/INFO-9-2-738.EN (4 February 2013), http://www.unictr.org/tabid/155/Default.aspx?id=1344 (accessed 4 May 2014).

176 See ICTR, Appeals Chamber, *Justin Mugenzi and Prosper Mugiraneza v. The Prosecutor*, 'Judgement', Case No. ICTR-99-50-A (4 February 2013), http://www.unictr.org/Portals/0/Case%5CEnglish%5CMugenzi%5CJudgment%5C130204-Appeal%20Judgment.pdf (accessed 4 May 2014), para 138.

177 See UNMICT, Press Release, 'Mechanism for International Criminal Tribunals (MICT) begins work in The Hague' (1 July 2013), http://unmict.org/news/2013/130701_PR10.html (accessed 5 May 2014).

178 See ICTR, Press Release, 'ICTR Prosecutor Hands Over Last Case File to Rwanda', ICTR/INFO-9-2-743.EN (24 July 2013), http://www.unictr.org/tabid/155/Default.aspx?id=1356 (accessed 5 May 2014).

179 The report can be found here: http://unmict.org/files/documents/annual_reports/130801-annual-report_en.pdf (accessed 5 May 2014).

180 See UNMICT, Press Release, 'President Meron presents first Annual Report to the United Nations General Assembly' (14 October 2013), http://unmict.org/news/2013/131014_PR15.html (accessed 5 May 2014).

other things, the important issue of fugitives. Indeed, almost 20 years after the Rwandan genocide, there are still nine individuals at large initially indicted by the ICTR. Three of them (Augustin Bizimana, Félicien Kabuga and Protais Mpiranya), if arrested, will be tried by the MICT and the cases of the remaining six (Fulgence Kayishema, Charles Sikubwabo, Ladislas Ntaganzwa, Aloys Ndimbati, Charles Ryandikayo and Phénéas Munyarugarama) have been referred to Rwanda.

#### 7.2.1.4 International Criminal Court

2013 was an eventful year for the International Criminal Court (ICC, the Court), in no small part due to the various developments in the cases related to the Kenyan situation, and the political and media interest generated by these cases. In February 2013, it became clear that 'OTP-4', a key witness for the Prosecution during the confirmation stages of the trial, had received a bribe to withdraw his evidence and in an interview with the Prosecution testified that he had lied while giving testimony prior to the confirmation stage. His evidence had been key in placing Muthaura at a series of organizational meetings related to the post-election violence. Both the Defence teams for Muthaura and Kenyatta argued that the cases had to be returned to the confirmation stage.[181] In response, the Prosecution argued that there was still substantial evidence against Kenyatta, but that "the witness whose statement is at issue was essential on the issue of Mr Muthaura's criminal responsibility and, in fact, was the only direct witness against him".[182] The Prosecutor conceded that Muthaura presented the "extremely rare case where it is appropriate to contemplate sending the case back to the Pre-Trial Chamber for reconsideration…"[183] At a status conference on 11 March 2013, Prosecutor Fatou Bensouda announced that her office was dropping all charges against Muthaura, stating that the evidentiary record

---

[181] See ICC, Trial Chamber V, *Situation in the Republic of Kenya, In the case of the Prosecutor v. Francis Kirimi Muthaura and Uhuru Muigai Kenyatta*, 'Defence Application to the Trial Chamber Pursuant to Article 64(4) of the Rome Statute to Refer the Preliminary Issue of the Confirmation Decision to the Pre-Trial Chamber for Reconsideration', Case No. ICC-01/09-02/11 (5 February 2013), http://www.icc-cpi.int/iccdocs/doc/doc1548545.pdf (accessed 4 June 2014); and ICC, Trial Chamber V, *Situation in the Republic of Kenya, In the case of the Prosecutor v. Francis Kirimi Muthaura and Uhuru Muigai Kenyatta* (hereinafter: *Prosecutor v. Muthaura and Kenyatta*), 'Defence Application pursuant to Article 64(4) for an order to refer back to Pre-Trial Chamber II or a Judge of the Pre-Trial Division the Preliminary issue of the Validity of the Decision on the Confirmation of Charges for an order striking out new facts alleged in the Prosecution's Pre-Trial Brief and Request for an extension of the page limit pursuant to Regulation 37(2)', Case No. ICC-01/09-02/11 (7 February 2013), http://www.icc-cpi.int/iccdocs/doc/doc1549410.pdf (accessed 4 June 2014), para 2.

[182] See ICC, Trial Chamber V, *Prosecutor v. Muthaura and Kenyatta*, 'Public redacted version of the 25 February 2013 Consolidated Prosecution response to the Defence applications under Article 64 of the Statute to refer the confirmation decision back to the Pre-Trial Chamber', Case No. ICC-01/09-02/11 (25 February 2013), http://www.icc-cpi.int/iccdocs/doc/doc1557330.pdf (accessed 4 June 2014), para 9.

[183] Ibid., para 44.

against him was no longer sufficient to secure a conviction. In the same statement, the Prosecution indicated that the case had presented "serious investigative challenges", including a "limited pool of potential witnesses…others who are unwilling to testify or provide evidence" and "limited cooperation" from the Government of Kenya.[184] In a press release following the decision, the Prosecutor stressed that this decision applied only to Muthaura and was based only on the specific facts of the Muthaura case, and not on any other considerations.[185] Slightly earlier in March 2013, Uhuru Kenyatta and William Ruto, two of the four defendants in the cases *The Prosecutor v. William Samoei Ruto and Joshua Arap Sang* and *The Prosecutor v. Francis Kirimi Muthaura and Uhuru Muigai Kenyatta* were elected President and Vice President of the Republic of Kenya, respectively, a result which was confirmed by Supreme Court of Kenya. Uhuru Kenyatta was inaugurated on 9 April 2013, and so became the second sitting head of state to be indicted by the ICC. A key issue that arose in the cases in the spring and summer months of 2013, was whether the two defendants, Ruto and Kenyatta, who now also had duties as heads of state, must be physically present throughout their trials. On 28 February 2013, the Defence teams for Ruto and Muthaura jointly filed 'Joint Defence Submissions on Legal Basis for the Accused's Presence at Trial via Video Link' ('Video Link Application'), requesting the Chamber to authorize the use of video link technology.[186] On 17 April 2013, Ruto requested to waive his right to be present during the trial. In the alternative he requested to participate via video link.[187] In an 18 June 2013 decision, Trial Chamber V (a) decided by majority, with Judge Olga Herrera Carbuccia dissenting, to grant the request conditionally, and excused Ruto from continuous presence at trial, except during opening and closing statements, statements from victims and if applicable, sentencing hearings, victim impact hearings, reparation hearings and "any other attendance directed by the Chamber".[188] However, on 25

[184] See ICC, Trial Chamber V, *Prosecutor v. Muthaura and Kenyatta*, 'Prosecution Notification of withdrawal of the charges against Francis Kirimi Muthaura', Case No. ICC-01/09-02/11 (11 March 2013), http://www.icc-cpi.int/iccdocs/doc/ICC-01-09-02-11-687.pdf (accessed 4 June 2014), para 11.

[185] See ICC, Press Release, 'Statement by ICC Prosecutor on the notice to withdraw charges against Mr Muthaura' (11 March 2013), http://www.icc-cpi.int/en_menus/icc/press%20and%20media/press%20releases/Pages/OTP-statement-11-03-2013.aspx (accessed 4 June 2014).

[186] See ICC, Trial Chamber V, *Prosecutor v. Muthaura and Kenyatta*, 'Joint Defence submissions on Legal Basis for the Accused's Presence at Trial via Video Link', Case No. ICC-01/09-02/11 (28 February 2013), http://www.icc-cpi.int/iccdocs/doc/doc1560298.pdf (accessed 4 April 2014).

[187] See ICC, Trial Chamber V, *Prosecutor v. Muthaura and Kenyatta*, 'Defence Request Pursuant to Article 63(1) of the Rome Statute', Case No. ICC-01/09-02/11 (17 April 2013), http://www.icc-cpi.int/iccdocs/doc/doc1580797.pdf (accessed 4 April 2014).

[188] See ICC, Trial Chamber V, *Prosecutor v. Muthaura and Kenyatta*, 'Decision on Mr Ruto's Request for Excusal from Continuous Presence at Trial', Case No. ICC-01/09-02/11 (18 June 2013), http://www.icc-cpi.int/iccdocs/doc/doc1605793.pdf (accessed 4 April 2014), para 3a.

October 2013, the Appeals Chamber unanimously reversed this decision, finding that the Trial Chamber had interpreted the scope of its discretion to excuse attendance too broadly, and that absence should be exceptional and decided on a case-by-case basis.[189] In the *Kenyatta* case, on 23 September 2013, Defence counsel filed a request that Kenyatta be conditionally excused from continuous presence at trial. On 18 October 2013 Trial Chamber V (b) conditionally granted the Defence request, "in order to permit him to discharge his functions of state as the executive President of Kenya; while his trial proceeds, as it must do, in this Court".[190] Similar to the Trial Chamber V (a) decision in the Ruto/Sang case, it was decided that Kenyatta must be present during opening and closing statements, during victim statements, during the delivery of judgment in the case and, if applicable, during sentencing, victim impact and reparation hearings.[191] On 28 October 2013, the Prosecutor asked Trial Chamber V (b) to reconsider its decision, or grant leave to appeal, in light of the recent Appeals Chamber decision reversing a similar decision in the Ruto/Sang case. On 26 November 2013, Trial Chamber V (b) reviewed its decision from a month prior, and in light of the "legal clarifications provided by the Appeals chamber in its recent judgment on the manner", held by majority that as a general rule, Kenyatta must be present at trial and that any future requests to be excused from attending parts of the trial would be considered on a case-by-case basis.[192] A further issue to be resolved prior to the opening of trial in both cases was the issue of where the trial should take place. On 24 January 2013, the Defence in the Ruto/Sang case, applied for a change of place where the Court shall sit for trial. Arguing that a similar request had been made and considered in 2012 in the Kenyatta case, and that "the two cases are inextricably linked in terms of their listing and it would be impractical to have the two trials heard in different places as far apart as The Hague and East Africa", the Defence requested that the venue be changed from The Hague to either Kenya or Tanzania, and that this change would

[189] See ICC, Trial Chamber V, *Prosecutor v. Muthaura and Kenyatta*, 'Judgment on the appeal of the Prosecutor against the decision of Trial Chamber V(a) of 18 June 2013 entitled Decision on Mr Ruto's Request for Excusal from Continuous Presence at Trial', Case No. ICC-01/09-02/11 (25 October 2013), http://www.icc-cpi.int/iccdocs/doc/doc1669852.pdf (accessed 4 April 2014), paras 46 and 63.

[190] See ICC, Trial Chamber V(B), *Prosecutor v. Muthaura and Kenyatta*, 'Decision on Defence Request for Conditional Excusal from Continuous Presence at Trial', Case No. ICC-01/09-02/11 (18 October 2013), http://www.icc-cpi.int/iccdocs/doc/doc1667182.pdf (accessed 4 April 2014), para 4.

[191] Ibid., para 5.

[192] See ICC, Press Release, 'Kenyatta case: ICC Trial Chamber V(b) reviews decision on presence of accused at trial' (26 November 2013), http://www.icc-cpi.int/en_menus/icc/press%20and%20media/press%20releases/Pages/PR965.aspx (accessed 4 April 2014).

be "in the respective interests of all the parties concerned".[193] On 3 June 2013, Trial Chamber V (a), after having obtained observations from the parties and participants in the Ruto/Sang case, as well as from the Government of Kenya and the Registrar of the ICTR, issued a recommendation to the Presidency that "it may be desirable to hold the commencement of trial and other portions thereof, to be determined at a later stage, in Kenya or, alternatively, in Tanzania", citing the potential benefits of holding the trial close to the locality where the alleged crimes were committed and as a means of bringing justice closer to the victims.[194] In a 15 July 2013 decision, issued after a discussion and a vote on the matter under Rule 100 of the ICC's Rules of Procedure and Evidence, which requires that all 18 ICC judges vote on a proposal to move the venue of the Court from The Hague, the ICC judges decided that the trials will be held in The Hague. They did not reach the required two-thirds majority necessary for a decision to change the location of the hearing. They stated that while in principle in favor of bringing ICC proceedings closer to the affected communities, they had reached their conclusion taking into account security, the cost of holding proceedings outside The Hague, the potential impact on victims and witnesses, the length of the proceedings, the potential impact on the perception of the Court and the impact on its ability to conduct and support other proceedings that are taking place simultaneously at the Court.[195] In a further development, prior to the start of trial in the *Ruto/Sang* case, the Prosecution on 22 July 2013 requested permission to amend the charges against Ruto and Sang by broadening the scope in relation to the crimes allegedly committed in the greater Eldoret area on 30 and 31 December 2007, but on 16 August 2013, Pre-Trial Chamber II rejected this request, deciding that it would unduly compromise the rights of the accused.[196] The Ruto/Sang trial opened on 10 September 2013, but was adjourned shortly after to allow Vice-President Ruto to deal with the Westgate mall attack in Kenya at the end of September. The start of the Kenyatta trial was postponed until early 2014, but on 19 December 2013, Prosecutor Fatou Bensouda communicated to Trial Chamber V (b) that witness P-0012 had admitted to providing false evidence regarding "the event at the heart of the case against the accused" and that they no longer intended to call

[193] See ICC, The Presidency, *Situation in the Republic of Kenya, In the case of the Prosecutor v. William Samoei Ruto and Joshua Arap Sang* (hereinafter: *Prosecutor v. Ruto and Sang*), 'Joint Defence Application for a Change of Place where the Court Shall Sit for Trial', Case No. ICC-01/09-01/11 (24 January 2013), http://www.icc-cpi.int/iccdocs/doc/doc1544498.pdf (accessed 5 April 2014), paras 23 and 25.

[194] See ICC, Trial Chamber V(A), *Prosecutor v. Ruto and Sang*, 'Recommendation to the Presidency on where the Court shall sit for trial', Case No. ICC-01/09-01/11 (3 June 2013), http://www.icc-cpi.int/iccdocs/doc/doc1599761.pdf (accessed 5 April 2014), paras 10 and 11.

[195] See ICC, Press Release, 'Ruto and Sang case: Trial to open in The Hague' (15 July 2013), http://www.icc-cpi.int/en_menus/icc/press%20and%20media/press%20releases/Pages/pr931.aspx (accessed 5 April 2014).

[196] See ICC, Pre-Trial Chamber II, 'Decision on the "Prosecution's Request to Amend the Updated Document Containing the Charges Pursuant to Article 61(9) of the Statute"', Case No. ICC-01/09-01/11 (16 August 2013), http://www.icc-cpi.int/iccdocs/doc/doc1634046.pdf (accessed 5 April 2014), para 42.

P-0012 as a witness. Separately, P-0011, another Prosecution witness, had informed the Office of the Prosecution (OTP) that he was no longer willing to testify at trial. With the loss of these two witnesses, the Prosecution considered that it no longer had sufficient evidence to proceed to trial and requested a 3-month adjournment of the 5 February 2014 trial date in order to pursue additional investigative steps.[197] In November 2013, the AU and Kenya attempted to secure a deferral of the Kenyan cases under the Security Council's powers as per Article 16 of the Rome Statute, but the draft resolution failed to secure the requisite nine votes in favor to pass.[198]

In other situations, on 16 January 2013, the OTP finalized the preliminary examination of the Situation in Mali, and having identified cases of sufficient gravity to warrant further action, the Prosecutor announced that her office would open an investigation into alleged crimes committed in Mali since January 2012. The Malian State referred the situation to the ICC in July 2012.[199]

On 14 May 2013, the Union of the Comoros referred the situation "with respect to the 31 May 2010 Israeli raid on the Humanitarian Aid Flotilla bound for Gaza Strip." As per Article 12(2)a of the Rome Statute, the ICC can exercise its jurisdiction over crimes committed on a vessel if the State of registration is a State Party to the Rome Statute.[200]

Early 2013 also began with the confirmation of charges hearing in the case against Laurent Gbagbo, the former President of Côte d'Ivoire. The hearing began on 19 February 2013 and ended a week later on 28 February 2013. The purpose of the confirmation of charges hearing in the Rome Statute framework is to establish whether there is enough evidence to establish substantial grounds to believe that the person committed the crimes charged. Three months later, in early June 2013, Pre-Trial I adjourned the confirmation of charges and requested that the Prosecutor consider providing further evidence or conducting a further investigation. The judges, with Judge Sylvia Fernández de Gurmendi dissenting,[201] found the evidence presented by the Prosecution insufficient, but they did not decline to confirm the charges against Laurent Gbagbo, because they found that there was some

---

197 See ICC, Trial Chamber V(B), *Prosecutor v. Muthaura and Kenyatta*, 'Notification of the removal of a witness from the Prosecution's witness list and application of an adjournment of the provisional trial date', Case No. ICC-01/09-02/11 (19 December 2013), http://www.icc-cpi.int/iccdocs/doc/doc1703998.pdf (accessed 5 April 2014).

198 See M. Nichols, 'Africa fails to get Kenya ICC trials deferred at the United Nations', *Reuters* (15 November 2013), http://www.reuters.com/article/2013/11/15/us-kenya-icc-un-idUSBRE9AE0S420131115 (accessed 4 June 2014).

199 See ICC, Press Release, 'ICC Prosecutor opens investigation into war crimes in Mali: "The legal requirements have been met. We will investigate."'(16 January 2013), http://www.icc-cpi.int/en_menus/icc/press%20and%20media/press%20releases/news%20and%20highlights/Pages/pr869.aspx (accessed 4 April 2014).

200 See ICC, Press Release, '2010 events on Comorian, Greek and Cambodian vessels: Situation assigned to ICC Pre-Trial Chamber I' (5 July 2013), http://www.icc-cpi.int/en_menus/icc/press%20and%20media/press%20releases/Pages/pr926.aspx (accessed 4 April 2014).

201 See 'Dissenting Opinion of Judge Silvia Fernández de Gurmendi' (3 June 2013), http://www.icc-cpi.int/iccdocs/doc/doc1599832.pdf (accessed 4 April 2014).

relevance and probative value to the evidence presented. Rather than declining to confirm the charges, they chose not to make a final determination, and provided the Prosecutor with the opportunity to provide further evidence by November 2013, providing the Prosecutor with an additional 6-month window. In the majority decision, the judges were critical of the Prosecutor's reliance on anonymous hearsay, as often contained in reports of nongovernmental organizations (NGOs) and press articles, with regard to key elements of the case.

> "Such pieces of evidence cannot in any way be presented as the fruits of a full and proper investigation by the Prosecutor…Even though NGO reports and press articles may be a useful introduction to the historical context of a conflict situation, they do not usually constitute a valid substitute for the type of evidence that is required to meet the evidentiary threshold for the confirmation of charges".[202]

In the timeline set out by the judges, it was envisioned that all parties would make written submissions in response to the additional evidence set out by the Prosecution, and that the Chamber would issue a decision on the confirmation of charges by April 2014.[203] However, in August 2013, the OTP appealed the 3 June 2013 decision to adjourn the confirmation of charges hearing and on 16 December 2013, the Appeals Chamber issued a decision upholding the Pre-Trial Chamber decision[204] and on 17 December 2013 set out a new calendar requiring the Prosecutor to submit to the Defence all evidence on which she intends to rely by 13 January 2014, with further proceedings extending into 2014. A second key development in the case against Laurent Gbagbo in 2013 was the ruling on an admissibility challenge, which was brought by Gbagbo's Defence on 15 February 2013. In the challenge, it was advanced that Laurent Gbagbo had in August 2011 been charged with and was being prosecuted for economic crimes allegedly committed during the post-electoral crisis in Côte d'Ivoire, and that these proceedings must be presumed to be ongoing on the national level. It was further advanced that the national proceedings against Gbagbo constitute the same case as the ICC case, because it related to the same context, the same general conduct and "the alleged will of Mr. Gbagbo to implement a policy to remain in power".[205] The admissibility challenge argued that

---

[202] See ICC, Pre-Trial Chamber I, *Situation in the Republic of Côte d'Ivoire, in the case of the Prosecutor v. Laurent Gbagbo* (hereinafter: *Prosecutor v. Gbagbo*), 'Decision adjourning the hearing on the confirmation of charges pursuant to Article 61(7)(c)(i) of the Rome Statute', Case No. ICC-02/11-01/11 (3 June 2013), http://www.icc-cpi.int/iccdocs/doc/doc1599831.pdf (accessed 5 April 2014), p. 16.

[203] Ibid., p 24.

[204] See ICC, Appeals Chamber, *Prosecutor v. Gbagbo*, 'Judgment on the appeal of the Prosecutor against the decision of Pre-Trial Chamber I of 3 June 2013 entitled "Decision adjourning the hearing on the confirmation of charges pursuant to Article 61(7(c)(i) of the Rome Statute"', Case No. ICC-02/11-01/11 (OA5) (16 December 2013), http://www.icc-cpi.int/en_menus/icc/situations%20and%20cases/situations/icc0211/related%20cases/icc02110111/court%20records/chambers/appeals-chamber/Pages/572.aspx (accessed 5 April 2014).

[205] See ICC, Pre-Trial Chamber I, *Prosecutor v. Gbagbo*, 'Decision on the "Requête relative à la recevabilité de l'affaire en vertu des Articles 19 et 17 du Statut"', Case No. ICC-02/11-01/11 (11 June 2013), http://www.icc-cpi.int/iccdocs/doc/doc1602934.pdf (accessed 5 April 2014), para 9.

there were numerous national prosecutions ongoing in relation to the post-electoral crisis and that these proceedings should indicate that Ivorian authorities were willing and able to carry out proceedings. In response, the Prosecution argued that even if national proceedings had been started, they had been suspended since Gbagbo's transfer to The Hague in November 2011. The OTP concluded that the Ivorian authorities had demonstrated a willingness to prosecute crimes on a national level, but that in transferring Gbagbo to The Hague, they had relinquished jurisdiction to the ICC. In addition, it advanced that the notion of 'substantially the same conduct' was too broad, and that the threshold should be whether "at a minimum, the national authorities are focused on the same course of conduct and series of events as the ICC, meaning that they are examining the person's criminal responsibility in the context of substantially the same incidents and underlying facts and allegations of criminal responsibility".[206] It was argued that the economic crimes with which Gbagbo may have been charged on a national level related to criminal conduct in obtaining the funds, but not the subsequent alleged use of those funds to contribute to the crimes against humanity which formed the basis of the ICC case.[207] Cote d'Ivoire had also requested authorisation to submit observations on the admissibility challenge, which was granted on 14 March 2013. In observations submitted on 28 March 2013, Cote d'Ivoire maintained that the case against Gbagbo was admissible because there were no "relevant proceedings against him at the national level" and that national authorities had in fact refrained from initiating proceedings against Gbagbo for violent crimes in view of the ICC proceedings.[208] On 11 June 2013, Pre-Trial Chamber I issued its decision rejecting the challenge and deciding that the case is still admissible before the ICC because there was no tangible proof that steps had been taken to prosecute Gbagbo nationally and that it had not been demonstrated that he was being tried for the same case or any other.[209]

In further developments related to the Cote d'Ivoire situation, on 30 September 2013, the judges of Pre-Trial Chamber I unsealed a warrant of arrest against Charles Blé Goudé, which was initially issued on 21 December 2011. This warrant was the third warrant of arrest issued in the situation in Cote d'Ivoire. The judges found that there are reasonable grounds to believe that, in the aftermath of the 2010 presidential elections in Cote d'Ivoire, pro-Gbagbo forces attacked the civilian population, systematically targeting civilians who were believed to support the opposing candidate. Charles Blé Goudé, an Ivorian national in his forties, allegedly belonged to Gbagbo's inner circle, and allegedly exercised joint control over the crimes and as the former leader of the Young Patriots, the youth wing of the pro-Gbagbo movement, made an essential contribution to the common plan to commit the crimes.

[206] Ibid., para 14.

[207] Ibid.

[208] Ibid., para 21.

[209] See ICC, Press Release, 'ICC Pre-Trial Chamber I rejects challenge to the admissibility of the case against Laurent Gbagbo' (11 June 2013), http://www.icc-cpi.int/en_menus/icc/press%20and%20media/press%20releases/Pages/pr917.aspx (accessed April 4 2014).

As per the warrant, he allegedly bears individual criminal responsibility, as indirect co-perpetrator, for four counts of crimes against humanity, namely murder, rape and other forms of sexual violence, persecution, and other inhumane acts, allegedly committed in the territory of Côte d'Ivoire between 16 December 2010 and 12 April 2011.[210]

Also on 30 September 2013, Côte d'Ivoire challenged the ICC case against Simone Gbagbo and requested a suspension of the arrest warrant against her and obligation to transfer, arguing that it is willing and able to try the former first lady before a national court.

On 18 March 2013, in an unprecedented occurrence, General Bosco Ntaganda, a suspect in the Democratic Republic of the Congo (DRC) situation, surrendered himself to the US embassy in Kigali, Rwanda and requested transfer to the ICC.[211] Bosco Ntaganda had been wanted since 2006 on charges of enlisting and conscripting child soldiers and using them to participate actively in hostilities in the DRC from July 2002 to December 2003. In 2012, Pre-Trial Chamber II issued a second arrest warrant containing additional charges for war crimes and crimes against humanity, stemming from evidence presented during the trial of Thomas Lubanga Dyilo, Bosco Ntaganda's superior. Working in cooperation, Rwandese, American and Dutch authorities facilitated Ntaganda's transfer to The Hague within a week of his surrender. Ntaganda was in ICC custody on 22 March 2014, and he first appeared before ICC judges on 26 March 2014. During this initial appearance, the judges confirmed the identity of Bosco Ntaganda and read out the charges against him, which he immediately denied, prompting Judge Ekaterina Trendafilova to explain to him that he did not need to enter a plea of guilty or innocent at this initial hearing.[212] The confirmation of charges hearing was set for September 2013 but was postponed until early 2014 after the Prosecution requested additional time to prepare for trial.[213]

In another case in the DRC situation, *The Prosecutor v. Germain Katanga and Mathieu Ngudjolo Chui*, Trial Chamber II had in late 2012 informed the parties that it was proposing a re-characterisation of facts relating to Germain Katanga's mode of liability from commission of a crime in the form of indirect co-perpetration (25 (3)(a) of the Rome Statute), to complicity in the commission of a crime by a group of persons acting with a common purpose. This decision did not concern Mathieu

---

[210] See ICC, Pre-Trial Chamber III, *Situation in the Republic of Côte d'Ivoire, In the case of The Prosecutor v. Charles Blé Goudé*, 'Warrant Of Arrest For Charles Blé Goudé', Case No. ICC-02/11-02/11 (21 December 2013), http://www.icc-cpi.int/iccdocs/PIDS/press/ICC-02-11-02-11-1-Reclass.pdf (accessed 5 April 2014), para 9.

[211] See 'Congo war crimes suspect surrenders at US embassy in Rwanda', supra n 37.

[212] See 'Bosco Ntaganda denies Congo atrocities at international criminal court', *The Guardian* (26 March 2013), http://www.theguardian.com/world/2013/mar/26/bosco-ntaganda-denies-congo-atrocities (accessed 4 April 2014).

[213] See ICC, Pre-Trial Chamber II, *Situation in the Democratic Republic of the Coungo, In the case of The Prosecutor v. Bosco Ntaganda*, 'Decision on the "Prosecution's Urgent Request to Postpone the Date of the Confirmation Hearing" and setting a New Calendar for the Disclosure of Evidence Between the Parties', Case No. ICC-01/04-02/06 (17 June 2013), http://www.icc-cpi.int/iccdocs/doc/doc1605646.pdf (accessed 4 April 2014).

Ngudjolo and effectively severed the charges and the cases against the two accused.[214] Mathieu Ngudjolo was acquitted of all charges against him at the end of 2012 and was released from ICC custody, but was detained by Dutch police shortly thereafter. Ngudjolo requested asylum to avoid repatriation to the DRC and was held in an alien retention center while his application was being processed.[215] On 3 May 2013, the District Court of The Hague ordered the release of Ngudjolo from the detention center at Schiphol Airport in the Netherlands on the basis that there cannot be continuous alien retention during an ongoing asylum procedure. Ngudjolo's former co-defendant Germain Katanga's Defence team appealed the decision to re-characterize the charges on 10 January 2013, arguing that the decision was "unlawful and inappropriate".[216] On 27 March 2013, the Appeals Chamber dismissed this appeal by majority, confirming the Trial Chamber decision to re-characterize the charges. The Appeals Chamber found that the timing of the Trial Chamber II decision, taken at the deliberation stage, and the scope of the proposed change to the mode of liability, were in conformity with the Regulations of the Court. The Chamber also found that the decision did not violate Katanga's right to a fair trial but did emphasize that the Trial Chamber must continue to be vigilant in protecting Katanga's rights—particularly, considering the advanced stage of proceedings, his right to be tried without undue delay.[217] On 19 November 2013, Trial Chamber II scheduled a hearing to deliver the judgment in the case *The Prosecutor v. Germain Katanga* on Friday 7 February 2014.[218]

Finally, also in relation to the DRC situation and the case *The Prosecutor v. Jean-Pierre Bemba Gombo* in particular, Judge Cuno Tarfusser issued a warrant of

---

[214] See ICC, Trial Chamber II, *Situation in the Democratic Republic of the Congo, in the case of The Prosecutor v. Germain Katanga and Mathieu Ngudjolo Chui*, 'Decision on the implementation of regulation 55 of the Regulations of the Court and severing the charges against the accused persons', Case No. ICC-01/04-01/07 (21 November 2012), http://www.icc-cpi.int/iccdocs/doc/doc1529337.pdf (accessed 4 April 2014).

[215] See ICC, Appeals Chamber, *Situation in the Democratic Republic of the Congo, in the case of The Prosecutor v. Mathieu Ngudjolo Chui*, 'Urgent application by Mathieu Ngudjolo's Defence seeking the Appeals Chamber's instructions on the modalities of preparation for the appeals procedure in view of Mathieu Ngudjolo's current situation (Article 67 of the Rome Statute)', Case No. ICC-01/04-02/12 (20 March 2013), http://www.icc-cpi.int/iccdocs/doc/doc1573711.pdf (accessed 4 April 2014), paras 4–5.

[216] See ICC, Appeals Chamber, *Situation in the Democratic Republic of the Congo, in the case of The Prosecutor v. Germain Katanga*, 'Defence's Document in Support of Appeal Against the Decision on the implementation of regulation 55 of the Regulations of the Court and severing the charges against accused persons', Case No. ICC-01/04-01/07 (10 January 2013), http://www.icc-cpi.int/iccdocs/doc/doc1539247.pdf (accessed 5 April 2014), para 12.

[217] See ICC, Press Release, 'Katanga case: Appeals Chamber confirms Trial Chamber II decision on potential modification of the form of responsibility' (27 March 2013), http://www.icc-cpi.int/en_menus/icc/press%20and%20media/press%20releases/Pages/pr892.aspx (accessed 4 June 2014).

[218] See ICC, Press Release, 'Katanga case: Judgment to be delivered on 7 February 2014' (19 November 2013), http://www.icc-cpi.int/en_menus/icc/press%20and%20media/press%20releases/Pages/ma146.aspx (accessed 5 April 2014).

arrest for Jean-Pierre Bemba Gombo, his lead counsel Aimé Kilolo Musamba, his case manager Jean-Jacques Mangenda Kabongo and Fidèle Babala Wandu (a member of the DRC Parliament and Deputy Secretary General of the Mouvement pour la Libération du Congo) and Narcisse Arido (a Defence witness) for offenses against the administration of justice allegedly committed in connection with the case of *The Prosecutor v Jean-Pierre Bemba Gombo*. A few days later, on 23 and 24 November 2013, Aimé Kilolo Musamba was arrested by Belgian authorities, Jean-Jacques Mangenda Kabongo was arrested by Dutch authorities, Narcisse Arido was arrested by the French authorities and the authorities of the DRC arrested Fidèle Babala Wandu. Aimé Kilolo Musamba and Fidèle Babala Wandu were transferred to the ICC Detention center in Scheveningen on 25 November 2013, while Jean-Jacques Mangenda Kabongo and Narcisse Arido were to be transferred to Scheveningen after the completion of national proceedings in France and the Netherlands, respectively. Jean Pierre-Bemba Gombo was already in the custody of the ICC. On 27 November 2013, Aimé Kilolo Musamba, Fidèle Babala Wandu and Jean-Pierre Bemba Gombo made their first appearance before the single Judge of Pre-Trial Chamber II, Judge Cuno Tarfusser, who verified the identity of the suspects, ensured they had been informed of the charges against them, and set a calendar for proceedings leading to the confirmation of charges.

In relation to the Sudan (Darfur) situation, on 6 March 2013, Trial Chamber IV decided that the trial in the case *The Prosecutor v. Abdallah Banda Abakaer Nourain and Saleh Mohammed Jerbo Jamus* was to begin on 5 May 2014, taking into account the necessary preparations needed to prevent interruption to the trial.[219] On 4 October 2013, Trial Chamber IV terminated the proceedings against Saleh Mohammed Jerbo Jamus, a former leader of the JEM rebel group who was to be tried for an attack on AU peacekeepers in 2007. Though there was no official death certificate, the judges decided that the evidence suggested that Jerbo was killed in North Darfur in April 2013.[220] President Omar Al-Bashir—wanted by the ICC for war crimes, crimes against humanity and genocide since 2009—remained at large, travelling to various countries and States Parties without arrest. For instance, in mid-July 2013, Al-Bashir travelled to Nigeria, prompting the President of the Assembly of States Parties to call upon Nigeria to respect its obligations under the Rome Statute, and causing Pre-Trial Chamber II to issue a request to Nigeria to immediately arrest Al-Bashir.[221] On 18 September 2013, ICC judges,

---

[219] See ICC, Press Release, 'Banda and Jerbo Trial to Start on 5 May 2014' (6 March 2013), http://www.icc-cpi.int/en_menus/icc/press%20and%20media/press%20releases/Pages/pr877.aspx (accessed 1 June 2014).

[220] See ICC, Press Release, 'Darfur Situation: Trial Chamber IV terminates proceedings against Saleh Jerbo' (4 October 2014), http://www.icc-cpi.int/en_menus/icc/press%20and%20media/press%20releases/Pages/pr950.aspx (accessed 1 June 2014).

[221] See ICC, Pre-Trial Chamber II, *Situation in Darfur, Sudan, In the case of* The Prosecutor v. *Omar Hassan Ahmad Al Bashir*, 'Decision Regarding Omar Al-Bashir's Visit to the Federal Republic of Nigeria', ICC-02/05-01/09 (15 July 2013), http://www.icc-cpi.int/iccdocs/doc/doc1619414.pdf (accessed 4 April 2014).

informed of Omar Al-Bashir's potential travel to the United States, invited the United States to arrest the President Al-Bashir and transfer him to the ICC.[222]

In the Libya situation, on 6 February 2013 Pre-Trial Chamber I decided that Libya remained under an obligation to surrender Abdullah Al-Senussi to the Court. The obligation to surrender Saif Al Islam Gaddafi had been postponed pending a decision on Libya's May 2012 challenge to the ICC jurisdiction over the case.[223] On 2 April 2013, Libya filed an admissibility challenge against the ICC case against Abdullah Al-Senussi, citing ongoing domestic investigations into alleged crimes committed by him in Libya.[224] In relation to the previous admissibility challenge by Libya against the ICC case against Saif Al Islam Gaddafi, on 31 May 2013, ICC Pre-Trial Chamber I rejected the challenge and ordered his surrender to the Court. The Chamber concluded that Libya's domestic investigation did not sufficiently cover the alleged crimes ('same conduct') as the ICC case. Though the judges acknowledged Libya's efforts to restore the rule of law domestically, they stressed that Libya continues to face difficulties in exercising judicial powers, citing the inability to secure Gaddafi into state custody as an example.[225] Libyan authorities appealed this decision on 7 June 2013 and requested a suspension of the surrender order of Saif Gaddafi to the court while a final decision on the admissibility challenge was pending. On 18 July 2013, the ICC Appeals Chamber rejected this request and on 23 July 2013, Gaddafi's (court-appointed) Defence requested that the Pre-Trial Chamber find that Libya has failed to cooperate with Court orders by deliberating to surrender Saif Al Islam Gaddafi to the Court and refer the matter to the UN Security Council. [226]

On 11 October 2013, ICC Pre-Trial Chamber I decided that the case against former Libyan head of intelligence Abdullah Al-Senussi was inadmissible before the ICC and that it was to proceed in Libya on the basis that Libyan authorities were both willing and able to effectively prosecute him. This decision marked the first

---

[222] See ICC, Press Release, 'Al Bashir case: ICC Judges invite the US to arrest the suspect and transfer him to the Court' (18 September 2013) http://www.icc-cpi.int/en_menus/icc/press%20and%20media/press%20releases/Pages/pr942.aspx (accessed 1 June 2014).

[223] See ICC, Pre-Trial Chamber I, *Situation in Libya, In the case of The Prosecutor v. Saif Al-Islam Gaddafi and Abdullah Al-Senussi*, 'Decision on the "Urgent Application on behalf of Abdullah Al-Senussi for Pre-Trial Chamber to order the Libyan Authorities to comply with their obligations and the orders of the ICC"', Case No. ICC-01/11-01/11 (6 February 2013), http://www.icc-cpi.int/iccdocs/doc/doc1549214.pdf (accessed 5 April 2014).

[224] See ICC, Pre-Trial Chamber I, *Situation in Libya, In the case of The Prosecutor v. Abdullah Al-Senussi*, 'Summary of the Decision on the admissibility of the case against Mr Abdullah Al-Senussi', http://www.icc-cpi.int/en_menus/icc/press%20and%20media/press%20releases/Documents/pr953/Summary%20AL-Senussi%20English.pdf (accessed 4 April 2014).

[225] See ICC, Press Release, 'ICC Pre-Trial Chamber I rejects Libyan challenge to the admissibility of the case against Saif Al Islam Gaddafi' (31 May 2013), http://www.icc-cpi.int/en_menus/icc/press%20and%20media/press%20releases/Pages/pr911.aspx (accessed 4 June 2014).

[226] See ICC, Press Release, 'ICC Appeals Chamber rejects the Libyan authorities' request to suspend the surrender of Saif Al-Islam Gaddafi to the Court' (18 July 2013), http://www.icc-cpi.int/en_menus/icc/press%20and%20media/press%20releases/Pages/pr934.aspx (accessed 4 June 2014).

time that ICC judges ruled in favour of a government challenge to ICC jurisdiction.[227] Abdullah Al-Senussi's Defence team appealed the decision on 17 October 2013 and requested that the decision be suspended pending a final ruling.[228]

With regards to ratifications and other institutional developments within the Court, in early 2013, on 15 January, Luxembourg became the fourth state party to ratify the amendments on the crime of aggression that were adopted at the 2010 Review Conference of the Court in Kampala, Uganda.[229] In later months, Estonia, Botswana and Germany followed suit, with ratifications on 28 March 2013 and 6 June, becoming the fifth, sixth and seventh state parties, respectively.[230] Towards the end of the year, on 1 October and 29 November, Andorra, Cyprus, Slovenia, Uruguay and Belgium ratified the amendments, with Belgium becoming the twelfth state party to ratify the amendments on the crime of aggression.[231] The Court may exercise jurisdiction over the crime of aggression when thirty states parties have ratified the amendments, and subject to a decision to be taken after 1 January 2017 by the States Parties. In other ratifications, on 18 March 2013, Cote d'Ivoire became the 122nd State Party to the Rome Statute, after having previously accepted the jurisdiction of the Court in 2003 and again in 2010.[232] In further institutional

---

[227] See ICC, Press Release, 'ICC Pre-Trial Chamber I decides that the Al-Senussi case is to proceed in Libya and is inadmissible before the ICC' (11 October 2013), http://www.icc-cpi.int/en_menus/icc/press%20and%20media/press%20releases/Pages/pr953.aspx (accessed 5 April 2014).

[228] See ICC, Appeals Chamber, *Situation in Libya In the case of The Prosecutor v. Saif Al-Islam Gaddafi and Abdullah Al-Senussi*, 'Appeal on behalf of Abdullah Al-Senussi against Pre-Trial Chamber I's 'Decision on the admissibility of the case against Abdullah Al-Senussi', and Request for Suspensive Effect', Case No. ICC-01/11-01/11 (17 October 2013), http://www.icc-cpi.int/iccdocs/doc/doc1666694.pdf (accessed 1 June 2014).

[229] See ICC, Press Release, 'Luxembourg ratifies amendments on the crime of aggression and Article 8' (17 January 2013), http://www.icc-cpi.int/en_menus/icc/press%20and%20media/press%20releases/Pages/PR870.aspx (accessed 4 April 2014).

[230] See ICC, Press Release, 'Estonia ratifies amendments to the Rome Statute on the crime of aggression and Article 8' (28 March 2013), http://www.icc-cpi.int/en_menus/icc/press%20and%20media/press%20releases/Pages/pr893.aspx (accessed 4 April 2014). See also ICC, Press Release, 'Botswana and Germany ratify amendments on the crime of aggression and Article 8' (10 June 2013), http://www.icc-cpi.int/en_menus/icc/press%20and%20media/press%20releases/Pages/pr916.aspx (accessed 4 April 2014).

[231] See ICC, Press Release, 'Andorra, Cyprus, Slovenia, and Uruguay ratify amendments to the Rome Statute on the crime of aggression and Article 8' (1 October 2013), http://www.icc-cpi.int/en_menus/icc/press%20and%20media/press%20releases/Pages/pr946.aspx (accessed 4 April 2014). See also ICC, Press Release, 'Belgium ratifies amendments to the Rome Statute on the crime of aggression and Article 8' (29 November 2013), http://www.icc-cpi.int/en_menus/icc/press%20and%20media/press%20releases/Pages/PR968.aspx (accessed 4 April 2014).

[232] See ICC, Press Release, 'ICC welcomes Cote d'Ivoire as new State Party' (19 March 2013), http://www.icc-cpi.int/en_menus/icc/press%20and%20media/press%20releases/Pages/PR968.aspx (accessed 4 April 2014); ICC, Situation in the Republic of Côte d'Ivoire, 'Declaration under Articles 12–3 of the Rome Statute' (18 April 2003), http://www.icc-cpi.int/NR/rdonlyres/CBE1F16B-5712-4452-87E7-4FDDE5DD70D9/279779/ICDE.pdf (accessed 4 April 2014); and ICC, Situation in the Republic of Côte d'Ivoire, 'Letter reconfirming the acceptance of the ICC

developments, the new Deputy Prosecutor James Stewart (Canada) was sworn in on 8 March 2013.[233] He was elected for a period of 9 years by the Assembly of States Parties on 16 November 2012 and will report directly to the Prosecutor Fatou Bensouda.

In November 2013, the 12th Assembly of States Parties (ASP) to the Rome Statute of the ICC took place in The Hague, the Netherlands. Reflecting on the Assembly in a talk at the Asser Institute on 12 December, Ambassador Tiina Intelmann stated that this ASP "has probably been the most political one—or at least addressing the most politically sensitive issues—ever". Several issues were addressed during this ASP, from the Court's 2014 budget, the Independent Oversight Mechanism, victims participation and (non-) cooperation and the tension between African states parties/the African Union and the Court. Crucially, the ASP began weeks after the AU and the Kenyan government failed to secure an Article 16 deferral of the Kenyan cases at the Security Council. At the request of the African Union, a special session featuring a panel discussion was scheduled to debate the issue of head of state immunity, and discussions on amendments to the ICC Rules of Procedure and Evidence governing presence at trial featured heavily.[234]

## *7.2.2 Hybrid*

### 7.2.2.1 EULEX Kosovo

As addressed in last year's *Year in Review*, on 24 November 2012, EULEX arrested well-known Kosovo politician Fatmir Limaj and other suspects for a re-trial in a case of alleged war crimes against Serbian prisoners of war and (Kosovo) Albanian civilians in or near Klecka (Kosovo) in 1999. On 18 April 2013, the re-trial began, with all ten defendants pleading not guilty.[235] On 17 September 2013, Limaj was

(Footnote 232 continued)
jurisdiction' (14 December 2010), http://www.icc-cpi.int/NR/rdonlyres/498E8FEB-7A72-4005-A209-C14BA374804F/0/ReconCPI.pdf (accessed 4 April 2014).

233 See ICC, Press Release, 'ICC's new Deputy Prosecutor James Stewart sworn in' (8 March 2013), http://www.icc-cpi.int/en_menus/icc/press%20and%20media/press%20releases/Pages/pr879.aspx (accessed 4 April 2014).

234 See 'Report on the 12th Session of the Assembly of States Parties to the Rome Statute', *Coalition for the International Criminal Court*, http://www.iccnow.org/documents/asp12_report.pdf (accessed 1 June 2014).

235 See S.U. Kim, 'Retrial begins against Kosovo politician accused of war crimes', *Jurist* (19 April 2013), http://jurist.org/paperchase/2013/04/retrial-begins-against-kosovo-politician-accused-of-war-crimes.php#.U2edGCiFH5N (accessed 5 May 2014).

again, for the third time, acquitted.[236] The EULEX judges opined that although the Prosecution's chief witness Zogaj, who committed suicide in 2011 (See again last year's *Year in Review*), could not testify, his information was unreliable and moreover, there was no independent evidence showing that Limaj committed the crimes of which he was accused.

In May 2013, another close ally of Kosovo Prime Minister Hashim Thaci, Sami Lushtaku, the mayor of Skenderaj, and four others, were arrested by EULEX and the Kosovo Police Special Operations Unit ROSU on suspicion of war crimes in the 1998–1999 war.[237] The men were charged with "war crimes against the civilian population in the form of violation of bodily integrity and health of civilians held in a KLA detention centre [...] also for [...] the killing of one civilian".[238]

And finally, on 8 November 2013, a EULEX prosecutor indicted 15 more defendants in the Mitrovica Basic Court, charging them with war crimes against civilians, including torture, mistreatment of prisoners and murder, that occurred at a KLA detention center in Likovac in 1998.[239]

#### 7.2.2.2 Extraordinary Chambers in the Courts of Cambodia

In 2013, considerable attention was paid at the Extraordinary Chambers in the Courts of Cambodia (ECCC) to the severance of Case 002, the case against Chea Nuon, former Chairman of the Democratic Kampuchea National Assembly and Deputy Secretary of the Communist Party of Kampuchea and Samphan Khieu, former Head of State of Democratic Kampuchea. Initially, Sary Ieng and his wife Thirith Ieng were also part of this case, but Thirith was declared unfit to stand trial and was released from provisional detention on 16 September 2012 (See last year's *Year in Review*) and Sary passed away on 14 March 2013.[240] On 8 February 2013, the Supreme Court Chamber of the ECCC annulled the 8 October 2012 Trial Chamber decision in which the latter denied, in part, to expand the scope of the first trial of Case 002 (Case 002/01).[241]

---

[236] See L. Klein Mullen, 'Kosovo politician again acquitted of war crimes charges', *Jurist* (18 September 2013), http://jurist.org/paperchase/2013/09/kosovo-politician-again-acquitted-of-war-crimes-charges.php#.U2eliCiFH5M (accessed 5 May 2014).

[237] See G. Redd, 'Allies of Kosovo PM probed over war crimes allegations', *Jurist* (24 May 2013), http://jurist.org/paperchase/2013/05/allies-of-kosovo-pm-probed-over-war-crimes.php#.U2eaFyiFH5M (accessed 5 May 2014).

[238] Ibid.

[239] See S. Adelgren, 'EULEX Kosovo prosecutor indicts 15 people for war crimes', *Jurist* (8 November 2013), http://jurist.org/paperchase/2013/11/sprk-indicts-15-for-war-crimes-at-kla-detention-center-in-1998.php#.U2epviiFH5N (accessed 5 May 2014).

[240] See ECCC, Office of Administration, Press Release, 'Accused Person Ieng Sary Dies' (14 March 2013), http://www.eccc.gov.kh/sites/default/files/media/ECCC%20PR%20DIC%20Ieng%20Sary%2014%20March%202013.pdf (accessed 5 May 2014).

[241] See ECCC, 'Supreme Court Chamber renders decision on appeal against scope of Case 002/01' (12 February 2013), http://www.eccc.gov.kh/en/articles/supreme-court-chamber-renders-decision-appeal-against-scope-case-00201 (accessed 5 May 2014).

The 8 February 2013 decision "was widely discussed in the media by the public and by NGOs. The views were varied and included reference to the health of the accused, the complexity of the trial as well as calls for the inclusion of additional factual allegations such as genocide, work sites, other execution sites beyond S-21 or forced marriages".[242] The Supreme Court Chamber noted that the original severance order of 22 September 2011 and later decisions on which the 2012 decision was based lacked clarity and reasoning and that the parties had not been given sufficient opportunity to be heard.[243] Nevertheless, this did not mean that the Trial Chamber could not reassess a mode of severance after inviting submissions from the parties and taking into account all relevant factors.[244] This is what happened; in February and March 2013, the Trial Chamber heard submissions from the parties and on 29 March 2013, it announced that Chea Nuon is fit to stand that trial, that Case 002 will be severed and that Case 002/01 will deal with the forced evacuation of Phnom Penh in April 1975, the second phase of forced population movement initiated from September 1975, and the execution of Lon Nol soldiers at the Tuol Po Chrey execution site in Pursat province.[245] A reasoned decision on this severance was issued on 26 April 2013,[246] and it was explained that "[t]he uncertainty of stable funding, the fragile health of NUON Chea and the advancing age of KHIEU Samphan, all influenced the decision not to hold a lengthy trial or to hear all the facts".[247] The notorious S-21 prison, for instance, was also not included in the scope of the case. Both the Co-Prosecutors (on 15 May) and Chea Nuon (on 27 May) filed appeals. The Co-Prosecutors argued that the case should include S-21 and Chea Nuon submitted

> that the Trial Chamber erred in deciding to sever Case 002 anew, and in failing to include charges relating to genocide and cooperatives and worksites in Case 002/001. He accordingly request[ed] the Supreme Court Chamber to annul the Impugned Decision with prejudice to future severance order, or, in the alternative, to expand of the scope of Case 002/01 such that it includes charges of genocide and those concerning crimes allegedly committed at cooperatives and working sites [original footnotes omitted].[248]

---

242 See ECCC, 'Trial Chamber issues reasoned decision on Case 002 severance' (26 April 2013), http://www.eccc.gov.kh/en/articles/trial-chamber-issues-reasoned-decision-case-002-severance (accessed 5 May 2014).

243 See 'Supreme Court Chamber renders decision on appeal against scope of Case 002/01', supra n 241.

244 Ibid.

245 See ECCC, 'Case 002 severed and Nuon Chea found fit to stand trial' (29 March 2013), http://www.eccc.gov.kh/en/articles/case-002-severed-and-nuon-chea-found-fit-stand-trial (accessed 5 May 2014).

246 For the decision, see http://www.eccc.gov.kh/sites/default/files/documents/courtdoc/2013-04-26%2016:43/E284_EN.PDF (accessed 5 May 2014).

247 See 'Trial Chamber issues reasoned decision on Case 002 severance', supra n 242.

248 See ECCC, Supreme Court Chamber, 'Decision on Immediate Appeals against Trial Chamber's Second Decision on Severance of Case 002. Summary of Reasons', Case File 002/19-09-2007-ECCC-TC/SC(28) (23 July 2013), http://www.eccc.gov.kh/sites/default/files/documents/courtdoc/2013-07-23%2016:57/E284_4_7_EN.PDF (accessed 5 May 2014), para 5.

Finally, on 23 July 2013, the Supreme Court Chamber dismissed these appeals. It denied Nuon's request to annul the severance order as the Trial Chamber's discretion to sever a case is broad and as the Trial Chamber's determination that renewed severance was required is not so unreasonable.[249] However, it also considered that the Trial Chamber had failed to comply with the Supreme Court Chamber's instructions "that renewed severance must entail a tangible plan for the adjudication of the entirety of the charges in the Indictment and due consideration to reasonable representativeness of the Indictment within the smaller trials [original footnotes omitted]".[250] This constituted an error of law and an error in the exercise of the Trial Chamber's discretion.[251] Nevertheless, the judges held:

> the Supreme Court Chamber considers that to order an expansion of Case 002/01 and to require the Trial Chamber to reconfigure its schedule would inevitably result in unnecessary delays. In the present circumstances, concerns of the effective management of the entirety of charges pending before the Trial Chamber prevail over the postulate that Case 002/01 be reasonably representative of the Indictment. The Supreme Court therefore considers that a more appropriate course of action at this state is to instruct that charges that should have been included within the scope of Case 002/01 will instead form part of the scope of Case 002/02 [meaning that Case 002/02 will at least comprise the charges related to S-21, a worksite, a cooperative and genocide], so as to render the combination of Cases 002/01 and 002/02 reasonably representative of the Indictment.[252]

Because of this, the appeals of both the Co-Prosecutors and Nuon to include additional charges in the scope of Case 002/01 were dismissed[253] and the Supreme Court Chamber decided that it was "imperative to establish a second panel within the Trial Chamber in order to ensure that Case 002/02 can commence as soon as possible after closing submissions in Case 002/01"[254] and thus instructed the ECCC's Office of the Administration "to immediately explore the establishment of a second panel of national and international judges within the Trial Chamber to hear and adjudicate Case 002/02".[255]

[249] Ibid., paras 6–7.

[250] Ibid., paras 8–9.

[251] Ibid., para 9.

[252] Ibid., para 11.

[253] Ibid., para 12.

[254] See ECCC, Supreme Court Chamber, 'Order Regarding the Establishment of a Second Trial Panel', File No. 002/19-09-2007-ECCC-TC/SC(28) (23 July 2013), http://www.eccc.gov.kh/sites/default/files/documents/courtdoc/2013-07-23%2017:14/E284_4_7_1_EN.PDF (accessed 5 May 2014), p. 2.

[255] Ibid.

#### 7.2.2.3 Special Court for Sierra Leone

After found guilty of aiding, abetting and planning the commission of certain crimes (on 26 April 2012) and sentenced to 50 years' imprisonment (on 30 May 2012) by Trial Chamber II of the Special Court for Sierra Leone (SCSL) (see last year's *Year in Review*), former Liberian resident Charles Taylor filed his appeal brief against both the Judgment and the Sentencing Judgment on 1 October 2012.[256] The Prosecution did the same.[257] The Defence brought forward the following six challenges. First, it challenged the Trial Chamber's assessment of the evidence and its finding of fact in several ground of appeal.[258] Second, it argued "that the Trial Chamber erred in law and in fact in finding that the RUF/AFRC had an operational strategy to commit crimes against the civilian population of Sierra Leone throughout the Indictment Period [original footnote omitted]".[259] Third, the Defence challenged the judges' findings on the elements of aiding and abetting and planning liability in a number of grounds.[260] Fourth, it challenged the conclusion that Taylor's *actus reus* and *mens rea* establish his criminal responsibility for aiding, abetting and planning the commission of the alleged crimes.[261] Fifth, the Defence asserted that irregularities in the judicial process occurred which constituted violations of Taylor's right to a fair and public trial.[262] And finally, the Defence argued that the judges erred in entering cumulative convictions and challenged the sentence.[263] The Prosecution made four complaints, the first two being that the judges failed to find that Taylor had also ordered and instigated the commission of crimes.[264] Third, it asserted that the judges erred in finding that the location of some crimes were not pleaded in the indictment and finally, it complained about the inadequacy of the sentence, arguing that Taylor should have received 80 years.[265] Almost all of these arguments were rejected by the Appeals Chamber in its judgment of 26 September 2013. For instance, as to the point of the Prosecution that Taylor had also ordered and instigated the commission of crimes, the judges of the Appeals Chamber noted:

---

256 See http://www.sc-sl.org/LinkClick.aspx?fileticket=R5js%2fPiBejc%3d&tabid=107 (accessed 6 May 2014).

257 See http://www.sc-sl.org/LinkClick.aspx?fileticket=RKV2Z8dIRLI%3d&tabid=107 (accessed 6 May 2014).

258 See SCSL, Appeals Chamber, *Prosecutor against Charles Ghankay Taylor*, 'Judgment', Case No. SCSL-03-01-A (26 September 2013), http://www.sc-sl.org/LinkClick.aspx?fileticket=t14fjFP4jJ8%3d&tabid=53 (accessed 6 May 2014), para 17.

259 Ibid., para 18.

260 Ibid., para 19.

261 Ibid., para 20.

262 Ibid., para 21.

263 Ibid., para 22.

264 Ibid., para 23.

265 Ibid.

> [A]iding and abetting liability fully captures Taylor's numerous "interventions" over a sustained period of 5 years, the variety of assistance he provided to the RUF/AFRC leadership in the implementation of its Operational Strategy and the cumulative impact of his culpable acts and conduct on the "tremendous suffering caused by the commission of the crimes" for which he is guilty. Planning liability likewise fully captures Taylor's additional culpable acts and conduct for the crimes committed during the Freetown Invasion. These descriptions of Taylor's culpable acts and conduct fully reflect the Trial Chamber's findings on Taylor's authority and leadership role [original footnotes omitted].[266]

However, it also allowed, in part, one ground of the Defence and revised "the Trial Chamber's Disposition for planning liability under Article 6(1) of the Statute by deleting Kono District under Counts 1–8 and 11".[267] Likewise, it allowed, in part, one ground of the Prosecution and held "that the Trial Chamber erred in law in finding that aiding and abetting liability generally warrants a lesser sentence than other forms of criminal participation".[268] As a result of this, the sentence of 50 years' imprisonment was confirmed. This cleared the way for Taylor's transfer to the UK, on 15 October 2013, where he will serve the remainder of his 50-year sentence.[269]

With the finalization of the Taylor case, the SCSL could start its process of dissolution. On 2 December 2013, and after 11 years of existence, the SCSL was formally closed.[270] During the official closing ceremony in Freetown, Miguel de Serpa Soares, Under-Secretary-General for Legal Affairs and United Nations Legal Counsel, representing the Secretary-General of the United Nations, remarked that "[t]he Special Court is the first of the United Nations and United Nations-assisted tribunals to complete its mandate and to fully hand over its rights and responsibilities to its successor residual institution".[271] This is the Residual Special Court for Sierra Leone, which was established by an agreement between the United Nations and the Government of Sierra Leone "to oversee the continuing legal obligations of the Special Court for Sierra Leone after its closure in 2013. These include witness protection, supervision of prison sentences, and management of the SCSL archives".[272] On 31 December 2013, the website of this Residual Special Court for Sierra Leone (www.rscsl.org), containing electronic records of the SCSL, was launched.

---

[266] Ibid., para 594.

[267] Ibid., XI. Disposition (p. 305).

[268] Ibid.

[269] See SCSL, Outreach and Public Affairs Office, Press Release, 'Charles Taylor Transferred to the UK for the Enforcement of his Sentence' (15 October 2013), http://www.sc-sl.org/LinkClick.aspx?fileticket=rHbdqmtDjKg%3d&tabid=53 (accessed 6 May 2014).

[270] See SCSL, Outreach and Public Affairs Office, Press Release, 'Government of Sierra Leone Hosts Formal Closing Ceremony for the Special Court' (3 December 2013), http://www.rscsl.org/Documents/Press/2013/pressrelease-120313b.pdf (accessed 6 May 2014).

[271] Ibid.

[272] See http://www.rscsl.org (accessed 6 May 2014).

#### 7.2.2.4 Special Tribunal for Lebanon

The year 2013 at the Special Tribunal for Lebanon (STL) was marked by, among other things, alleged witness intimidation, the initial proceedings against Merhi and the preparations for the trial phase in the case *Ayyash et al.*

On 22 January 2013, the STL "denounce[d] in the strongest possible terms any attempts at witness intimidation", in view of Lebanese media reports claiming to reveal the identities of individuals who could testify before the STL as witnesses.[273] It therefore came as no surprise that the STL condemned, again "in the strongest possible terms",[274] the fact that in early April, the hacker group "Journalists for the Truth" broke into the website of the newspaper Al Mustaqbal, posting a list of 167 alleged witnesses and directing visitors to its own website.[275] The STL noted that "[t]hose behind the website purporting to unveil the "truth", are in grave breach of journalistic ethics and employ questionable methods such as Internet hacking"[276] and warned that "[a]ny attempt to knowingly and willfully interfere with the judicial process, including disclosure of confidential material or threatening, intimidating, or otherwise interfering with potential witnesses, is taken very seriously by the four organs of the Tribunal".[277] On 29 April, Judge Baragwanath, acting as the Contempt Judge for the month of April, announced that an amicus curiae would be appointed by the Registrar to investigate "three incidents which could potentially be considered interference with the administration of justice through publication of alleged witness identities".[278]

As to the second development, on 10 October 2013, Pre-Trial Judge Daniel Fransen ordered the lifting of the confidentiality of the indictment against Hassan Habib Merhi, subject to certain redactions.[279] This indictment, submitted for confirmation on 5 June 2013 by the Prosecution and confirmed by the Pre-Trial Judge

---

[273] See STL, Press Release, 'STL condemns media reports on alleged witness identities' (22 January 2013), http://www.stl-tsl.org/en/media/press-releases/22-01-2013-stl-condemns-media-reports-on-alleged-witness-identities (accessed 25 May 2014).

[274] See STL, Press Release, 'Tribunal condemns attempts to interfere with judicial process' (11 April 2013), http://www.stl-tsl.org/en/media/press-releases/tribunal-condemns-attempts-to-interfere-with-judicial-process (accessed 25 May 2014).

[275] See M. Simons, 'Hackers Post Witness List in Trial on Ex-Premier's Death', *The New York Times* (13 April 2013), http://www.nytimes.com/2013/04/14/world/middleeast/hackers-reveal-witness-names-in-hariri-murder-trial.html?_r=0 (accessed 25 May 2014).

[276] See 'STL condemns media reports on alleged witness identities', supra n 273.

[277] Ibid.

[278] See STL, Press Release, 'Tribunal to launch investigation in alleged witness intimidation' (29 April 2013), http://www.stl-tsl.org/en/media/press-releases/29-04-2013-tribunal-to-launch-investigation-in-alleged-witness-intimidation (accessed 25 May 2014).

[279] See STL, Pre-Trial Judge, *The Prosecutor v. Hassan Habib Merhi*, 'Order on Partially Lifting the Confidentiality of the Indictment Against Mr. Hassan Habib Merhi', Case No. STL-13-04/I/PTJ (10 October 2013), http://www.stl-tsl.org/index.php?option=com_k2&Itemid=760&id=2906_97ff8ed01cba5f60a4e4dd9109c4f8bd&lang=en&task=download&view=item (accessed 25 May 2014).

on 31 July 2013, charges Merhi with five counts for his involvement in the 14 February 2005 terrorist attack in Beirut, which killed Lebanese former Prime Minister Rafik Hariri and 21 other persons, and injured 226 persons.[280] The same day, it was decided to initiate a 30-day public advertisement phase to locate and inform Merhi of his charges and rights.[281] This was without any result. Consequently, on 20 December 2013, the Trial Chamber decided to hold the Merhi trial *in absentia*, after it found that Mehri had absconded or otherwise could not be found and that all reasonable steps had been taken to secure his appearance before the STL and to inform him of the charges by the Pre-Trial Judge.[282]

Finally, 2013 was characterized by the preparations for the start of the actual trial in the case *Ayyash et al.* Although initially provisionally scheduled to begin on 25 March 2013, Pre-Trial Judge Daniel Fransen postponed, on 21 February 2013, the start of the trial, among other things because "[h]e found that the Prosecution ha[d] not yet disclosed the entirety of the material to the Defence, and that the Defence ha [d] not yet been able to access certain material disclosed by the Prosecution due to technical issues.[283] On 28 October 2013, the *Ayyash* case file was transferred to the Trial Chamber,[284] and on 10 December, the judges of the Trial Chamber scheduled the start of the trial for 16 January 2014.[285]

---

[280] See STL, Pre-Trial Judge, *The Prosecutor v. Hassan Habib Merhi*, 'Public Redacted Indictment', Case No. STL-13-04/I/PTJ (5 June 2013), http://www.stl-tsl.org/index.php?option=com_k2&Itemid=760&id=2907_e7e1d4e4756a3bf6c966c14c165507ce&lang=en&task=download&view=item (accessed 25 May 2014).

[281] See STL, Press Release, 'STL Indicts Hassan Habib Merhi in 14 February 2005 Beirut attack' (10 October 2013), http://www.stl-tsl.org/en/media/press-releases/10-10-2013-stl-indicts-hassan-habib-merhi-in-14-february-2005-beirut-attack (accessed 25 May 2014).

[282] See STL, Trial Chamber, *Prosecutor v. Hassan Habib Merhi*, 'Decision to Hold Trial *In Absentia*', Case No. STL-13-04/I/TC (20 December 2013), http://www.stl-tsl.org/index.php?option=com_k2&Itemid=760&id=3165_d03aa7736e4045e952eec3bb897f9ba9&lang=en&task=download&view=item (accessed 25 May 2014), para 4.

[283] See STL, Press Release, 'Pre-Trial Judge postpones trial date' (21 February 2013), http://www.stl-tsl.org/en/media/press-releases/pre-trial-judge-postpones-trial-date (accessed 25 May 2014).

[284] See STL, Press Release, 'Pre Trial Judge transfers the complete Ayyash et al. case file to Trial Chamber' (28 October 2013), http://www.stl-tsl.org/en/media/press-releases/28-10-2013-pre-trial-judge-transfers-the-complete-ayyash-et-al-case-file-to-trial-chamber (accessed 25 May 2014).

[285] See STL, Trial Chamber, *Prosecutor v. Salim Jamil Ayyash, Mustafa Amine Badreddine, Hussein Hassan Oneissi and Assad Hassan Sabra*, 'Scheduling Order', Case No. STL-11-01/PT/TC (10 December 2013), http://www.stl-tsl.org/index.php?option=com_k2&Itemid=633&id=3098_747019f209906001b1452467eba16425&lang=en&task=download&view=item (accessed 25 May 2014).

## 7.2.3 *Domestic*[286]

### 7.2.3.1 Bangladesh

In Dhaka, Bangladesh, the International Crimes Tribunal (ICT) continued its work investigating and prosecuting suspects of international crimes committed during the 1971 Bangladesh Liberation War. The oft-criticized[287] ICT is trying persons who allegedly collaborated with Pakistani forces who tried to prevent Bangladesh (then East Pakistan) from becoming an independent state. Many suspects are linked to the opposition party Jamaat-e-Islami (JI), which opposed the independence of Bangladesh from Pakistan.

Whereas in 2012, the first indictments were issued and trials commenced (see last year's *Year in Review*), 2013 was characterized by many convictions and (heavy) sentences. The first verdict by the ICT was handed down on 21 January 2013, when Abul Kalam Azad, also known as "Bachchu Razakar", was sentenced to death *in absentia* (he was said to have fled to Pakistan), after the ICT found him guilty of genocide and crimes against humanity.[288] On 5 February 2013, the second verdict was issued, this time against JI assistant secretary-general Abdul Quader Mollah, also known as the 'Butcher of Mirpur'. He was tried for, among other things, the killing of hundreds of unarmed civilians (crimes against humanity),[289] and received life in prison, which, given the serious charges, led to "the biggest mass demonstration the country ha[d] seen in 20 years".[290] As a result of these protests, which demanded the death penalty for Mollah, the Bangladesh Parliament amended the 1973 Act regulating the ICT, enabling the state to appeal a life sentence and seek the death penalty.[291] On 17 September 2013, the Supreme Court

[286] Although it was already mentioned in the very first footnote to this article that this *Year in Review* cannot be comprehensive in scope, this goes *a fortiori* for the domestic context, where more and more cases on international humanitarian law and international criminal law are adjudicated. The current (domestic) section will therefore only select a few cases. More analyses of national cases can be found at the T.M.C. Asser Instituut's International Crimes Database (http://www.internationalcrimesdatabase.org), where one will also find analyses of cases adjudicated by hybrid and international tribunals.

[287] See, e.g., K. Iliopoulos, 'Bangladesh: A Free and Fair War Crimes Tribunal?', *Crimes of War* (26 August 2010), http://www.crimesofwar.org/commentary/bangladesh-a-free-and-fair-war-crimes-tribunal (accessed 1 June 2014).

[288] The judgment can be found here: http://bangladeshtrialobserver.files.wordpress.com/2012/12/full_judgement_azad.pdf (accessed 1 June 2014).

[289] The judgment can be found here: http://bangladeshwarcrimes.blogspot.nl/2013/02/5-feb-2013-mollah-final-judgment-part-1.html (accessed 1 June 2014).

[290] See T. Anam, 'Shahbag protesters versus the Butcher of Mirpur', *The Guardian* (13 February 2013), http://www.theguardian.com/world/2013/feb/13/shahbag-protest-bangladesh-quader-mollah (accessed 1 June 2014).

[291] See International Commission of Jurists, Press Release, 'Bangladesh: Abdul Quader Mollah death sentence violates international law' (17 September 2013), http://www.icj.org/bangladesh-abdul-quader-mollah-death-sentence-violates-international-law/ (accessed 1 June 2014).

of Bangladesh indeed reversed the verdict of the ICT, sentencing Mollah to death,[292] and on 12 December 2013, Mollah was hanged, making him the first person convicted by the ICT to be executed.[293] Obviously, not only the death penalty as such, but also the retroactive application of the law was heavily criticized, as being incompatible with international principles of fair trial.[294]

Other severe verdicts were issued in 2013, against JI leader Delwar Hossain Sayedee (sentenced to death on 28 February 2013 for crimes against humanity),[295] against former JI leader Gholam Azam (about whom the judges stated that he deserved the death penalty, but given his age (91) and illness, was 'merely' sentenced, on 15 July 2013, to 90 years' imprisonment for, among other things, crimes against humanity),[296] against JI secretary-general Ali Ahsan Mohammed Mujahid (sentenced to death on 17 July 2013 for crimes against humanity),[297] against MP for the Bangladesh Nationalist Party (BNP) Salauddin Quader Chowdhury (sentenced to death on 1 October 2013 for crimes against humanity and genocide),[298] against BNP leader Abdul Alim (sentenced to life imprisonment (taking into account his age and illness), on 9 October 2013, for genocide and crimes against humanity),[299] and against JI members Chowdhury Mueen Uddin and Ashrafuzzaman Khan (sentenced on 3 November 2013 to death, *in absentia*, for crimes against humanity).[300]

---

292 See Th. Donovan, 'Bangladesh top court sentences opposition leader to death', *Jurist* (17 September 2013), http://jurist.org/paperchase/2013/09/bangladesh-top-court-sentences-opposition-leader-to-death.php (accessed 1 June 2014).

293 See M. Sadique, 'Bangladesh Islamist Abdul Kader Mullah hanged for war crimes', *BBC News* (12 December 2013), http://www.bbc.com/news/world-asia-25356034 (accessed 1 June 2014).

294 See 'Bangladesh: Abdul Quader Mollah death sentence violates international law', supra n 291. See also 'Bangladesh: Post-Trial Amendments Taint War Crimes Process', *Human Rights Watch* (14 February 2013), http://www.hrw.org/news/2013/02/14/bangladesh-post-trial-amendments-taint-war-crimes-process (accessed 1 June 2014).

295 See '28 Feb 2013: Sayedee Convicted of 8 out of 20 Charges, Sentenced to Death', *The Bangladesh Trial Observer* (28 February 2013), http://bangladeshtrialobserver.org/2013/02/28/28-feb-2013-sayedee-convicted-of-8-out-of-20-charges-sentenced-to-death/#more-842 (accessed 1 June 2014).

296 See '15 July 2013: Gholam Azam Found Guilty—Sentenced to 90 years', *The Bangladesh Trial Observer* (15 July 2013), http://bangladeshtrialobserver.org/2013/07/15/15-july-2013-gholam-azam-found-guilty-sentenced-to-90-years/ (accessed 1 June 2014).

297 The judgment can be found here: http://bangladeshtrialobserver.files.wordpress.com/2013/07/aammujahid-judgment.pdf (accessed 1 June 2014).

298 The judgment can be found here: http://www.dropbox.com/s/4xgmkc6xnoxk71c/chowdhury_judgement_1Oct2013.pdf (accessed 1 June 2014).

299 The judgment can be found here: http://www.satp.org/satporgtp/countries/bangladesh/document/papers/Verdict_Abdul_Alim.pdf (accessed 1 June 2014).

300 The judgment can be found here: http://www.dropbox.com/s/3xckpr73pyzap4p/bangladesh_tribunal_chowdhury_mueenuddin_judgment.pdf (accessed 1 June 2014).

#### 7.2.3.2 Bosnia and Herzegovina

Like in 2012, the War Crimes Section of the Court of Bosnia and Herzegovina (BiH) was very active in 2013, issuing many decisions. However, only a small selection of developments can be highlighted here.

On 11 January 2013, Trial Panel of Section I for War Crimes of the Court of BiH, found Božidar Kuvelja guilty, in first instance, of crimes against humanity for his role in the 1995 Srebrenica massacre and sentenced him to 20 years' imprisonment.[301] Kuvelja, a former Bosnian Serb police officer, was found to have searched for Bosnian Muslims, and

> [a]fter seizing the victims from their homes, Kuvjela [*sic*] assisted members of his police unit in their transport to a warehouse collection point known as 'the White House' where they were detained and subjected to physical abuse. The following day, Kuvjela [*sic*] then helped to separate the victims by sex, whereupon he and the others began the systematic execution of more than a thousand Muslim men and boys.[302]

This sentence was confirmed in appeal on 16 September 2013.[303]

On 29 March 2013, the same trial panel found the Montenegrin Veselin Vlahović guilty, in first instance, of crimes against humanity (persecution), and sentenced him to 45 years' imprisonment, the most stringent sentence the Court of BiH has ever imposed.[304] According to the judges, Vlahović, as member of the paramilitary forces of the Republika Srpska, persecuted in 1992 the civilian non-Serb population of a Sarajevo suburb, by killing 31 people, raping countless Bosniak and Croat women and torturing and robbing non-Serbs.[305]

Then, in the summer of 2013, the Court of BiH suffered a serious set-back when the European Court of Human Rights determined, on 18 July 2013, that the proceedings against Abduladhim Maktouf, who had earlier been convicted of war crimes and sentenced to 5 years' imprisonment,[306] and Goran Damjanović, who had earlier been convicted of war crimes and sentenced to 11 years'

---

[301] See Court of Bosnia and Herzegovina, 'Božidar Kuvelja sentenced to 20 years in prison' (14 January 2013), http://www.sudbih.gov.ba/index.php?id=2667&jezik=e (accessed 1 June 2014).

[302] See B. Minegar, 'Ex-police officer sentenced to 20 years for role in Srebrenica massacre', *Jurist* (11 January 2013), http://jurist.org/paperchase/2013/01/ex-police-officer-sentenced-to-20-years-for-role-in-srebrenica-massacre.php (accessed 1 June 2014).

[303] See Court of Bosnia and Herzegovina, 'Trial Verdict confirmed in relation to Božidar Kuvelja' (26 November 2013), http://www.sudbih.gov.ba/index.php?id=2984&jezik=e (accessed 1 June 2014).

[304] See Court of Bosnia and Herzegovina, 'Veselin Vlahović sentenced to a long-term imprisonment of 45 years' (29 March 2013), http://www.sudbih.gov.ba/?id=2749&jezik=e (accessed 1 June 2014).

[305] See S. Paulsworth, 'Bosnia court sentences Montenegro paramilitary leader to 45 years', *Jurist* (29 March 2013), http://jurist.org/paperchase/2013/03/bosnia-court-sentences-montenegro-paramilitary-leader-to-45-years.php (accessed 1 June 2014).

[306] The judgment can be found here: http://www.sudbih.gov.ba/files/docs/presude/2006/Maktouf_ENG_KPZ-32-05.pdf (accessed 2 June 2014).

imprisonment,[307] had violated Article 7 of the European Convention of Human Rights ('No punishment without law'). This was because the two men had been sentenced under provisions of the 2003 Criminal Code of BiH (for war crimes committed during the 1992–1995 war), whereas the sentencing provisions of the 1976 Criminal Code of the former Socialist Federal Republic of Yugoslavia should have been applied.[308] The judges held:

> Admittedly, the applicants' sentences in the instant case were within the latitude of both the 1976 Criminal Code and the 2003 Criminal Code. It thus cannot be said with any certainty that either applicant would have received lower sentences had the former Code been applied (…). What is crucial, however, is that the applicants could have received lower sentences had that Code been applied in their cases. (…) [S]ince there exists a real possibility that the retroactive application of the 2003 Code operated to the applicants' disadvantage as concerns the sentencing, it cannot be said that they were afforded effective safeguards against the imposition of a heavier penalty, in breach of Article 7 of the Convention.[309]

As a result of this human rights violation, the Court of BiH scheduled new trials in early October, not only for Maktouf and Damjanović, but also Goran Damjanović's brother, Zoran Damjanović, who did not file an application with the European Court.[310]

It was clear immediately that the European Court's ruling "could set a precedent for more retrials in the Balkan country",[311] which was exactly what happened: it quickly encouraged ten more men, namely Slobodan Jakovljević (sentenced to 28 years for genocide), Aleksandar Radovanović (sentenced to 32 years for genocide), Branislav Medan (sentenced to 28 years for genocide), Brane Džinić (sentenced to 32 years for genocide), Milenko Trifunović (sentenced to 33 years for genocide), Petar Mitrović (sentenced to 28 years for genocide), Nikola Andrun (sentenced to 18 years for war crimes against civilians), Milorad Savić (sentenced to 21 years for war crimes against civilians), Mirko (son of Špiro) Pekez (sentenced to 14 years for war crimes against civilians), Mirko (son of Mile) Pekez (sentenced to 29 years for war crimes against civilians), to complain on the same grounds.[312] On 22 October 2013, the Constitutional Court of BiH indeed upheld the appeals of the men, found the human rights violation pursuant to Article 7 of the ECHR and

---

[307] The judgment can be found here: http://www.sudbih.gov.ba/files/docs/presude/2007/X-KRZ-05-107_od_18_06_2007_-_Drugostepena_presuda_-_eng.pdf (accessed 2 June 2014).

[308] See ECtHR, Grand Chamber, *Case of Maktouf and Damjanović v. Bosnia and Herzegovina (Applications nos. 2312/08 and 34179/08)*, 'Judgment' (18 July 2013), http://hudoc.echr.coe.int/sites/eng/pages/search.aspx?i=001-122716 (accessed 2 June 2014), para 76.

[309] Ibid., para 70.

[310] See L. Laing, 'Bosnia court reopens trial on war crimes convicts', *Jurist* (10 October 2013), http://jurist.org/paperchase/2013/10/bosnia-court-reopens-trial-on-war-crimes-convicts.php (accessed 2 June 2014).

[311] See D. Sito-Sucic, 'Bosnia to retry three war crimes convicts after European court ruling', *Reuters* (9 October 2013), http://www.reuters.com/article/2013/10/09/us-bosnia-court-warcrimes-idUSBRE9980P220131009 (accessed 2 June 2014).

[312] See Court of Bosnia and Herzegovina, 'Prison sentences suspended' (19 November 2013), http://www.sudbih.gov.ba/index.php?id=2977&jezik=e (accessed 2 June 2014).

ordered the war crimes court to reach a new decision, as a result of which the Appellate Division of the war crimes court suspended the prison sentences and released the men,[313] this to the anger of the victims' relatives and friends.

And others followed, such as Zrinko Pinčić (sentenced to nine years for war crimes against civilians).[314] It was reported that "[a]ccording to legal expert Goran Simic, the EU court decision could lead to annulment of up to 50 similar cases that include almost 70 convicts".[315]

Nevertheless, re-trials commenced and new sentences were issued, such as against the brothers Goran and Zoran Damjanović on 13 December 2013 (six years and six months, and six years, respectively)[316] and against Mirko (son of Špiro) Pekez and Milorad Savić on 18 December 2013 (10 years and 15 years, respectively).[317]

#### 7.2.3.3 Denmark

In last year's *Year in Review*, the Danish case against T., a school inspector and teacher who allegedly acted as the head of a death squad during the Rwandan genocide, was discussed. After Rwanda had requested T's extradition in February 2012, the Danish Minister of Justice, on 29 June 2012, decided that T. was to be extradited to Rwanda.[318] T. challenged this decision in court, but both in first instance (19 November 2012) and in appeal (22 March 2013), the decision to extradite was affirmed.[319] He subsequently challenged the appeals decision at the Danish Supreme Court, but on 6 November 2013, also the Supreme Court held that T.'s extradition to Rwanda was lawful.[320] Among other things, the judges found that T.'s argument that he would risk being subjected to torture or inhuman treatment or that his trial would be unfair in Rwanda had to be dismissed. In doing so, they referred to the *Ahorugeze v. Sweden* judgment of the European Court of

---

313 Ibid.

314 See Court of Bosnia and Herzegovina, 'Prison sentence for Zrinko Pinčić suspended' (4 December 2013), http://www.sudbih.gov.ba/index.php?id=2999&jezik=e (accessed 2 June 2014).

315 See 'Bosnia releases 10 war crime convicts under EU court ruling', *AFP/Global Post* (19 November 2013), http://www.globalpost.com/dispatch/news/afp/131119/bosnia-releases-10-war-crime-convicts-under-eu-court-ruling (accessed 2 June 2014).

316 See Court of Bosnia and Herzegovina, 'First-instance Verdict handed down in the reopened proceedings for the Acused [*sic*] Goran and Zoran Damjanović' (13 December 2013), http://www.sudbih.gov.ba/index.php?id=3024&jezik=e (accessed 2 June 2014).

317 See Court of Bosnia and Herzegovina, 'Appeals Verdict handed down in the case v. Mirko Pekez et al.' (18 December 2013), http://www.sudbih.gov.ba/index.php?id=3036&jezik=e (accessed 2 June 2014).

318 See the case's analysis on the International Crimes Database: http://www.internationalcrimesdatabase.org/Case/1215 (accessed 3 June 2014).

319 Ibid.

320 The decision can be found here: http://www.internationalcrimesdatabase.org/upload/ICD/Upload1215/200131106_Danish_Supreme_Court_decision_on_extradition_to_Rwanda.pdf (accessed 3 June 2014).

Human Rights of 27 October 2011,[321] where the judges noted: "Nor has any evidence been submitted or found which gives reason to conclude that there is a general situation of persecution or ill-treatment of the Hutu population in Rwanda."[322] The Danish judges, following up on this, opined:

> The Supreme Court has no information that provides a basis for any other assessment. There is moreover no information about special conditions concerning T according to which he should be at risk of persecution or inhuman treatment contrary to section 6(1) or (2) of the Extradition Act or Article 3 of the Human Rights Convention.[323]

As to the fair trial issue, the European judges in *Ahorugeze* concluded that "there is no sufficient indication that the Rwandan judiciary lacks the requisite independence and impartiality"[324] and that "the applicant, if extradited to stand trial in Rwanda, would not face a real risk of a flagrant denial of justice."[325] In the same vein, the judges of the Danish Supreme Court held that there are "no grounds to assume that if extradited to Rwanda, T would receive treatment that would constitute a flagrant denial of his right to a fair trial."[326]

#### 7.2.3.4 France

Also in France, decisions involving the Rwandan genocide were issued in 2013. On 22 January 2013, Innocent Musabyimana was arrested on charges of genocide and crimes against humanity.[327] After Rwandan Prosecutors requested Musabyimana's extradition, a French appeals court in Paris decided on 13 November 2013 that he could indeed be sent to Rwanda.[328] The same was decided for Claude Muhayimana, accused of participating in killings and other crimes against humanity, and

---

[321] The judgment can be found here: http://hudoc.echr.coe.int/sites/eng/pages/search.aspx?i=001-107183 (accessed 3 June 2014).

[322] Ibid., para 90.

[323] See p. 8 of the Supreme Court's order, which can be found here: www.internationalcrimesdatabase.org/upload/ICD/Upload1215/200131106_Danish_Supreme_Court_decision_on_extradition_to_Rwanda.pdf (accessed 4 June 2014).

[324] See para 125 of the judgment, which can be found here: http://hudoc.echr.coe.int/sites/eng/pages/search.aspx?i=001-107183 (accessed 3 June 2014).

[325] Ibid., para 129.

[326] See p 10 of the Supreme Court's order, which can be found here: www.internationalcrimesdatabase.org/upload/ICD/Upload1215/200131106_Danish_Supreme_Court_decision_on_extradition_to_Rwanda.pdf (accessed 4 June 2014).

[327] See S. Posner, 'Rwanda genocide suspect arrested in France', *Jurist* (25 January 2013), http://jurist.org/paperchase/2013/01/rwanda-genocide-suspect-arrested-in-france.php (accessed 8 June 2014).

[328] See S. Franklin, 'France appeals court approves extradition of Rwandan genocide suspects', *Jurist* (13 November 2013), http://jurist.org/paperchase/2013/11/france-appeals-court-approves-extradition-of-rwanda-genocide-suspects.php (accessed 8 June 2014).

about whom a lower French court in Rouen already decided in March 2012 that he could be sent to Rwanda.[329]

Moreover, on 29 March 2013, Pascal Simbikangwa, a former Rwandan Army captain and head of the Central Intelligence during the Rwandan genocide, and detained by the French government since 2008, was ordered to stand trial in France for complicity in genocide and crimes against humanity,[330] possibly paving the way for the first French trial of a Rwandan person allegedly involved in the 1994 genocide.

And a few days later, French police officials in Toulouse arrested Tite Barahira, a former Rwandan leader, for conspiracy to commit genocide.[331]

Finally, on 11 July 2013, Laurent Serubuga, a Hutu ex-colonel, was arrested in the north of France on the basis of an international arrest warrant in connection to the 1994 genocide. However, on 12 September 2013, a French appeals court in Douai rejected his extradition to Rwanda, holding that "because the crimes of which Serabuga [*sic*] was accused occurred more than 10 years ago, the claims were barred by the statute of limitations. Additionally, the court held that at the time when the crimes were committed, genocide and crimes against humanity were not against the laws of Rwanda".[332]

#### 7.2.3.5 Guatemala

In the case against General Efraín Ríos Montt, the country's former head of state (between March 1982 and August 1983) (see again last year's *Year in Review*), many developments occurred. On 28 January 2013, Judge Miguel Angel Galvez, the first-instance judge of High Risk Court "B", overseeing the preliminary phase of the trial after Judge Carol Patricia Flores, the first-instance judge of High Risk Court "A", had been recused by an appeals court on 23 November 2011,[333] ordered Efraín

---

[329] See J. Davies, 'France approves first extradition to Rwanda', *Jurist* (31 March 2012), http://jurist.org/paperchase/2012/03/france-approves-first-extradition-to-rwanda.php (accessed 8 June 2014).

[330] See 'France orders first Rwandan genocide trial', *France24* (3 April 2013), http://www.france24.com/en/20130402-france-rwanda-genocide-trial-pascal-simbikangwa/ (accessed 8 June 2014).

[331] See J. Votava, 'Rwanda genocide suspect arrested in France', *Jurist* (3 April 2013), http://jurist.org/paperchase/2013/04/rwanda-genocide-suspect-arrested-in-france-1.php (accessed 8 June 2014).

[332] See L. Klein Mullen, 'France court rejects request to extradite former Rwanda colonel', *Jurist* (12 September 2013), http://jurist.org/paperchase/2013/09/france-court-rejects-request-to-extradite-former-rwanda-colonel.php (accessed 8 June 2014). The judgment can be found here (in French): http://www.francerwandagenocide.org/documents/SerubugaArret12septembre2013.pdf (accessed 8 June 2014).

[333] See 'Efrain Rios Montt & Mauricio Rodriguez Sanchez before the national courts of Guatemala'; 'Who's Who', *International Justice Monitor*, http://www.ijmonitor.org/efrain-rios-montt-and-mauricio-rodriguez-sanchez-whos-who/ (accessed 7 June 2014): "In Guatemala, the individual judges who oversee the preliminary hearings (first instance judges) are distinct from the three-judge panel of judges who oversee the trial (sentencing court). There are only two High Risk Courts in Guatemala, "A" and "B"."

Ríos Montt, who is tried together with his former head of intelligence José Mauricio Rodríguez Sánchez, "to stand trial on charges of genocide and crimes against humanity stemming from the killing of more than 1,700 villagers of Mayan ancestry".[334] On 11 March 2013, the Constitutional Court rejected an *amparo* filed by Montt and Sanchez which claimed that the 1986 amnesty should bar the prosecution[335] and on 19 March 2013, the historic trial commenced before a three-judge panel of the First High-Risk Tribunal A, headed by Judge Yassmin Barrios. Navi Pillay, the UN High Commissioner for Human Rights, welcomed the start and noted that "[t]his is the first time, anywhere in the world, that a former head of State is being put on trial for genocide by a national tribunal".[336] However, the months that followed showed many obstacles in the proceedings: on 17 April 2013, Judge Patricia Flores issued a notification of the decision of almost one year old by the Supreme Court which determined as invalid the recusal request that led to the replacement, on 23 November 2011, of Judge Flores by Judge Galvez (see above).[337] The Supreme Court's decision of 23 May 2012[338] "order[ed] that the applicant is restored to the legal situation prior to the recusal resolution".[339] Because of this, Judge Flores annulled the trial on 18 April, holding that all actions taken since 23 November 2011 were invalid.[340] However, the day after, the First High-Risk Tribunal A, headed by Barrios, noted that Flores had exceeded her authority.[341]

---

334 See S. Franklin, 'Former Guatemala dictator to stand trial for genocide', *Jurist* (29 January 2013), http://jurist.org/paperchase/2013/01/former-guatemala-dictator-to-stand-trial-for-genocide.php (accessed 7 June 2014).

335 See 'Efrain Rios Montt & Mauricio Rodriguez Sanchez before the national courts of Guatemala'; 'Timeline', *International Justice Monitor*, http://www.ijmonitor.org/efrain-rios-montt-and-mauricio-rodriguez-sanchez-timeline/ (accessed 7 June 2014).

336 See UN Office of the High Commissioner for Human Rights, Press Release, 'Pillay hails start of genocide trial in Guatemala' (18 March 2013), http://www.ohchr.org/en/NewsEvents/Pages/DisplayNews.aspx?NewsID=13155&LangID=E (accessed 3 June 2014).

337 See 'Efrain Rios Montt & Mauricio Rodriguez Sanchez before the national courts of Guatemala'; 'Timeline', supra n 335.

338 See ibid. why it took so long: "The defense appealed and the Constitutional Court confirmed the Supreme Court's decision on December 13, 2012. News reports state that a three-judge panel of the appellate court reportedly recognizes this resolution on March 13, 2013. As a matter of course, it took until April 2013 for the notification of the final decision concerning the illegality of the prior recusal to reach Judge Flores, and until April 17, 2013 for Judge Flores to notify the parties."

339 Ibid.

340 See S. Paulsworth, 'Trial halted for former Guatemala leader accused of genocide', *Jurist* (20 April 2013), http://jurist.org/paperchase/2013/04/trial-for-former-guatemala-leader-accused-of-genocide-halted.php (accessed 7 June 2014).

341 See J. Deisher, 'Guatemala judge reverses suspension of trial against former president', *Jurist* (20 April 2013), http://jurist.org/paperchase/2013/04/guatemala-judge-reverses-suspension-of-trial-against-former-president.php (accessed 7 June 2014).

Nevertheless, it did still suspend the proceedings pending Constitutional Court review. On 23 April 2013, the Guatemalan Constitutional Court ordered Barrios to send the case back to Flores, who had to "resolve the limited and technical question of whether defense evidence was incorporated properly and how to incorporate it".[342] On 9 May 2013, the landmark trial was concluded and already the day after, the verdict was issued; he 86-year-old Ríos Montt was sentenced to 50 years in prison for the crime of genocide and 30 years for crimes against humanity. Presiding Judge Barrios stated that Montt was fully aware of plans to exterminate the indigenous Ixil population during his 1982–1983 rule. The First High-Risk Tribunal A cancelled any alternative measures and ordered his immediate detention.[343] UN experts welcomed the judgment, with the UN Working Group on Enforced or Involuntary Disappearances saying that "this verdict represents a breakthrough in the fight against impunity and demonstrates that no one today can be above the law".[344] On 13 May 2013, the Tribunal, during a hearing on reparations for victims, ordered the government to apologize to the Ixil Maya for the genocide committed by Montt.[345] In addition, it also ordered the government to declare 23 March, the day Montt seized power in 1982, to be the National Day Against Genocide.[346] However, complications reemerged very quickly, when on 20 May 2013, only 10 days after the conviction and only 3 days after the 718-page judgment was issued, Guatemala's Constitutional Court annulled the trial judgment and set the trial back to where it was on 19 April 2013.[347] On 27 May 2013, the divided Constitutional Court re-affirmed its ruling partially annulling the trial, in a more detailed clarification issued by the three-judge majority.[348] In addition, and much to the dismay of many, it

[342] See B. Lynch, 'New judge to preside over trial of Guatemala ex-dictator', *Jurist* (24 April 2013), http://jurist.org/paperchase/2013/04/new-judge-to-preside-over-trial-of-guatemala-ex-dictator.php (accessed 7 June 2014).

[343] See the case analysis on the International Crimes Database at: http://www.internationalcrimes database.org/Case/948 (accessed 7 June 2014).

[344] See UN Office of the High Commissioner for Human Rights, Press Release, 'Guatemala: "Justice, the best guarantee to prevent the recurrence of atrocities"—UN experts' (15 May 2013), http://www.ohchr.org/FR/NewsEvents/Pages/DisplayNews.aspx?NewsID=13330&LangID=E (accessed 7 June 2014).

[345] See J. Cremeans, 'Guatemala court: government must apologize for acts of genocide', *Jurist* (15 May 2013), http://jurist.org/paperchase/2013/05/guatemala-court-government-must-apologize-for-acts-of-genocide.php (accessed 7 June 2014).

[346] Ibid.

[347] See E. LaForgia, 'Guatemala court voids ex-dictator Rios Montt's genocide conviction', *Jurist* (21 May 2013), http://jurist.org/paperchase/2013/05/guatemala-court-voids-ex-dictator-rios-montts-genocide-conviction.php (accessed 7 June 2014).

[348] See the case analysis on the International Crimes Database at: http://www.internationalcrimes database.org/Case/948 (accessed 7 June 2014).

reconsidered the question whether the 1986 amnesty should bar the proceedings (see again above).[349] Due to the fact that the First High-Risk Tribunal A had already issued a verdict, it was forced to recuse itself from the case.[350] On 4 June 2013, the other high-risk tribunal in Guatemala—First High-Risk Tribunal B—was assigned to the case. The trial then was expected to start in 2014, as the schedule of the Tribunal, presided over by Judge Irma Jeannette Valdez Rodas, was booked until April 2014.[351] On 11 June 2013, Montt was released from the military medical centre and placed under house arrest and in November 2013, it was reported that the Montt trial would restart in January 2015.[352]

#### 7.2.3.6 Norway

On 14 February 2013, Sadi Bugingo was sentenced to 21 years' imprisonment, the longest prison term in Norway, by the Oslo City Court for his role in the 1994 Rwandan genocide.[353] According to the judges, Bugingo was an accomplice to the murders of between 1,000 and 2,000 people.[354] Although Bugingo claimed he had nothing to do with the genocide and in fact, tried to save lives during the massacre, the judges apparently found the witnesses testifying against him more credible.[355] After having heard the verdict, Bugingo appealed on the spot.[356]

#### 7.2.3.7 Senegal

Also for the *Habré* case, 2013 was an important year. After the Senegalese National Assembly had adopted laws establishing the Extraordinary African Chambers (EAC) within the existing Senegalese court structure in Dakar, opening the way for

[349] See E. MacLean, 'One Month After Guatemala's Constitutional Court Intervenes to Challenge Rios Montt Genocide Conviction: Amnesty Back on the Table, New Trial Court Booked Till Mid-2014, and Rios Montt Back Home', *International Justice Monitor* (18 June 2013), http://www.ijmonitor.org/2013/06/one-month-after-guatemalas-constitutional-court-intervenes-to-challenge-rios-montt-genocide-conviction-amnesty-back-on-the-table-new-trial-court-booked-till-mid-2014-and-rios-montt-back-ho/ (accessed 7 June 2014).

[350] See the case analysis on the International Crimes Database at: http://www.internationalcrimesdatabase.org/Case/948 (accessed 7 June 2014).

[351] Ibid.

[352] See M. Slater, 'Guatemala court to restart genocide trial of former dictator in January 2015', *Jurist* (6 November 2013), http://jurist.org/paperchase/2013/11/guatemala-court-to-restart-genocide-trial-of-former-dictator-in-january-2015.php (accessed 7 June 2014).

[353] See N. Berglund, 'Court convicts Rwandan defendant', *News in English.no* (14 February 2013), http://www.newsinenglish.no/2013/02/14/court-convicts-rwandan-defendant/ (accessed 8 June 2014).

[354] Ibid.

[355] Ibid.

[356] Ibid.

a trial against Hissène Habré in Senegal (see last year's *Year in Review*), and after the EAC were officially opened on 8 February 2013,[357] Habré was arrested on 30 June 2013[358] and charged with war crimes, torture and crimes against humanity on 2 July 2013.[359] On 18 July 2013, more than 1,000 victims filed for civil party status, requesting the EAC to officially recognize them as parties with an interest in the matter.[360] Between 20 August and 2 September 2013, EAC investigative judges and prosecutors, in cooperation with Senegalese police officers and the Chadian authorities, conducted an investigatory mission to Chad, among other things to hear statements from victims and witnesses and to conduct on-site investigations.[361] A second mission was organized between 30 November and 22 December 2013.[362] In the meantime, in court, Habré challenged the jurisdiction of the EAC before the ECOWAS Court of Justice, arguing that the EAC were not legitimate and that Habré could not get a fair trial,[363] However, the ECOWAS Court of Justice, on 5 November 2013, "held that it did not have jurisdiction to rule on the application because the Extraordinary African Chambers were established pursuant to a treaty between Senegal and the African Union".[364]

#### 7.2.3.8 Serbia

On 22 February 2013, the trial chamber in the Higher Court in Belgrade convicted several members of the so-called "Sima's Chetniks" paramilitary group for war crimes against Roma civilians in the summer of 1992 in the village of Skočić near

---

357 See B. Minegar, 'Senegal opens court to try former Chad dictator', *Jurist* (8 February 2013), http://jurist.org/paperchase/2013/02/senegal-opens-court-to-try-former-chad-dictator.php (accessed 7 June 2014).

358 See 'Senegal police arrest Chad former leader Hissene Habre', *BBC News* (30 June 2013), http://www.bbc.com/news/world-africa-23119658 (accessed 7 June 2014).

359 See S. Franklin, 'Former Chad dictator charged with war crimes', *Jurist* (3 July 2013), http://jurist.org/paperchase/2013/07/former-chad-dictator-charged-with-war-crimes.php (accessed 7 June 2014).

360 See G. Redd, 'Victims of former Chad dictator seek to participate in trial', *Jurist* (19 July 2013), http://jurist.org/paperchase/2013/07/victims-of-former-chad-dictator-seek-to-participate-in-trial.php (accessed 7 June 2014).

361 See 'Chronology of the Habré Case', *Human Rights Watch* (13 March 2014), http://www.hrw.org/news/2012/03/09/chronology-habr-case (accessed 7 June 2014).

362 Ibid.

363 See 'Senegal: Case Against Habré Set to Continue. ECOWAS Court Rejects Chad Ex-Dictator's Bid to Halt Proceedings', *Human Rights Watch* (5 November 2013), http://www.hrw.org/news/2013/11/05/senegal-case-against-habre-set-continue-0 (accessed 7 June 2014).

364 See 'Chronology of the Habré Case', supra n 361. The judgment can be found here (in French): http://www.courtecowas.org/site2012/pdf_files/decisions/judgements/2013/HISSEIN%20HABRE_c_REPUBLIC_OF_SENEGAL2013.pdf (accessed 7 June 2014).

Zvornik (BiH).[365] Zoran Stojanović and Zoran Đurđević were sentenced to 20 years' imprisonment each, Zoran Alić and Tomislav Gavrić to 10 years each, Dragana Đekić and Đorđe Šević to five years each,[366] and Damir Bogdanović to two years.[367] Zoran Alić was released from detention, but he is to remain in his place of residence.[368] According to the judges, Zoran Đurđević, Zoran Stojanović, Zoran Alić, Đorđe Šević and Dragana Đekić destroyed on 12 July 1992 the mosque of Skočić and then gathered 32 Roma civilians, most of them women and children, in one house and (sexually) abused several of them and killed one person.[369] After that, they brought them to Malešić village, where they separated three young girls from the rest.[370] Zoran Đurđević, Zoran Stojanović and Zoran Alić and others subsequently transported the others to a pit near the village of Šetići, and killed 27 of them, including seven children.[371] In the months that followed, the three girls were used as (sex) slaves by the members of the group.[372]

### 7.2.3.9 The Netherlands

In the case of Yvonne Basebya (see last year's *Year in Review*), the District Court of The Hague found on 1 March 2013 that Basebya was guilty of incitement to genocide on multiple occasions.[373] She was sentenced to six years and eight months of imprisonment, the maximum sentence possible for the crime of incitement to genocide on multiple accounts.[374] Basebya was acquitted of the other charges because the evidence could not prove her involvement beyond a reasonable doubt.[375] The fact that Yvonne Basebya had incited youth during the meetings of the CDR, the *Coalition pour la Défense de la République*, the Hutu extremist party, was not sufficient to hold her criminally responsible for the ensuing violence

---

[365] See 'Reactions to Judgment in Skočić Case', *Humanitarian Law Center* (22 February 2013), http://www.hlc-rdc.org/?p=22538&lang=de (accessed 7 June 2014).

[366] "Since Đorđe Šević was already legally sentenced to 15 years in prison for another felony (war crime), he was sentenced to a conjoint prison term of 15 years." See the report of the case by the attorney of one of the victims: http://www.hlc-rdc.org/wp-content/uploads/2013/10/Skocic-Case-22.02.2013.pdf (accessed 7 June 2014).

[367] See 'Reactions to Judgment in Skočić Case', supra n 365.

[368] Ibid.

[369] See the report of the case by the attorney of one of the victims, supra n 366.

[370] Ibid.

[371] Ibid.

[372] Ibid.

[373] See the case analysis on the International Crimes Database at: http://www.internationalcrimesdatabase.org/Case/971 (accessed 7 June 2014), where one can find the verdict of the District Court of The Hague (in Dutch), the summary of the verdict (in Dutch, English and French) and the motivation of the verdict (in French).

[374] Ibid.

[375] Ibid.

committed by those young people.[376] Yvonne Basebya is the first Dutch citizen—she came to the Netherlands in October 1998 and on 7 December 2004 she obtained Dutch nationality—to be convicted for her involvement in the Rwandan genocide and the first person to be convicted of incitement to genocide in the Netherlands.[377] On 28 June 2013, both the National Public Prosecutor's Office and the Defence decided not to appeal the judgment, which means that the verdict of the District Court of The Hague is final.[378]

And in another Dutch case involving the Rwandan genocide, the case of Joseph Mpambara, the Dutch Supreme Court affirmed, on 26 November 2013, the conviction and sentence to life long imprisonment of the accused by the Court of Appeal of The Hague in 2011.[379] Mpambara, who was a member of the Interahamwe militia in Rwanda in 1994 and who sought asylum in the Netherlands in 1998, was initially convicted in 2009 for torture only, but the Court of Appeal of The Hague also found him guilty of war crimes and increased his initial 20 years' imprisonment to life imprisonment.[380] Mpambara appealed at the Supreme Court, arguing that this judgment—especially the use of evidence from witnesses he could not examine and the issuance of a life sentence—was in violation of his fundamental rights as found in the European Convention on Human Rights, namely his rights to a fair trial and to protection against inhumane treatment.[381] However, the Supreme Court found the grounds of appeal unfounded, dismissed Mpambara's appeal, and confirmed the judgment and sentence of the Court of Appeal.[382]

Finally, in two groundbreaking civil judgments, in the cases *The Netherlands v. Nuhanović* and *The Netherlands v. Mustafić*, the same Dutch Supreme Court found on 6 September 2013 the State of the Netherlands responsible for the death of three Muslim men during the Srebrenica massacre. The case is historic, as it "marks the first time an individual government has been held to account for the conduct of its peacekeeping troops operating under a UN mandate".[383] The case was filed by

---

[376] Ibid.

[377] Ibid.

[378] Ibid.

[379] See the case analysis on the International Crimes Database at: http://www.internationalcrimesdatabase.org/Case/1217 (accessed 7 June 2014), where one can find the judgment and the conclusion of the Advocate-General (in Dutch). For the judgment of the District Court of 23 March 2009, see the case analysis on the International Crimes Database at: http://www.internationalcrimesdatabase.org/Case/759 (accessed 7 June 2014) and for the judgment of the Court of Appeal of 7 July 2011, see the case analysis on the International Crimes Database at: http://www.internationalcrimesdatabase.org/Case/1218 (accessed 7 June 2014).

[380] Ibid.

[381] Ibid.

[382] Ibid.

[383] See 'Netherlands Supreme Court hands down historic judgment over Srebrenica genocide', *Amnesty International* (6 September 2013), http://www.amnesty.org/en/news/netherlands-supreme-court-hands-down-historic-judgment-over-srebrenica-genocide-2013-09-06 (accessed 8 June 2014).

Hasan Nuhanović and by the family of Rizo Mustafić. Hasan Nuhanović was in the employment of the UN as an interpreter at the compound in Potočari where the Dutch troops, Dutchbat, were stationed, who held a UN pass and who was on the list of local personnel who could be evacuated together with Dutchbat.[384] Conversely, Rizo Mustafić was employed by the Srebrenica municipal authority and was seconded to the Dutch, for whom he worked as an electrician at the compound.[385] After the fall of the enclave, Hasan Nuhanović's father Ibro, mother Nasiha and brother Muhamed sought refuge in the compound, but were told to leave, after which they were murdered by the Bosnian-Serb army or related paramilitary groups.[386] Rizo Mustafić, his wife and their two children, who were also not on the list of local personnel, were told to leave as well.[387] Shortly afterwards, Rizo Mustafić was murdered. It was argued in court that Dutchbat acted wrongfully by not taking Nuhanović's family and Rizo Mustafić and his family with them when they evacuated, instead sending them away. On 10 September 2008, the District Court of The Hague denied the claim, holding that the Dutch Government could not be held responsible because the peacekeepers were operating in Bosnia under a UN mandate.[388] However, on 5 July 2011, the Court of Appeal of The Hague quashed the judgment of the District Court, finding that the conduct was indeed attributable to the Netherlands and that it had acted wrongly.[389] The Supreme Court had to solve two questions: can Dutchbat's actions be attributed to the State of the Netherlands and second, were Dutchbat's actions wrongful?[390] The first question was answered in the affirmative, with the Supreme Court explaining that public international law allows conduct to be attributed not only to the UN (in charge of the peace mission), but also to the State because the latter had effective control over Dutchbat's disputed conduct.[391] As to the second question, the challenge against the decision of the Court of Appeal that Dutchbat's conduct was wrongful under the law of BiH, was unsuccessful.[392] The State advocated for judicial restraint in the review of Dutchbat's conduct, but according to the Supreme Court, this would mean that there would be virtually no scope for the courts to assess the conduct of a troop contingent in the

---

384 See Supreme Court of the Netherlands, 'State responsible for death of three Muslim men in Srebrenica' (6 September 2013), http://www.rechtspraak.nl/Organisatie/Hoge-Raad/Nieuws/Pages/State-responsible-for-death-of-three-Muslim-men-in-Srebrenica.aspx (accessed 8 June 2014).

385 Ibid.

386 Ibid.

387 Ibid.

388 See the case analysis of the *Nuhanović* judgment on the International Crimes Database at: http://www.internationalcrimesdatabase.org/Case/1005 (accessed 7 June 2014), where one can also find an English version of the judgment.

389 Ibid.

390 Ibid.

391 Ibid.

392 Ibid.

context of a peace mission, which was unacceptable, though it acknowledged that a court assessing the conduct in retrospect must make allowance for the fact that the decisions in questions were taken under great pressure in a war situation.[393] As a result, the Supreme Court concluded that the Dutch State was indeed responsible for the death of three Muslim men (Nuhanović's father Ibro and brother Muhamed and Rizo Mustafić) from Srebrenica.[394]

## 7.3 Arms Control and Disarmament

### *7.3.1 Conventional Weapons*

#### 7.3.1.1 Arms Trade Treaty Text

In April, the UN General Assembly adopted the Arms Trade Treaty (ATT).[395] From the UN website, this treaty is meant for "regulating the international trade in conventional arms, from small arms to battle tanks, combat aircraft and warships. The treaty will foster peace and security by thwarting uncontrolled destabilizing arms flows to conflict regions. It will prevent human rights abusers and violators of the law of war from being supplied with arms. And it will help keep warlords, pirates, and gangs from acquiring these deadly tools".[396] The ATT was adopted on 2 April by the General Assembly with a vote of 154-3-23; at the time of publication, it has 118 signatories and 40 ratifications.[397] The treaty will enter into force 90 days following the date of deposit of the instrument of ratification of the 50th State party to the treaty.[398]

---

[393] Ibid.

[394] Ibid. As to Nasiha, the mother of Hasan, the Supreme Court concluded: "The Court of Appeal has found that the allegation that the State acted wrongfully towards Nasiha Nuhanović has not been sufficiently substantiated. It has gone on to find that as a woman Nasiha did not—according to Nuhanović—have anything to fear from the Serbs and in the absence of further explanation, which is lacking, there does not appear to be any reason why Dutchbat was not entitled to allow her to leave the compound. The Court of Appeal's ruling in relation to the State's conduct towards Nasiha has not been disputed in the cassation proceedings." See para 3.5.3 at p. 14 of the English version of the judgment, which can be found here: http://www.asser.nl/upload/documents/20130909T125927-Supreme%20Court%20Nuhanovic%20ENG.pdf (accessed 8 June 2014).

[395] See Arms Trade Treaty, New York, 2 April 2013 *United Nations Treaty Series* available from http://unoda-web.s3.amazonaws.com/wp-content/uploads/2014/03/Ch_XXVI_08.pdf#page=22. (accessed 12 June 2014).

[396] See UN Office of Disarmament Affairs website, http://www.un.org/disarmament/ATT/. (accessed 12 June 2014).

[397] Ibid.

[398] Arms Trade Treaty, Article 22(1), supra n 395, p. 16

### 7.3.1.2 Small Arms and Light Weapons

In 2012, the second UN conference to review the 2001 Programme of Action on trafficking in small arms and light weapons met and ultimately "adopted a consensus outcome document that highlighted the international community's renewed commitment to preventing, combating and eradicating the illicit trade".[399] In 2013, the UN Secretary General undertook a review with the purpose of taking "stock of current and emerging concerns in the control and regulation of small arms, in particular in relation to the issues under the purview of the Security Council, and provides an analysis of measures taken to address those concerns." He published his recommendations in a report, as a follow-up to his report from 2011.[400] A sampling of the 15 recommendations included:

1. "The Security Council should, in mandating any peacekeeping operation, planning post-conflict peacebuilding and considering the possible lifting of an arms embargo, take into consideration the capacity of States to exert effective control over their existing arms and ammunition stockpiles and future imports with a view to preventing such weapons from being diverted to the illicit market."[401]
2. "I encourage all Member States to make every effort to secure arms and ammunition stockpiles from diversion. I encourage the Security Council to ensure that peacekeeping and peacebuilding missions are mandated to assist host countries in their stockpile management."[402]
3. "The Security Council should consider, on a case-by-case basis, the relevance of new technologies, such as time limitation or geographical limitation devices, or biometric or radio frequency identification, to improve weapons stockpile management and reduce diversion of weapons into illicit use."[403]
4. "I encourage regular information exchange between the informal expert group on the protection of civilians of the Security Council, the Office for Disarmament Affairs and other relevant United Nations entities, as appropriate, including the Office of the Special Representative for Children and Armed Conflict, the

[399] UN General Assembly 'Review Conference Adopts Text Renewing Commitment to Prevent, Combat, Eradicate Illicit Trade in Small Arms, Light Weapons', Press Release (7 September 2012) http://www.un.org/News/Press/docs/2012/dc3389.doc.htm (accessed12 June 2014).

[400] See UN Secretary General Report on Small Arms, (22 August 2013) (S/2013/503) http://www.un.org/ga/search/view_doc.asp?symbol=S/2013/503 (accessed 12 June 2014).

[401] Ibid. at 3.

[402] Ibid. at 6.

[403] Ibid.

Office of the Special Representative on Sexual Violence in Conflict, the United Nations Children's Fund and the United Nations Entity for Gender Equality and the Empowerment of Women".[404]
5. "I encourage Member States that have not done so to sign and ratify the Arms Trade Treaty as soon as possible in order to ensure its early entry into force and subsequent implementation".[405]

The Security Council passed Resolution 2117 in September regarding small arms and light weapons echoing many of the recommendations of the Secretary General.[406]

### *7.3.2 Nuclear Weapons*

On February 12, the Democratic People's Republic of Korea staged a nuclear test in violation of several resolutions. This test came approximately two months after a December test, both of which were quickly met with condemnation from various countries as well as the Security Council and the UN Secretary General. Ban Ki-Moon called the test "deplorable" and expressed that he was "gravely concerned about the negative impact of this deeply destabilizing act on regional stability as well as the global efforts for nuclear non-proliferation".[407]

The Security Council passed Resolution 2087 in response, condemning the violations of earlier resolutions, calling for a cessation of ballistic missile-launch activity, and placing a travel ban and/or asset freeze on several prominent figures in the DPRK government.[408] In a March Resolution (2094), the Security Council imposed further sanctions on various individuals.[409]

---

404 Ibid. at 8.

405 Ibid. at 9.

406 See UN Security Council Resolution 2117 (26 September 2013) http://www.un.org/en/ga/search/view_doc.asp?symbol=S/RES/2117(2013) (accessed 12 June 2014).

407 See E. Payne, 'World leaders react to N. Korea's nuclear test', *CNN* (12 February 2013) http://edition.cnn.com/2013/02/12/world/north-korea-nuclear-reax/ (accessed 12 June 2014).

408 See Security Council Resolution 2087 (22 January 2013) http://www.securitycouncilreport.org/atf/cf/%7B65BFCF9B-6D27-4E9C-8CD3-CF6E4FF96FF9%7D/s_res_2087.pdf (accessed 12 June 2014).

409 See Security Council Resolution 2094 (7 March 2013) http://www.securitycouncilreport.org/atf/cf/%7B65BFCF9B-6D27-4E9C-8CD3-CF6E4FF96FF9%7D/s_res_2094.pdf (accessed 12 June 2014).

### 7.3.3 Non-Proliferation and the International Atomic Energy Agency

#### 7.3.3.1 Iran

After the urging of the IAEA for Iran to engage with the body, talks were set to start at the beginning of 2013. However, in January, after two days of planned inspections, the talks fell through because the IAEA claimed they were not granted the access to the facilities necessary to perform their checks. They rescheduled the talks for February. After further delays, and several months of negotiations, a deal was reached in late 2013 between the P5+1 countries (US, UK, France, Russia, China and Germany) and Iran, including a freeze and rollback of the nuclear program in Iran in exchange for decreased economic sanctions.[410] It is the first formal agreement between Iran and the US in 34 years.[411] In November, the IAEA estimated it would need more funding to verify the agreement and talks have continued into 2014.[412]

### 7.3.4 Chemical Weapons

#### 7.3.4.1 Syria

In March and April, allegations surfaced that chemical weapons were being used in the armed conflict in Syria. BBC compiled a timeline:[413]

> *19 March: "Syria's state news agency Sana reported that "terrorists" had fired a rocket "containing chemical materials", killing 16 people in the Khan al-Assal area of Aleppo province. Sana published photographs of what it claimed were victims, although they appeared to show no obvious signs of exposure to chemical weapons. The official death toll rose to 31…On the same day as the attack in Khan al-Assal, activists uploaded videos purporting to show victims of*

410 See A. Gearan and J. Warrick, 'World powers reach nuclear deal with Iran to freeze its nuclear program', *The Washington Post* (24 November 2014) http://www.washingtonpost.com/world/national-security/kerry-in-geneva-raising-hopes-for-historic-nuclear-deal-with-iran/2013/11/23/53e7bfe6-5430-11e3-9fe0-fd2ca728e67c_story.html (accessed 12 June 2014).

411 See D. Blair, 'Iran nuclear deal agreed at Geneva', *The Telegraph* (24 November 2013) http://www.telegraph.co.uk/news/worldnews/middleeast/iran/10470716/Iran-nuclear-deal-agreed-at-Geneva-talks.html (accessed 12 June 2014).

412 See F. Dahl, 'IAEA says may need more money to help implement Iran nuclear deal', *Reuters* (28 November 2013) http://www.reuters.com/article/2013/11/28/us-iran-nuclear-iaea-idUSBRE9AR0AT20131128 (accessed 12 June 2014).

413 See BBC News: 'Syria: What we know', (24 September 2013) http://www.bbc.co.uk/news/world-middle-east-23927399 (accessed 12 June 2014).

*a bombardment in the village of al-Otaybeh near Damascus in the aftermath of an alleged bombardment using chemical weapons."*

*24 March: "The Local Co-Ordination Committees, a network of activists in Syria, said in its summary for 24 March that two people had been killed and "dozens" injured when Adra was shelled with "chemical phosphorus" bombs."*

*13 April: A London-based human rights organization reported that "two women and two children had been killed by poisoning from "gases from bombs dropped by an aircraft on the Sheikh Maqsoud neighbourhood...Footage that later appeared online appeared to show patients frothing at the mouth and twitching, both symptoms of exposure to nerve gas."*

*29 April: "Eyewitnesses say canisters were dropped from a helicopter above the town. Eight people were admitted [to the hospital]....They appear to be vomiting and have breathing problems."*

*21 August: "Rockets with toxic agents were launched at the suburbs of the Ghouta region early on 21 August killing hundreds, Syrian opposition activists claimed." These last claims were later validated that it was, indeed, the nerve agent sarin that was used in several of these attacks.*[414]

In response, UN Secretary General announced a probe into the attacks.[415] It was not clear at the outset which side of the conflict was using the chemical weapons (if not both). In September, the UN announced that its inspection team would enter Syria to investigate the evidence from 14 strikes. The Organization for the Prohibition of Chemical Weapons would also undertake an inspection. Rights groups as well as Ban Ki-Moon noted that these strikes against civilians amounted to crimes against humanity.[416] The UN Independent Report found evidence of the use of sarin gas on Syrian civilians,[417] making the use of sarin gas a potential war crime.[418] And in December, the same Independent Mission found that not only

[414] See 'United Nations Mission to Investigate Allegations of the Use of Chemical Weapons in the Syrian Arab Republic Report on the Alleged Use of Chemical Weapons in the Ghouta Area of Damascus on 21 August 2013' http://www.un.org/disarmament/content/slideshow/Secretary_General_Report_of_CW_Investigation.pdf (accessed 12 June 2014).

[415] See 'Off-the-Cuff: Secretary-General's Press Encounter on Syrian Government Request', (21 March 2013) http://www.un.org/sg/offthecuff/index.asp?nid=2745 (accessed 12 June 2014).

[416] See J. Deisher, 'UN SG accuses Assad of crimes against humanity', *Jurist* 1(4 September 2013) http://jurist.org/paperchase/2013/09/un-sg-accuses-assad-of-crimes-against-humanity.php (accessed 12 June 2014).

[417] See 'United Nations Mission to Investigate Allegations of the Use of Chemical Weapons in the Syrian Arab Republic Report on the Alleged Use of Chemical Weapons in the Ghouta Area of Damascus on 21 August 2013' supra n 414.

[418] See J. Levs and H. Yans, '"War Crime": UN finds sarin used in Syrian chemical weapon attack', *CNN* (17 September 2013) http://edition.cnn.com/2013/09/16/politics/syria-civil-war/ (accessed 12 June 2014).

during the 14 strikes they had investigated, but evidence had surfaced that chemical weapons had been used on several additional occasions throughout the duration of the Syrian armed conflict.[419]

## 7.4 Miscellaneous

### 7.4.1 *Organization of the Prohibition of Chemical Weapons Wins Nobel Peace Prize*

For its extensive efforts to eliminate chemical weapons, the Hague-based OPCW was the Nobel Peace Prize winner for 2013. Upon receipt for the prize, OPCW's Director-General, Ahmet Üzümcü, shared a statement:

> Our organization was tasked to verify the elimination of chemical weapons from the world and to encourage all nations to adhere to this hard-earned norm. We have since then worked with quiet determination to rid the world of these heinous weapons—weapons which have been used to horrific effect throughout the twentieth century, and, sadly, in our own time too. Events in Syria have been a tragic reminder that there remains much work yet to be done. Our hearts go out to the Syrian people who were recently victims of the horror of chemical weapons. Today we are engaged in work which is meant to ensure that this atrocity is not repeated.[420]

### 7.4.2 *International Committee of the Red Cross Celebrates 150 Years*

The International Committee of the Red Cross celebrated its 150th anniversary in 2013 with the theme of "150 Years of Humanitarian Action." A number of events were launched around the world in connection with this milestone and more information about the anniversary can be found on the ICRC's website.[421]

[419] See UN News Centre, 'UN team finds 'credible information' on more cases of chemical weapons use in Syria', (12 December 2013). http://www.un.org/apps/news/story.asp?NewsID=46730&Cr=syria&Cr1=#.Uqsh62RDu3M (accessed 12 June 2014).

[420] See Organization for the Prohibition of Chemical Weapons, 'Statement by the OPCW Director-General on the 2013 Nobel Peace Prize', (11 October 2013) http://www.opcw.org/news/article/opcw-receives-2013-nobel-prize-for-peace/ (accessed 12 June 2014).

[421] See International Committee of the Red Cross, '150 Years of Humanitarian Action', http://www.icrc.org/eng/who-we-are/history/150-years/index.jsp (accessed 11 June 2014).

### 7.4.3 *Strengthening Compliance with IHL Initiative*

The Swiss Government and the ICRC joined together to establish the initiative on Strengthening Compliance with IHL in 2011. The aims of this initiative are: "undertaking consultation and research on possible ways to improve compliance with IHL through the establishment of more effective international mechanisms" with the rationale that

> [u]nfortunately, IHL continues to be violated frequently by both States and non-State armed groups. If IHL was [sic] better respected, there would be less suffering. At present, for example, IHL lacks effective means of identifying, preventing and halting violations while they are occurring. The mechanisms within IHL that do exist are rarely, if ever used. Moreover, they are only applicable in international armed conflict, whereas the majority of conflicts are now non-international.[422]

They define compliance broadly as:

> observance and implementation of IHL. The initiative that is underway aims to strengthen compliance by means of enhancing the effectiveness of existing mechanisms where possible and examining the creation of new ones. It can therefore be differentiated from a wider range of activities aimed at promoting respect for IHL, including diverse forms of prevention activity, international dispute settlement and international criminal justice mechanisms.[423]

Two meetings of this initiative occurred in 2013 (April, June), and in December, the Chair's Conclusions were published.[424] The initiative continues into 2014.

### 7.4.4 *Red Cross/Red Crescent November Statutory Meetings in Sydney*

In November, Sydney, Australia hosted to the 19th General Assembly of the International Federation of Red Cross and Red Crescent Societies (IFRC) and Council of Delegates meeting of the Red Cross Red Crescent Movement. The meetings were a gathering of the leaders of the Movement from all National

---

422 See International Committee of the Red Cross, 'Strengthening compliance with international humanitarian law (IHL): The work of the ICRC and the Swiss government' (30 April 2014), http://www.icrc.org/eng/what-we-do/other-activities/development-ihl/strengthening-legal-protection-compliance.htm (accessed 11 June 2014).

423 Ibid.

424 See Swiss/ICRC Initiative on Strengthening Compliance with IHL, Preparatory Discussion in view of the third Meeting of States (2014) Geneva, 16-17 December 2013 'Chair's Conclusions', http://www.icrc.org/eng/assets/files/2014/2013-12-chairs-conclusions-december-2013.pdf (accessed 11 June 2014).

Societies, the IFRC and the ICRC and presented opportunities to discuss humanitarian challenges facing the world today and to plan for the future of the Movement. The website of the event also has more information.[425]

### 7.4.5 *Second Part of the Turkel Commission Report*

The second part of the Turkel Commission Report was published in February, entitled: "Israel's Mechanisms for Examining and Investigating Complaints and Claims of Violations of the Laws of Armed Conflict According to International Law".[426] The Turkel Commission was a commission of inquiry set up by the Israeli government to investigate the "Maritime Incident of 31 May 2010" and specifically the three following issues: (a) The security circumstances in which the naval blockade on the Gaza Strip was imposed and whether the blockade complies with the rules of international law; (b) Whether the actions carried out by Israel to enforce the naval blockade on May 31, 2010, complied with the rules of international law and (c) The actions carried out by the organizers and participants of the flotilla and their identities.[427] the Gaza Blockade and the situation on the Turkish ship, the *Mavi Marmara*, known informally as the Gaza Flotilla Raid. The mandate of the inquiry was to investigate the legality of the Israeli blockade as well as the Israeli Navy's actions during the raid. Allegations of war crimes and international law breaches also fell under the mandate of the inquiry to investigate. For an in-depth analysis of the second part of the report, see Michelle Lesh's Chap. 6 of this book.

## References

Amnesty International (2013) Report 2013: the state of the world's human rights. http://files.amnesty.org/air13/AmnestyInternational_AnnualReport2013_complete_en.pdf. Accessed 28 May 2014

Human Rights Watch (2013) World report 2012. www.hrw.org/sites/default/files/wr2013_web.pdf. Accessed 28 May 2014

---

[425] See Website, Red Cross and Red Crescent, Sydney 2013, http://www.rcrcmeetings.org/sydney2013/ (accessed 11 June 2014).

[426] The Public Commission to Examine the Maritime Incident of 31 May 2010, Second Report—The Turkel Commission, 'Israel's Mechanisms for Examining and Investigating Complaints and Claims of Violations of the Laws of Armed Conflict According to International Law' (February 2013), http://www.turkel-committee.gov.il/files/newDoc3/The%20Turkel%20Report%20for%20website.pdf (accessed 11 June 2014).

[427] The Public Commission to Examine the Maritime Incident of 31 May 2010, The Turkel Commission Report Part One, http://www.jewishvirtuallibrary.org/jsource/Society_&_Culture/TurkelCommission.pdf (accessed 11 June 2014), p. 2.

Human Rights Watch (2014) World report 2013. www.hrw.org/sites/default/files/wr2014_web_0.pdf. Accessed 28 May 2014

Sivakumaran S (2012) Law of non-international armed conflict. Oxford University Press, Oxford

Walker A (2012) Special report: what is boko haram? United States Institute of Peace. www.usip.org/files/resources/SR308.pdf. Accessed 10 June 2014

# Part III
# Essays on the Boundaries of the Battlefield

On 10 and 11 January 2013, the T.M.C. Asser Instituut and the International Centre for Counter-Terrorism—The Hague (ICCT), in cooperation with the International Humanitarian and Criminal Law Platform, the Konrad Adenauer Stiftung, the Municipality of The Hague and The Netherlands Ministry of Foreign Affairs organised a two-day symposium entitled *The Boundaries of the Battlefield: A Critical Look at the Legal Paradigms and Rules in Countering Terrorism*. During the symposium, 27 top panellists and moderators from academia, civil society, governments, the military and multilateral organisations discussed the contours of various approaches states take against non-state actors with the goal of countering terrorism. Specifically, the symposium addressed issues related to uses of force and how these may affect and define the geographic and temporal scope and limitations of the laws of armed conflict in relation to counter-terrorism. Besides this main theme, which operates within the armed conflict paradigm, the symposium also discussed and assessed the law-enforcement paradigm.

The following is a collection of (non-peer-reviewed) contributions reflecting on the symposium and its various aspects. The first, from Jessica Dorsey and Christophe Paulussen, outlines and elaborates on a number of key questions raised during the conference relating to the temporal and geographical limitations of armed conflict, the interplay between international humanitarian law and international human rights law, as well as the use of drones, the law enforcement approach to counter-terrorism and the possible need for a new framework for countering terrorism. Other essays from Gilles De Kerchove and Christiane Höhn, Laurie Blank, Terry Gill, Peter Margulies and Matthew Sinnott are in-depth reflections on various other aspects of the symposium.

# Chapter 8
# Boundaries of the Battlefield: A Critical Look at the Legal Paradigms and Rules in Countering Terrorism

**Jessica Dorsey and Christophe Paulussen**

**Abstract** On 10 and 11 January 2013, the T.M.C. Asser Institute and the International Centre for Counter-Terrorism—The Hague (ICCT), in cooperation with the International Humanitarian and Criminal Law Platform, the Konrad Adenauer Stiftung, the Municipality of The Hague and the Netherlands Ministry of Foreign Affairs organised a two-day symposium entitled The Boundaries of the Battlefield: A Critical Look at the Legal Paradigms and Rules in Countering Terrorism. During the symposium, twenty-seven top panellists and moderators from academia, civil society, governments, the military and multilateral organisations discussed the contours of various approaches states take against non-state actors with the goal of countering terrorism. Specifically, the symposium addressed issues related to uses of force and how these may affect and define the geographic and temporal scope and limitations of the laws of armed conflict in relation to counter-terrorism. Besides this main theme, which operates within the armed conflict paradigm, the symposium also discussed and assessed the law-enforcement paradigm. Specifically, this paper elaborates on a number of key questions raised during the conference; these relate to the temporal and geographical limitations of armed conflict, the interplay between international humanitarian law and international human rights law, as well as the use of drones, the law enforcement approach to counter-terrorism and the possible need for a new framework for countering terrorism.

---

Jessica Dorsey, J.D., LL.M., is a researcher in international humanitarian law, international human rights law and international criminal law at the T.M.C. Asser Institute and a Ph.D. candidate at the University of Amsterdam. j.dorsey@asser.nl and Dr. Christophe Paulussen, LL.M., M.Phil., is a senior researcher international humanitarian law/international criminal law at the T.M.C. Asser Instituut. c.paulussen@asser.nl.

---

J. Dorsey · C. Paulussen (✉)
T.M.C. Asser Institute, The Hague, The Netherlands
e-mail: c.paulussen@asser.nl

J. Dorsey
e-mail: j.dorsey@asser.nl

 
T.D. Gill et al. (eds.), *Yearbook of International Humanitarian Law 2013*,
Yearbook of International Humanitarian Law 16, DOI 10.1007/978-94-6265-038-1_8

**Keywords** *Jus ad bellum* · *Jus in bello* · International human rights law · International humanitarian law · Law enforcement · Counterterrorism · Counterinsurgency · Drones · Armed conflict

## Contents



## 8.1 Introduction

On 10 and 11 January 2013, the T.M.C. Asser Institute and the International Centre for Counter-Terrorism—The Hague (ICCT), in cooperation with the International Humanitarian and Criminal Law Platform, the Konrad Adenauer Stiftung, the Municipality of The Hague and the Netherlands Ministry of Foreign Affairs organised a two-day symposium entitled *The Boundaries of the Battlefield: A Critical Look at the Legal Paradigms and Rules in Countering Terrorism.*[1]

[1] See T.M.C. Asser Institute website for more information about the symposium: http://www.asser.nl/events.aspx?id=325. Accessed 4 June 2014.

During the symposium, twenty-seven top panellists and moderators from academia, civil society, governments, the military and multilateral organisations discussed the contours of various approaches states take against non-state actors with the goal of countering terrorism. Specifically, the symposium addressed issues related to uses of force and how these may affect and define the geographic and temporal scope and limitations of the laws of armed conflict in relation to counter-terrorism. Besides this main theme, which operates within the armed conflict paradigm, the symposium also discussed and assessed the law-enforcement paradigm.

This research paper aims to highlight the main issues that were addressed during the symposium and in doing so, will follow the titles of the six panels:

- Whenever War?: Temporal Limitations to Armed Conflict (Sect. 8.2);
- Wherever War?: Geographic Limitations to Armed Conflict (Sect. 8.3);
- International Humanitarian Law and International Human Rights Law: Menu à la Carte? (Sect. 8.4);
- A Case Study on Targeted Killings and Drones (Sect. 8.5);
- Law Enforcement Approach in Counter-Terrorism (Sect. 8.6); and finally
- The Way Forward: The Need for a New Framework for Counter-Terrorism? (Sect. 8.7).[2]

A conclusion will be provided with a very brief summary of the symposium, including the areas that are in need of further research (Sect. 8.8). This specific paper does not allow for a comprehensive summary of all the different matters that were discussed during these two days,[3] but it addresses a selection of a few important questions raised and conclusions reached, including relevant background information.

During the symposium, one participant remarked that the relevance of such conferences was that they help to interpret the law and demonstrate just how far it can be stretched. Indeed, in the words of Professor Terry Gill, the keynote speaker of the first day: "If the legal community does not come up with some kind of consensus, then I am afraid that policymakers will use what they find most expedient. As lawyers we have a responsibility or we run the risk of becoming irrelevant".

## 8.2 Whenever War?: Temporal Limitations to Armed Conflict

### 8.2.1 Introduction

The first panel was designed to address issues surrounding the temporal limitations to armed conflict, exploring the moments at which an armed conflict begins and ends, especially with respect to cross-boundary conflicts between state and non-state

[2] See Annex 1 for the programme of the symposium and Annex 2 for the list of speakers.

[3] The authors and T.M.C. Asser Press intend to explore opportunities for follow-up activities.

actors, the main focus of the symposium. Three main issues were explored in this panel: (1) the concept of "naked" self-defence and the *jus ad bellum* considerations in counter-terrorism, (2) the evolving concept of "imminence" with respect to self-defence, and (3) temporal considerations of armed conflict.

### 8.2.2 Discussion

The first issue addressed by the panel was that of "naked" self-defence, a concept defined as "resorting to force in self-defence, but in ways in which the means and levels of force used are not part of an armed conflict, as a matter of the technical law of war. Those circumstances include self-defence uses of force against non-state actors, such as individual terrorist targets, which do not yet rise to the NIAC [non-international armed conflict] threshold".[4] In March 2010, US State Department legal adviser Harold Koh endorsed this notion when he stated that the legal standards of necessity, distinction and proportionality apply in this resort to self-defence.[5] Anderson says Koh arrived at this via customary international law rather than from obligations stemming directly from the technical laws of armed conflict.[6]

This particular notion of "naked" self-defence has been met with criticism, both outside the symposium[7] as well as during the panel discussion. For example, the point was raised that such a concept or interpretation of self-defence would be a misreading of international law and that the use of the self-defence paradigm does not mean that international humanitarian law (IHL) or international human rights law (IHRL) frameworks can be escaped. When state consent is questionable (e.g., Pakistan's consent to drone strikes, where consent is not clear), self-defence might permit going past Article 2(4) of the UN Charter; however, it would not justify a disregard for IHL and IHRL—these frameworks remain applicable with their corresponding provisions (e.g., threshold for armed conflict and imminence). Additionally, this particular notion or interpretation of self-defence as the US purports to use, raised important questions regarding the roles and obligations of non-state actors, problems with state sovereignty, and the role of human rights within the armed conflict context as well as outside of it. One, perhaps controversial, remark was that the US may have felt as though it needed to use the law of armed conflict paradigm after 9/11 in order to detain and kill people who were not related to a conflict, and therefore the "war on al Qaeda" framework was implemented and complemented by this idea of "naked" self-defence in order to fulfil policy goals. This recalls Terry Gill's opening remarks of the symposium regarding his fear that without a legal consensus, policymakers would act out of expediency.

---

4 Anderson 2011, p. 8.

5 Koh 2010.

6 Anderson 2011, p. 8.

7 Milanovic 2010a, b.

One panellist expressed regret that concepts specifically related to *jus ad bellum* were continually being mixed with those under *jus in bello*, while the two paradigms are meant to be kept separate. In his view, that mixture convolutes the discussion.[8] He opined that "naked" self-defence was purely theoretical—to really get to the crux of the matter, one must look at the facts on the ground to see whether IHL applies (i.e., whether there is an armed conflict).

Another issue is that regarding whether force can be used against terrorist suspects in anticipatory or pre-emptive self-defence before an armed attack has taken place; and, in the case of pre-emptive self-defence, even as a response to a persistent threat under which it is unclear when the attack will precisely take place but is unlikely to take place imminently.[9] Under the *Caroline* doctrine, anticipatory self-defence is recognised but limited to those cases in which an armed attack is imminent.[10] This is the case when "the necessity of that self-defence is instant, overwhelming, and leaving no choice of means, and no moment of deliberation". This is the standard of imminence traditionally accepted in customary international law.

However, John Brennan, then Assistant to the US President for Homeland Security and Counter-Terrorism, has argued that there is increasing recognition by the international community that, when fighting terrorism, a more flexible understanding of "imminence" is appropriate.[11]

The issue to be debated is at what point a terrorist threat is "imminent". Brennan argues that a flexible approach must be taken towards the imminence concept in the terrorism context, for a terrorist threat differs from traditional conflicts.[12] On the one hand, al Qaeda does not have a traditional command structure, its members do not wear uniforms or carry arms openly, leading one to say they do not meet the requisite organisational criteria outlined in IHL. On the other hand, al Qaeda is capable of attacking unexpectedly and causing significant civilian and military damage, likening their acts to hostilities, which could be governed by IHL. According to Brennan, this calls for a broader possibility to strike against terrorists out of self-defence and therefore a broader concept of imminence.[13]

The US argues that a pattern of behaviour over several years can form an imminent threat when alleged terrorists had previously planned, conspired and perhaps acted in other places.[14] One panellist opined that the US government has

---

[8] See also Blank 2011; Corn 2012; Okimoto 2011.

[9] Alston 2010, para 45.

[10] Greenwood 2009, para 7.

[11] Brennan 2011. Additionally, a recently leaked White Paper from the US Department of Justice has surfaced reiterating this notion of imminence, but going even a step further: "First, the condition that an operational leader present an "imminent" threat of violent attack against the United States does not require the United States to have clear evidence that a specific attack on U.S. persons and interests will take place in the immediate future". Searchable text of the White Paper available at: www.en.wikipedia.org/wiki/020413_DOJ_White_Paper.

[12] Ibid.

[13] Ibid.

[14] Ibid.

used this standard but defined it beyond recognition. What John Brennan has said, and what a recently leaked White Paper from the US Department of Justice reiterates, is that its use needs to be broad and flexible—but this has led to a situation of too broad and too flexible that is beyond any *Caroline* manifestation of imminence. Another panellist stated that the exception formed in Article 51 of the UN Charter is for an imminence likened to tanks massing on the border of one country aimed at another. In this panellist's view, the post-9/11 approach has been to de-couple imminence from the idea that an armed attack would happen by supplanting it with the idea that great harm might happen and the concept of this occurring was so bad, the temporal element of self-defence must be relaxed—essentially for security reasons. The majority of the panellists agreed that when it came to the imminence requirement, a careful, measured and strict interpretation was advised in order to prevent attacks and reprisals.

The question becomes whether the broadening of the principle of imminence has, to an extent, indeed become recognised by the international community or if it is forecasted to do so in the (near) future. This segues nicely into the third main issue discussed in the panel: temporal considerations of armed conflict.

When trying to define the beginning or ending of an armed conflict, many challenges arise, especially regarding conflicts between a state and a non-state actor. Derek Jinks has outlined guidelines about the initiation and cessation of armed conflict as well as defining what an armed conflict actually is.[15] He writes that regarding the initiation, international armed conflict (IAC) is more straightforward.[16] In case of a NIAC, one can turn to Common Article 3 of the Geneva Conventions, which provides that in armed conflicts not of an international character, minimum standards apply to each party. One integral issue identified in the literature is that there is no authoritative definition of armed conflict. The International Law Association's Use of Force Committee concluded a five-year study into this issue and delivered its findings in the 2010 Committee Report. In that report, the committee confirmed that at least two characteristics are found with respect to all armed conflicts: (1) the existence of organised armed groups that are (2) engaged in fighting of some intensity. In addition to these minimum criteria respecting all armed conflict, IHL includes additional criteria so as to classify conflicts as either international or non-international in nature.[17]

---

[15] Jinks 2003. See also Brooks 2004.

[16] This is based on the fact that the Geneva Conventions apply in full to "all cases of declared war or of any other armed conflict which may arise between two or more of the High Contracting Parties, even if the state of war is not recognised by one of them", or in "any cases of partial or total occupation of the territory of a High Contracting Party". Essentially, as Jinks points out, "Hostilities between states are, for the most part, governed by the laws of war irrespective of the intensity, duration, or scale of the conflict".

[17] ILA 2010.

With regard to the end of the application of IHL, in both IACs and NIACs, the general rule is that IHL applies until the "general close of military operations".[18] However, the point at which that occurs, especially with regard to a conflict between a state and a non-state actor, is not clear. A peace treaty (though uncommon) is the clearest method of ending a conflict.[19] But even in the absence of such a peace treaty, a complete cessation of hostilities and a de facto resumption of normal relations between the parties may occur.[20]

During the symposium, one panellist remarked that it is never easy to draw a line at the beginning or the end of armed conflict but the correct law nevertheless must be applied.[21] Another thought the relevant question was not necessarily about the beginning or end, but rather whether there is an IAC or a NIAC in any given situation.[22] Yet another reiterated that the need for organisation criteria applies and though the question is difficult regarding when to apply IHL, it is an important one that should not be abandoned.[23] Finally, the discussion with respect to the temporal dimension refocused on the US, demonstrating that the US government cites situations that occurred pre-9/11 in its justification of this current conflict with al

---

[18] However, there are exceptions: the obligation to repatriate persons protected under the Third (POWs) and Fourth (Civilians) Geneva Conventions triggered by the "cessation of active hostilities" and the obligations of occupying powers extend beyond the "general close of military operations".

[19] Jinks 2003, p. 3.

[20] Ibid. He writes: "[I]t is important to note that many commentators have suggested that the 'general close of military operations' standard is distinct from the 'cessation of active hostilities' standard. The latter refers to the termination of hostilities—the silencing of the guns—whereas the former refers to the complete cessation of all aggressive military maneuvers. On this reading, an 'armed conflict' might persist beyond the 'cessation of active hostilities.'"

[21] One panellist pointed out that even in the absence of a clear definition of armed conflict, the panellist would still be in favour of applying IHL—though of course torture and killing of prisoners of war is and remains illegal under all circumstances.

[22] The panellist went on to elaborate that in a NIAC there must be much more evidence of a conflict higher than IAC's threshold of hostilities based on the fact that states did not desire to tie their hands when it came to controlling internal disturbances. He illustrated his point by employing the following hypothetical situation: that with Pakistan's consent, the US killed an individual in Pakistan. This would not amount to an IAC, given that Pakistan consented, but traditionally it would not be seen as a NIAC either, and this goes back to the earlier comment about why US desires the whole world to be a battlefield—to treat al Qaeda as a single entity—for expediency, again harking back to Terry Gill's point. He also used the example of Israel-Hezbollah as a cross-border NIAC and asked: can you even qualify something as disparate as the "global war on terror" as a NIAC. No, not in its entirety, he argued. This may be true for some of the situations but not all. And that means that not every person killed by a drone strike is killed in a NIAC.

[23] With respect to Afghanistan, the criterion of intensity also matters—and once it is classified as an armed conflict, it remains so until a conclusion of peace. Even if there is an armed conflict, however, that does not mean the *jus ad bellum* becomes obsolete, especially when desiring to export the armed conflict to a third country. Either you have consent or you do not. If you have consent, one panellist's views were that IHRL will apply because a host-state cannot accept a third state's violations of IHRL as this would violate its own human rights obligations. Without consent, there are *jus ad bellum* restrictions as well.

Qaeda, going back to 1996 with Osama Bin Laden's *fatwa*.[24] Regarding the end of hostilities, some officials say "when Al-Qaeda has degraded to such an extent it is much more difficult to carry out an attack".[25] The US and NATO plan to drawdown troops in Afghanistan by the end of 2014,[26] and it will be interesting to see how the rest of the conflict on-going between the US and al Qaeda morphs once that occurs. Without the most solid link until now to an existing IAC, it remains to be seen what kind of legal framework the US will try to use once the IAC with Afghanistan draws to a close.[27]

## 8.3 Wherever War?: Geographical Limitations to Armed Conflict

### *8.3.1 Introduction*

The idea behind this panel was to discuss issues related to the geographic scope of armed conflict, such as: where can a war be fought? Where is the battlefield in an armed conflict (i.e., does it have a territorial scope tied to a nation state or a geographic region)? Is an armed conflict related to a "hot battlefield" or does the conflict follow the participants wherever they may go? Does the consent of a territorial state matter in the use of force when a member of a non-state actor group finds him/herself there? The use of analogy between IAC and NIAC was also explored. Three main issues were identified in the discussion during the symposium: (1) the implication of territorial state consent, (2) the issue of the "hot battlefield", and (3) combatant status and location of hostilities.

---

[24] Osama Bin Laden's Fatwa, declaring a "holy war" against America and the West, 1996, translated into English, available at: http://www.pbs.org/newshour/updates/military/july-dec96/fatwa_1996.html. Accessed 4 June 2014.

[25] However, it was noted by the panellist, this can also pose problems especially with respect to terrorism as it can take as few as one or two people planning and executing an attack. So in that sense, it was a concern that this construction of a conflict with al Qaeda would never end. But on 30 November 2012, Department of Defense General Counsel Jeh Johnson stated: "on the present course, there will come a tipping point…at which so many of the leaders and operatives of al Qaeda and its affiliates have been killed or captured, and the group is no longer able to attempt or launch a strategic attack against the United States, such that al Qaeda as we know it, the organization that our Congress authorized the military to pursue in 2001, has been effectively destroyed". Johnson added that "[a]t that point, we must be able to say to ourselves that our efforts should no longer be considered an "armed conflict" against al Qaeda". He also insisted, however, that he offered "no prediction about *when* this conflict will end, or whether we are…near the 'beginning of the end.'" Johnson 2012.

[26] See Spetalnick and Ryan 2012.

[27] For more information on the various comments and coverage of the end of the conflict between the US and al Qaeda, see the "End of War Timeline" on Lawfare, available at: http://www.lawfareblog.com/the-end-of-war-timeline/. Accessed 4 June 2014.

### 8.3.2 Discussion

Consent provided by the territorial state (state A) to the state seeking to use force (state B) against non-state actors present in state A precludes the violation of the sovereignty of state A.[28] In other words, the use of force by one state on the territory of another is allowed when that state thereto consents and the violation of Article 2 (4) of the UN Charter's prohibition on the use of force is precluded.

However, whether consent has been given can be difficult to determine. Posner sets out what he calls "coercive consent".[29] The US justifies its use of drone attacks in Pakistan against terrorists there through Pakistan's consent. Publicly and officially, however, Pakistan has opposed the use of drones on its territory.[30] Nonetheless, the US claims such consent was given, and infers further and continuing consent from the fact that the "Pakistani military continues to clear airspace for drones and doesn't interfere physically with the unpiloted aircraft in flight".[31] To do otherwise would be risky, according to Posner, and Pakistan is not in the position to actually do something about the attacks.[32] Recently, the UN Special Rapporteur on the Promotion and Protection of Human Rights and Fundamental Freedoms while Countering Terrorism, Ben Emmerson, conducted a country visit to Pakistan and after meeting with several government representatives concluded: "The position of the Government of Pakistan is quite clear. It does not consent to the use of drones by the United States on its territory and it considers this to be a violation of Pakistan's sovereignty and territorial integrity",[33] though this statement has been met with some critical reception.

A further issue then becomes whether consent can be inferred and what risks come with it. Regarding consent in international law, in the *Armed Activities* case before the International Court of Justice (ICJ), JudgeTomka stated that when the use of armed force is a lawful exercise of the right to self-defence,the force used falls outside of the scope of Article 2(4)'s prohibition. Andre de Hoogh remarks that "this view appears to mischaracterise the relationship that exists between Articles 2 (4) and 51, which is one of general prohibition and justification. Any use of armedforce necessarily falls within the scope of the prohibition, more so when territorial integrity is interpreted to mean territorial inviolability".[34] And he points to the Court's conclusion that Uganda violated the prohibition, to illustrate that "Article 2(4) does not exclude certain specific armed measures or activities from its

[28] ICJ, *Case Concerning Armed Activities on the Territory of the Congo (Democratic Republic of the Congo v. Uganda)*, Judgment, (2005) ICJ Rep 168, p. 227, para 165.

[29] Posner 2012.

[30] Pakistani officials have made several statements deploring the drone deployment, Randall 2012.

[31] Posner 2012.

[32] Ibid.

[33] OHCHR 2013.

[34] De Hoogh 2006.

scope".[35] Therefore, this kind of use of force needs some kind of justification (e.g., either self-defence or Security Council authorisation). This is only relevant when considering consent. As De Hoogh points out, "if the territorial State agrees to the use of armed force by another State on its territory, e.g., to suppress armed bands or pursue terrorists, there will not be a violation of Article 2(4) because such force will not be against the territorial integrity or political independence of the former State, nor inconsistent with the purposes of the United Nations".[36]

During the symposium, the case-by-case basis approach regarding classification of conflict was a theme that returned to this particular topic in order to assess the type of conflict, and analyse where it is occurring rather than trying to assign a "blurry" concept of a battlefield to it. It was posited that the concept of consent in IHL takes away the possibility of classifying the conflict as an IAC, but then the intensity and organisation of the parties must be examined in order to see whether a situation rises to the threshold of a NIAC—where IHL would govern—or not—where IHRL and the law enforcement paradigm would be more appropriate. In conclusion, it was offered that it is not the consent, but rather the facts on the ground that determine the classification of an armed conflict.

Regarding the issue of the "hot battlefield", John Brennan has addressed the US' position regarding the geographic scope of armed conflict. He made reference to al-Qaeda's leadership base as being in Pakistan and that the "affiliated forces" are "in places like Pakistan, Yemen, and countries throughout Africa".[37] This serves to concretise some ideas about how the US perceives the battlefield (i.e., naming particular countries where operations have already happened or may yet occur). Brennan directly addressed the geographic scope by stating that the US was not "restricted solely to 'hot' battlefields like Afghanistan" as the armed conflict with al-Qaeda allows the US to use force against these non-state actors under a self-defence regime, but without the requirement to do "a separate self-defence analysis each time".[38]

One panellist remarked that with non-state actors, it is easy for conflicts to spread and therefore we should link the physical footprint (i.e., where the non-state actors find themselves) to the on-going conflict.[39] Panel discussion further identified the fact that there is a widespread use of the term "hot battlefield" without it

---

[35] Ibid.

[36] Ibid.

[37] Brennan 2011.

[38] Ibid.

[39] One panellist gave examples of a related string of attacks or attempted attacks in order to illustrate the point: the attack in 1998 on the USS Cole, the US embassy in Kenya, the shoe bomber. Because Somalia is very close to Yemen, there are reasonable reports that it has been used as a staging ground and training ground, making it a legitimate basis for extending the territory to include this area. To take steps reasonably tailored to address this particular physical footprint, a state has a right to, in a tailored fashion, respond to threats that are posed in another state when proportional. The problem in this case however was that the response was not proportional—it was a glorified territory grab. For more on this issue, see Norton-Taylor 2012.

even being mentioned in the Geneva Conventions. When describing the permissible boundaries, one panellist remarked that the question really revolved around the distance allowable from the hot battlefield and thought that a training facility located, for example, in Somalia, ought to be legitimately classified as part of the battlefield, mainly based in using the law of neutrality by analogy.[40]

Another issue that arose relates to the status of the combatant and the location of hostilities. The crux of the issue is whether the conflict follows a participant wherever he may be found. The US position is that killing suspected members of al-Qaeda in today's conflict is, by analogy, just as legally defensible as killing Japanese General Yamamoto in the Second World War.[41] "For the United States (and others that adopt this position), once a state is in an armed conflict with a non-state armed group, that conflict follows the members of that group wherever they go, as long as the group's members continue to engage in hostilities against that state (either on the 'hot battlefield' or from their new location.)".[42] This has been challenged by some scholars because applying IAC standards in a NIAC by analogy is inherently problematic.[43] Additionally, according to the International Committee of the Red Cross (ICRC), the US theory that "a person directly participating in hostilities in relation to a specific ongoing NIAC 'carries' that armed conflict with him to a non-belligerent state by virtue of continued direct participation (the nexus requirement) and remains targetable under IHL" is a novel view in contrast with the underlying object and purpose of the Geneva Conventions.[44] This is demonstrated in the same ICRC report, given that the legal expansion of this theory allows for an application of the rules governing the conduct of hostilities to a globally limitless battlefield.[45]

In discussion, one panellist found the idea that the conflict follows the participant very problematic given that this construct was not envisioned by the Geneva Conventions or the subsequent protocols. Going back to Common Article 3 of the Geneva Conventions (which states that each party to the conflict shall be bound to apply, as a minimum, certain provisions, "[i]n the case of armed conflict not of an international character occurring in the territory of one of the High Contracting Parties"), he argued, it says "in the territory of *one* of the High Contracting Parties" not two or three. Additional Protocol II stipulates "in the territory of *a* High Contracting Party" which is slightly more flexible. In looking at the Afghanistan/Pakistan situation, spill over is geographically problematic. The panellist urged the audience to look at attacks on a case-by-case basis, so those in Pakistan remained separate from those in Afghanistan. The next step is to then ask the requisite

---

40 For an overview of the argumentation regarding the applicability of neutrality law to contemporary armed conflicts with non-state actors, see Chang 2011.

41 See also Goldsmith 2011; Tabin 2011.

42 Deeks 2011.

43 See generally Heller 2011a, b; Ingber 2011.

44 ICRC 2011, p. 22.

45 Ibid. See also Blank 2010.

questions: is this a new IAC? If there is consent from the territorial state (see discussion on consent on pp. 7–8), this might make a difference in classification of the conflict (NIAC vs. IAC), but again, it is not the consent, it is the facts on the ground that determine the decision involving classification of the armed conflict.

Another panellist offered three relevant different operational lenses to view the issue through: prospectively (where can a soldier go?), real-time (where can a soldier find his/her enemy?) and post hoc accountability (what law applies?), while also emphasising that the answers to these questions may depend on who is trying to answer them. A military perspective might say that a global battlefield is preferable—an easy answer, but not necessarily the right one. The level of threat perceived will also have a bearing on what decisions are made, as you cannot divorce law from policy. Looking to the fundamentals of the law can be helpful when IHL is not clear in that lawyers must balance principles of IHL.[46] One conclusion may be that "geographical limitations cannot be found on a map" as one panellist suggested. Another panellist reiterated an idea already discussed: the real question is whether there is an IAC or a NIAC, and there is a need for careful analysis on a case-by-case basis, rather than an overly broad application of IHL across the entire globe. If there is a NIAC, is it indigenous and where is the NIAC located? Only once you have answered this can IHL be applied, and it is applied, geographically, across the entire territory of hostilities.[47] Yet another panellist thought that it was not up to IHL to govern the geographical scope of armed conflict but that this was rather a *jus ad bellum* question about where force was being used and whether the amount of force rose to the requisite intensity and organisation, in which case IHL follows the hostilities rather than determines them.

Regarding the notion of status, in a NIAC only those who directly participate in hostilities (DPH) might be targeted under international law. The ICRC published a study on guiding the interpretation of DPH in 2009 and posits that DPH implicates "individual (civilian) involvement of a person in hostilities (i.e., the resort by the parties to the conflict to means and methods of injuring the enemy)".[48] But it does not stop there. In this interpretive guidance, the conclusions drawn about civilians taking direct part in hostilities have the following three constitutive elements: (1) a threshold of harm must be reached, (2) there must be direct causation by the direct

[46] Military necessity when thinking about IHL is a threat-driven approach. That is one tool for undermining the narrow geographical idea. How would the principle of humanity be relevant? There is a lot of protective aspects of IHL so it is important in this sense that the conflict would have a broad scope. In pure principles of humanity—you do not want to live in a conflict zone—you want to limit the conflict zone. You need to look at what the law is trying to achieve.

[47] See Statement by ICRC's Washington D.C. Legal Advisor Daniel Cohen, "Why and how IHL applies in Syria" (27 July 2012), available at: http://intercrossblog.icrc.org/blog/why-and-how-ihl-applies-syria. Accessed 4 June 2014. In pertinent part: "As a matter of legal principle, when a NIAC between two or more parties occurs, the geographical scope of application of IHL/LOAC covers the whole territory of the affected State".

[48] Melzer 2009, pp. 51–52; This distinction is also apparent in Article 15(1)(b) GCIV.

participant to have reached this harm, and (3) there must be a belligerent nexus between one party causing the harm to another party to the conflict.

In terms of other statuses assigned to individuals involved in hostilities, it must be said that membership within a particular group, such as al-Qaeda, cannot be based on "abstract affiliation, family ties, or other criteria prone to error, arbitrariness or abuse".[49] Instead, it must depend on whether one's "continuous function corresponds to that collectively exercised by the group as a whole, namely the conduct of hostilities on behalf of a non-State party to the conflict".[50] This continuous combat function role is crucial to distinguishing those who fight in an organised armed group from those who directly participate in hostilities on a merely spontaneous, sporadic or unorganised basis, or who assume exclusively political, administrative or other non-combat functions.[51]

## 8.4 International Humanitarian Law and International Human Rights Law: Menu à La Carte?

### *8.4.1 Introduction*

When there is an armed conflict, the question arises about which law is applicable. This raises additional questions such as the extraterritorial applicability of certain human rights treaties, principles of non-derogation, and ideas about whether IHL is the *lex specialis* and therefore always controls within an armed conflict or if there can be concurrent application of IHRL in certain situations or times where IHRL fully controls in an *in bello* framework. Two main issues were explored in-depth in the panel session: (1) IHL as *lex specialis* or IHRL as *lex generalis* in counter-terrorism, and (2) the complementarity of IHL and IHRL via the discussion of the killing of Osama Bin Laden. However, as the issues were handled with such synchronicity, the overlap dictates that they are handled concurrently in this paper.

### *8.4.2 Discussion*

In terms of the US conflict with al-Qaeda, Ohlin has set out the discussion in US federal courts on the application of the Authorization to Use Military Force (AUMF) by Congress for the President to fight the war on terror.[52] The Justice Department of the Obama Administration claims that the AUMF should be

---

[49] Ibid.

[50] Ibid.

[51] Ibid.

[52] Ohlin 2012a.

interpreted in a manner consistent with international law, that the AUMF gives the President authority in accordance to what is allowed under international law and IHL specifically. Within the support of this view another disagreement is apparent: there are those that claim that the AUMF should be interpreted both in light of IHL *and* IHRL. For Ohlin this is an impossible position because IHL is a *lex specialis* "in the sense that it displaces other bodies of law, including domestic criminal law, with a set of radically different norms based on reciprocity, namely that combatants can kill each other with impunity but must protect civilians and others *hors de combat*".[53] He claims further that the ICRC is of the opinion that both IHL and IHRL can apply at the same time based on the Israeli Supreme Court's *Targeted Killings* case. Ohlin dismisses this by pointing to the fact that there is no other precedent.[54]

In response, Gabor Rona states that international jurisprudence accepts the logic and necessity of applying IHRL in times of armed conflict, while the explicit terms of both instruments are in accordance with each other.[55] Ohlin's response was that the rule exclusion means that if there is an applicable rule of IHL on a specific issue, then IHL applies and IHRL does not,[56] pointing again to the Israeli Supreme Court *Targeted Killings* case.[57] The Court there applied a rule of IHL that allows the targeting of civilians taking DPH. However, the Court went further and concluded that a civilian taking DPH cannot be attacked when other less harmful means can be employed. The Court seems then to be reading IHRL norms on proportionality into the IHL proportionality norm applicable in that case. To Ohlin this kind of co-applicability, where IHRL and IHL apply to the same rule, is strange because, in his view, IHL is *lex specialis* and it always displaces IHRL when there is overlap in armed conflict situations. Concluding, he agrees that there exist *lacunae* in the relative scope of IHL and IHRL application to be filled by international law, but this is no reason to scrap the idea of concurrent application altogether.

The killing of Osama Bin Laden in May 2011 by US Navy Seals raised issues on the applicability of IHL and/or IHRL standards. The issue was whether the legality of the killing depended on the question whether Bin Laden could have been captured through non-lethal means rather than killed and if that would have been the preferred measure.[58] Starting from the premise that both IHL and IHRL apply to

---

[53] Ibid.

[54] He disagrees with the concurrent application of IHRL and IHL for three reasons. First, the most basic principles of IHRL such as the right to life do not make sense in armed conflict. Second, IHL is a much older body of norms that govern the humane treatment of prisoners and others *hors de combat*. Lastly, he points to the fact that states continue to develop IHL in the area of humane treatment; something that would not be necessary if IHRL applies.

[55] Rona 2012.

[56] Ohlin 2012b.

[57] Israeli Supreme Court, *The Public Committee against Torture in Israel and the Palestinian Society for the Protection of Human Rights and the Environment v. The Government of Israel ("Targeted Killings Case")*, Judgment (HCJ 769/02), 13 December 2006.

[58] Milanovic 2011.

this killing, Milanovic sets out in his article the relationship between both legal regimes. Under IHL, targeting takes place on the basis of status, meaning that Bin Laden, either as a combatant or a civilian taking DPH, could be attacked at any time while the status persists as long as he is not *hors de combat.* Under IHL there is no necessity requirement for attacking a target that has such a status so there is no obligation to first use non-lethal means or to capture or detain before going for the kill. This is different under IHRL, which proscribes the use of non-lethal means primarily, and only if those means are not practically feasible, can lethal use of force be lawful. Depending on the facts, the killing of Osama Bin Laden could be lawful where the risk to the life of others, including that of the US soldiers, in attempting to capture him alive and the risk of escape outweighed his right to life. The killing would not have been lawful only on the basis that it was vastly easier to kill him than to capture and prosecute him.[59]

The real disagreement now lies in how norms of IHL and IHRL should interact.[60] Models of co-application exist according to Milanovic. One is based on the *Nuclear Weapons* Advisory Opinion of the ICJ and would be that any IHL-compliant taking of life is *by definition* not arbitrary for the purpose of Article 6 of the International Covenant on Civil and Political Rights (ICCPR).[61] IHL is then used to interpret Article 6 ICCPR as a norm of IHRL, though other IHRL norms do not leave such interpretative space.

Another model asks the question whether IHRL sets additional requirements for the lawfulness of a killing under IHL and whether these requirements can be less stringent than those developed in human rights jurisprudence in and for times of peace.[62] Milanovic would cautiously answer yes to both questions. The question whether we can expect militaries to abide by more stringent and humane rules than what is strictly necessary under IHL depends on treaty interpretation. The Israel Supreme Court *Targeted Killings* decision is an example where the Court held that a capture-before-kill requirement of IHRL was needed because of the degree of control the Israeli military exercises over the occupied territories.[63] This is the

---

[59] Ibid.

[60] In his contribution, Milanovic sets out several competing models. The first one is one of separation advocated by the US government in its war on terror. Even if these bodies of law do not exclude each other technically, IHL as a *lex specialis* rules out IHRL application. Milanovic believes this view is incorrect because of the derogation clauses found in IHRL treaties, these treaties' object and purpose and the jurisprudence of the ICJ. A second model advocated by O'Connell takes the following view: (1) terrorism is a crime; (2) crime should be dealt with by law enforcement and so (3) targeted killings are generally illegal as they are not available methods under law enforcement (except in extreme circumstances). (Ibid.) Milanovic also views O'Connell's model as incorrect as there is no legal barrier between armed conflict and law enforcement and between IHL and law of peace, meaning that IHL will apply whenever its criteria are met.

[61] Ibid.

[62] Ibid.

[63] Ibid. For more on the capture versus kill discussion, see Goodman 2013a. Additionally, surrounding this article, there has been rich discussion on legal blogs. See Anderson 2013 for a summary of various posts, and see Goodman 2013b.

preferable approach according to Milanovic because it shows a reflection of the object and purpose of IHL and IHRL treaties in their best light, while at the same time reflecting the demands of universality of human rights and practical considerations of effectiveness. The question remains: how far should IHL allow IHRL into its domain without compromising itself?[64]

During discussion at the symposium, one panellist stated that the international legal community has reached the point in 2013 that the answer the ICJ gave in its 1996 *Nuclear Weapons Advisory Opinion* is no longer sophisticated enough. In IHRL, killing is a last resort. IHL is actually about killing people in order to win battles and wars and there are cases where the two bodies of law will contradict. The killing of Bin Laden is one prime example. If we assume this killing took place within an IHL conflict, and that he was targetable because of his status (e.g., continuous combat function), he can still be killed. In IHRL this is not the case. Another panellist stated that the *lex specialis* has always been a rule of interpretation to establish priorities enacted by the same legislator, which is not the case for these two distinct sets of laws. Yet another wondered what the "gaps" were in IHL. If they are present, would they be filled with IHRL? These questions and more were analysed and discussed before concluding that more work must be done with the development of the application of IHL and IHRL.

## 8.5 A Case Study on Targeted Killings and Drones

### *8.5.1 Introduction*

Against these discussions and theoretical background, this panel looked at a specific and concrete case study on targeted killings and drones.

First of all, it was observed that drones, as a weapons system, are not inherently unlawful: they are not indiscriminate and do not cause unnecessary suffering. In fact, drones could be more precise as they can stay longer in the air surveilling the target and can gather more information before attacking the target. Their accuracy was also mentioned, although this point was also questioned.[65]

However, their *use* in specific situations may be unlawful and needs to be considered on a case-by-case basis. The three main problems identified with respect to targeted killings and drones concern (1) the *jus ad bellum*, (2) the personal

---

[64] Ibid.

[65] Cf. Report of the International Human Rights and Conflict Resolution Clinic 2012, which concluded: "In the United States, the dominant narrative about the use of drones in Pakistan is of a surgically precise and effective tool that makes the US safer by enabling "targeted killing" of terrorists, with minimal downsides or collateral impacts. This narrative is false [original footnote omitted]" (Ibid, p. v.).

dimension (i.e., the person that is being targeted)—again something that has to be considered on a case-by-case basis, and (3) accountability and transparency.[66]

### 8.5.2 Discussion

Concerning the topic of the *jus ad bellum*, the point was made that the US is blurring the lines between the *jus ad bellum* and the *jus in bello* when it uses both paradigms at the same time ("we are in an armed conflict *and* act under self-defence") without elaborating on the specifics to justify targeted strikes in counter-terrorism operations. It was noted that blurring can lead not only to less clarity for the soldiers (and hence to less mission effectiveness) as the permissiveness of IHL is blurred, but also to a weakening of IHRL norms/less protection.

In the context of the *jus ad bellum*, the topic of imminence (discussed above, see Panel 1 of the symposium or Sect. 8.2 of this chapter), was again addressed. One panellist, referring to a recent article,[67] argued that this concept must be reframed and that the probability of an attack, the scale of a planned attack and the question whether this is the last opportunity to disrupt the attack must be considered. (This "last clear chance doctrine" may temporally not be very close to the actual attack, but may be the last chance to interrupt). A further element in attacking in self-defence for purpose of stopping an attack can be not only the targeting of those responsible but also of those who provide material support essential to the attack, such as the manufacturer of bombs.

On the other hand, the point was made that the US administration uses the concept of imminence as a justification for force, not out of what it perceives to be legal necessity but as a matter of government policy, and that the concept of imminence generally has two parts: an impending attack, and a specific and identifiable attack that is about to happen. The idea of an impending attack (e.g., with regard to weapons of mass destruction) may justify a loosening of the requirement for imminence. But this will not be the situation in many counter-terrorism cases.

The concept of naked self-defence (see again Panel 1 of the symposium or Sect. 8.2 of this chapter) was revisited and it was generally concluded that this concept is not very useful as it is straddling two things, namely trying to justify the use of force in another country and trying to justify the use of force against a target. The consensus was that it should be abandoned. In any case, naked self-defence

[66] Note that also another, less legal problem, was identified, namely that they represent the furthest extension of the individualisation of armed conflict and the epitome of a "remote-controlled" armed conflict. On the other hand, the point was made that drones are perhaps the most personalised form of warfare, as the operator follows the target around for extended periods of time prior to the killing and also sees his/her target dead as a confirmation. Indeed, there are studies showing that drone operators suffer similar psychological problems as 'ordinary' soldiers, see, e.g., Bumiller 2011.

[67] Bethlehem 2012.

cannot provide any legal basis to assess questions such as what individual to target, what kinds of weapons to use and so on.

When discussing the topic of personal dimension, the so-called "kill lists", which have caused deep concern in the media, were addressed. Nevertheless, from an IHL point of view, such lists, it was argued, are not necessarily problematic (that is: provided it is agreed that IHL is applicable, for instance in Afghanistan). In fact, IHL even *requires* such individual tests to be conducted in order to ensure adherence to IHL and target only those directly participating in combat. The main problem is of course that this is the case when IHL applies (in the case of an armed conflict) and that in many targeting situations, the US may not be engaged in an armed conflict.

It was stressed that sometimes, the wrong questions are asked or answers are not found in the right contexts. According to one panellist, there is a need to clarify what the real problems are. Within IHL, this means identifying an armed conflict in the first place. However, IHL does not apply to many drone strikes. If IHL does not apply, the question is "what does"? In such situations, resorting to IHRL has often been defended. It was stressed that IHRL does allow for the lethal use of force albeit with more red tape. There must be clearer reasons and planning processes involved, but in extreme situations, IHRL does not prohibit shoot-to-kill, see, for instance the *McCann* case.[68] Does it exclude situations where other people may get killed? While the IHRL test is stricter than the IHL test, this is of course still possible.

When a person from the audience asked how IHRL is applicable when drone strikes occur outside a state's jurisdiction, a panellist responded with another question: could it be that no law is applicable? If the basic principles of IHL do not apply, other paradigms such as law enforcement or IHRL need to be used: it cannot be that there is a black hole here, that no law can be applied. Another panellist noted that the idea that killing from a distance is not regulated by IHRL (see e.g., the *Banković* case, where it was decided that the rights of the European Convention on Human Rights are in principle territory-based)[69] is wrong and that it only invites people to do exactly that: killing from a distance. According to this panellist, there is a big problem with basing applicability of IHRL to the distance between the attacker and the victim. It is also important to consider the interplay between the two. One needs a contextual approach here. In this panellist's view, IHRL carries

---

[68] See ECtHR (Grand Chamber), *McCann and Others v. The United Kingdom*, Judgment (Appl. No. 18984/91), 27 September 1995.

[69] See ECtHR (Grand Chamber), *Case of Banković and Others v. Belgium and Others*, Decision as to the Admissibility of Appl. No. 52207/99, 12 December 2001, para 61: "The Court is of the view (...) that Article 1 of the Convention ["The High Contracting Parties shall secure to everyone within their jurisdiction the rights and freedoms defined in Section I of this Convention."] must be considered to reflect this ordinary and essentially territorial notion of jurisdiction, other bases of jurisdiction being exceptional and requiring special justification in the particular circumstances of each case".

more weight the further one goes away from the battlefield. There is a definite need to explore the interplay between IHRL and IHL.[70]

Finally, as to accountability and transparency, one panellist talked about transparency in the US context and noted that the US determined 11 years ago that the law enforcement framework was no longer adequate. However, it was never analysed or asked why this was the case. According to this panellist, the US is currently "seduced" (in the words of Robert Grenier, the former head of the CIA's Counterterrorism Center) by drones, which are creating more enemies than killing them.[71] As to the involvement of CIA operatives in drone attacks, it was remarked that those within that organisation who carry out targeted killings have sometimes been termed "unlawful combatants".[72] Whereas this is incorrect[73]—there is in principle no problem with the CIA targeting individuals—this DPH by civilians can have consequences, such as the fact that there is no immunity from prosecution under domestic law and that they themselves may be targeted and killed.[74] For this panellist, the covert nature of the operations was especially problematic.[75] Some judicial bodies in the US have acknowledged that there are problematic issues with regards to the limits of power of the government to, on the one hand, acknowledge targeted killings but not to disclose information on the other. Basically, the issue of drones, according to this panellist, boils down to a "trust us" approach by the government. However, it was argued that calls for more information and transparency as well as investigations to ensure clarity are justified.

With regards to transparency, another speaker pointed out that it is often claimed that mainly senior al-Qaeda leaders are targeted, although in practice it appears that

---

[70] In this context, a question was asked from the audience whether the Declaration of Turku was a possible starting point for addressing the limbo between IHL and IHRL. However, it was remarked that this declaration is too general and impossible to operationalise. See Declaration of Minimum Humanitarian Standards, *reprinted in* Report of the Sub-Commission on Prevention of Discrimination and Protection of Minorities on its Forty-sixth Session, Commission on Human Rights, 51st Sess., Provisional Agenda Item 19, at 4, UN Doc. E/CN.4/1995/116 (1995) (Declaration of Turku), available at: http://www1.umn.edu/humanrts/instree/1990b.htm. Accessed 4 June 2014.

[71] See Harris 2012.

[72] See, e.g., O'Connell 2010, p. 22.

[73] See for this controversy more generally Alston 2010, para 70; and "U.S. House of Representatives. Committee on Oversight and Government Reform. Subcommittee on National Security and Foreign Affairs. Subcommittee Hearing: "Drones II", Wednesday, April 28, 2010. Rayburn House Office Building. Written Testimony Submitted By Kenneth Anderson (26 April 2010), paras 16–36, available at: http://www.fas.org/irp/congress/2010_hr/042810anderson.pdf. Accessed 4 June 2014.

[74] See also 'Written Testimony of Hina Shamsi, Senior Advisor to the Project on Extrajudicial Executions, Center for Human Rights and Global Justice, New York University School of Law. Before the U.S. House of Representatives Committee on Oversight and Government Reform, Subcommittee on National Security and Foreign Affairs. Hearing on "Rise of the Drones II: Examining the Legality of Unmanned Targeting" (28 April 2010), no longer available on House Oversight Committee website; http://ow.ly/yajj8. Accessed 18 June 2014; Alston 2010, para 71.

[75] Indeed, states may use intelligence operatives for such operations as to shield them from IHL and IHRL transparency and accountability requirements. Alston 2010, para 73.

most are low-level suspected militants who are involved in insurgencies against their own governments rather than against the US or its allies.[76] Moreover, in Pakistan and Yemen, the US frequently calls victims of targeted killings "combatants" unless there is clear evidence after the fact that a victim was not a combatant. Such investigations, however, are rarely conducted.

The investigation point was also taken up by another panellist, noting the apparent impunity and lack of oversight and accountability in drone activity. One of the biggest problems is of course that there is not much information from the ground and that estimates about civilian casualties vary. If there is no information, then how can investigations be triggered? It was argued that if the US conducted clear investigations into the bigger cases of targeted killings, there would be less controversy in the media and less involvement of or pressure from IHRL bodies.

Another panellist noted, however, that it is very difficult to investigate incidents in a place like Pakistan where the US does not have control, and that in other countries such as Afghanistan, there have arguably even been artificial inflations of civilian casualties by other victims dropped at the scene after the attack.

It was wondered, while agreeing that the difficult reality of such investigations on the ground must be taken into account, how there are indeed so many inconsistencies by different parties in estimating civilian deaths caused by drone strikes. This speaker noted that there is a need to consider whose responsibility and whose burdens of proof such investigations are.[77]

## 8.6 Law Enforcement Approach in Counter-Terrorism

### *8.6.1 Introduction*

In the previous panel, the link with the law enforcement approach to countering terrorism was briefly made. Although this conference had a focus on situations of armed conflict, this panel took a different approach and looked at countering non-state actors within the law enforcement paradigm. Can terrorism be effectively countered via the normal peacetime procedures of arresting, detaining and prosecuting suspects?

### *8.6.2 Discussion*

It was remarked that prior to 9/11, the law enforcement approach was the prominent mode for counter-terrorism operations in the US. After 9/11, the military paradigm

[76] See also Report of the International Human Rights and Conflict Resolution Clinic 2012, p. 31.

[77] A few interesting recommendations in that respect can be found in the report of the Human Rights Clinic 2012.

took over, but the law enforcement paradigm continued to loom in the background. 9/11 gave rise to reforms, most notably surveillance laws, to aid the intelligence community to anticipate acts of terrorism (think of the Patriot Act). However, between 9/11 and the first inauguration of Obama, things flipped in the US. As law enforcement efforts got better, they were criticised for not being "tough" enough. If there was doubt, one had to detain militarily. Military committees were created by Presidential fiat. Despite a reform of the US Justice Department and a lot of positive changes, problems regarding secrecy and transparency remained.

According to this panellist, with the war in Afghanistan winding down and al-Qaeda deteriorating, the law enforcement approach is set to re-gain its prominence.[78] However, there are serious problems in the law enforcement domain, which are not solely confined to the US. One could, for example, think of charging under the material support statute. The *Holder v. Humanitarian Law Project* decision[79] has been telling with regards to the dangers involved in using criminal law. According to the Center for Constitutional Rights, the US Supreme Court in this case ruled to criminalise speech. The Center stated that "[a]ttorneys say that under the Court's ruling, many groups and individuals providing peaceful advocacy could be prosecuted".[80] While the decision is limited, it indicated that law enforcement can sweep up the protected freedom of expression.

One panellist noted that militaries are uncomfortable with unclear legal mandates, and that there is no luxury in discussing law extensively in the practical setting of military reality. This speaker was of the opinion that in armed conflicts, the law is clear. It is based on IHL (IAC or NIAC) and all the customary law that applies. In the context of hostilities, there is no place for IHRL. It is regulated by the law of armed conflict. The speaker was also of the opinion that one should stick to

---

[78] See speech Johnson 2012: "In the current conflict with al Qaeda, I can offer no prediction about *when* this conflict will end, or whether we are, as Winston Churchill described it, near the "beginning of the end". I do believe that on the present course, there will come a tipping point—a tipping point at which so many of the leaders and operatives of al Qaeda and its affiliates have been killed or captured, and the group is no longer able to attempt or launch a strategic attack against the United States, such that al Qaeda as we know it, the organization that our Congress authorized the military to pursue in 2001, has been effectively destroyed. At that point, we must be able to say to ourselves that our efforts should no longer be considered an "armed conflict" against al Qaeda and its associated forces; rather, a counter-terrorism effort against *individuals* who are the scattered remnants of al Qaeda, or are parts of groups unaffiliated with al Qaeda, for which the law enforcement and intelligence resources of our government are principally responsible, in cooperation with the international community—with our military assets available in reserve to address continuing and imminent terrorist threats". Another panellist was of the opinion that the 'rebirth' of the law enforcement approach would have especially been true if the Benghazi attacks of 11 September 2012 had not occurred, which required a high level of organisation, coordination and sophistication. However, the Benghazi attacks showed that al Qaeda still poses a danger as a group with striking capabilities. This is, in the view of this speaker, why there is a need to continue to use the war paradigm, even if there are no major al Qaeda attacks in the coming years.

[79] Supreme Court of the United States, *Holder v. Humanitarian Law Project*, Certiorari to the United States Court of Appeals for the Ninth Circuit, No. 08-1498 (21 June 2010).

[80] Center for Constitutional Rights 2010.

these obligations under the law of armed conflict. Hence, it was advised not to start mixing laws, as the capture-rather-than-kill approach suggests,[81] as it will not be helpful for the soldiers on the ground. There should be a clear division between IHL and IHRL and their application. In the opinion of this panellist, the war paradigm should continue to apply in counter-terrorism operations amounting to an armed conflict.

Another panellist noted that according to Article III of the US Constitution, civilian courts should—and indeed are—the preferred option for trying terrorism suspects in the US, where the vast majority were prosecuted in civilian courts.[82] However, sometimes this is not feasible, for example, when a soldier captures someone on the battlefield. Echoing the view of the previous panellist, this speaker also felt that the military are not equipped to gather evidence, nor are they available to testify in court, and so on. If suspects are going to be released because of these circumstances, then what is the point of having this trial? And the answer is not making the soldiers more like police officers—they have enough to deal with. As such military commissions can be the right answer for certain trials.

Nevertheless, this point was also challenged. One speaker pointed out that crimes are a problem to be dealt with by law enforcement, and armed conflict should be dealt with via hostilities. When you call the fight against terrorism a war, you make the adversaries equal, whereas they are simply criminals. This gives them advantages and favours the idea of identification—of belonging to a party—whereas they should merely be seen as individuals. This panellist did not agree that the military should not be able to apply IHRL. Even in an armed conflict, you might have to apply the law enforcement paradigm, for instance *vis-à-vis* protesting civilians. Furthermore, the disadvantages of law enforcement, according to this panellist, can also be overcome within IHRL: States can derogate from IHRL in counter-terrorism situations. Interestingly, a military advisor in the audience noted that it is the military commander who can take the capture-rather-than-kill decision and that despite there not being any obligation under IHL to capture, in practice, this is frequently done for a variety of reasons. This advisor stressed that IHRL is as necessary as IHL for soldiers.

One speaker noted that Europe uses the traditional law enforcement approach when it comes to countering terrorism (with the exception of clear and specific armed conflicts such as in Afghanistan). According to this panellist, the law is not a question of choice, but based on the situation. In Europe we do not have a war so it is based on the criminal justice framework, an effective system (as is evidenced by

---

[81] Cf. Melzer 2009, p. 82: "[W]hile operating forces can hardly be required to take additional risks for themselves or the civilian population in order to capture an armed adversary alive, it would defy basic notions of humanity to kill an adversary or to refrain from giving him or her an opportunity to surrender where there manifestly is no necessity for the use of lethal force".

[82] See also Herodotou 2012: "To anyone who doubts the ability of federal courts to effectively handle terrorism-related cases, know this: since September 11, there have been 494 convictions in federal court. (…) By contrast, the military commissions at Guantanamo have convicted only seven people since their inception".

the hundreds of prosecutions of terrorist suspects) and a sustainable and successful route that does not lead to further radicalisation. According to this speaker, terrorist acts can be prevented by criminalising conduct before the attack occurs and there are currently also considerations to criminalise the travel of foreign fighters to participate in training camps.

## 8.7 The Way Forward: The Need for a New Framework for Counter-Terrorism?

### *8.7.1 Introduction*

Influenced and informed by all previous panels, this last session gave the experts a forum to reflect on the conference's discussions and contributions in order to parse a way forward regarding future approaches to counter-terrorism.

### *8.7.2 Discussion*

It has been argued that terrorism brings a new kind of war that cannot fit perfectly within existing international law. This leads to the opinion that the law of war needs to be adapted to encompass this new kind of war. Are the existing *jus ad bellum* and *jus in bello* adequate to counter terrorism? Or should they be adapted to the new kind of war between states and terrorist non-state actors?[83] In other words, is there a need perhaps for a new protocol to the Geneva Conventions to encapsulate the idea of a transnational armed conflict (a third category) and prescribe new rules for countering terrorism, or does the *lex lata* (both IHL and IHRL) sufficiently cover all potential situations in countering terrorism?

The first panellist urged to look at existing *lex lata* and to improve it in the sense of better means of cooperation and implementation. There is a lot of overlap between the various branches (IHL, IHRL) and one has to look into similarities and complementarities. In doing so, it is not of primary importance to look into specifics, but rather to attempt and consider what we would like to achieve internationally and multilaterally. Hence, this speaker did not think that the current framework is in need of change but that we need a better understanding of its different branches.

The second panellist noted that it is a mistake to believe that we must do something because of urgent necessities. The current interpretations and development of our legal frameworks are decisive for the future. When one applies the law in a sober way (as lawyers do without agenda), then very reasonable results will be

83 See for more information Paulussen 2012a.

attained. The cry for a new law is the sign of desperation, rather than a sober analysis of what the law says and what it calls for. We need to cope with changing situations under the existing legal frameworks, which are sufficient. The speaker warned not to mess around with the law of armed conflict. Do not believe that armed conflicts belong to the past; armed conflicts will continue to exist in the future and perhaps counter-terrorism is the exception rather than a rule. It might be true that there are some grey areas, but these uncertain areas are not too big to just change what has been built up in 150 years.

Another participant agreed with this and argued that many of the problems may be a matter of fixing policy rather than law. It is important to remember the function and purpose of each different area of law—IHL is a set of rules set up to regulate armed conflict, and IHRL is set up to regulate the government and its inhabitants—while avoiding a blurring of boundaries. There are indeed a few grey areas (e.g., military detention, fair trial rights and the use of lethal force outside the realm of armed conflict) and there is room for further development and clarification here, but they do not warrant new laws. The current frameworks are sufficient.

The next panellist likewise argued that he is not in favour of rewriting the laws of armed conflict because the current legal frameworks are sufficient for the situations faced today on the ground. Nevertheless, there is a need to better understand and adjust to changing situations. This speaker noted that it should be considered how current rules are interpreted, for instance with respect to detention, the *jus ad bellum*, and the use of drones outside the context of an armed conflict.[84] On these issues, there are simply not yet answers nor interpretations of the current legal framework that are sufficiently clear and satisfactory, or which enjoy a broad consensus. A further argument for taking a new look at our current legal setting is that there has been a growing international shift and increased discussion about the expansion or flexibility of what an armed conflict is. We should therefore rein this in before a precedent about armed conflict is established. In short: this speaker was not talking about a new agreement, but about a better interpretation of the current agreements and how the current frameworks inter-relate.

The international shift was also identified by the next speaker, who went one step further. According to this panellist, the world is witnessing the development of a distinct corpus of counter-terrorism law. Even though it seems that al-Qaeda is degrading, terrorism, in this speaker's view, is not going to disappear in the near future. To deal with this very unconventional threat, very unconventional responses have been used. Some modifications, for better or worse, have been sloppily drawn

[84] Cf. Bianchi and Naqvi 2011, p. 380, writing about the targeting of suspected terrorists by CIA-operated drones: "The problem (…) does not seem to lie in the rules on proportionality or distinction as such, but rather in the way they are being applied or, as in the case of the drone attacks, in the issue whether IHL rules or international human rights standards should apply to certain factual situations. Therefore, even though there is no apparent need for the law to be revised, further clarification of how to properly apply these principles in complex contexts would appear to be an area of fruitful development".

up. But, the panellist continued, it appears that states are learning from some of those mistakes and are adapting, which may lead to a new corpus of law.

In this context, an interesting observation was made from the audience, namely, that any new framework for addressing terrorism may be difficult given that the international community cannot even agree on a definition of terrorism.[85] Nevertheless, it was also noted that the lack of a definition of terrorism should perhaps not be over-exaggerated; even without an internationally agreed definition, the international community has been able to conclude 13 sectoral conventions on terrorist-related activities.

The final speaker concluded that existing bodies of law are adequate. According to this panellist, it is not correct to say that many countries accept new modifications to the existing frameworks, to the contrary. There is currently no sufficient state practice to suggest that a new paradigm has emerged. What *is* important though is to establish more clearly which countries are using these new measures.

The moderator of this final panel summarised the current debate saying that there are several positions supporting the idea that the current legal frameworks are adequate, but that there is also the view that (customary) law is perhaps developing in a certain direction. In the latter instance, it was noted, it has to be ascertained in what direction this will continue to develop and which the influential states are in shaping this shift. While these two basic positions may seem different, the dichotomy is not overly strong since law is never fixed but ever evolving. With this in mind, there is clearly a need for more clarity on this issue, and these shifts and developments should be closely monitored.

## 8.8 Conclusion

This two-day symposium covered a range of issues that continue to be important in the on-going debate about using force in counter-terrorism operations against non-state actors.

The first day looked at the geographic and temporal scope of armed conflict along with the interplay of international humanitarian law and international human rights law. As outlined above, though much progress was made through the panels and discussion, we were able to identify three main areas that still need attention. The first is the definition of armed conflict as a legal concept. Though it may seem strange that such a common term as armed conflict is not precisely defined in international treaty law, that is the case. A definition with respect to non-international armed conflict has been used by the ICTY (from its *Tadic* judgement[86] Jurisdiction, Appeals Chamber (IT-94-1-AR72), 2 October 1995, para 70, which, in

[85] See for more information Paulussen 2012b.

[86] ICTY, *Prosecutor v. Dusko Tadić*, Decision on the Defence Motion for Interlocutory Appeal on.

pertinent part states: "whenever there is [...] protracted armed violence between governmental authorities and organised armed groups or between such groups within a State".) but controversy still remains about the precise requirements for "protracted" violence as well as the level of organisation of the armed groups required. Another area that would benefit from additional research is the effect of consent on uses of force against non-state actors. Section 8.3.2. above outlines some of the particular issues, one of which questions what precisely constitutes consent from a state and at what point might it be adjudged that a previously given consent no longer exists. These issues may become more and more relevant as conflicts with non-state actors working from territories of states without a clear and centralised government (i.e., Somalia) increase. The final issue from the symposium's first day that deserves further research is the need for a clearer understanding of the role for IHRL in armed conflict and the interplay of IHRL and IHL in counter-terrorism operations.

The second day's panels, exploring drones, targeted killings, the law enforcement paradigm in countering terrorism and forging a way forward also identified three main areas that would benefit from further research and analysis: First of all, it was often heard that controversial weapon systems such as drones are not necessarily problematic, but that in many situations in which they are used, there might not even be an armed conflict situation in the first place. Hence, what is important is to get more clarity on the basic starting point, meaning on the question when (temporal boundaries) and where (geographical boundaries) one can qualify a certain factual situation on the ground as an armed conflict. It was also reiterated that more research is needed on the interplay between IHL and IHRL, again a point that was already alluded to during the first day of the symposium. Finally, and regarding one of the most important questions—are the existing *jus ad bellum* and *jus in bello* adequate to counter terrorism or should they be adapted to the new kind of war between states and terrorist non-state actors?—two views were identified: The first was that the current legal frameworks are sufficient (even though it might be useful to get more clarity on how the current rules are interpreted and applied to new situations, for instance with respect to detention, the *jus ad bellum* and the use of drones outside the context of an armed conflict). The second was that (customary) law is perhaps already developing in a certain direction and that, if this is indeed the case, it is time to examine in what direction this will continue to develop and which the influential states are in shaping this shift.

Echoing the statement made at the beginning of the symposium, it should be reiterated that if the legal community does not want policy makers to provide the answers regarding these pertinent questions, it must come up with answers itself to guide the policy. This symposium aimed at constituting a new step in that important direction.

## Annex 1: Programme Symposium

| **Day 1: Thursday** | **10 January, 2013** |
|---|---|
| 09:30–10:00 | Registration/Coffee and Tea |
| 10:00–10:05 | Opening and Announcements, Christophe Paulussen |
| 10:05–10:15 | Keynote, Terry Gill |
| 10:15–11:00 | **Panel I**: *Whenever War?*: *Temporal Limitations to Armed Conflict* Panellists: Dieter Fleck, Marco Milanovic, Wolff Heintschel von Heinegg, Tom Ruys, Joanne Mariner Moderator: Terry Gill |
| 11:00–11:45 | Discussion |
| 11:45–13:30 | Lunch |
| 13:30–14:15 | **Panel II**: *Wherever War?*: *Geographic Limitations to Armed Conflict* Panellists: Laurie Blank, Noam Lubell, Jelena Pejic, Michael Lewis, Peter Margulies, Robert Heinsch Moderator: Wouter Werner |
| 14:15–15:00 | Discussion |
| 15:00–15:30 | Coffee/Tea Break |
| 15:30–16:15 | **Panel III**: *International Humanitarian Law and International Human Rights Law*: *Menu à la Carte?* Panellists: Joanne Mariner, Marko Milanovic, Marco Sassòli, Jann Kleffner, William Schabas, Paul Ducheine Moderator: Theo van Boven |
| 16:15–17:00 | Discussion |
| 17:00–17:15 | Summary and Announcements, Jessica Dorsey |
| 19:00–22:00 | Dinner for panellists |

| **Day 2: Friday 11** | **January, 2013** |
|---|---|
| 09:30–10:00 | Registration/Coffee and Tea |
| 10:00–10:05 | Opening and Announcements, Christophe Paulussen |
| 10:05–10:15 | Keynote, Gilles de Kerchove |
| 10:15–11:00 | **Panel IV**: *A Case Study on Targeted Killings and Drones* Panellists: Hina Shamsi, Noam Lubell, Peter Margulies, Laurie Blank, Anthony Dworkin Moderator: Liesbeth Lijnzaad |
| 11:00–11:45 | Discussion |
| 11:45–13:30 | Lunch |
| 13:30–14:15 | **Panel V**: *Law Enforcement Approach in Counter-Terrorism* Panellists: Christiane Höhn, Marco Sassoli, Michael Lewis, Chris De Cock, William Banks Moderator: Nico Schrijver |
| 14:15–15:00 | Discussion |
| 15:00–15:30 | Coffee/Tea Break |

| | |
|---|---|
| 15:30–16:15 | **Panel VI**: The Way Forward: The Need for a New Framework for Counter-Terrorism?[87]Panellists: Anthony Dworkin, Christiane Höhn, Wolff Heintschel von Heinegg, Dieter Fleck, William Banks Moderator: Andre Nollkaemper |
| 16:15–17:00 | Discussion |
| 17:00–17:15 | Summary and Closing Remarks, Jessica Dorsey |
| 17:15–19:00 | Reception |

## Annex 2: Speakers Symposium

**William C. Banks**, Board of Advisors Distinguished Professor of Law; Professor of Public Administration and International Affairs; Director, Institute of National Security and Counter Terrorism, Syracuse University

**Laurie Blank**, Professor Emory Law School, Director, IHL Center at Emory University

**Theo van Boven**, Professor Emeritus of International Law, Maastricht University

**Chris de Cock**, Chief Operational Law Section, Belgian Ministry of Defence

**Jessica Dorsey**, Researcher, TMC Asser Institute, PhD candidate University of Amsterdam, Research Fellow, International Center for Counter-Terrorism—The Hague

**Paul Ducheine**, Associate Professor of Cyber Operations, Dutch Defence Academy; Legal Advisor to the Netherlands Army Legal Service

**Anthony Dworkin**, Senior Policy Fellow at European Council on Foreign Relations, executive director Crimes of War Project, member Terrorism/Counter-Terrorism Advisory committee of Human Rights Watch

**Dieter Fleck**, Editor *Handbook of IHL*, co-editor of *The Handbook of the International Law of Military Operations;* formerly with the German Defence Ministry.

**Terry Gill**, Professor of International Law, University of Amsterdam; Military Professor, Netherlands Defence Academy

**Wolff Heintschel von Heinegg**, Professor Public International Law, European University Viadrina, Frankfurt

**Robert Heinsch**, Assistant Professor, Grotius Centre for International Legal Studies, Leiden University

**Christiane Höhn**, Advisor to the EU Counter-Terrorism Coordinator

---

87 Dworkin 2009.

**Gilles de Kerchove**, EU Counter-Terrorism Coordinator

**Jann Kleffner**, Head of International Law Centre and Associate Professor of International Law, Swedish National Defence College; Assistant Professor of Law, University of Amsterdam

**Michael W. Lewis**, Professor of Law, Ohio Northern University Claude Pettit College of Law

**Liesbeth Lijnzaad**, Extraordinary Professor Maastricht University, Legal Advisor, Dutch Ministry of Foreign Affairs

**Noam Lubell**, Professor in the School of Law, University of Essex

**Peter Margulies**, Professor of Law, Roger Williams University School of Law

**Joanne Mariner**, Human Rights Program Director, Hunter College CUNY; recently appointed as Senior Crisis Response Advisor, Amnesty International (from 1 February 2013)

**Marko Milanovic**, Lecturer in Law, University of Nottingham School of Law

**Andre Nollkaemper**, Professor of Public International Law and Vice Dean for Research at the Faculty of Law, University of Amsterdam; External Advisor to the Dutch Minister of Foreign Affairs and Vice President of the Board of European Society of International Law

**Christophe Paulussen**, Senior Researcher International Humanitarian Law and International Criminal Law, T.M.C. Asser Institute; Coordinator of the International Humanitarian and Criminal Law Platform and Research Fellow at the International Centre for Counter-Terrorism—The Hague

**Jelena Pejic**, Legal Advisor at the ICRC Legal Division, Geneva

**Tom Ruys**, Attorney at the Brussels Bar (Stibbe, PG European and Competition Law), Senior member of the Leuven Centre for Global Governance Studies and lecturer in Public International Law

**Marco Sassòli**, Professor of International Law and Director of the Department of International Law and International Organization, University of Geneva; Chairman of the Board of Geneva Call

**William A. Schabas**, Professor of International Law, Middlesex University (London); Professor of International Humanitarian Law and Human Rights, Leiden University; Emeritus Professor of Human Rights, National University of Ireland Galway; Honorary Chairman, Irish Centre for Human Rights

**Nico Schrijver**, Professor of International Law, Leiden University

**Hina Shamsi**, Director, ACLU National Security Project

**Wouter Werner**, Professor of International Law, Free University Amsterdam

## References

Alston P (2010) Report of the special rapporteur on extrajudicial, summary or arbitrary executions. UN Doc. A/HRC/14/24/Add.6

Anderson K (2011) Targeted killing and drone warfare: how we came to debate whether there is a 'legal geography of war'. Washington College Law Research Paper No. 2011-16

Anderson K (2013) Jens Ohlin posts response to Ryan Goodman on paper on capture over kill. www.opiniojuris.org/2013/03/08/jens-ohlin-posts-response-to-ryan-goodman-paper-on-capture-over-kill. Accessed 4 June 2014

Bethlehem D (2012) Self-defense against an imminent or actual armed attack by nonstate actors. Am J Int Law 106:770–777

Bianchi A, Naqvi Y (2011) International humanitarian law and terrorism. Hart Publishing, Oxford, pp 770–777

Blank L (2010) Defining the battlefield in contemporary conflict and counter-terrorism: understanding the parameters of the zone of combat. Georgia J Int Comp Law 39(1):1–38

Blank L (2011) A new twist on an old story: lawfare and the mixing of proportionalities. Case W Reserve J Int Law 43(3):707–738

Brennan J (2011) Remarks addressing the Harvard Law School Brookings conference. www.lawfareblog.com/2011/09/john-brennans-remarks-at-hls-brookings-conference. Accessed 4 June 2014

Brooks E (2004) War everywhere: rights, national security law, and the law of armed conflict in the age of terror. Univ Pennsylvania Law Rev 153(675):695–702

Bumiller E (2011) Air force drone operators report high levels of stress. www.nytimes.com/2011/12/19/world/asia/air-force-drone-operators-show-high-levels-of-stress.html?_r=0. Accessed 4 June 2014

Center for Constitutional Rights (2010) Supreme court ruling criminalizes speech in material support law case. www.ccrjustice.org/newsroom/press-releases/supreme-court-ruling-criminalizes-speech-material-support-law-case. Accessed 4 June 2014

Chang K (2011) Enemy status and military detention in the war against Al-Qaeda. Texas Int Law J 47(1):1–73

Corn G (2012) Self-defense targeting: blurring the line between jus ad bellum and the jus in bello. Int. Law Stud 88:57–92

De Hoogh A (2006) The armed activities case: unasked questions, proper answers. www.haguejusticeportal.net/index.php?id=2510. Accessed 4 June 2014

Deeks A (2011) Pakistan's sovereignty and the killing of Osama Bin Laden. www.asil.org/insights/volume/15/issue/11/pakistans-sovereignty-and-killing-osama-bin-laden. Accessed 4 June 2014

Dworkin A (2009) Beyond the "war on terror": towards a new transatlantic framework for counter-terrorism, European Council on foreign relations policy brief. http://ecfr.eu/content/entry/counter_terrorism_eu_us_dworkin/. Accessed 4 June 2014

Goldsmith J (2011) A just act of war. www.nytimes.com/2011/10/01/opinion/a-just-act-of-war.html?_r=3&ref=opinion. Accessed 4 June 2014

Goodman R (2013a) The power to kill or capture enemy combatants. Eur J Int Law 24(3):819–853

Goodman R (2013b) Goodman responds to Heller on capture v. kill. www.opiniojuris.org/2013/04/01/guest-post-goodman-responds-to-heller-on-capture-v-kill. Accessed 4 June 2014

Greenwood C (2009) The Caroline. Max Planck encyclopaedia of public international law. www.mpepil.com. Accessed 4 June 2014

Harris P (2012) Drone attacks create terrorist safe havens, warns former CIA official. www.guardian.co.uk/world/2012/jun/05/al-qaida-drone-attacks-too-broad. Accessed 4 June 2014

Heller K (2011a) The law of neutrality does not apply to the conflict with Al-Qaeda, and it's a good thing too: a response to Chang. Texas Int Law J 47(1):115–141

Heller K (2011b) The folly of comparing Al-Awlaki to admiral Yamamoto. http://www.opiniojuris.org/2011/10/01/the-folly-of-comparing-al-awlaki-to-admiral-yamamoto. Accessed 4 June 2014

Herodotou K (2012) Let the numbers do the talking: federal courts work. http://www.humanrightsfirst.org/press-release/let-numbers-do-talking-federal-courts-work-infographic. Accessed 4 June 2014

Human Rights Clinic (2012) Colombia Law School, Report of the "counting drone strike deaths". http://www.web.law.columbia.edu/sites/default/files/microsites/human-rights-institute/files/COLUMBIACountingDronesFinal.pdf. Accessed 4 June 2014

ICRC (2011) International humanitarian law and the challenges of contemporary armed conflict. www.icrc.org/eng/assets/files/red-cross-crescent-movement/31st-international-conference/31-int-conference-ihl-challenges-report-11-5-1-2-en.pdf. Accessed 4 June 2014

ILA (2010) Use of force committee report. www.ila-hq.org/download.cfm/docid/2176DC63-D268-4133-8989A664754F9F87. Accessed 4 June 2014

Ingber R (2011) Untangling belligerency from neutrality in the conflict with Al-Qaeda. Texas Int Law J 47(1):75–114

International human rights and conflict resolution clinic (2012), Stanford Law School and global justice clinic, New York University School of Law. Living under drones. Death, injury, and trauma to civilians from US drone practices in Pakistan. http://www.livingunderdrones.org/wp-content/uploads/2013/10/Stanford-NYU-Living-Under-Drones.pdf. Accessed 4 June 2014

Jinks D (2003) The temporal scope of application of international humanitarian law in contemporary conflicts. www.hpcrresearch.org/sites/default/files/publications/Session3.pdf. Accessed 4 June 2014

Johnson J (2012) The conflict against Al Qaeda and its affiliates: how will it end? www.lawfareblog.com/2012/11/jeh-johnson-speech-at-the-oxford-union. Accessed 4 June 2014

Koh H (2010) The Obama administration and international law. www.state.gov/s/l/releases/remarks/139119.htm. Accessed 4 June 2014

Melzer N (2009) Interpretive guidance on the notion of direct participation in hostilities under international humanitarian law. www.icrc.org/eng/assets/files/other/icrc-002-0990.pdf. Accessed 4 June 2014

Milanovic M (2010a) Drones and targeted killings: can self-defence preclude their wrongfulness? www.ejiltalk.org/drones-and-targeted-killings-can-self-defense-preclude-their-wrongfulness. Accessed 4 June 2014

Milanovic M (2010b) More on drones, self-defense, and the Alston report on targeted killings. www.ejiltalk.org/more-on-drones-self-defense-and-the-alston-report-on-targeted-killings. Accessed 4 June 2014

Milanovic M (2011) When to kill and when to capture? http://www.ejiltalk.org/when-to-kill-and-when-to-capture. Accessed 4 June 2014

Norton-Taylor R (2012) Somalia is training ground for British would-be terrorists, report warns. www.guardian.co.uk/uk/2012/feb/07/somalia-training-ground-british-terrorism. Accessed 4 June 2014

O'Connell M (2010) Unlawful killing with combat drones: a case study of Pakistan, 2004–2009. Notre Dame Law School, Legal Studies Research Paper 09-43

OHCHR (2013) Pakistan: statement by the UN special rapporteur on human rights and counter-terrorism. www.ohchr.org/en/NewsEvents/Pages/DisplayNews.aspx?NewsID=13148&LangID=E. Accessed 4 June 2014

Ohlin J (2012a) IHL and IHRL. www.liebercode.org/2012/01/ihl-and-ihrl.html. Accessed 4 June 2014

Ohlin J (2012b) Response to Gabor Rona. www.liebercode.org/2012/01/response-to-gabor-rona.html. Accessed 4 June 2014

Okimoto K (2011) The distinction and relationship between jus ad bellum and jus in bello. Hart Publishing, Oxford

Paulussen C (2012a) Testing the adequacy of the international legal framework in countering terrorism: the war paradigm. www.icct.nl/publications/icct-papers/testing-the-adequacy-of-the-international-legal-framework-in-countering-terrorism-the-war-paradigm. Accessed 4 June 2014

Paulussen C (2012b) Impunity for international terrorists? Key legal questions and practical considerations. www.icct.nl/download/file/ICCT-Paulussen-Impunity-April-2012.pdf. Accessed 4 June 2014

Posner E (2012) Obama's drone dilemma. www.slate.com/articles/news_and_politics/view_from_chicago/2012/10/obama_s_drone_war_is_probably_illegal_will_it_stop_.single.html. Accessed 4 June 2014

Randall E (2012) Pakistan says no more drones. www.theatlanticwire.com/global/2012/01/pakistan-says-no-more-drones/47674. Accessed 4 June 2014

Rona G (2012) A response to Ohlin about IHL and IHRL. www.opiniojuris.org/2012/01/17/a-response-to-ohlin-about-ihl-and-ihrl. Accessed 4 June 2014

Spetalnick M, Ryan M (2012) NATO sets "irreversible" but risky course to end Afghan war. http://ca.reuters.com/article/topNews/idCABRE84J02C20120521?sp=true. Accessed 4 June 2014

Tabin J (2011) The Awlaki precedent. www.spectator.org/blog/27553/awlaki-precedent. Accessed 4 June 2014

# Chapter 9
# Some Thoughts on the Relationship Between International Humanitarian Law and International Human Rights Law: A Plea for Mutual Respect and a Common-Sense Approach

**Terry D. Gill**

**Abstract** This essay provides a commentary on the ongoing discussion of the relationship between the two legal regimes and attendant paradigms of hostilities and law enforcement in armed conflict. The discussion has, to an extent, taken the form of a disconnect between the IHL and IHRL communities. In order to get past this, a plea is made here to apply basic well established tools of legal methodology, to apply both regimes within their respective scope of application and to utilise common sense in determining which regime is the most relevant to a particular situation. This is in the interest of legal coherence and maintaining respect for the law, as well as in the interest of the persons the law is meant to protect.

**Keywords** Relationship international humanitarian law and international human rights law · Applicability · Interpretation · Legal methodology

## Contents



---

T.D. Gill is Professor of Military Law at the University of Amsterdam and the Netherlands Defence Academy. This contribution has been published in the *Liber Amicorum* for Dr. Leo Zwaak, Y. Haek et al. (eds.) *The Realisation of Human Rights: When Theory Meets Practice*, Intersentia Publishers (2014) and is reproduced here with the kind permission of the editors. It formed the basis of the author's comments as a keynote speaker at the 'Boundaries of the Battlefield' symposium in January 2013, which are reproduced here in slightly more comprehensive form. All websites were last accessed 10/05/2013.

---

T.D. Gill (✉)
University of Amsterdam, Amsterdam, The Netherlands
e-mail: T.D.Gill@uva.nl



T.D. Gill et al. (eds.), *Yearbook of International Humanitarian Law 2013*,
Yearbook of International Humanitarian Law 16, DOI 10.1007/978-94-6265-038-1_9

## 9.1 Introduction

The relationship and interplay between international humanitarian law (IHL) and international human rights law (IHRL) has become a topic that has received considerable attention in policy debates, judicial decisions and academic opinion over the past two decades.[1] This short essay does not pretend to provide an in-depth analysis of the way this relationship has developed through the case law and official standpoints of human rights courts and supervisory bodies, nor will it attempt to reproduce the viewpoints of various authors in detail and subject these to a critical analysis. Still less does it set out to provide a comprehensive answer to how all questions which can arise in the application of these two sub-disciplines of international law should be resolved. Instead, its basic purpose is to set out a number of observations and criteria which could assist in determining how the two bodies of law interact, and how they could be applied in practice with a view to promoting a fruitful interaction between IHL and IHRL, promoting protection of victims and vulnerable groups in armed conflict and in other military operations outside a situation of armed conflict, while at the same time taking account of the realities of armed conflict and of military considerations.

The essay will first set out the basic object and purpose of both sub-disciplines and provide some observations concerning the basic terms of their applicability. It will then briefly discuss the main approaches to determining their mutual relationship and interaction, including, in particular, the role of the principle of *lex specialis derogat legi generali* (the *lex specialis* principle), both as a means of interpretation and as an instrument for resolving conflicts between legal rules and regimes when they occur. It will then apply the above to two situations and normative paradigms: the conduct of hostilities and the maintenance of public order and law enforcement. It will conclude with a number of final observations relating to the basic purpose of the essay as set out above.

[1] Various decisions by the ICJ, by human rights tribunals and bodies, and academic publications have dealt with this relationship. See, *inter alia*, ICJ, *Legality of the Threat or Use of Nuclear Weapons,* Advisory Opinion (1996) ICJ Rep 226, para 25; ICJ, *Legal Consequences of the Construction of a Wall in the Occupied Palestinian Territories*, Advisory Opinion (2004) ICJ Rep 136, para 102 *et seq.*; ICJ, *Case Concerning Armed Activities on the Territory of the Congo (Democratic Republic of the Congo v. Uganda*), Judgment (2005) ICJ Rep 168, pp. 242–245, paras 216–221; HRC 2004 General Comment No. 31; Droege 2007; Hampson 2008; Kleffner 2011; Sassòli and Olson 2008; Doswald-Beck 2011.

## 9.2 Basic Purposes and Applicability

Both IHL and IHRL are sub-disciplines of public international law and share a number of basic characteristics as a result, such as what their respective sources and subjects are, common principles and rules of interpretation and concepts such as jurisdiction and responsibility for breaches of international obligations. As such, both are governed primarily by multilateral international conventions and international customary law, and additionally by other sources of international law. Both relate primarily to States as the prime actors in the international legal system, but also and increasingly to a variety of non-State actors, albeit in somewhat different ways, with IHL having a more horizontal structure of obligations between belligerents, while IHRL is more vertically structured as obligations resting upon a State in relation to persons subject to its jurisdiction.

The basic purpose of IHL is and always has been two-fold. First, to regulate and —to some degree—mitigate the conduct of hostilities between belligerent parties; and second, to provide protection to specific categories of persons and to certain objects, which are either particularly vulnerable or which require an enhanced degree of care or protection (such as medical installations and transports) and persons in the hands of or under the control of the adversary. The law of war, to use its more traditional name, is one of the oldest branches or sub-disciplines of international law and has its roots in both natural law concepts and doctrine, and in ethical, professional and proto-legal codes of conduct incorporating notions of military honour and chivalry, which date back centuries. By the eighteenth century, it had become a customary set of legal rules and principles, which were codified over the course of the nineteenth and twentieth centuries into a dense set of rules and obligations in a number of international conventions, many of which have long had or have more recently obtained customary status. It is based on a number of basic principles, the two most important of which are the principle of military necessity and the principle of humanity. The former allows for the application of force, including lethal force, and the infliction of injury, damage and destruction, which is required for realising the objectives of the conflict, *within* the limits imposed by humanitarian law. The latter prohibits the use of weapons and methods of combat that inflict unnecessary suffering and/or are inherently indiscriminate in nature. It additionally provides for special regimes of protection for specific categories of persons who have been rendered helpless or have fallen into the hands or under the control of the adversary. None of the rules and prohibitions contained in it is susceptible to derogation.[2]

The basic purpose of IHRL is to provide the citizens and inhabitants of a particular State with a number of freedoms and protection from arbitrary or discriminatory interference and treatment by the State and its agents, and to require the State to provide a legal framework to secure these rights and freedoms, as well as (to undertake) to provide essential social, economic and cultural safeguards and

[2] See, e.g., Kleffner 2011, pp. 51–52.

security to its population. It has some of its roots in the period of the Enlightenment, with respect to basic civil and political rights and freedoms, and some in the gradual provision of primary education, social legislation and workers' rights, starting from the late nineteenth century. Its codification at the international level came after the Second World War, and its development has gained in momentum and importance during the last decades of the twentieth century. It is based on a number of international and regional conventions, and certain of its provisions have obtained customary status, some of which may be derogated from in times of emergency.[3]

IHL is applicable to all parties to an armed conflict of either an international or non-international nature, irrespective of the motivations of the parties, or the legality (or lack thereof) of the recourse to force by either of them. The former type of conflict refers to any clash between the armed forces of two or more States, or any occupation by a State of another State's territory, whether total or partial, irrespective of whether such occupation is forcibly resisted. The latter refers to hostilities between a State and (an) armed group(s), or between armed groups within a State, of an organised, intensive and protracted nature. This includes armed rebellion, armed insurrection and civil war, but does not extend to situations of mob violence, riots and criminal activity. In temporal and geographical terms, an international armed conflict occurs from the outbreak of hostilities or onset of an occupation until a peace agreement is reached, or a sustained and general cessation of hostilities occurs. It applies within the territory of the belligerent States and also applies within the 'international commons' (all maritime areas and airspace not forming part of the territory of a non-belligerent State) wherever and whenever hostilities and other military operations extend to such areas. The territory of non-belligerent or neutral States is inviolable unless one of the belligerent parties conducts operations from neutral territory and the neutral State fails to take adequate measures to halt such operations after being called upon to do so by the injured party.

Non-international armed conflicts take place normally within the confines of a single State, but in some cases can spill over into the territory of a neighbouring State (or States) to the extent that an armed group displaces or is displaced to another State's territory and conducts operations from there without being prevented from doing so by the authorities of the State whence it conducts such operations.[4] A non-international conflict commences when the material conditions for the existence of a non-international armed conflict (organisation and intensity and protracted nature of hostilities) are fulfilled and ends upon the conclusion of a peace agreement between the government and opposing armed groups, or when the material conditions are no longer fulfilled.

---

[3] Ibid, pp. 65–66.

[4] The material threshold for armed conflict was authoritatively stated in the decision of the Appeals Chamber in ICTY, *Prosecutor v. Dusko Tadić*, Decision on Defence Motion for Interlocutory Appeal on Jurisdiction, Appeals Chamber (IT-94-I-AR72), 2 October 1995, para 70. For the applicability of IHL in geographical terms see, e.g., Greenwood 2008, pp. 59–62.

IHRL applies at all times within a State's territory, or with respect to areas or persons within its jurisdiction or under its effective control. Aside from permissible derogations, it does not cease to apply during armed conflict and will apply to extraterritorial military operations, within the context of an armed conflict, or below the threshold thereof, to the extent that either a particular geographical area or persons are under its jurisdiction or effective control, irrespective of whether such jurisdiction is exercised lawfully.[5]

## 9.3 Main Approaches to the Relationship and Interaction Between IHL and IHRL

While the discourse relating to the relationship between IHL and IHRL is an ongoing process, it is fair to say that there are basically three main approaches relating to how the two sub-disciplines relate to and interact with each other. The traditional approach in international law up to comparatively recently was that the law of peace, including human rights law, applied in peacetime and that the law of war and of neutrality applied in wartime. That is reflected inter alia in traditional international law textbooks up to and including the first two decades of the period after the Second World War, and in international conventions and practice of that period. In the present, this strict separation is still adhered to by only a handful of States, most notably the US and Israel, which have taken the view that during armed conflict, IHL is the sole basis of legal obligations for parties to the conflict, and/or that IHRL is not applicable, or in any case is wholly set aside by IHL in the context of (extraterritorial) military operations. Another approach that is put forward by certain academics and human rights advocates is that IHL is a branch of human rights law and that to the extent they differ, it is necessary to adjust and apply IHL with a view to make it conform more closely to human rights standards, particularly in the context of non-international armed conflicts. This is sometimes referred to broadly as 'the humanisation of IHL'. A third approach, which at present seems to reflect prevailing opinion and practice, is that the two bodies of law are basically complementary and in the event that they actually collide, to apply the rule which is most specific and relevant to the issue at hand. This is sometimes referred to by reference to the general principle of law known as the *lex specialis* principle, referred to previously in the introduction. In my view, the third approach is the most persuasive and coherent for a number of reasons.[6]

---

[5] Kleffner 2011, pp. 68–69 and accompanying notes.

[6] The 'separationist' approach of the US and Israel, whereby IHRL is considered either inapplicable to armed conflict or is presumed to be consistently overridden by IHL, is referred to by, inter alia, Hampson 2008, p. 559. The 'humanisation 'or 'pacification' of IHL approach is epitomised by, inter alia, Schabas 2007; Doswald-Beck 2011, pp. 112–113, where she refers to 'an IHL mentality, which tends towards a *lex specialis* approach that in effect marginalizes human rights law'. The mainstream approach, which sees the two bodies of law as essentially

On the one hand, a strict 'separationist' approach is not only outmoded, but also inaccurate as a matter of law, as it is clear that human rights conventions are clearly intended to apply in armed conflict and contain provisions that allow either for derogation or accommodation of IHL in situations of armed conflict. Moreover, it would also seem clear on the basis of consistent jurisprudence by human rights courts and other national and international courts and tribunals, that human rights law and conventions are applicable in any situation in which a State or its agents exercise jurisdiction or control over territory or individuals. There is no reason, in principle, why this would not be the case in the context of an armed conflict, although this does not necessarily answer the question as to *when* such jurisdiction or control is established, a point to which I will return subsequently. On the other hand, the second approach ignores the distinct nature and function of the two bodies of law and most notably ignores the incontrovertible fact that States have seen fit to devise a specific body of law to apply to situations of armed conflict and continue to develop and apply it to the present day. Leaving aside the fact that IHL and IHRL do not share a common historical development, and despite a degree of overlap are framed and structured differently, they are distinct in their basic functions and approaches, notwithstanding certain undeniable shared basic principles and purposes. IHL is essentially a balance between humanitarian and military considerations. Ignoring the latter, while solely or primarily concentrating on the former, undermines one of its basic purposes and tenants, which is to mitigate the effects of war while not preventing the conduct of hostilities, including the application of force within the accepted confines of the law and the treatment of certain categories of persons, such as prisoners of war and civilians in occupied territory, which balances both sets of considerations. If parties to an armed conflict feel the law ignores or unduly underplays military considerations, they may well choose to ignore the law entirely as a means of ensuring success on the battlefield. This would obviously be counterproductive and at variance with what both legal regimes are intended to prevent.

This in a nutshell is why the third approach seems to be the most rational and coherent solution. More to the point, it reflects both the essential reality of armed conflict and the fact that States have clearly devised two separate—but essentially complementary—bodies of law to deal with that reality. To the extent that they collide, it makes sense to apply the rule which most closely relates to or was specially devised to apply to a particular situation and/or which provides the most detailed regulation of what is allowed or prohibited. The term *lex specialis* more or less corresponds to this, but if one finds the term confusing or misleading, it could be referred to by any other name, thereby achieving the same result and taking account of what States intended and best fits the situation.

---

(Footnote 6 continued)
complementary, whereby *lex specialis* is a means of resolving conflicts between conflicting norms when these occur, is expressed, inter alia, in the decisions of the ICJ referred to in supra n 1, as well as by various authors, e.g., Droege 2007, p. 312 *et seq.*; Kleffner 2011, pp. 72–75; Melzer 2011, pp. 43–44.

The *lex specialis* principle has engendered considerable discussion and, in my view, a significant degree of needless confusion since it was referred to by the international Court of Justice (ICJ) as a means of determining what determines an arbitrary deprivation of life in relation to the use of nuclear weapons (or by implication any situation of hostilities) in its *Nuclear Weapons* advisory opinion in 1996.[7] Some argue that the Court on the basis of that statement had determined that IHL as a whole and in every situation of armed conflict would be the more specific body of law and would therefore have precedence over IHRL in any situation where there was a (potential) conflict between them, or even that IHRL is, on the basis of the principle, inapplicable in armed conflict. Others denied that *lex specialis* was a general principle of law, opined that it was ambiguous and incapable of resolving the question of the interrelationship of the two bodies of law, argued that the ICJ reversed its opinion in subsequent case law, which failed to specifically mention it, or argued that application of the *lex specialis* principle would result in the marginalisation of IHRL and therefore should be rejected.[8] In my view, none of these positions is correct, and the subsequent confusion and jockeying for precedence between IHL lawyers and human rights advocates is both misguided and counterproductive.

In looking at the relationship between the two bodies of law and what the function of the *lex specialis* principle is in the context of that relationship, it is important to bear in mind what the ICJ actually said, and to see the principle in perspective. The ICJ neither said that IHL will always take precedence in every situation and with regard to any issue, nor did it say that the entire relationship between IHL and IHRL is governed by it. Likewise, no considered reading of the two bodies of law will result in the finding that they are fundamentally incompatible or constantly at variance with each other's basic purposes and principles, or even, for that matter, that they inevitably will collide and provide for conflicting obligations on many matters. To be sure, there are some important differences in their respective functions and, in some instances, there is a greater or lesser degree of collision between specific provisions allowing or prohibiting a particular conduct or course of action, but it is both inaccurate as well as counterproductive to overemphasise this degree of collision, just as it is to ignore their specific functions or pretend that they wholly coincide on all matters.

The starting point is that in interpreting and applying two bodies of law which are relevant and applicable to a given situation is to apply both to the fullest extent

[7] *Legality of the Threat or Use of Nuclear Weapons*, supra n 1.

[8] In addition to the sources advocating either a 'separationist' or a 'humanisation' approach cited in supra n 6, see, e.g., Milanović 2010. Milanović argues that *lex specialis* and other methods of interpretation are of limited value in resolving the normative relationship between IHL and IHRL, and further sees the purpose of the latter body of law as further humanising IHL both by applying IHRL in a way to not only fill gaps left open by IHL, but to 'change some outcomes that are in fact determined by IHL by introducing human rights rules and arguments into the equation'. Needless to say, I disagree with both contentions and positions on the basis of the arguments set out in this essay.

possible, with due regard for their specific functions, and emphasising their mutual compatibility unless it is clear there is in fact a conflict between specific provisions or obligations. Without a clear intention on the part of States to view a specific body of law as overriding or setting aside the other in all situations, there are no grounds for doing so. Likewise, it is clear that if a specific provision or subset of provisions are specifically designed to regulate a particular matter, they must be given all due consideration and, where necessary, precedence. Consequently, a court will take account of what the specific provisions of each set of applicable obligations provide and use all means of interpretation, including, but not limited to, any specific principle of interpretation, such as the *lex specialis* principle, to ensure that both bodies of law are given the maximum effect possible. Where a specific matter is dealt with in detail, it will apply those detailed provisions without ignoring the obligations which arise from another applicable legal source or body of law, to the extent that there is no clear conflict between them. If conflict should arise, a court will examine what the provisions provide on the basis of their ordinary meaning, taking account where necessary of the intentions of the parties and the purposes of both, and make use of all relevant tools and principles of interpretation and legal methodology to arrive at a solution which gives maximum possible effect to both as intended by the parties and which reconciles any conflicting obligations in a coherent and logical fashion, and takes account of all relevant circumstances. Hence, a court will make use of general legal principles of interpretation whenever necessary, alongside the well-established methods of treaty interpretation, such as the textual, historical or teleological methods. Such general principles of interpretation include, alongside the previously mentioned *lex specialis* principle, the notion that whenever possible, full effect must be given to the intentions of the parties and legal instruments must be reconciled to the maximum extent possible to avoid legal gaps or confusion, which is reflected in the legal maxim of *ut res magis valeat quam pereat*.[9] Taken together, these mean that in the absence of clear intention to the contrary, both bodies of law must be given all due consideration; that the fullest possible effect should be given to both; that rules specifically designed for a particular subject matter or situation should be given special consideration and weight; and that in the event of an actual collision of obligations, the most specific obligation will prevail (to the extent necessary) over obligations of a more general nature, including more general obligations which are of a later origin.

In short, the *lex specialis* principle is neither a 'trump card', nor a mystic formula which defies explanation or application, but rather is part of a whole bundle or system of well-established legal means of interpretation, and methods of reconciling legal instruments and conflicts of obligation when they actually arise. It should not be viewed in isolation and is neither a means of marginalisation of legal obligations, nor an indication that one body of law inevitably will prevail over another. It

[9] This maxim is a tool of interpretation which can be summarised as follows: 'such an interpretation is to be adopted that the measure may take effect rather than fail'. See: US Legal Definitions, available at: www.definitions.uslegal.com/i/interpretatio-fienda-est-ut-res-magis-valeat-quam-pereat/.

depends entirely upon whether there is an actual conflict between obligations or sets of obligations whether it will be used as a means of conflict resolution. To the extent there is no conflict, it is part of a system of legal interpretation which aims at emphasising the complementary obligations arising from parallel legal instruments or bodies of law and additionally gives added weight to provisions which have been specifically intended to apply to a particular situation. In applying this system to the relationship between IHL and IHRL, it is important to bear a number of basic considerations in mind: first, that both bodies of law are applicable in principle to any armed conflict within the conditions, and temporal and geographical scope of applicability set out above. When, for any reason, only one body of law is applicable to a particular situation (for example, when IHRL is inapplicable due to lack of jurisdiction or control over persons or territory, or IHL ceases to be applicable because the threshold conditions for the existence of an armed conflict are no longer met), no question of parallel application or conflict arises and only one body of law will be relevant. Second, whenever both bodies of law are applicable, they will complement each other and fill any gaps that occur, and should be interpreted and applied in such a way as to give both maximum possible effect. Third, where a specific set of rules has been implemented to apply to a particular situation, such as the rules pertaining to the conduct of hostilities in IHL (which is all the ICJ was referring to in *Nuclear Weapons*), or the rules pertaining to due process and fair trial guarantees in IHRL (which are only mentioned but not worked out in IHL), they should receive special consideration in applying both bodies of law, even when there is no actual collision between specific provisions. To do otherwise is to ignore the clear intention of the parties. Fourth, in specific cases where there is a clear clash of obligations arising from one body of law with those from the other, the more specific rule should be given precedence to the extent necessary to resolve the specific conflict. However, where no actual conflict of obligation exists, none should be inferred and the previously mentioned consideration of the complementary character of the two should be given all possible application. For example, humane treatment of prisoners of war (POWs) or civilian security detainees under the Third and Fourth Geneva Conventions is complemented by rules of IHRL prohibiting torture and other forms of inhumane treatment. There is little or no conflict of obligation and no reason why both should not apply in parallel. However, provisions of IHRL relating to the right of *habeas corpus* of persons in custody would be set aside in relation to such persons, while special provisions of IHRL relating to the treatment of children in detention would complement IHL rules relating to detention and be specially relevant to the treatment of captured child soldiers. In the former case, it is clear that a detailed regime relating to POWs has been devised with the purpose of comprehensively regulating their treatment and that the application of *habeas corpus*, as provided in IHRL, would be incompatible with that regime (although IHL contains its own provisions relating to determining the status of captured persons whenever there is any doubt relating thereto). In the latter case, IHL contains few specific rules relating to child detainees and IHRL not only complements those which do exist, but provides a much more extensive set of standards of protection specifically devised for this particular group and, as such, qualifies as *lex specialis* in that particular context. Hence, *lex specialis* is not the exclusive preserve of either body of law, but will depend upon the particular subject matter and what the intentions of the parties are. Sometimes this will result in more protection, but sometimes the contrary will be the case. Moreover, it forms but part of a whole system of interpretation and conflict resolution between norms.

These examples indicate that the specific factual circumstances also play a role in determining the relationship between the two bodies of law. We will now turn to applying that to two specific types of situations that occur in armed conflict.

## 9.4 The Application of IHL and IHRL in the Context of Hostilities and Law Enforcement in Armed Conflict

By and large, two main factual and normative paradigms are relevant in the context of an armed conflict, whether international or non-international in nature. These are the paradigm of hostilities and the paradigm of law enforcement.[10] The former refers to the application of the means and methods of warfare between the parties to an armed conflict. This occurs whenever there are armed clashes and similar activities relating to such confrontations between the parties in the context of an armed conflict. Although 'hostilities' are not specifically defined under IHL, they are intrinsic to an armed conflict and have the aim of weakening the military potential and achieving the submission (either total or partial) of the adversary. The conduct of hostilities involves the conducting of attacks (defined in IHL as any act of violence directed against the adversary, whether offensive or defensive in nature), and other related activities, such as deployment, manoeuvres, reconnaissance, and direct logistical support and supply of such activities. It is governed by the rules and principles of international (humanitarian) law relating to such activities, which form the legal paradigm of hostilities. Hostilities can only take place within the context of an armed conflict, which involves two or more organised parties with some kind of recognisable command structure, and is a factual situation which exists whenever the means and methods of warfare are actually applied between members of opposing forces with a view to directly effecting the adversary's military operations and/or preventing one's own military operations from being adversely effected. Consequently (and this is a point that is of essential importance), the paradigm of hostilities will only be relevant in the context of an armed conflict, within the temporal and geographic confines set out above, to the extent that there is a factual situation of lack of control over either persons or territory (or both) which require the application of the means and methods of warfare. While the (legal) paradigm of hostilities is intrinsic to any armed conflict, it is by no means synonymous with the entire legal regime pertaining to armed conflict and forms but one

---

[10] See Melzer 2011 for detailed treatment of the two (legal) paradigms.

part of the humanitarian law of armed conflict. Many activities and situations which form part of any armed conflict, such as the exercise of authority over persons or territory, the maintenance of public order and the detention or internment of persons, such as POWs, do not form part of the paradigm of hostilities, even though they are governed by IHL, alongside other applicable rules of international law.

The other factual and legal paradigm relevant to armed conflict is the paradigm of law enforcement. This refers to all activities connected to the exercise of authority over persons or territory; the maintenance of public order; and the suppression of criminal or subversive activity outside the conduct of hostilities. The legal paradigm of law enforcement refers to all rules and principles of international law relating to and regulating such activities, some of which pertain to international humanitarian law, and others which derive from IHRL, international criminal law or general international law. It includes such matters as maintaining and preventing breakdown in public order; the exercise of public authority over persons or territory, including over occupied territory under effective control; the investigation, apprehension and arrest of persons involved in or suspected of criminal or subversive activity outside the conduct of hostilities; and the detention and treatment of captured, interned or arrested persons and the curtailment or deprivation of their liberty and freedom of movement. Unlike the paradigm of hostilities, it can occur both inside and outside the context of an armed conflict, but the rules of IHL relating to this paradigm are only relevant within the context of an armed conflict.

The conduct of hostilities implies lack of control over either persons or territory. The occurrence of organised armed confrontation and clashes, the presence of enemy forces and the need to apply the means and methods of warfare to (re)assert control and achieve the submission of the adversary or prevent it from achieving the same, all are clear indications of a lack of effective control. In the context of an international armed conflict, this will be the case whenever and wherever one party has either not (yet) succeeded in overcoming organised resistance in a particular area, where it is not (yet) or no longer capable of exercising public authority, or has temporarily or permanently withdrawn or lost control over territory, persons or objects formerly under its control. In the context of a non-international armed conflict, there is a (rebuttable) presumption that the government of the territorial State where the conflict is taking place will exercise jurisdiction over all its territory, except where it is no longer capable of doing so for a shorter or longer period of time. This can be because (a portion of) its territory has come under the control of rebel or insurgent forces, or it is prevented from exercising any degree of public authority over persons or territory due to hostile activity or a general breakdown of State authority. Consequently, in most situations in which hostilities are conducted and ongoing in the context of an international armed conflict, there will be no jurisdiction over territory outside of situations of occupation, although this will not always preclude the existence of jurisdiction over persons under the physical control of one of the parties, such as when combatants/fighters or civilians fall into the hands of the opposing party. In the context of non-international armed conflict, while there will be *de jure* jurisdiction over a State's 'own' territory, it will be incapable of being exercised in areas under rebel or insurgent control and may be incapable of being exercised in areas which are contested. However, this too will not preclude the existence of jurisdiction over persons who are under the control of State forces.

It should also be stressed that in either international or non-international armed conflict, the mere ability to direct fire upon a particular military object or opposing forces does not in itself constitute effective control. Hostilities always imply the employment of force against opposing forces and military objects with a variety of weapons (systems), from a greater or shorter distance. The mere ability to do this does not equate with exercising 'jurisdiction' over them in the absence of other factors, such as the ability to exercise authority and control over either persons or territory. Likewise, the fact that one party to a conflict may have a predominance in military terms (more effective weapons, tactics or leadership and/or numerical superiority) and is able to prevail in a particular situation or engagement with opposing forces, or for that matter consistently prevails in most, or even all engagements, does not translate into exercising jurisdiction, until such time as organised resistance has ceased or has been overcome, and effective control is established over persons or territory. To the extent that lack of control coincides with lack of jurisdiction, which, as set out above, will always be the case in the context of an international armed conflict, except in relation to a State's own territory in so far as this is uncontested, or situations of belligerent occupation of hostile territory which is uncontested. By contrast, in the context of non-international armed conflict, the territorial State will possess jurisdiction over its territory, except where hostilities are ongoing or in areas in which it has temporarily or permanently lost control to opposing forces, or as a result of inability to exercise public authority. In either situation, a lack of control would translate into a lack of de facto jurisdiction and would prevent the applicability of international human rights law. To the extent jurisdiction (is presumed to) exist(s) and hostilities occur, the rules relating to the conduct of hostilities would take precedence over other rules on the basis of the system of interpretation set out above. While not all jurisprudence of human rights bodies consistently points to this conclusion, some does, and, in any case, there is a lack of consistency and clarity, both between different human rights tribunals and bodies, and even with regard to the same tribunal or body in different decisions. Sometimes this is the result of differing circumstances, which should clearly always be taken into account, but in other situations it would seem that either procedural considerations, such as the fact that the State in question has failed to enter a derogation from the application of a particular human rights convention, or a reluctance or inability on the part of the tribunal or body to apply IHL rules relating to the conduct of hostilities, is the underlying reason for such lack of consistency and clarity.[11]

[11] On the differing approaches to the question of effective control and extraterritorial applicability of human rights in general between the European and Inter-American human rights systems, and in some cases between decisions of the same human rights body, see Kleffner 2011, pp. 70–71, and accompanying notes.

In all situations in which effective control is exercised or is capable of being exercised, there is de facto or *de jure* jurisdiction, and consequently, IHRL will apply alongside any relevant provisions of IHL to either the use of force to exercise and maintain such control, or in the treatment of persons. Since the maintenance of public order and the exercise of authority over persons and territory also form part of IHL, the two bodies of law will apply in tandem, taking into account the rules of interpretation as outlined above and the specific factual circumstances, which will determine the degree of control present at a particular point in time or relating to a specific situation. The paradigm of hostilities will apply whenever and wherever opposing forces are capable of operating, and conducting attacks and directly related military operations, even if this is in territory (ostensibly) under the control of the other party. For example, a raid carried out by the opposing party's special operations forces deep in enemy-held territory to capture or kill a specific person or group of persons, or capture or neutralise a particular installation, would be subject to the paradigm of hostilities, notwithstanding the territorial control of the other party. This is because the situation requires the application of that paradigm for both parties. If, on the other hand, to use a frequently cited example, a particular rebel or insurgent commander were present on government controlled territory and incapable of conducting hostilities (say because he was visiting his family in the capital city), the use of force in effecting his capture would be subject to the law enforcement paradigm, simply because the State and its agents are capable of doing so without having to resort to the 'means and methods of warfare' to effect an arrest. If he resisted or attempted flight, the same rules (that is, those of IHRL) would govern under which circumstances any use of (potentially) lethal force would be justified. The fact that he was a member of opposing forces, which would normally justify his being targeted without warning, would be secondary in those circumstances because of the possession of effective control and the lack of any requirement to resort to the paradigm of hostilities to maintain such control. This is the consequence of the relationship between the two bodies of law, their basic functions and purposes, and the system of interpretation of their parallel application referred to above, and not because of 'restrictive military necessity' arising from IHL, or any presumed superiority of one body of the law over the other. It is essentially a matter of 'common sense', as well as of sound legal interpretation to apply the paradigm which best fits the particular situation, notwithstanding the formal applicability of either regime. In the first example, the paradigm of hostilities is applicable, notwithstanding that the State where the raid is being conducted has territorial control in its territory, which makes the regime of IHRL otherwise applicable outside the conduct of hostilities; in the second example, law enforcement is the applicable paradigm because of State control over that portion of its territory, despite the formal applicability of IHL to the entire territory where the conflict is taking place.[12] While admittedly it is comparatively easy to determine

[12] The example of the rebel commander visiting his family in government-controlled territory figured repeatedly in the discussions of the Expert Group, which was tasked to attempt to clarify

which paradigm is applicable in these two examples, and in some cases, the decision will not always be so clear, this does not mean that the problems which may arise are insolvable, or that rules appropriate to the situation cannot be devised and applied. These give precedence where precedence is due and provide for a reasonable solution, which recognises the basic purposes of both bodies of the law, and takes account of both human rights and humanitarian requirements, without ignoring military and security considerations.

## 9.5 Some Concluding Observations

The relationship and interaction between any two bodies of law or sets of obligations is governed by well-established principles of legal methodology and interpretation, and there is no reason why this system should not apply or cannot be applied to the relationship between IHL and IHRL as two parallel, complementary, but distinct legal sub-disciplines of public international law. If this is done in a rational way, which takes account of the purposes and functions of both branches, there is no reason why this should not result in solutions which are coherent, consistent and which do justice to both bodies of law, and to the obligations States have undertaken to meet and are legally bound by. In doing so, the specific functions and purpose of both bodies of law must be given all due consideration. In many situations, there is no conflict between the obligations arising under both bodies of law and, to the extent they are both applicable in temporal or geographic terms, or in relation to a particular person or category of persons, both can and will apply alongside each other and should be given all possible effect. Where only one body of law is applicable, the other should not be applied and no question of possible conflict between them will arise. Where both are applicable and conflict arises between a specific (set of) obligation(s), the rules most relevant, which provide the most detailed set of obligations in relation to a specific situation and set

(Footnote 12 continued)
the notion of 'Direct Participation in Hostilities' by the ICRC between 2003 and 2008. The resulting 'Interpretive Guidance on the Notion of Direct Participation in Hostilities under International Humanitarian Law', issued independently by the ICRC outside the Expert Group in 2009, relied upon a concept of 'restrictive military necessity' rather than, but without prejudice to, human rights law, to apply to such situations. This has caused a significant degree of controversy, but since the mandate of the ICRC and the Expert Group was to clarify the notion of 'direct participation in hostilities' from within IHL, rather than enter into an examination of the parallel application of IHL and IHRL and the relationship between the two bodies of law, this controversy does not directly relate to whether, when and why IHRL would apply in such a situation. As a member of the 'Expert Group', I took part in the discussions and experienced first-hand what I saw then and see now as a needless competition and jockeying for precedence between (some) IHL and IHRL lawyers. I have experienced the same phenomenon on various occasions since then at other conferences, which is what brought me to consider writing this plea for a more 'common sense approach'.

of factual considerations, will have precedence to the extent necessary to resolve any conflict. This translates into a considered application of a system of interpretation, which includes, but is not limited to the *lex specialis* principle, both as part of a broader system of interpretation and as a means of conflict resolution, when, but only when, conflict actually arises between them and/or it is clear that a specific set of obligations has been devised to apply to the situation in question.

To me, the incessant competition and jockeying for precedence by humanitarian law and human rights lawyers and advocates is unnecessary, incorrect as a matter of law, and is dangerously counterproductive. One should recall that the basic purpose of both IHL and IHRL in the context of an armed conflict is to provide the maximum degree of protection possible to persons who are at risk and are vulnerable to abuse, while recognising the extraordinary nature and reality of armed conflict. Whether one likes it or not, 'war' is a situation which has occurred throughout history and which is likely to continue to occur for the foreseeable future. If the law is to have any influence on policy makers and those who (are supposed to) apply the law under extreme conditions and provide for any degree of mitigation of the effects of armed conflict and protection for the persons who need it most in such situations, it must be seen as clear, coherent and consistent and, at the same time, workable and realistic in relation to the circumstances of armed conflict. That will not be the case if IHL and IHRL lawyers consistently come up with conflicting interpretations and applications of the applicable law, or, even worse, question each other's relevance and motives. If that happens, the most likely result will be that the law is either cynically adapted to fit a particular policy, or will be ignored altogether. That would be nothing less than a brevet of incompetence and irrelevance for both 'sides' in the debate and would be the worst possible outcome for the persons both branches of the law are intended to protect.

## References

Doswald-Beck L (2011) Human rights in times of conflict and terrorism. Oxford University Press, Oxford

Droege C (2007) The interplay between International Humanitarian Law and International Human Rights Law in situations of armed conflict. Isr Law Rev 40(2):310–355

Greenwood C (2008) The area of war. In: Fleck D (ed) The handbook of International Humanitarian Law. Oxford University Press, Oxford, pp 59–62

Hampson F (2008) The relationship of International Humanitarian Law and Human Rights Law from the perspective of a human rights treaty body. Int Rev Red Cross 90(871):549–572

HRC (2004) General comment no. 31, the nature of the general obligation imposed on states parties to the covenant states of emergency (29 March 2004). UN Doc. CCPR/C/21/Rev.1/Add.13

Kleffner J (2011) Human rights and Humanitarian Law: general issues. In: Gill TD, Fleck D (eds) The handbook of the international law of military operations. Oxford University Press, Oxford, pp 51–77

Melzer N (2011) Conceptual distinctions and overlaps between law enforcement and the conduct of hostilities. In: Gill TD, Fleck D (eds) The handbook of the International Law of military operations. Oxford University Press, Oxford, pp 33–49

Milanović M (2010) A norm conflict perspective on the relationship between international humanitarian law and human rights law. J Confl Sec Law 14(3):459–483

Sassòli M, Olson L (2008) The relationship between international humanitarian and human rights law where it matters: admissible killing and internment of fighters in non-international armed conflicts. Int Rev Red Cross 90(871):599–627

Schabas W (2007) Lex specialis? Belt and suspenders? The parallel operation of human rights law and the law of armed conflict, and the conundrum of jus ad bellum. Isr Law Rev 40(2):592–613

# Chapter 10
# Counter-Terrorism and International Law Since 9/11, Including in the EU-US Context

**Gilles De Kerchove and Christiane Höhn**

**Abstract** The article by EU Counter-Terrorism Coordinator Gilles de Kerchove and his adviser Christiane Höhn provides an inside view into the EU's practices and views related to counter-terrorism and international law. It explains the EU's criminal justice approach to the fight against terrorism and provides arguments for the effectiveness of this response in practice. The authors set out the tools for regional law enforcement and judicial cooperation the EU has adopted since 9/11, based on the principle of mutual recognition, as well as EU-US cooperation in this area. It also looks at the role of the military in the fight against terrorism. In a second part, the article deals with questions related to the international legal framework for the fight against terrorism, such as the existence of not of an armed conflict in the legal sense against Al Qaeda. It also explains relevant initiatives in the EU-US context, including the EU-US legal advisers' dialogue, the EU framework to support the closure of Guantánamo and the EU input to the implementing provisions of the National Defense Authorization Act.

**Keywords** European Union · Counter-terrorism · Terrorism · Criminal justice · Law enforcement · EU-US relations · EU-US legal advisers dialogue · United States · International law · International humanitarian law · Human rights law · Guantanamo · National defense authorization act · Remotely piloted aircraft systems · Detainees · Principle of mutual recognition

---

Gilles De Kerchove is the European Union (EU) Counter-Terrorism Coordinator (CTC). Dr. Christiane Höhn is adviser to the EU CTC. The views expressed in this article are those of the authors alone and do not necessarily reflect the views and positions of the Council of the European Union.

---

G. De Kerchove (✉) · C. Höhn
Council of the European Union, Brussels, Belgium
e-mail: gilles.dekerchove@consilium.europa.eu

C. Höhn
e-mail: christiane.hoehn@consilium.europa.eu



T.D. Gill et al. (eds.), *Yearbook of International Humanitarian Law 2013*,
Yearbook of International Humanitarian Law 16, DOI 10.1007/978-94-6265-038-1_10

## Contents



## 10.1 Introduction

The US is the EU's most important partner in the fight against terrorism.[1] Strong EU-US cooperation is indispensable to fight terrorism effectively. The EU Member States strongly rely on the US for the fight against terrorism. Since 9/11, many EU-US tools have been adopted for the fight against terrorism, such as EU-US Mutual Legal Assistance and Extradition Agreements, cooperation agreements between the US and the EU agencies Europol and Eurojust, EU-US Passenger Name Record (PNR) and Terrorist Financing Tracking Program (TFTP) agreements. The EU is working in particular with the Department of State, the Department of Justice, the Department for Homeland Security (transport security, prevention of radicalization, foreign fighters,[2] PNR) and the Treasury Department (terrorist financing), as well as with the White House. EU-US cooperation on counter-terrorism (CT) capacity building in third countries is strong, as is cooperation in the UN and Global Counterterrorism Forum (GCTF) contexts. Best practices are shared and cooperation is close in challenging

[1] For more details see De Kerchove 2011.

[2] Persons from Western or other countries travelling to conflict zones, in particular Syria, to join terrorist groups in the fight there.

areas such as the prevention of radicalization and foreign fighters, which have become a serious threat over the past year. Measures to fight the threat to civil aviation have been aligned and strengthened on both sides of the Atlantic, including related to cargo after the attempted attack by explosives hidden in cargo from Yemen in 2009. Cooperation to fight terrorist financing is strong as well.

Although the interpretation of international law sometimes differs, the EU and the US share the view that international law has to be respected in the fight against terrorism. The EU has expressed concerns about the number of policies adopted in the context of the so-called "Global War on Terror" and the "global war/armed conflict against Al Qaeda" in the legal sense since 9/11. Changes which resulted in more legal rights for detainees have started to occur during the Bush Administration, such as the so-called McCain Amendment (legislation) clarifying that the prohibition of cruel, inhuman and degrading treatment also applies extraterritorially, decisions by the US Supreme Court which extended some legal rights and protections to Guantánamo detainees and the wish expressed by President Bush to close Guantánamo. The EU has welcomed further policy changes by President Obama such as the decision to close Guantánamo within a year, the end of "enhanced interrogation techniques" and the end of secret detention. However, divergent approaches on some issues related to the fight against terrorism and some questions remain.

This article sets out a number of issues related to counter-terrorism and international law since 9/11. Special emphasis is put on the criminal justice approach, the cornerstone of the European CT effort and also one of the most successful policy options used by the US in the fight against terrorism.

## 10.2 The Criminal Justice Approach to the Fight Against Terrorism

The EU and the Member States use and promote a criminal justice approach for the fight against terrorism, including Al-Qaeda (AQ) related terrorism. This has not changed after 9/11. The fight against terrorism is carried out by the civilian actors: intelligence services, which operate outside the EU context, according to Article 4 of the Treaty of the European Union; police; law enforcement; judicial actors (investigators, prosecutors, judges) and the prison system. The CT efforts are geared towards preventing attacks and investigation and prosecution. It is a task not only for the Ministers of the Interior, but also for the Ministers of Justice.[3] Challenges remain, both in the national and the EU context. The criminal justice response has to adapt to new operating methods of the terrorist groups, such as advocating lone-actor attacks (the most deadly of which was committed in July 2012 in Oslo by Anders Breivik, a Norwegian right-wing extremist who killed 77 people and wounded 151) and traveling to hotspots such as Syria to join terrorist groups there.

[3] See, e.g., CTC 2010.

To improve the criminal justice response across the EU, Directorate-General (DG) Justice is financing a project carried out by the French *Ecole Nationale de la Magistrature*, in cooperation with the EU CTC and several other EU Member States, where since December 2013 European CT investigators, prosecutors and judges share best practices on challenges such as the terrorism and drugs nexus, use of intelligence as evidence, cooperation of judicial players with intelligence agencies, the military and emergency response after an attack. After conclusion of the project, the EU CTC will bring the outcomes to the attention of policy makers.

### 10.2.1 Context of the Fight Against Terrorism in the EU and the Member States

Before 9/11, a number of EU Member States already had a long history and experience in fighting terrorism that had produced many victims, including inter alia the Irish Republican Army (IRA) in Northern Ireland, the Euskadi Ta Askatasuna (ETA) in Spain and France, the Red Army Faction (RAF) in Germany and the Red Brigades in Italy. Given the fact that the terrorist threat was different in the various EU Member States (no terrorist organization operated all across Europe) and that Justice and Home Affairs (JHA) was only added to the EU's remit with the Maastricht Treaty in 1993, the fight against terrorism was mainly dealt with at the national level and not at the EU level. This changed after 9/11, as AQ-related terrorism now threatened all EU Member States.

In the aftermath of 9/11, terrorism was the main driving force behind the adoption of a number of EU tools in the JHA area, which were not necessarily CT specific but also covered other forms of serious crime, both inside the EU and within the US. Terrorism received the attention of the EU Heads of State and Government. In 2004, after the attacks in Madrid, the European Council created the post of the EU Counter-Terrorism Coordinator (CTC),[4] the mandate of which was set out by the European Council in the Stockholm Programme[5] after entry into force

[4] European Council Declaration to Combat Terrorism 2004. The European Council emphasises that a comprehensive and strongly coordinated approach is required in response to the threat posed by terrorism. The European Council accordingly agrees to the establishment of the position of a Counter-Terrorism Coordinator. The Coordinator, who will work within the Council Secretariat, will coordinate the work of the Council in combating terrorism and, with due regard to the responsibilities of the Commission, will maintain an overview of all the instruments at the Union's disposal with a view to regular reporting to the Council and effective follow-up of Council decisions.

[5] The Stockholm Programme—An open and secure Europe serving and protecting citizens, adopted by the European Council on 10–11 December 2009 (Council Doc. 17024/09). The European Council reaffirms the importance of the role of the EU Counter-Terrorism Coordinator in ensuring implementation and evaluation of the Counter-Terrorism Strategy, coordinating counter-terrorism work within the Union, and fostering better communication between the Union and third countries.

of the Lisbon Treaty. In 2005, after the attacks in London, the European Council adopted the EU Counter-Terrorism Strategy.[6] While the Member States have the main responsibility regarding the fight against terrorism, the EU plays a supporting role. Internal security has become a shared competence in the Lisbon Treaty.

### *10.2.2 Strategic Reasons for the Criminal Justice Approach*

Both before and after 9/11, the EU and its Member States have taken a criminal justice response to terrorism. Terrorism is a crime that needs to be investigated and prosecuted. Treating terrorism as the crime that it is de-glorifies terrorists and shows them as the criminals they are (they would rather be seen as combatants and martyrs). It also avoids terrorist groups using counter-terrorism measures as propaganda tools leading to radicalization and recruitment to terrorism—as for example President Obama has said happens with Guantánamo. (Perceived) double standards pose the risk of feeding into the terrorist narrative. A criminal justice response, which provides the terrorist suspects with full respect of human rights, rule of law and fundamental freedoms, defends our Western values and does not change who we are as societies because of the terrorist threat. The terrorists want us to change and provoke us to betray our values in the response. Maintaining the traditional criminal justice paradigm and using regular criminal courts to try terrorists does not give the terrorist groups this victory. Criminal trials are also important for the victims.

To be effective in the long term, CT policy requires full respect of human rights, rule of law and international law.[7] This is why the EU CT Strategy is "the European Union's strategic commitment to fight terrorism globally while respecting human rights." The criminal justice response is also set out in the EU CT Strategy under the "Pursue" pillar:

> We will further strengthen and implement our commitment to disrupt terrorist activity and pursue terrorists across borders. Our objectives are to impede terrorists' planning, disrupt their networks and the activities of recruiters to terrorism, cut off terrorists' funding and access to attack materials, and *bring them to justice*, while continuing to respect human rights and international law.

### *10.2.3 The Criminal Justice Response in the Context of the UN and the Council of Europe*

The criminal justice response to the fight against terrorism has also been recognized and required of the UN Member States by the UN Security Council, despite recognition of the "inherent right to self-defense", which has been used by some as an

[6] European Council 2005.

[7] See Søvndal et al. 2012, p. 247.

argument against the criminal justice approach to terrorism: In Resolution 1368 of 12 September 2001, the UN Security Council

> calls on all States to work together urgently to *bring to justice* the perpetrators, organizers and sponsors of these terrorist attacks and stresses that those responsible for aiding, supporting or harboring the perpetrators, organizers and sponsors of these acts will be held accountable.

In the key, legally binding resolution 1373 of 28 September 2001 "Threat to international peace and security caused by terrorist acts", the UN Security Council acted under Chapter VII and

> decide[d] also that all States shall: Ensure that any person who participates in the financing, planning, preparation or perpetration of terrorist acts or in supporting terrorist acts *is brought to justice* and ensure that, in addition to any other measures against them, *such terrorist acts are established as serious criminal offences in domestic laws* and regulations and that the punishment duly reflects the seriousness of such terrorist acts; afford one another the greatest measure of assistance in connection with *criminal investigations or criminal proceedings* relating to the financing or support of terrorist acts, including assistance in obtaining evidence in their possession necessary for the proceedings.

The UN CT conventions also set out a criminal justice response.

The criminal justice response is also taken by the Council of Europe, which had already adopted the Convention for the Suppression of Terrorism in 1977 and adopted the Convention on Prevention of Terrorism in 2005. Both set out various terrorist crimes and provisions for international cooperation in criminal matters.

### *10.2.4 EU Tools to Strengthen the Criminal Justice Response to CT in Europe Since 9/11*

After 9/11, this included the adoption of additional legislation creating a powerful legal framework. In the EU, instruments have been adopted both at the national and the EU level. Because of the suppression of border controls inside the Schengen zone, flanking measures are necessary to facilitate law enforcement and justice cooperation across borders.

In order to create the same minimum standards for the definition of the terrorist crimes across the EU, in 2002 the EU Framework Decision on Combating Terrorism[8] was adopted and updated in 2008[9] (to cover new behaviors such as public provocation to commit terrorist offenses in particular on the internet, recruitment for terrorism and training for terrorism, as well as implementing the Council of Europe Convention on the Prevention of Terrorism). EU Member States are legally obliged

---

[8] Council Framework Decision 2002/475/JHA of 13 June 2002 on combating terrorism, *OJ* 2002 L 164/3.

[9] Council Framework Decision 2008/919/JHA of 28 November 2008 amending Framework Decision 2002/475/JHA on combating terrorism, *OJ* 2008 L 330/21.

to transpose these into national legislation. The Commission will publish an implementation report about the transposition of the Framework Decision in the Member States in the autumn of 2014. With these common minimum requirements for criminalization of terrorist offenses across the EU the situation that terrorists commit a crime in one EU Member State and then travel to another Member State where the act is not punishable is avoided. Hence, the Framework Decisions close potential gaps in the response and have played a major role in strengthening the CT legal framework. Contrary to the UN, the EU has a common legal definition of the terrorist intent, although the material law offences, such as sabotage, are not harmonized.

The material terrorist crimes are not static, but have to evolve along with the threat. The EU needs to reflect upon whether the current crimes are still sufficient, or whether an updating of the Framework Decision is necessary to reflect the phenomena of lone-actor terrorism (which cannot be covered by membership in a terrorist group) and foreign fighters—European citizens and residents who travel to hotspots such as Syria to receive terrorist training and join terrorist groups there and fight with them. While some Member States have adopted legislation to deal with the latter phenomenon, such as explicitly criminalizing the membership in a terrorist organization abroad, the EU Framework Decision criminalizes only providing terrorist training, but not receiving it. Adapting the Framework Decision would produce a common EU legal framework, which facilitates cooperation, also in the context of the EU agencies.

One counter-argument used against the criminal justice response is that it cannot prevent attacks but it only serves to convict the perpetrators after an attack has been committed. This is not true; in the EU and Council of Europe context, a number of preparatory offenses have been created, which criminalize inherently dangerous behavior before an attack is committed, such as public provocation to commit a terrorist attack, membership in a terrorist organization, etc. As set out above, the UN Security Council also requires criminalization of preparatory acts.

On the other hand, some human rights advocates argue that the terrorist crimes now go too far and kick in too early by not requiring an attack to have happened. However, there are crimes in other areas than CT that also criminalize inherently dangerous behavior as such, for example membership of a criminal organization, drunken driving or conspiracy to commit a serious crime. This is a known concept of criminal law. If a criminal justice response is advocated, the legal framework and therefore also the material crimes have to provide the necessary tools to allow the disruption of attacks and convictions before an attack is committed. All terrorist offenses, however, require a number of objective and subjective elements and have to respect human rights, such as freedom of speech, freedom of thought, principle of legality and certainty of crimes, etc. It is also important to note that the EU CT legislation is not overbroad. For example, the broad crime of "material support to terrorism", which in the US context concerns the providers of humanitarian assistance, as all forms of support is criminalized, does not exist in the same way in the EU. The EU legislation criminalizes "participating in the activities of a terrorist group, including by supplying information or material resources, or by funding its activities in any way, *with knowledge of the fact that such participation will contribute to the criminal activities of the terrorist group*". The requirement of contribution to the criminal activities of the terrorist group narrows the criminalization, so that, for example, provision of humanitarian assistance in areas where terrorist groups operate is not prohibited nor negatively affected by EU CT legislation.[10]

EU CT measures are being reviewed by the European Court of Justice (which, since the Lisbon Treaty, with a transitional period of 5 years until 1 December 2014 for Maastricht and Amsterdam instruments, is also competent in the JHA area), the EU Charter for Fundamental Rights applies. All CT measures of EU Member States are subject to the review of the European Court of Human Rights (ECtHR), so that external human rights review takes place. With the accession of the EU to the European Convention of Human Rights, the ECtHR will also be able to review EU CT measures. Since 9/11, there have been numerous cases related to terrorism, which in some cases have required policy adjustments (such as, for example, in the sanctions area). This shows the strong impact of the human rights jurisprudence on CT in Europe. In addition to the judicial review, the European Parliament is now competent to adopt legislation in internal security, and therefore CT, in co-decision with the Council, so that the democratic legitimacy has been strengthened.

In addition to the material criminal offenses, the EU has created tools for cross-border cooperation in law enforcement and criminal justice that are based on the principle of mutual recognition in criminal matters and go way beyond traditional mutual legal assistance and extradition. The European Arrest Warrant[11] replaces extradition and has shortened the time to transfer a terrorist suspect to another EU Member State from sometimes over a decade (for example Rahid Ramda, the mastermind of to the 1995 terrorist attacks against the public transport system in Paris,[12] was arrested in London in 1995 and extradited to France in 2005. He was convicted in France in 2007 and is now serving a life sentence) to a few weeks (for example, Osman Hussein/Hamdi Isaac, one of the perpetrators of the London bombings of July 2005, was arrested in Italy at the end of July 2005 and extradited to the UK in September 2005, based on a European Arrest Warrant. He has since been convicted in the UK).

In the area of evidence, the principle of mutual recognition has been progressively implemented: the Framework on execution of orders freezing property and evidence (2003)[13] applied the principle of mutual recognition to the freezing orders

---

[10] For more details see Mackintosh and Duplat 2013; Norwegian Refugee Council 2012.

[11] Council Framework Decision 2002/584/JHA of 13 June 2002 on the European Arrest Warrant and the surrender procedures between Member States, *OJ* 2002 L 190/1.

[12] Perpetrated by the Algeria-based Armed Islamic Group (GIA). Between July and October 1995, several bombs and other explosives killed 8 people and wounded over 100 mainly at metro and RER stations.

[13] Council Framework Decision 2003/577/JHA of 22 July 2003 on the execution in the European Union of orders freezing property or evidence, *OJ* 2003 L 196/45.

(but transfers had to be asked separately). The European Evidence Warrant (2008)[14] applied to existing evidence and was complementary to the Mutual Legal Assistance Agreement (MLA).[15] The recently adopted European Investigation Order[16] goes a lot further and applies also to the collection of evidence. It creates a comprehensive system for obtaining evidence in cases with cross-border dimension.

> The goal of the directive is to allow member states to carry out investigative measures at the request of another Member State on the basis of mutual recognition. The investigative measures would, for example, include interviewing witnesses, obtaining of information or evidence already in the possession of the executing authority, and (with additional safeguards) interception of telecommunications, and information on and monitoring of bank accounts. The new rules would replace the current patchwork of legal provisions in this area with a single new instrument aiming to make judicial cooperation on investigations faster and more efficient. It will introduce automatic mutual recognition of investigation orders and limit the grounds for refusal by another EU state to execute the order, while at the same time providing legal remedies to protect the defense rights of concerned persons.[17]

Controlled deliveries carried out in another Member State are regulated by Article 12 EU MLA, the Schengen Implementation Convention[18] as well as the Naples II Convention[19] for customs.

The EU agencies Europol[20] and Eurojust[21] have been created and strengthened and the legal framework for Joint Investigation Teams[22] between several Member States has been created. In the context of Eurojust, in addition to strategic and tactical meetings, where investigations and prosecutions related to a particular terrorist threat (such as the Kurdistan Worker's Party (PKK), foreign fighters) are shared, case coordination meetings are possible which allow for real time coordination of arrests across EU Member States, for example. The Terrorism Convictions

---

[14] Council Framework Decision 2008/978/JHA of 18 December 2008 on the European evidence warrant for the purpose of obtaining objects, documents and data for use in proceedings in criminal matters, *OJ* 2008 L 350/72.

[15] Council Act of 29 May 2000 establishing in accordance with Article 34 of the Treaty on European Union the Convention on Mutual Assistance in Criminal Matters between the Member States of the European Union, *OJ* 2000 C 197/1.

[16] Directive 2014/41/EU of the European Parliament and of the Council of 3 April 2014 regarding the European Investigation Order in criminal matters, *OJ* 2014 L 130/1.

[17] European Council 2014.

[18] The Schengen acquis—Convention implementing the Schengen Agreement of 14 June 1985 between the Governments of the States of the Benelux Economic Union, the Federal Republic of Germany and the French Republic on the gradual abolition of checks at their common borders, *OJ* 2000 L 239/19.

[19] Council Act of 18 December 1997 drawing up, on the basis of Article K3 of the Treaty on European Union, the Convention on mutual assistance and cooperation between customs administrations, *OJ* 1998 C 24/1.

[20] Europol is the European Union's law enforcement agency, see: http://www.europol.europa.eu/.

[21] Eurojust stimulates and improves the coordination of investigations and prosecutions between the competent authorities in the Member States, see: http://eurojust.europa.eu/Pages/home.aspx.

[22] Council Framework Decision 2002/465/JHA of 13 June 2002 on joint investigation teams, *OJ* 2002 L 162/1.

Monitor provides an overview over terrorism trials and judicial arguments throughout the EU. Europol provides support and expertise with regard to collection, sharing and analysis of information, support to specific investigations and centers of excellence, such as EC 3 on cybercrime and the Check the Web project, which provides analysis to Member States of jihadist websites. As the terrorist groups operate across borders, cooperation in the context of Europol and Eurojust facilitates the response by investigators and prosecutors across Europe.

This is the most advanced form of regional cooperation in this area worldwide, and has started to inspire other regions to develop similar tools. One example is that the African Union has started to work on an African Arrest Warrant.

### *10.2.5 EU-US Judicial and Law Enforcement Cooperation Tools*

After 9/11, the judicial and law enforcement cooperation has also been strengthened among the EU and the US: a modern legal framework covering all 28 EU Member States has been created with the entry into force of the EU-US Mutual Legal Assistance and Extradition Agreements and cooperation agreements between the US and Europol and Eurojust. The US now has a liaison officer with Europol and a liaison prosecutor with Eurojust and participates in meetings and case coordination where relevant. It can also initiate case coordination for specific cases.

### *10.2.6 Effectiveness of the Criminal Justice Response to Terrorism in Practice*

The criminal justice response to terrorism has proven effective on both sides of the Atlantic. Numerous terrorists have been convicted in regular criminal courts to long sentences, including before attacks were committed, both in EU Member States and in the US.

President Obama said in May 2013:[23]

> Much of our best counterterrorism cooperation results in the gathering and sharing of intelligence, the arrest and prosecution of terrorists. And that's how a Somali terrorist apprehended off the coast of Yemen is now in a prison in New York. That's how we worked with European allies to disrupt plots from Denmark to Germany to the United Kingdom. That's how intelligence collected with Saudi Arabia helped us stop a cargo plane from being blown up over the Atlantic. These partnerships work [...] Our courts have convicted hundreds of people for terrorism-related offenses, including some who are more dangerous than most GTMO detainees.

[23] President Obama, National Defense University Speech on US drone and counter-terrorism policy (23 May 2013), available at: http://www.nytimes.com/2013/05/24/us/politics/transcript-of-obamas-speech-on-drone-policy.html?pagewanted=all&_r=0. Accessed 30 April 2014.

Attorney General Eric Holder issued the following statement on 20 May 2014 in response to a federal jury in Manhattan unanimously reaching a guilty verdict against Abu Hamza al-Masri, who had been extradited from the UK and was convicted to life for a number of AQ-related terrorist related offenses committed around the world in a regular Article III (civilian) federal court in New York:

> In both word and deed, Abu Hamza supported the cause of violent extremism. His conviction is as just as it was swift. This case is all the more noteworthy since it continues a trend of successful prosecutions of top terrorism suspects in our federal court system. With each efficiently delivered guilty verdict against a top al Qaeda-linked figure, the debate over how to best seek justice in these cases is quietly being put to rest.

The criminal investigations and trials led to the collection of valuable information on the terrorist groups and networks. Criminal trials provide incentives for the terrorist suspects to cooperate and provide information, which interrogations in other contexts do not, such as reduction of sentences. In spite of strict rules for evidence, the regular civilian courts were able to convict a high number of terrorists. After the London and Madrid attacks, the law enforcement and criminal justice response was taken to these large-scale attacks. In Spain, the perpetrators of the Madrid attacks have been convicted in fair and successful trials, which do not serve the terrorists as propaganda material. In Norway, the trial of Breivik provided a strong counter-narrative to the terrorist narrative—the legal system provided all the rights and protections to the terrorist who had committed atrocious attacks, and nevertheless was able to convict him with a life sentence.

Since 9/11, many terrorists have successfully been convicted in US courts, including terrorists arrested overseas. The US government has provided many arguments for the effectiveness of the regular criminal justice system to deal with AQ-related terrorism, including a number of high profile convictions to life sentences. However, resistance in parts of the US population and Congress to using regular Article III courts to try foreign terrorist suspects remains strong.

Given the concept of the transnational armed conflict in the legal sense with AQ and associated forces in which the US sees itself, criminal trials are only one of several tools which can be chosen by the US Administration to incapacitate terrorists. The other tools in the US arsenal are (indefinite) law of war detention without trial (based on the armed conflict in the legal sense with AQ and associated forces) and trial in Military Commissions for foreign terrorist suspects as well as targeted killings abroad. Hence, the—difficult—criminal justice path where a conviction has to be gained in Court is optional; "easier" options are available (evidence rules are more relaxed in Military Commissions, which are legally only allowed to try aliens, not US citizens). With regard to AQ-related terrorist suspects, going through the criminal justice process with all the procedural guarantees for the defendant is not required to receive the result of long-term detention. The question remains, though, about what this optional toolbox approach means for a rule of law society and its fundamental human rights guarantees.

This optional approach, together with rhetoric since 9/11 that a war in the legal sense is needed to fight AQ-related terrorism, might be the cause for political opposition to regular civilian trials in the US that does not exist in Europe. Attempts in Congress to prohibit criminal trials for foreign terrorist suspects were only narrowly defeated and the National Defense Administration Act 2012 created a default for military detention of alien terrorist suspects having attempted to commit or committed an attack (see below). Let's look at the various arguments in turn:

- *Terrorist suspects are unlawful enemy combatants and should be treated according to the laws of war.* A transnational war against AQ is not an internationally recognized concept. It was not the US approach before 9/11, either. Terrorists want to be treated as combatants and not criminals, so one plays their game if one does so. The concept of "unlawful enemy combatant" is not a recognized concept under international humanitarian law (IHL).
- *Foreign terrorist suspects do not deserve the procedural rights and protections under the US Constitution.* Discrimination between US persons and aliens with regard to CT tools creates resentment, also among allies. It provides the impression of double standards, which are used in the terrorist narrative. If certain tools, such as Military Commissions, are not deemed fit for purpose to try US citizens under the US Constitution, it is difficult to convince an international audience of their fairness. As John McCain famously said: "It is about who we are, not about who the terrorists are." We must not let ourselves be provoked to abandon rule of law and human rights, our core values, in our response to terrorism. Having to prove guilt beyond a reasonable doubt according to fair procedures is a cornerstone of the rule of law. How does one know that somebody is a terrorist suspect if it is not established with credible evidence? Experience has shown that mere assertions have sometimes proven not to be sustainable. The alternatives to regular civilian trials are not good policy choices: long term or indefinite detention has proven to be politically unsustainable, as it raises questions with regard to human rights and fairness. Not only President Obama, but also the Bush Administration announced the goal of wanting to close Guantánamo in 2006. The political cost of this detention center has been high and the difficulties closure show the problems that long term offshore detention without trial can cause. There have been extremely few convictions in Military Commissions; there were many hurdles and legal challenges; most trials ended by plea bargains with short sentences. Compared to regular Article III Courts, objectively, the performance of Military Commissions has been poor. In addition, there are questions related to discrimination, fairness and human rights, which risk increasing if and when the death penalty is used there. Martyrs risk being created.
- *Regular criminal trials work for terrorist attacks committed at home, but it is not possible to do this for terrorists and terrorist acts overseas.* This is contradicted by the facts. While in 2001 the US Criminal Code indeed had not covered terrorist crimes committed abroad, as in the EU, the legislation has been changed and now has extraterritorial effect. The international legal framework

(UN CT conventions, UN Security Council Resolutions, Mutual Legal Assistance and Extradition Treaties) covers the scenario that terrorist suspects have to be extradited, that mutual legal assistance from third countries is necessary. With the similar problem of drug trafficking, the US Drug Enforcement Agency has shown that a law enforcement and criminal justice approach works internationally. Lessons can be learnt here, how the agents work with partner countries to establish evidence and prepare prosecutions abroad and in the US. With Europe, the cooperation could even be more advanced: The EU-US Mutual Legal Assistance and Extradition agreement (MLAE) allows the US to participate in Joint Investigation Teams with EU Member States, which means that US agents could participate in European investigations if it were to be so decided. In the context of Europol and Eurojust, the US has the full benefit of the close intra-EU cooperation, in which it can participate. FBI officers (LEGAT —legal attachés) and liaison prosecutors are placed in US embassies around the world, which could be mobilized for investigations and prosecutions.

- *Interrogations are necessary for intelligence purposes to avoid attacks. This is not possible in the context of a law enforcement/criminal justice approach.* As demonstrated above, there are no incentives for the suspect to cooperate outside a criminal trial where he could get benefits in view of sentencing. Enhanced interrogation techniques to force confessions have now also been banned in the US. Experience of terrorist trials have shown that in the context of the investigations and prosecutions, a wealth of knowledge about the terrorist organizations and their functioning is found, as the agents are forced to collect the evidence. In the criminal justice context, the prohibition to force the suspect to incriminate himself is important, hence he needs to be informed that he can remain silent (Miranda warning in the US), which is not the case in other forms of interrogation. However, as pointed out above, there are incentives to cooperate. In addition—we do not comment here on the lawfulness of this—the US seems to have found ways to deal with intelligence collection before transferring suspects to the regular criminal justice system, where "clean teams" provide the warnings (such as in the case of Wasame, who was first interrogated for intelligence purposes on a US navy vessel and later transferred to the US for trial).
- *Evidence related to some dangerous Guantánamo detainees is not admissible in Article III Courts.* This is a legacy problem, to which interrogation techniques no longer authorized might have contributed. This legacy problem should not determine future policy beyond Guantánamo.

In addition, there is the risk that third countries with a weak rule of law and human rights record follow the example of using long-term military detention for terrorist suspects. In those cases, the definition of terrorism is often overbroad and includes the political opposition.

For all these reasons, we fully support the policy of the US Administration in favor of criminal terrorism trials in regular Article III Courts.

### 10.2.7 EU-US Cooperation to Strengthen the Criminal Justice Response to Terrorism Around the World

In 2014, the EU-US Joint Summit Statement[24] said:

> We welcome our increasingly close cooperation in building the capacity of partner countries to counter terrorism and violent extremism within a framework of rule of law, particularly in the Sahel, Maghreb, Horn of Africa region and Pakistan.

It is a priority for both the EU and the US to work with partner countries affected by terrorism to strengthen their criminal justice response. In many of these countries, the criminal justice system needs strengthening to be able to convict terrorists within a reasonable timeframe in fair trials. The whole criminal justice chain needs to be beefed up. The human rights obligations related to the fight against terrorism and fair trials are set out in the International Covenant on Civil and Political Rights (ICCPR) and the Convention against Torture. Over the years, numerous UN soft laws by human rights treaty bodies, resolutions, etc., as well as rulings by the International Court of Justice have shed more light on how the various human rights provisions are interpreted, including with regard to special investigation techniques, where also the Council of Europe has developed guidelines.

In the context of the GCTF, co-chaired by the US and Turkey, one of the five working groups is devoted to criminal justice and the rule of law. In this context, the GCTF with 30 Members from around the world has adopted the "Rabat Memorandum on Good Practices for Effective Counterterrorism Practice in the Criminal Justice Sector", which sets out good practices for evidence-based prosecutions. In 2014, the International Institute for Justice and the Rule of Law will start operating in Malta, which is being set up in the GCTF context and aims at assisting interested countries, in particular those turning their back on repressive approaches to terrorism, in North, West and East Africa and the Middle East.

Both the EU and the US have criminal justice capacity-building projects in third countries. The EU is financing a project with UN Office on Drugs and Crime/UN Counter Terrorism Executive Director (UNODC/UNCTED) on "Rule of law-based prosecutions in the Maghreb", assisting the countries in the Maghreb to strengthen evidence based prosecution, instead of relying on confessions where the risk of torture and ill-treatment exists. The EU has another project with UNODC/UNCTED in Nigeria. With the CT Sahel and other justice projects, the EU is providing support to the specialized CT criminal justice poles in the Sahel countries. In Pakistan, the EU is contributing to the UK's Counter-Terrorism Associated Prosecution Reform Initiative (CAPRI) project, which aims at strengthening the criminal justice response.

---

[24] EU-US Summit Statement (26 March 2014), available at: http://www.eeas.europa.eu/statements/docs/2014/140326_02_en.pdf. Accessed 30 April 2014.

### 10.2.8 The Role of the Military in the Fight Against Terrorism

The general criminal justice approach does not mean that the EU Member States do not use the military overseas to fight terrorism, where appropriate. To the contrary, EU Member States have actively contributed to international efforts:

For example, they have contributed troops to Afghanistan and participated in military counter-terrorism patrolling/surveillance operations such as NATO's Operation Active Endeavour in the Mediterranean, in the context of which suspicious ships are localized and visited. This is NATO's only current Article 5 operation. Under Operation Active Endeavour, NATO ships patrol the Mediterranean and monitor shipping to help detect, deter and protect against terrorist activity. The mission is described in the following way by NATO[25]:

> NATO forces have hailed over 100,000 merchant vessels and boarded some 155 suspect ships. By conducting these maritime operations against terrorist activity, NATO's presence in these waters has benefited all shipping traveling through the Straits by improving perceptions of security. NATO is helping to keep seas safe, protect shipping and control suspect vessels. Moreover, this operation is also enabling NATO to strengthen its relations with partner countries, especially those participating in the Alliance's Mediterranean Dialogue.

France took the lead to help Mali to push back terrorist groups that had taken over the North of Mali in 2013 and moved towards the South in January 2014. For example, French military forces are stationed in the Sahel and can assist the governments of the region, where appropriate. Special forces of EU Member States can also intervene in hostage situations. Rules of engagement are often very strict.

Hence, the military has a role in the fight against terrorism, in particular overseas in situations of armed conflict, such as in Afghanistan or Mali.

The international law framework applicable to CT efforts overseas is determined on a case-by-case basis. EU Member States do not see themselves in a global war against AQ and associated forces. When some actions against terrorism take place in the context of an armed conflict in a given area, IHL applies. The international legal requirements for the extraterritorial use of force have to be met. In situations that do not reach the threshold of an armed conflict, armed forces operate in a law enforcement environment.

There are different scenarios, including the following:

The fight against terrorism is part of an armed conflict in a given territory, such as, for example, in Afghanistan and Mali, where terrorist groups are among the non-State actors participating in the conflict. In this case, the use of military force is justified when the *ius ad bellum* requirements are met for the extraterritorial use of force (for example authorization by the UN Security Council or invitation/consent

[25] NATO, Operation Active Endeavour, see: http://www.mc.nato.int/ops/Pages/OAE.aspx. Accessed 30 April 2014.

of the State on the territory of which the conflict takes place) and the *ius in bello* (IHL) is respected.

A new challenge is how the military and prosecution cooperate in such conflict zones, either to facilitate terrorist trials at home or in the host country. This is an issue, for example, in Afghanistan and Mali. After the end of the armed conflicts, terrorist suspects would have to be released if evidence had not been collected which would allow convictions in Court. Prosecutions would be for terrorist offenses such as membership in a terrorist group or terrorist acts (independent of the armed conflict or prior to it). However, it has to be kept in mind that under IHL the attack of military objectives during an armed conflict, even by non-State actors, is not a war crime, nor a terrorist attack. The US is very advanced on this cooperation between the military and law enforcement/criminal justice and has embedded prosecutors with military forces. The aspects of evidence collection in the context of military operations for civilian trials need to be further explored.

Given difficult territory and weakness of the internal security forces, in some countries, for example in the desert zones of the Sahel, military forces and not the police or gendarmerie carry out law enforcement functions. The EU in its civilian EUCAP Sahel Niger Common Security and Defense Policy (CSDP) mission is working with all security forces in Niger who carry out civilian law enforcement functions, including the military, and training them on evidence collection and other matters, which promotes "judiciarisation". Over time, reliance on the military for civilian functions is problematic, so that assistance should be provided to transfer the task to robust civilian police forces, such as the gendarmerie. In Mali, the importance of strengthening the civilian forces in a rule of law society has been recognized by the EU: After EU Training Mission in Mali (EUTM) Mali, a military CSDP training mission for the Malian army, the EU is now also launching EUCAP Mali, a civilian mission to train the civilian security forces.

## 10.3 The International Legal Framework for the Fight Against Terrorism and the EU-US Legal Advisers' Dialogue

### *10.3.1 The EU-US Legal Advisers' Dialogue*

With the release of a number of US legal memos in 2004, it became clear that the CT policies since 9/11 had been based on certain interpretations of international law. While the EU had initially been slow in reacting to US policies such as Guantánamo, secret detention and enhanced interrogation techniques, in early 2006, thanks to Jim Cloos, at the time director of Transatlantic Relations in the Council Secretariat, and Ferdinand Trauttmansdorff, the Legal Adviser of the Austrian Ministry of Foreign Affairs, despite caution from many sides, an interesting and productive dialogue was started with the participation of the Legal Advisers of the

Ministries of Foreign Affairs of the EU Member States (COJUR), EU institutions and the Legal Adviser of the US State Department, John Bellinger.[26] Prior to this dialogue, there had not been detailed discussion about the interpretation of international law in the CT context, neither within COJUR nor with the US, despite the fact that international law is one of the underpinnings of EU foreign policy. The dialogue allowed participants to gain an in-depth understanding of CT policies, interpretation of international law related to CT, relevant Court rulings, policy changes, etc., as well as to ask questions and express concerns among international law experts. Upon request by the US Legal Adviser Bellinger, the EU side developed for the first time a common interpretation of relevant international legal principles related to the fight against terrorism, which was transmitted to the US and which allowed an identification of areas of agreement, disagreement and areas for further discussion. This dialogue was continued twice a year with Harold Koh, the Legal Adviser of the State Department under the Obama Administration, and continues today.

The dialogue was welcomed for the first time in the EU-US Summit Statement of 21 June 2006[27] at the Vienna summit, during the Austrian Presidency:

> Consistent with our common values, we will ensure that measures taken to combat terrorism comply fully with our international obligations, including human rights law, refugee law and international humanitarian law. We attach great importance to our ongoing in-depth dialogue on our common fight against terrorism and our respective domestic and international legal obligations.

The 2007 EU-US Summit stated[28]:

We will continue and deepen our ongoing dialogue on international law principles relevant to our common fight against terrorism which has contributed to a better understanding of our respective legal frameworks and should help us to work together to combat terrorism.

The 2008 EU-US Summit Declaration[29] also included a reference to the dialogue:

> We agree that the fight against international terrorism raises important legal questions. We have continued and deepened our dialogue on international law principles, relevant to our common fight against terrorism. Our dialogue contributes to a better mutual understanding of our respective legal frameworks and helps us work together more effectively.

26 In November 2005, during a speech at the Atlantic Council on "Transatlantic Approaches to the International Legal Regime in an Age of Globalization and Terrorism", Bellinger had urged greater dialogue between the US and Europe on international law issues. See: http://www.state.gov/s/l/2005/87203.htm.

27 EU-US Summit Statement (21 June 2006), available at: http://www.consilium.europa.eu/ueDocs/cms_Data/docs/pressData/en/er/90176.pdf. Accessed 30 April 2014.

28 EU-US Summit Statement on Promoting Peace, Human Rights and Democracy Worldwide (30 April 2007), available at: http://www.eeas.europa.eu/us/sum04_07/statement_political_security_issues.pdf. Accessed 30 April 2014.

29 EU-US Summit Declaration (10 June 2008), available at: http://www.consilium.europa.eu/uedocs/cms_Data/docs/pressdata/en/er/101043.pdf. Accessed 30 April 2014.

In June 2009, the EU and the US made the following statement about the dialogue[30]:

> Taking into account that the action against international terrorism raises important legal questions, we recognize the importance of deepening our dialogue on international legal principles relevant to combating terrorism. In particular, we will continue working together in semi-annual meetings involving the COJUR, representatives of the General Secretariat of the Council of the European Union and the European Commission, and the U.S. Department of State Legal Adviser, with the objective of furthering an improved mutual understanding of our respective legal frameworks, and developing common ground from which we can work more effectively in combating terrorism.

## *10.3.2 Relevant International Legal Issues Related to the Fight Against Terrorism*

The relevant international legal issues with regard to CT include the following themes:

### 10.3.2.1 Existence of an Armed Conflict in the Legal Sense Against AQ?

A cornerstone of the US response after 9/11 has been the Congressional Authorization for the Use of Military Force (AUMF), which states:

> The President is authorized to use all necessary and appropriate force against those nations, organizations, or persons he determines planned, authorized, committed, or aided the terrorist attacks that occurred on September 11, 2001, or harboured such organizations or persons, in order to prevent any future acts of international terrorism against the United States by such nations, organizations or persons.

This authorization has been broadly interpreted and is provided as the reason for the US approach since 9/11 of a "war", or an "armed conflict" in the legal sense against AQ. Initially the political concept was a broad "global war on terror" (which has now been abandoned and which was not a legal concept).[31] Since 9/11, the US sees itself in a legal state of armed conflict with AQ and associated forces.

John Bellinger said in 2006:[32]

---

[30] US-EU Joint Statement on Closure of Guantánamo Bay And Future Counterterrorism Cooperation (15 June 2009), available at: http://www.state.gov/r/pa/prs/ps/2009/06a/124796.htm. Accessed 30 April 2014.

[31] Bellinger, London School of Economics Speech (31 October 2006), available at: http://www.state.gov/s/l/2006/98861.htm. Accessed 30 April 2014. "We do not believe that we are in a legal state of war with every terrorist group everywhere in the world. Rather, the United States uses the term "global war on terrorism" to mean that all countries must strongly oppose, and must fight against, terrorism in all its forms, everywhere around the globe".

[32] Ibid.

> We believe that the United States was and continues to be in an armed conflict with al Qaida, one that is conceptually and legally distinct from the conflict with the Taliban in Afghanistan. It cannot reasonably be argued that the conflict with al Qaida ended with the closure of al Qaida training camps and the assumption of power by a new government in Afghanistan. Al Qaida's operations against the United States and its allies continue not only in and around Afghanistan but also in other parts of the world. And because we remain in a continued state of armed conflict with al Qaida, we are legally justified in continuing to detain al Qaida members captured in this conflict [...] I am aware that many Europeans do not agree that we are in a war with al Qaida at all.

The view of an armed conflict with AQ has been maintained by the Obama Administration:

John Brennan, Assistant to the President for Homeland Security and Counter-terrorism, said in September 2011[33]:

> First, our definition of the conflict. As the President has said many times, we are at war with al-Qa'ida. In an indisputable act of aggression, al-Qa'ida attacked our nation and killed nearly 3,000 innocent people. And as we were reminded just last weekend, al-Qa'ida seeks to attack us again. Our ongoing armed conflict with al-Qa'ida stems from our right—recognized under international law—to self defense. An area in which there is some disagreement is the geographic scope of the conflict. The United States does not view our authority to use military force against al-Qa'ida as being restricted solely to 'hot' battlefields like Afghanistan...Others in the international community—including some of our closest allies and partners—take a different view of the geographic scope of the conflict, limiting it only to the 'hot' battlefields.

President Obama said in 2013[34]:

> We have now been at war for well over a decade... Under domestic law, and international law, the United States is at war with al Qaeda, the Taliban, and their associated forces. We are at war with an organization that right now would kill as many Americans as they could if we did not stop them first.

In terms of rhetoric, the "global war against Al Qaeda" and now is an "armed conflict against Al Qaeda and associated forces not restricted to Afghanistan", which, in substance, seems be the same. According to the US, this conflict is of a non-international character. The US Supreme Court ruled in *Hamdan v. Rumsfeld*[35] that there was a non-international armed conflict with AQ in Afghanistan (however, the case was about Afghanistan and a Guantánamo detainee captured there and did not touch on the question whether there is an armed conflict with AQ beyond Afghanistan. Similarly, in the Supreme Court decision *Hamdi v. Rumsfeld* the law

---

33 Brennan, Remarks addressing the Harvard Law School Brookings Conference (16 September 2011), available at: http://www.whitehouse.gov/the-press-office/2011/09/16/remarks-john-o-brennan-strengthening-our-security-adhering-our-values-an. Accessed 30 April 2014.

34 Speech President Obama, supra n 23.

35 *Hamdan v. Rumsfeld*, 548 U.S. 557 (2006).

of war detention of a Guantánamo detainee captured in the context of the armed conflict in Afghanistan was at stake and only this narrow situation was decided).[36]

This war paradigm means that the fight against AQ and "associated forces" (other than AQ in the Arabian Peninsula it is unclear which regional affiliates of AQ are included, as this is classified information) is conducted under the laws of war (IHL). This is different from a law enforcement/criminal justice/human rights-based framework for the fight against terrorism: under IHL detention for security purposes is possible without trial until the end of the conflict and targeting (killing) of combatants and civilians actively participating in hostilities, including collateral damage, is allowed.

Therefore, the question whether the fight against AQ takes place under IHL or law enforcement rules, hence the existence or not of an armed conflict, is a crucial one.

One of the central questions since 9/11 has been the existence and the scope of a transnational armed conflict against AQ.

The International Criminal Tribunal for the Former Yugoslavia (ICTY) determined in the *Tadic* case[37] that

> an armed conflict exists whenever there is a resort to armed force between States or protracted armed violence between governmental authorities and organized armed groups or between such groups within a State.

Therefore, the existence of a non-international armed conflict depends on two cumulative requirements: on the level of hostilities (intensity of violence and duration) and the level of organization of the non-state armed group that would be a party to the conflict. To determine in practice whether or not a conflict exists, according to ICTY, is thus

> a factual criterion, the assessment of which depends on an examination of events on the ground. Pursuant to international jurisprudence, indicative factors for assessment include the number, duration and intensity of individual confrontations, the type of weapons and other military equipment used, the number and calibre of munitions fired, the number of persons and types of forces partaking in the fighting, the number of casualties, the extent of material destruction, and the number of civilians fleeing combat zones. The involvement of the UN Security Council may also be a reflection of the intensity of a conflict.[38]

---

[36] *Hamdi v. Rumsfeld*, 542 U. S. 507 (2004). "For purposes of this case, the enemy combatant that [the Government] is seeking to detain is an individual who, it alleges, was part of or supporting forces hostile to the United States or coalition partners *in Afghanistan and who engaged in an armed conflict against the United States there.* We therefore answer only the narrow question before us: whether the detention of citizens falling within that definition is authorized".

[37] ICTY, *Prosecutor v. Dusko Tadić*, Decision on the Defence Motion for Interlocutory Appeal on Jurisdiction, Appeals Chamber (IT-94-I-AR72), 2 October 1995, para 70.

[38] ICTY, *Prosecutor v. Ramush Haradinaj* et al., Judgment Trial Chamber (IT-04-84-T), 3 April 2008, para 49; ICRC 2011, pp. 8–9.

These criteria are used to distinguish "an armed conflict from banditry, unorganized and short-lived insurrections, or terrorist activities, which are not subject to IHL."[39]

The EU does not share the view about the existence of a transnational conflict against AQ, which would mean a global battlefield. Instead, just as the International Committee of the Red Cross (ICRC) has done,[40] the EU has taken a case-by-case approach. The traditional criteria for determining whether or not an armed conflict exists have to apply: when in a given area hostilities are of such intensity that they cross the threshold to armed conflict and the parties are sufficiently organized, an armed conflict takes place there, to which IHL applies, such as in Afghanistan or Mali. Hence, if acts of terrorism are part of a specific armed conflict, IHL applies. Outside the context of an armed conflict, different national and international instruments related to, inter alia, criminal law enforcement, suppression of acts of terrorism and mutual legal assistance in criminal matters as well as human rights law apply.

AQ and "associated" forces are often only loosely linked, and while they are active in many countries around the globe, including in Europe, the level of hostilities in most countries does not reach the threshold required for armed conflict.[41] Taking a case-by-case approach, situations arise where IHL applies to the fight against terrorism in specific contexts, when the level of hostilities and the organization of the parties reaches a certain threshold. The existence of an armed conflict needs to be determined based on law and fact. In addition to non-international armed conflicts taking place within the territory of a single state, it may be argued that there are also spillover armed conflicts to the territory of a neighboring State.

President Obama has declared that at some point in the future the US war against AQ must end:

> The AUMF is now nearly 12 years old. The Afghan war is coming to an end. Core al Qaeda is a shell of its former self. Groups like AQAP must be dealt with, but in the years to come, not every collection of thugs that labels themselves al Qaeda will pose a credible threat to the United States. Unless we discipline our thinking, our definitions, our actions, we may be drawn into more wars we don't need to fight, or continue to grant Presidents unbound powers more suited for traditional armed conflicts between nation states…Our systematic effort to dismantle terrorist organizations must continue. But this war, like all wars, must end.[42]

This shift back to the traditional law enforcement approach would be very welcome, as it would align again the EU and US response.

---

[39] ICTY, *Prosecutor v. Dusko Tadić*, Opinion and Judgment in First Instance, Trial Chamber (IT-94-1-T), 7 May 1997, para 562.

[40] Interview with ICRC President Maurer, "The use of armed drones must comply with laws" (10 May 2013), available at: http://www.icrc.org/eng/resources/documents/interview/2013/05-10-drone-weapons-ihl.htm. Accessed 30 April 2014.

[41] See also Alston 2010.

[42] Speech President Obama, supra n 23.

There are also a number of important legal issues related to the lawfulness of extraterritorial use of force (*ius ad bellum*), which are not further discussed in this article.

#### 10.3.2.2 Relationship Between IHL and Human Rights Law? Extraterritorial Application of Human Rights Law?

In order to determine the applicable legal framework for the fight against terrorism, in particular the application of human rights law, it is important to know whether human rights law applies extraterritorially: The International Court of Justice has stated that the ICCPR applies in respect of acts done by a State in the exercise of its jurisdiction outside its own territory.[43] The US does not recognize extraterritorial application of the ICCPR.

Another issue is the relationship between IHL and human rights law. The International Court of Justice has stated that the protection offered by human rights conventions does not cease in case of armed conflict, save through the effect of derogation provisions of the relevant conventions. As regards the relationship between IHL and human rights law, there are thus three possible situations: some rights may be exclusively matters of IHL, others may be exclusively matters of human rights law, yet others may be matters of both these branches of international law.[44]

#### 10.3.2.3 Legal Protections of Detainees

Other legal issues are procedural rights of detainees, international law obligations related to transfers of detainees and protections of detainees under IHL. In the EU's view, as a minimum, the protections contained in Common Article 3 of the Geneva Conventions and Article 75 AP I, which is regarded as customary law, apply both in international and in non-international armed conflict.

The EU expressed its position with regard to CT and human rights in Council Conclusions in December 2006:

> The EU remains firmly committed to the absolute prohibition of torture, cruel, inhuman or degrading treatment and punishment. It guides our own actions and we raise our concerns with third countries. In this context, the Council reiterates that human rights, refugee law and international humanitarian law have to be respected and maintained when combating terrorism. The Council will continue to follow closely developments with regard to human rights in combating terrorism and take adequate measures for their protection. The existence of secret detention facilities where detained persons are kept in a legal vacuum is not in conformity with international humanitarian and human rights law.[45]

---

[43] ICJ, *Legal Consequences of the Construction of a Wall in the Occupied Palestinian Territory*, Advisory Opinion, (2004) ICJ Rep 136, para 111.

[44] Ibid, para 106.

[45] Council of the European Union 2006.

### 10.3.3 EU Support to the Closure of Guantánamo

The EU had expressed concerns about Guantánamo in the past. Guantánamo illustrates long-term or even indefinite law of war detention policies of terrorist suspects without trial.

The EU welcomed the policy changes announced by President Obama immediately after taking office: The intended closure of Guantánamo within a year, the end of secret detention, the end of "enhanced interrogation techniques" and the review of detention, interrogation and transfer policies.

> We welcome the determination of the United States of America to close the facility together with other steps taken, including the intensive review of its detention, transfer, trial and interrogation policies in the fight against terrorism and increased transparency about past practices in regard to these policies, as well as the elimination of secret detention facilities.[46]

Given the importance of the review, the EU made a written contribution to the Detention Policy Task Force created by President Obama (letter by the President of the General Affairs and Foreign Relations Council to the US Attorney-General and US Secretary of Defense as co-chairs of the Task Force and participation by the EU CTC in a briefing of the Task Force).

In order to support the closure of Guantánamo about which President Obama had said:

> GTMO has become a symbol around the world for an America that flouts the rule of law. Our allies won't cooperate with us if they think a terrorist will end up at GTMO,[47]

the EU set up a framework to facilitate acceptance of Guantánamo detainees by EU Member States. Within six months, despite the political sensitivities, in close cooperation with the US Administration, the framework, led by the EU CTC and the Commission (DG JHA), was set up. It consisted of Council Conclusions[48] setting up a system for information exchange among Member States and Schengen partners before and after acceptance of ex-detainees (this was crucial as the free movement within Schengen means that security of other Schengen partners is at stake as well) and a joint statement with the US,[49] which provided the political framework for such acceptance. Based on the framework, around two-dozen detainees have been accepted by EU Member States, which is a lot given that only one detainee was moved to the US for trial.

The Council Conclusions highlight the importance of addressing the detention policies underlying Guantánamo:

---

[46] US-EU Joint Statement on Closure of Guantánamo Bay and Future Counterterrorism Cooperation, supra n 30.

[47] Speech President Obama, supra n 23.

[48] Council of the European Union 2009.

[49] US-EU Joint Statement on Closure of Guantánamo Bay and Future Counterterrorism Cooperation, supra n 30.

> Wishing to lend its support to this process against the background of a thorough review of US counter-terrorism policies consistent with the rule of law and international law in the expectation that the underlying policy issues would be addressed.

In the Joint Statement, EU and US also stated the following:

> Depending on the outcomes of the US policy review processes we might explore, including in the context of our regular dialogue among Legal Advisers, the possibility of developing a Set of Principles that might serve as a common reference point within the context of our shared efforts to counter terrorism.

Such a Set of Principles has not yet been developed. In the future, perhaps after the end of the US war against AQ, it would be useful to develop such a document. The more the views on the principles are aligned across the Atlantic, the closer CT cooperation can be.

### *10.3.4 The National Defense Authorization Acts (NDAA) 2012 and 2013*

The EU was concerned about the CT provisions of the NDAA 2012, which not only included restrictions to transfer Guantánamo detainees, but also for the first time set out explicitly in law the possibility for long term law of war detention without trial for terrorist suspects and even required mandatory military detention without trial of foreign terrorist suspects having attempted or committed an attack, including on US soil. Military detention would be the default, civilian trials in regular Article III Courts would only be possible with derogations. This approach adopted by Congress would have gone further than the war paradigm under President Bush ever did. Just like the EU, the US Administration was concerned about this law and at least obtained the requirement in the law that the President could develop implementing regulations for the mandatory military detention provision.

Upon request, the EU provided input to the US Administration as to how such mandatory military detention not only raised concerns under international law, including discrimination against aliens, but would also pose serious problems for transatlantic CT cooperation, as European security, law enforcement and justice personnel may not cooperate or exchange information if this could lead to such military detention of terrorist suspects who would require a criminal justice response in Europe. Based on European input, the US Administration developed implementing regulations, which exclude such mandatory military detention in the case of problems of CT cooperation with allies. Up until today, there have not been problems. This is a good example of excellent EU-US cooperation. The EU reiterated its concerns in the context of the NDAA 2013, including the obstacles to Guantánamo closure that this legislation posed.

## 10.4 Remotely Piloted Aircraft Systems (RPAS)

The EU has recognized RPAS as critical both in the military and civilian fields and has become, through interested Member States, active in the development of RPAS and airspace integration. The European Council stated in December 2013[50]:

> The European Council remains committed to delivering key capabilities and addressing critical shortfalls through concrete projects by Member States, supported by the European Defence Agency. Bearing in mind that the capacities are owned and operated by the Member States, it welcomes…the development of Remotely Piloted Aircraft Systems (RPAS) in the 2020–2025 timeframe: preparations for a programme of a next-generation European Medium Altitude Long Endurance RPAS; the establishment of an RPAS user community among the participating Member States owning and operating these RPAS; close synergies with the European Commission on regulation (for an initial RPAS integration into the European Aviation System by 2016); appropriate funding from 2014 for R&D activities…

Activities of the European Defense Agency are set out in a fact sheet.[51] In April 2014, the Commission has presented a Communication on airspace integration of civilian RPAS.[52] EU research projects fund technology development and related issues. The EU Military Committee has recently adopted a military concept for RPAS, where it sets out potential use of RPAS in EU CSDP operations. This concept identifies five scenarios where RPAS could be used in the context of EU crisis management operations, and is focusing on surveillance and reconnaissance.

The European Parliament is also interested in RPAS and has adopted a resolution in February 2014[53] calling on the Council to adopt a common position on the use of armed drones and to promote greater transparency and accountability regarding their use, both regarding the legal basis and operational responsibility.

The EU's position is that RPAS, or drones, have to be used in full respect of international law, but there is no EU position on the interpretation of international law related to RPAS.

In the statement on behalf of the EU at the EP Plenary Session on Wednesday 26 February 2014, Greek Deputy Foreign Minister Kourkoulas said:

> The use of drones has raised some concerns on the respect of human rights and international law. Their use while countering terrorism has already been raised and questioned by the UN Special Rapporteur on the Promotion and Protection of Human Rights and Fundamental Freedoms. Our position is clear: we have to ensure that any use will be consistent with both European and international law. It is not the technology but its use that is key.

RPAS have to be distinguished from Lethal Autonomous Robots (LAR)[54]:

---

[50] European Council 2011.

[51] European Defence Agency 2013.

[52] European Commission 2014.

[53] European Parliament Resolution 2014/2567(RSP) of 25 February 2014 on the use of armed drones, RC/1021121EN.doc.

[54] See also for legal questions related to both and the distinction UNIDR 2013.

With RPAS, the target selection and the launching of the strike are under human control. Therefore, under IHL, RPAS are no different from weapons launched from manned aircraft. The technology as such is lawful under IHL, RPAS can respect IHL, a position also taken by the ICRC. Some argue that RPAS can respect the principle of distinction even better than traditional fighter aircraft due to greater precision. According to the ICRC, this may be possible but there are no data to confirm this yet. The use of RPAS, not the technology, is decisive.

LAR, on the other hand, can select and engage targets without further intervention by a human operator. There is an autonomous choice regarding selection of a target and use of lethal force by the robot. As set out in a recent report by the UN Special Rapporteur of Extrajudicial Killings and Summary Executions Heyns,[55] there are a number of concerns under international law about LARs and their decision-making. There are questions about whether LARs have the capability to respect IHL, in particular the principle of distinction which requires judgment. There are also ethical questions to leave the decision to kill to a robot. For example, Heyns mentions

> the question of the extent to which they can be programmed to comply with the requirements of international humanitarian law and the standards protecting life under international human rights law. Beyond this, their deployment may be unacceptable because no adequate system of legal accountability can be devised, and because robots should not have the power of life and death over human beings.

LARs have not been deployed yet and their implications and potential restrictions are discussed in the context of the Convention on Certain Conventional Weapons (CCW).

International law questions related to RPAS arise for example related to the RPAS infrastructure—host State support is necessary to base RPAS, launch and recover them, and to base nearby search and rescue forces. Over-flight rights are necessary in transit countries, access to satellites is needed by host and transit countries. With regard to surveillance by RPAS, the question about the scope and potential extraterritorial application of Article 17 ICCPR arises, as well as of the data protection and privacy obligations of the consenting host State.

In armed conflict, such as in Afghanistan, RPAS do not raise any fundamental new legal questions compared to the use of manned military aircraft. IHL applies. Combatants and civilians directly participating in hostilities may be targeted and the principles of distinction, proportionality and precaution need to be respected. There is a difficulty to apply these principles in practice given difficulty of identification and mingling with civilians. There is an obligation to carry out investigations for suspected war crimes and provide accountability for those, as well as transparency.

---

[55] Heyns 2013a.

Targeted killings are a controversial policy enabled and facilitated by RPAS. Targeted killings are *not* included as a potential use for RPAS in the EU military concept. UN Special Rapporteurs Emmerson[56] and Heyns[57] have set out a number of international legal questions and concerns related to targeted killings in recent reports. As for every extraterritorial use of force, a two-step analysis of the lawfulness is necessary: one related to the lawfulness of inter-State use of force (*ius ad bellum*/State sovereignty) and one in determination of the legal framework governing the use of force against persons (*ius in bello*/IHL in armed conflicts, and human rights law outside of armed conflict). The EU does not have a position on the international legal framework with regard to targeted killings yet.

## 10.5 Conclusion

Since 9/11, the EU has maintained and promoted the criminal justice approach to the fight against terrorism. While EU-US CT cooperation has been strong since 9/11, a number of questions have arisen in relation to international law. Given the close relationship, these could be productively discussed among the EU and the US. The EU has welcomed the policy changes which bring both sides closer together, including the end of a number of controversial policies adopted after 9/11 and renewed emphasis on using the regular criminal justice system to try terrorist suspects. The EU and its Member States have assisted in the closure of Guantánamo by facilitating and accepting a considerable number of detainees in order to support the shift in policies. The dialogue with the US has also allowed to clarify the EU's own views on the international legal questions related to the fight against terrorism. We need to be aware that the CT policies of the EU, the Member States and the US serve as examples to third countries.

The tools for the criminal justice response have been strengthened since 9/11, loopholes have been closed, with the EU having created the most advanced regional model of cooperation based on the principle of mutual recognition, which is much faster and more efficient than traditional MLAE. The cooperation among criminal justice professionals on both sides of the Atlantic is strong and the track record of the criminal justice system to successfully deal with AQ related terrorism is convincing.

---

56 Emmerson 2013, 2014.

57 Heyns 2013b.

Both the EU and the US might want to reflect upon how we could better communicate about this most successful tool to bring terrorists behind bars without leading to radicalization so that the criminal justice response will be generally supported in the political discourse on both sides of the Atlantic.

## References

Council of the European Union (2006) Conclusions on general affairs and external relations. www.consilium.europa.eu/ueDocs/cms_Data/docs/pressData/en/gena/92122.pdf. Accessed 30 April 2014

Council of the European Union (2009) Conclusions on the closure of the Guantánamo Bay detention centre. www.consilium.europa.eu/uedocs/cmsUpload/108299.pdf. Accessed 30 April 2014

CTC (2010) Judicial dimension of the fight against terrorism—recommendations for action (28 September 2010). Doc. 13318/1/10 REV 1

De Kerchove G (2011) Preface. In: Pawlak P (ed) The EU-US security and justice agenda in action, Chaillot paper no. 127. EU Institute for Security Studies, Paris

Emmerson B (2013) Interim report of the special rapporteur on the promotion and protection of human rights and fundamental freedoms while countering terrorism (18 September 2013). UN Doc. A/68/389

Emmerson B (2014) Report of the special rapporteur on the promotion and protection of human rights and fundamental freedoms while countering terrorism (11 March 2014). UN Doc. A/HRC/25/59

European Council (2014) Fact sheet: Council adopts the "European investigation order" directive. www.consilium.europa.eu/uedocs/cms_data/docs/pressdata/en/jha/141495.pdf. Accessed 30 April 2014

European Council (2005) The European Union counter-terrorism strategy (30 November 2005). Doc. 14469/4/05 REV 4

European Council (2004) Declaration to combat terrorism. www.consilium.europa.eu/uedocs/cmsUpload/DECL-25.3.pdf. Accessed 30 April 2014

European Council (2011) Conclusions on common security and common defence policy. www.consilium.europa.eu/uedocs/cms_data/docs/pressdata/en/ec/140214.pdf. Accessed 30 April 2014

European Defence Agency (2013) Fact sheet on remotely piloted aircraft systems. www.european-council.europa.eu/media/1299819/2013-11-18-factsheet_rpas_high_.pdf. Accessed 30 April 2014

European Commission (2014) Final communication from the commission to the European parliament and the Council, A new era for aviation: opening the aviation market to the civil use of remotely piloted aircraft systems in a safe and sustainable manner. http://ec.europa.eu/transport/modes/air/doc/com(2014)207_en.pdf. Accessed 30 April 2014

Heyns C (2013a) Report of the special rapporteur on extrajudicial, summary or arbitrary executions (9 April 2013). UN Doc. A/HRC/23/47

Heyns C (2013b) Report of the special rapporteur on extrajudicial, summary or arbitrary executions (13 September 2013). UN Doc. A/68/382

ICRC (2011) International humanitarian law and the challenges of contemporary armed conflicts. www.icrc.org/eng/assets/files/red-cross-crescent-movement/31st-international-conference/31-int-conference-ihl-challenges-report-11-5-1-2-en.pdf. Accessed 30 April 2014

Mackintosh K, Duplat P (2013) Study of the impact of donor counter-terrorism measures on principled humanitarian action. www.nrc.no/arch/_img/9682778.pdf. Accessed 30 April 2014

Norwegian Refugee Council (2012) Principles in practice: safeguarding humanitarian action. www.nrc.no/arch/_img/9677774.pdf. Accessed 30 April 2014

Søvndal V, De Kerchove G, Emmerson B (2012) Remembering the victims of terrorism: a collective commitment to respect for human rights. Eur Hum Rights Law Rev 3:247–248

United Nations Institute for Disarmament Research and Geneva Academy of International Humanitarian Law and Human Rights (2013) Summary of discussions of the experts meeting on armed drones and robots under International Law. http://www.unidir.org/files/medias/pdfs/summary-of-discussions-eng-0-557.pdf. Accessed 30 April 2014

# Chapter 11
# Debates and Dichotomies: Exploring the Presumptions Underlying Contentions About the Geography of Armed Conflict

**Laurie R. Blank**

**Abstract** An examination of the growing literature on the topic of the geography of armed conflict suggests that the differences of opinion, between and among academics, policymakers and military lawyers, for example, are nearly intractable. Statements about the propriety of a certain target under the law of armed conflict are often met by pronouncements regarding the role of jus ad bellum in cabining the use of force in the territory of another state or the restrictive parameters of the international human rights/law enforcement regime for addressing individuals who pose a threat or danger to others. Indeed, one might easily conclude that the participants in these debates are simply operating in entirely separate analytical paradigms, leading to interesting and challenging intellectual discussions but not to productive conversations that advance the analysis and move beyond the debate to effective potential resolution of a complicated and multi-layered issue. However, unlike pornography or terrorism, where notwithstanding a myriad of different definitions, "you know it when you see it", little agreement exists even on whether there is a specific, definable geography of armed conflict at all. To help move beyond this impasse, this article explores the presumptions underlying the ongoing debates regarding the geography of armed conflict, in an effort to untangle the debates and provide new opportunities and venues for discussion—and thus to help advance the development of the law of armed conflict and other relevant bodies of law. These presumptions appear in particular in four dichotomies that inherently help drive the debates but are brushed aside or not taken into consideration: law versus policy; authority versus obligation; territory versus threat; and submission of the collective enemy versus elimination of an individual threat. For each or any of these dichotomies, the lens through which one views the contrasting positions will then have a significant—if not determinative—effect on considerations and

---

Laurie R. Blank is Director of the International Humanitarian Law Clinic, Emory University School of Law.

---

L.R. Blank (✉)
International Humanitarian Law Clinic, Emory University School of Law,
Atlanta, GA 30322-2770, USA
e-mail: lblank@emory.edu



T.D. Gill et al. (eds.), *Yearbook of International Humanitarian Law 2013*,
Yearbook of International Humanitarian Law 16, DOI 10.1007/978-94-6265-038-1_11

conclusions regarding questions of geography and the battlefield. As a result, recognizing these dichotomies and understanding how they impact the current discourse is critical to any effective conversation, whether in the academic or policy arenas.

**Keywords** Law of war · Law of armed conflict · International humanitarian law · Battlefield · Armed conflict · Geography · Targeted killing · Targeted strikes · Jus in bello · Jus ad bellum · Rules of engagement

## Contents



## 11.1 Introduction

An examination of the growing literature on the topic of the geography of armed conflict suggests that the differences of opinion, between and among academics, policymakers and military lawyers, for example, are nearly intractable. Statements about the propriety of a certain target under the law of armed conflict are often met by pronouncements regarding the role of *jus ad bellum* in cabining the use of force in the territory of another state or the restrictive parameters of the international human rights/law enforcement regime for addressing individuals who pose a threat or danger to others. Indeed, one might easily conclude that the participants in these debates are simply operating in entirely separate analytical paradigms, leading to interesting and challenging intellectual discussions but not to productive conversations that advance the analysis and move beyond the debate to effective potential resolution of a complicated and multi-layered issue. However, unlike pornography or terrorism, where notwithstanding a myriad of different definitions, "you know it when you see it", little agreement exists even on whether there is a specific, definable geography of armed conflict at all.

In many cases, what seem to be extensive and vigorous debates about the geography of armed conflict, or the "boundaries of the battlefield", are in fact debates about entirely different questions that get subsumed within or masked by the *au courant* topic of geography. Three questions in particular underlie most of the geography debates and, upon closer examination, appear to be the actual issue or issues at the center of the debate: where can force be used; how should conflicts between a state and entities not located wholly within the boundaries of that state be characterized; and how can force be used, that is, what law governs how (not whether or when) a state or other party uses force in pursuit of its goals. These and other issues remain the source of extensive and contentious debate, particularly between the United States and several of its allies in Europe and elsewhere, but talking about them through the lens of a debate on the geography of armed conflict does not contribute to effective resolution or minimization of the existing debate. In effect, when one person talks about geography of conflict with an eye to how one frames the scope of a non-international armed conflict—that is, a characterization of conflict question—and another is focused on whether the involved state can use force across the border in the territory of a neighboring state—that is, a *jus ad bellum* question—the conversation ultimately is akin to ships passing in the night.

To help move beyond this impasse, this chapter explores the presumptions underlying the ongoing debates regarding the geography of armed conflict, in an effort to untangle the debates and provide new opportunities and venues for discussion—and thus to help advance the development of the law of armed conflict (LOAC) and other relevant bodies of law. These presumptions appear in particular in four dichotomies that inherently help drive the debates but are brushed aside or not taken into consideration: law versus policy; authority versus obligation; territory versus threat; and submission of the collective enemy versus elimination of an individual threat. For each or any of these dichotomies, the lens through which one views the contrasting positions will then have a significant—if not determinative—effect on considerations and conclusions regarding questions of geography and the battlefield. As a result, recognizing these dichotomies and understanding how they affect the current discourse is critical to any effective conversation, whether in the academic or policy arenas. Sections 11.2 through 11.5 of this chapter examine these dichotomies in turn to explore how they distort the overt debate over geography or simply render that debate ineffective. It is also useful to consider how these dichotomies and presumptions overlap and the common themes that flow throughout, such as the frequent conflation of *jus ad bellum* and *jus in bello* when discussing the lawfulness of and parameters governing the use of force against non-state entities located outside the boundaries of the state.[1]

## 11.2 Law and Policy

Throughout 2011 and 2012, the Obama Administration engaged in a remarkable series of public speeches by top legal advisors and national security advisors that appeared to offer extensive explanation of the international legal principles governing the use of drone strikes against al-Qaeda operatives in various locations around the globe, as well as related counterterrorism measures. In May 2013, the

[1] For further discussion of this issue, see Blank 2012; Corn 2012.

Obama Administration released a fact sheet on *U.S. Policy Standards and Procedures for the Use of Force in Counterterrorism Operations Outside the United States and Areas of Active Hostilities*,[2] which provides information about counterterrorism policy standards and procedures, particularly with regard to the use of force. These extensive efforts to purportedly expound on the international legal parameters for U.S. counterterrorism operations offer—perhaps instead—an excellent example of the dichotomy between and conflation of law and policy.

Policy and strategic considerations are without a doubt an essential component of understanding contemporary military operations and the application of LOAC during armed conflict. However, it is equally important to distinguish between law and policy, and to recognize when one is driving analysis versus the other. LOAC—otherwise known as the law of war or international humanitarian law—governs the conduct of both states and individuals during armed conflict. It seeks to minimize suffering in war by protecting persons not participating in hostilities and by restricting the means and methods of warfare.[3] LOAC applies during all situations of armed conflict, with the full panoply of the Geneva Conventions and customary law applicable in international armed conflict (conflicts between two states) and a more limited body of conventional and customary law applicable during non-international armed conflict (conflicts between a state and a non-state armed group or between two or more non-state armed groups). In all circumstances, therefore, LOAC provides the basic framework for all actions, obligations, and privileges; it is, in essence, the outer parameters for all military conduct.

Strategic policy determines the goals of the overall operation and of specific missions and will be based on a range of national security objectives, domestic policy goals or constraints, and the needs of coalition operations or other multilateral considerations. Law and policy come together directly in the rules of engagement (ROE), which are tactical instructions to military forces regarding the parameters for executing their mission. ROE are based on three key components: law, strategy and policy—the legal framework of LOAC, the military needs of strategy and

---

[2] The White House 2013.

[3] ICRC 2004. The law of armed conflict is codified primarily in the four Geneva Conventions of 12 August 1949 and their Additional Protocols. See Geneva Convention for the Amelioration of the Condition of the Wounded and Sick in Armed Forces in the Field, opened for signature 12 August 1949, 75 UNTS 31 (entered into force 21 October 1950) (hereinafter: GCI); Geneva Convention for the Amelioration of the Condition of Wounded, Sick and Shipwrecked Members of Armed Forces at Sea, opened for signature 12 August 1949, 75 UNTS 85 (entered into force 21 October 1950) (hereinafter: GCII); Geneva Convention Relative to the Treatment of Prisoners of War, opened for signature 12 August 1949, 75 UNTS 135 (entered into force 21 October 1950) (hereinafter: GCIII); Geneva Convention Relative to the Protection of Civilian Persons in Time of War, opened for signature 12 August 1949, 75 UNTS 287 (entered into force 21 October 1950) (hereinafter: GCIV); Protocol Additional to the Geneva Conventions of 12 August 1949, and Relating to the Protection of Victims of International Armed Conflicts, opened for signature 12 December 1977, 1125 UNTS 3 (entered into force 7 December 1978) (hereinafter: API); Protocol Additional to the Geneva Conventions of 12 August 1949, and Relating to the Protection of Victims of Non-International Armed Conflicts, opened for signature 12 December 1977, 1125 UNTS 609 (entered into force 7 December 1978) (hereinafter: APII).

operational goals, and the national command policy of the U.S. The relationship between LOAC and ROE demonstrate the interaction between law and policy during military operations: LOAC forms the basic parameters for the conduct of hostilities and the treatment of persons and objects during armed conflict; ROE operate within that framework to set the rules for the use of force in the circumstances of the particular military mission at hand, the operational imperatives and national command policy.

In the debates about the potential geographic boundaries of armed conflict, law and policy are intertwined nearly irrevocably, making any clear delineation of the reasoning behind any particular argument difficult to identify. Indeed, seemingly lost amidst the political discourse and policy debates is the fact that "armed conflict" is a legal term of art, one introduced to avoid the political manipulations enabled by the earlier use of the word "war",[4] while "battlefield" is an operational euphemism for the place where armed hostilities are taking place and does not even appear as a defined term in military doctrine.[5] And yet "armed conflict" and "battlefield" have become linked and have even begun to morph into a legal conception of the "battlefield" that is not based in LOAC, which does not explicitly provide specific geographic parameters for armed conflict.

Distinguishing between law and policy—and, in the same manner, between law and rhetoric—is therefore essential to understanding how the debate about the geography of armed conflict has developed and is developing. Historically, there has not necessarily been a direct match between the concept of the legal parameters for action during conflict and the actual location of fighting. Oppenheim's classic treatise explains that the "region of war", or the area where belligerents are *permitted* to prepare and execute hostilities, is distinct from the "theater of war", the location where hostilities are *actually* taking place.[6] This notion—that the area where combat is actually occurring is not necessarily co-extensive with the area where there is authority to engage in combat—has been both lost and, more interestingly, seemingly reversed in some ways in recent years. As Oppenheim's explanation evinces, parties to a conflict might not engage in hostilities in all places where they could do so in accordance with international law. Strategic and operational choices about where to engage enemy forces must comport with and stay within the boundaries of international law, but do not have to extend out to the full parameters allowable under the law. In the context of international armed conflict, this framework remains

[4] See Uhler et al. 1958 ("The substitution of this much more general expression for the word 'war' was deliberate. It is possible to argue almost endlessly about the legal definition of 'war' […] The expression 'armed conflict' makes such arguments less easy".).

[5] The closest term in the *Department of Defense Dictionary of Military and Associated Terms* is "theater of war," which is "[d]efined by the President, Secretary of Defense, or the geographic combatant commander as the area of air, land, and water that is, or may become, directly involved in the conduct of major operations and campaigns involving combat." See Joint Chiefs of Staff, Joint Publication 1-02: Department of Defense Dictionary of Military and Associated Terms (15 December 2013), available at: www.dtic.mil/doctrine/new_pubs/jp1_02.pdf, p. 292.

[6] Oppenheim 1952, paras 70–71.

the governing paradigm under LOAC: an international armed conflict takes place wherever the forces of the belligerent parties meet, which can be anywhere—including the high seas and possibly outer space—except the territory of neutral parties. The law of neutrality thus defines the relationship between states engaged in an international armed conflict and states not participating and, in traditional conflicts, provides the boundaries for the conduct of hostilities.[7]

Non-international armed conflicts—most notably many contemporary conflicts pitting states against terrorist groups—significantly challenge traditional frameworks for understanding the parameters of the zone of combat. Simply superimposing the approach applicable in international armed conflict onto conflicts with terrorist groups does not provide any means for creating geographically-driven conceptions of the battlefield. Indeed, although the law of neutrality's fundamental principles and goals are clear, it traditionally applies only in international armed conflict, when the primary protagonists are states. Even if one were to attempt to use the belligerency-neutrality framework as an analogy, traditional conceptions of belligerency and neutrality do not effectively address the complex spatial and temporal nature of terrorist attacks and states' responses, leaving open fundamental questions about where the conflict with terrorist groups does and can take place. Thus,

> [a]lthough it is uncontested that [LOAC] applies to the conduct of 'battlefield hostilities' between the parties to an armed conflict, the territorial parameters of the battlefield and the range of actions that fall within the remit of hostilities are neither defined in conventional [LOAC] nor beyond debate.[8]

For example, an important preliminary question is whether there can even be one overarching conflict between a state and a transnational armed group, or whether such hostilities are instead better understood as a series of localized conflicts between or among state actors and discrete groups that may or may not be linked in some way by ideology, operational methodology, or other connections.[9] Uncertainty about the geographic scope of armed conflict involving transnational armed groups leads to a variety of analytical and implementation challenges with regard to LOAC, human rights law, *jus ad bellum*, and other relevant legal regimes.[10] At a minimum, the hard-to-define parameters of an ongoing armed conflict with terrorist groups raise serious concerns about which areas—and how many areas—are being

---

[7] Convention Respecting the Rights and Duties of Neutral Powers and Persons in Case of War on Land (Hague Convention V), opened for signature 18 October 1907, 36 Stat. 2310 (entered into force 26 January 1910), Chap. 1 (defining boundaries and responsibilities of neutral powers).

[8] Lubell and Derejko 2013.

[9] The ICRC takes the latter approach and does not accept the notion of a transnational conflict, but rather looks at the level of hostilities in a particular state to determine whether the situation in that area meets the threshold for an armed conflict. If adopted, this analytical method obviates the need to determine the geographical parameters of a conflict between a state and one or more transnational armed groups not located in any particular area. Instead, this method allows its proponents to conclude that certain states are experiencing armed conflict and others are not.

[10] For a comprehensive discussion of LOAC and the problem of defining the battlefield, see Blank 2010.

subsumed within an area of armed conflict and the authority to use lethal force as a first resort. As more and more areas are viewed as part of the "zone of combat", more innocent civilians will face the consequences of hostilities, whether those are unintended death, injury, or property damage.

In the context of conflict between a state and a transnational armed group, such as the conflict between the United States and al Qaeda over the past decade, both the geographic contours of that conflict and the nature of the interaction between law and policy are quite different. Indeed, in the face of the complex and heretofore unresolved question of whether and how LOAC sets geographic boundaries to a non-international armed conflict, policy and rhetoric have often seemed to stretch beyond —or even operate somewhat out of concert with—the law. At first, for example, the rhetoric of a "war on terror" used for most of the 2000–2010 decade in the United States seemed to lead directly to a conclusion that the world is a global battlefield—that wherever a terrorist operative is found is part of the zone of combat.[11] The policy goal was to disable al Qaeda wherever it, or its operatives, were found, which then drove how the law was interpreted and communicated. The presentation of a global war or global battlefield thus eliminated the need to consider or debate where the conflict was taking place, because it was taking place everywhere.

Another consequence was the conflation of law and policy—the policy of "taking the fight" to al Qaeda wherever it could be found quickly translated into a legal conception of a global armed conflict, one that had never been considered before. This conflation of law and policy rears its head regularly in debates over the geography of armed conflict; the debate often seems to be between a formalized legal interpretation (non-international armed conflicts are limited to the territory of the High Contracting Party in which they are occurring) and a policy-driven approach (allowing an enemy operative to "get out of the game" simply by crossing a border is highly illogical and strategically unsound). In essence, until the two sides of this debate begin to converse on the same level, rather than on two different wavelengths of law and policy without recognizing the difference, the debate will continue to go round and round with little effective contribution to the development of the law or policy.

The contrast between this view of the battlefield with respect to targeting and the U.S. characterization of geography with respect to detention is particularly telling. In contrast to the assertion of an extensive "battlefield" for the purposes of targeting al Qaeda and other terrorist operatives in a wide variety of locales around the world, the United States has taken a much more narrow view of the "battlefield" in cases stemming from detention at Guantanamo Bay, Bagram and other detention facilities. U.S. courts have consistently referred to the United States as "outside a zone of combat",[12] "distant from a zone of combat",[13] or not within any "active [or formal]

[11] The view of the Bush Administration was: "Our [W]ar on [T]error will be much broader than the battlefields and beachheads of the past. The war will be fought wherever terrorists hide, or run, or plan." See Roth 2004 (quoting President Bush's statement made on 29 September 2001).

[12] *Padilla v. Rumsfeld*, 352 F.3d 695 (2d Cir. 2003), 698.

[13] *Padilla v. Hanft*, 547 U.S. 1062 (2006) (Ginsburg, J., dissenting), 1064.

theater of war",[14] even while recognizing the novel geographic nature of the conflict. In *Al Maqaleh v. Gates*, for example, both the D.C. District Court and the Court of Appeals for the D.C. Circuit distinguished between Afghanistan, "a theater of active military combat",[15] and other areas outside Afghanistan (including the United States), which are described as "far removed from *any* battlefield".[16] This contrast demonstrates the challenge of mixing law and policy rhetoric—although terms such as "battlefield" or "combat zone" are descriptive and not legal, as noted above, they have taken on a legal context in many situations. Although the contrast between the U.S. assertion in the targeting arena and its characterizations in the detention context demonstrates that these conceptions of geography are policy-driven and case-specific, they nonetheless have spawned an extensive conversation and debate about the geographic boundaries of armed conflict—without the initial step of first examining whether there is even a legal issue regarding the geography of armed conflict.

Other examples of policy masquerading as law followed as well, such as the characterization of detention at Guantanamo as "law of war detention", or the application of LOAC targeting principles to the use of force in self-defense. With both of these examples, policy decisions were characterized as law and legal analysis, continuing to muddy the parameters of any conversation about the geography or boundaries of conflict. As I have written elsewhere, the so-called "law of war detention" at Guantanamo Bay does not necessary comport with the conception of detention under the law of war, making the legal label a misnomer.[17] Nonetheless, labeling the detention of an individual as "law of war detention" suggests that such person was captured in the course of an armed conflict, thus extending the armed conflict to wherever that person was captured.

With regard to the use of force in self-defense, the seemingly principled claim that the United States will follow the LOAC principles of distinction, proportionality and precautions in targeting individuals in self-defense also uses law to erode legal distinctions—between armed conflict (where LOAC applies) and not armed conflict, (where LOAC does not apply)—and to conflate law and policy. In effect, "the legal logic through which the battlespace is extended beyond the declared zone of combat in Afghanistan [or other areas of conflict] is itself infinitely extendible".[18] LOAC does not apply to a use of force outside of an armed conflict, by definition, because there is no armed conflict. Pronouncing that LOAC targeting principles apply—particularly when presented in a positive light—therefore extends armed conflict rules to situations that are not armed conflict and thus appears to extend the spatial arena of the armed conflict as a result as well. The same problem of a debate

[14] *Boumediene v. Bush*, 553 U.S. 723 (2008), 770.

[15] *Al Maqaleh v. Gates*, 605 F.3d 84 (D.C. Cir. 2010), 88.

[16] *Al Maqaleh v. Gates*, 604 F. Supp. 2d 205 (D.D.C. 2009), 229 (emphasis added) (holding that individuals captured in Afghanistan and detained at the Bagram Theater Internment Facility are not entitled to habeas corpus and specifically distinguishing between detained battlefield enemy belligerents and individuals apprehended outside the zone of combat operations).

[17] See Blank 2011.

[18] Gregory 2011, p. 241.

on two separate wavelengths appears here as a result: one may contest the U.S. authority to use force in self-defense against an individual or group posing a threat or launching attacks; another counters by asserting that the U.S. is using force in compliance with LOAC's targeting principles and therefore the use of force is legal. The latter argument does not actually answer the former, but it has been offered a sufficient number of times that it has begun to change the discourse by conflating legal regimes and essentially morphing the conversation into one about boundaries and geography rather than authority, legal parameters and obligation.

## 11.3 Authority *versus* Obligation

LOAC is a law of both authority and obligation. This duality is manifested primarily in the delicate balance between military necessity and humanity that lies at the heart of LOAC.[19] Military necessity "justifies those measures not forbidden by international law which are indispensable for securing the complete submission of the enemy as soon as possible".[20] Accordingly, military necessity provides the normative basis for employing those measures necessary to bring an enemy to submission, including the application of deadly combat power. Military necessity is therefore a principle of authority: the authority to use force to accomplish strategic and national security goals.[21] The principle of humanity—also referred to as the principle of unnecessary suffering—aims to minimize suffering in armed conflict. To that end, the infliction of suffering or destruction not necessary for legitimate military purposes is forbidden. The principle of humanity thus provides an essential counterbalance to the authority to employ measures to defeat an enemy in armed conflict. In practice, humanity serves as the foundation for two critical limits on the authority to inflict suffering in the context of armed conflict: the prohibition against subjecting an opponent to superfluous injury or unnecessary suffering; and the obligation to ensure the humane treatment of any person (even a captured enemy) who is no longer or never was actively participating in armed hostilities.[22]

---

19 See, e.g., Dinstein 2004, p. 17 (explaining that LOAC "takes a middle road, allowing belligerent States much leeway (in keeping with the demands of military necessity) and yet circumscribing their freedom of action (in the name of humanitarianism)").

20 US Department of the Army Field Manual 1956, pp. 3–4.

21 It is important to note, nonetheless, that the principle of military necessity contains its own essential constraints because it prohibits any acts that are forbidden by LOAC.

22 See UK Ministry of Defence Joint Service Manual 2004, paras 2.4–2.4.3. This principle of humanity is the central focus of the four 1949 Geneva Conventions and is implemented through numerous LOAC treaty provisions. These include the prohibition against the use of any type of coercion against a prisoner of war or civilian internee; the obligation to search for and collect the wounded and sick and ensure that priority of medical care is based solely on medical considerations; the obligation to search for and collect the shipwrecked at sea; the obligation to provide notice of capture of enemy personnel to the enemy state through a neutral intermediary; the obligation to facilitate the efforts of neutral relief agencies; the extensive immunities from attack

Effective application of and adherence to LOAC demands attention to both the authority and the obligation aspects of the law. LOAC authorizes the use of lethal force as first resort against enemy persons and objects within the parameters of the armed conflict.[23] It also provides, based on treaty provisions and the fundamental principle of military necessity, for the detention of enemy fighters and civilians posing imperative security risks.[24] Along with these authorities, however, come obligations—such as the obligation to use force in accordance with the principles of distinction and proportionality,[25] the obligation to protect civilians and those no longer fighting from the ravages of war to the extent possible, and the obligation to treat all persons humanely. Thus, while a soldier may lawfully target an enemy soldier during armed conflict, that same soldier must protect that same enemy individual once he or she is *hors de combat* due to wounds, sickness or detention. A state has the authority to detain enemy personnel without charge until the end of the hostilities, but it has a corresponding obligation to ensure that such detained personnel are held far from active hostilities and provided with appropriate food, shelter and medical care, among other obligations.[26]

When these two components of authority and obligation fall out of sync, significant shortcomings in LOAC's effectiveness are evident. A prime—and recent—example was the Bush Administration's assertion of the authority inherent in LOAC to target and detain enemy operatives while denying any commensurate obligation from LOAC with regard to the nature and conditions of that detention. Seeking to use the authority LOAC grants without also assuming the obligations LOAC mandates created a fundamental imbalance in the application of the law and the protection of persons and had an equally detrimental effect on the perception of the U.S. as acting extra-legally in its conflict with al Qaeda and pursuit of other counterterrorism objectives.[27]

---

(Footnote 22 continued)
afforded to places engaged in medical functions; and even the obligation to maintain and record the location of interment of the enemy dead.

[23] See Corn 2009a, pp. 1352–1353 ("[A]rmed conflict is defined by the authority to use deadly force as a measure of first resort").

[24] See Article 4 GCIII (describing various prisoner of war categories); Articles 42, 78 GCIV (permitting internment).

[25] The principle of distinction mandates that all parties to a conflict distinguish between those who are fighting and those who are not and that parties only target those who are fighting. In addition, fighters, including soldiers, must distinguish themselves from innocent civilians. See Article 48 API. The principle of proportionality states that parties must refrain from attacks where the expected civilian casualties will be excessive in relation to the anticipated military advantage. See Article 51(5)(b) API.

[26] See generally GCIII and GCIV with respect to detention of prisoners of war and enemy civilians during conflict.

[27] Corn 2009b, p. 4 ("the authority of the LOAC would be asserted to provide the legal basis for the execution of military operations against al Qaeda—an entity considered to be engaged in an armed conflict with the United States; however, unlike their Taliban counterparts who could at least in theory claim the protections of the LOAC (because they were captured in the context of what the United States ultimately conceded was an inter-state armed conflict), al Qaeda captive

The current debates about the geographic parameters of a conflict between a state and a transnational terrorist group are revisiting this disconnect between the authority and obligation prongs of LOAC. Almost without exception, every discussion or official speech about the boundaries of conflict focuses on where the U.S. (or another state, potentially) can or cannot use force against enemy operatives. That is, the debate is driven entirely by questions regarding the authority LOAC provides to use deadly combat power against a member of the opposing force: when, where and under what circumstances can force be used, and against whom (i.e., which persons fall into the category of the enemy force). This single-minded focus holds true not only for those who assert broad parameters for a transnational non-international armed conflict, but also—interestingly—for those who argue that the geographic parameters of conflict must be narrowly conceived. Everyone, it seems, from the Obama Administration[28] to the United Nations Special Rapporteur on Extrajudicial, Summary, or Arbitrary Executions,[29] to academics on both sides of the debate,[30] looks only to targeting when debating the boundaries of conflict. Lost in the extensive back and forth is any consideration of how far LOAC's protective obligations extend, or any examination of whether the parameters of LOAC's obligations during conflict could offer useful hints for understanding the geography of conflict.

This omission is particularly notable given that the primary judicial pronouncement on the geographic reach of conflict focused on the reach of LOAC's protective framework. In fact, in *Prosecutor v. Tadić*, the International Tribunal for the Former Yugoslavia (ICTY) explicitly viewed LOAC's protective obligations as potentially far greater in geographic reach than the exercise of authority inherent in the conduct of hostilities. As the Tribunal explained,

> [a]lthough the Geneva Conventions are silent as to the geographic scope of international 'armed conflicts', the provisions suggest that at least some of the provisions of the Conventions apply to the entire territory of the Parties to the conflict, not just to the vicinity of actual hostilities. Certainly, some of the provisions are clearly bound up with the hostilities and the geographical scope of those provisions should be so limited. Others, particularly those relating to the protection of prisoners of war and civilians are not so limited.[31]

---

(Footnote 27 continued)
were afforded no such claim to LOAC protections because the conflict they engaged in defied classification under either Common Article 2 or 3").

28 See Koh, Annual Meeting of the American Society of International Law Speech (25 March 2010), available at: http://www.state.gov/s/l/releases/remarks/139119.htm; Brennan, Woodrow Wilson International Center for Scholars Speech (30 April 2012), available at: http://www.wilsoncenter.org/event/the-efficacy-and-ethics-us-counterterrorism-strategy; Holder, Remarks at Northwestern University School of Law Speech (5 March 2012), available at: http://www.justice.gov/iso/opa/ag/speeches/2012/ag-speech-1203051.html.

29 Alston 2010.

30 See, e.g., O'Connell 2010; Anderson 2010; Lewis 2012.

31 ICTY, *Prosecutor v. Dusko Tadić*, Decision on the Defence Motion for Interlocutory Appeal on Jurisdiction, Appeals Chamber (IT-94-I-AR72), 2 October 1995, para 68.

The Tribunal used an equally broad approach to LOAC's protective reach in internal armed conflicts.[32] Indeed, the Tribunal relied specifically on the language pertaining to detention and the protection of those who have been detained or whose liberty has been restricted, as a guide, noting that "the relatively loose nature of the language 'for reasons related to such conflict', [in Additional Protocol II] suggests a broad geographical scope".[33] The issue, in *Tadić* and other ICTY judgments addressing the geographical parameters of LOAC's application in the former Yugoslavia, was often whether LOAC's obligations of humane treatment and protection for civilians and persons *hors de combat* applied even where no hostilities were taking place. The Tribunal's answer, repeatedly, was affirmative: "there does not have to be actual combat activities in a particular location for the norms of international humanitarian law to be applicable".[34] Considering this statement in the context of current debates about the use of force against al Qaeda operatives and associated forces in various locales around the globe highlights that these debates remain solely within the context of the authority prong of LOAC.

At first glance, one might assume that those arguing for a broad, or even unlimited, geographic scope to armed conflict are acting on a presumption that LOAC is about authority, while those arguing for a narrow geographic scope act on a presumption that LOAC is about obligation. However, unlike the other presumptions discussed in this chapter, here both sides seem to be starting from the same presumption—LOAC as authority—but then use that presumption to reach entirely opposite results. In effect, the failure to remember that LOAC is always a combination of authority and obligation, a balance between military necessity and humanity, leaves both sides of the debate arguing from an incomplete foundation. Those who see authority as the justification for a broad geographic scope must, at the same time, be willing to grant that broad geographic scope to LOAC's protective obligations; those who see authority as the reason to constrain the boundaries of conflict should, notwithstanding the goal of limiting the authority to use force, recognize that that narrow geographic scope can restrict LOAC's ability to protect potential victims of conflict and hostilities from a variety of harms and deprivations that result from combat and combat-related activities.

## 11.4 Territory *versus* Threat

A third set of presumptions that invariably stymies comprehensive examination and analysis of geography and conflict—if there are boundaries to armed conflict and, if so, what they are—rests on alternate views of conflict as a spatial construct or as an

[32] Ibid, para 69.

[33] Ibid.

[34] ICTY, *Prosecutor v. Zejnil Delalić et al.*, Judgment Trial Chamber (IT-96-21-T), 16 November 1998, para 185.

enemy- or party-centered construct. These differing approaches to conceptualizing armed conflict result in vastly different conclusions about where that conflict takes place and, perhaps more important, how the "space" of that conflict moves and changes over time and in response to developments.

Common Article 3 provides the most direct linkage between the existence or characterization of armed conflict and geographical areas, speaking of "an armed conflict not of an international character occurring in the territory of one of the High Contracting Parties […]"[35] The spatial understanding of international armed conflict is also tied directly to territory, with the law of neutrality determining which areas constitute part of the battlespace and which are off-limits, so to speak, as neutral territory. However, it is in the realm of non-international armed conflict, particularly conflicts between a state and a non-state entity operating outside the boundaries of that state, where the presumptions truly drive the debate. For some engaging in this debate, territory is the primary starting point for all analysis of armed conflict and the application of LOAC. From this standpoint,

> [a]rmed conflicts inevitably have a limited and identifiable territorial or spatial dimension because human beings who participate in armed conflict require territory in which to carry out intense, protracted, armed exchanges.[36]

In effect, the territorially-bound view of conflict sees armed conflict as fighting that occurs in limited areas, with firm boundaries between those areas and everywhere else, where LOAC does not apply. This territorially-based view of conflict is directly related to the interpretation of Common Article 3 that limits non-international armed conflict altogether to conflicts occurring solely within the boundaries of a single state, what might otherwise be termed internal conflicts. The Bush Administration thus argued in a January 2002 memo addressing the application of LOAC to Taliban and al Qaeda detainees, "common Article 3 addresses only non-international conflicts that occur within the territory of a single state party, again, like a civil war".[37] As a result, it "would not reach an armed conflict in which one of the parties operated from multiple bases in several different states".[38]

Enemy forces, particularly transnational terrorist organizations, do not adhere to strict geographical lines and boundaries, however. Pragmatically, threat and the concomitant need to respond to that threat will always be the primary consideration driving the strategic, operational, and tactical calculus:

> Armed conflict is a threat-driven concept, arising when the threat necessitates resort to combat power, and extending to wherever the operational and tactical opportunity to produce a militarily valuable effect on the enemy arises.[39]

---

[35] Common Article 3 of the 1949 Geneva Conventions.

[36] O'Connell 2009, p. 858.

[37] US Department of Justice, Memorandum for Alberto R. Gonzales, Counsel to the President, and William J. Haynes II, General Counsel of the Department Defense (22 January 2002), available at: http://www.washingtonpost.com/wp-srv/nation/documents/012202bybee.pdf.

[38] Ibid.

[39] Corn 2013, p. 82.

The U.S. military's concept of "effects-based operations" illustrates this directly: the desired strategic, operational, and tactical effects drive the military mission, and these effects are in turn dictated by threat capabilities, dispositions, and vulnerabilities.[40] Failure to account for the role of threat and the requisite response to that threat in the planning and execution of military operations leaves the law disconnected from the reality of military operations and strategy. The simple example of the militant in Afghanistan who crosses the border but still directs attacks against coalition forces highlights the impracticality of the overly territorial-driven analysis of the parameters of armed conflict. The militant still poses a threat and remains engaged in the conflict, yet defining the conflict solely by the geographical borders of the state theoretically renders him immune from attack under LOAC authority to use force in a first resort and therefore grants him safe haven.[41]

However, a focus on threat to the exclusion of numerous other important factors in the analysis of enemy groups, operational dynamics and geographical considerations can lead to an equally irrational characterization of armed conflict and concomitant authority. Certainly every individual or group who poses a threat is not necessarily part of an ongoing armed conflict, even if that conflict occurs transnationally in some way. The U.S. took this approach, however, in the immediate aftermath of 9/11 when President Bush pronounced that "[o]ur war on terror will be much broader than the battlefields and beachheads of the past. The war will be fought wherever terrorists hide, or run, or plan".[42] Even recognizing the critical role that threat plays in the strategic, operational and tactical implementation of armed conflict, the rhetoric of the entire world as a battlefield and every possible terrorist as an enemy in that conflict raises the specter of warfare unlimited by either legal or geographical parameters, where threat itself becomes

[40] See, e.g., Herndon et al. 2004, p. 26 (analyzing effects-based operations, "[a] process for obtaining a desired strategic outcome or 'effect' on the enemy through the synergistic, multiplicative and cumulative application of the full range of military and nonmilitary capabilities" (citation and internal quotation marks omitted)).

[41] See Lubell and Derejko 2013, p. 10 ("the extension of IHL beyond the immediate geographical and temporal spheres of hostilities is necessary to prevent attempts by the Parties to an armed conflict to evade the reach of IHL by relocating individuals and directing operations away from the immediate sphere of hostilities"). See also Rise of the Drones II: Examining the Legality of Unmanned Targeting, Hearing Before the Subcomm. on National Security and Foreign Affairs of the H. Comm. on Oversight and Government Reform, 111th Cong, 2nd Sess. 4–5 (2010) (statement of Lewis, Professor, Ohio Northern University Pettit College of Law) (noting that "the proposed geographic restrictions allow the individual to obtain the same immunity by crossing an international border and avoiding law enforcement while remaining active in an organization that targets civilians"); Discussion of the Bin Laden raid, Sect. 11.5 infra.

[42] Roth 2004.

divorced from armed conflict and the distinction between wartime and peacetime is lost.[43]

The overly zealous rhetoric of the "war on terror" in the first several years after 9/11 combined with the emphasis on territorial conceptions of conflict among critiques of the U.S. approach led to an exclusive focus on territory and geography in identifying the parameters of conflict and authority. Divorcing a geographic analysis from the fundamental nature of military operations and decision-making can make the law less practical in the immediate sense. In particular, this effect has the potential to be a recipe for uncertainty and unpredictability operationally, and divorces legal authority from operational practice and necessity. The failure to view questions about the parameters of conflict through a totality of the circumstances approach—taking into account LOAC, threat perception, national strategy, sovereignty and many other factors—risks producing a situation in which international legal scholars overlook the practicalities of military operations and practitioners consequently begin to see the law as irrelevant. Neither offers positive prospects for LOAC to accomplish its key purposes during armed conflict.

## 11.5 Elimination of Individual Threat *versus* Submission of the Collective Enemy

The final set of presumptions that distort and hijack the debates about the characterization and geographic reach of armed conflict centers on the perception of the enemy individual and the nature of the force used in response. One premise is that an individual is attacked in order to eliminate the particular threat that he or she poses; the other asserts that enemy operatives in an armed conflict are attacked as part of an effort to defeat the enemy in the collective sense. The natural extension of the former premise is that individuals can only be attacked on the basis of an individualized threat determination; the latter, that they can be attacked on the basis of their status as members of the opposing forces. These opposing presumptions stem from and also lead to vastly different conceptions of the enemy, the actions needed to defeat or disable that enemy, and the requisite authority to accomplish that goal.

Before elaborating on how these presumptions affect the debates over geography and conflict, it is important to understand how they have come to be set in opposition to each other in the context of the parameters of armed conflict. For the past several years, the United States has relied on both armed conflict and self-defense as

[43] See Blank 2012 (discussing the risks of conflating armed conflict with self-defense as justifications for the use of force against non-state actors); Corn 2013, p. 85 ("Nonetheless, the concept of armed conflict of international scope conducted against a loosely organized non–State opponent—a typology of armed conflict resulting in the increasingly common characterization of 'transnational armed conflict,'—certainly creates the perception, if not the reality, of authority overreach").

legal justifications for targeted strikes outside of the zone of active combat in Afghanistan. The use of both justifications at the same time, without careful distinction delimiting the boundaries between when one applies and when the other applies, poses serious questions. For example, when the U.S. targets a member of al-Shabaab in Somalia, U.S. explanations generally offer no guidance for determining if that strike is considered part of a broader armed conflict with al Qaeda in which al-Shabaab is part of al Qaeda or some type of associated forces or if it is justified because that individual militant poses an imminent threat to the U.S. that cannot be deterred or eliminated in any other way. In the case of targeted strikes in the current international environment of armed conflict and counterterrorism operations occurring at the same time, in particular, the mixing of legal justifications raises significant concerns about both current implementation and future development of the law.[44] No less, it is these very targeted strikes and the authority asserted in conjunction with these and future strikes that triggers much of the debate over the geographic parameters of conflict.

Outside armed conflict, the use of force against an individual or group who poses a threat takes place within the parameters of the international law of self-defense, in which force can only be used where necessary and proportionate to the goal of repelling or deterring an armed attack or imminent armed attack.[45] In the counterterrorism scenario, targeted strikes are used to neutralize a non-state actor who poses a threat to the security of the responding state—by planning, and potentially launching, a terrorist attack against the state, the state's interests, or the state's nationals. Effective counterterrorism seeks to prevent such attacks, not only to identify and attack those responsible after the fact. The two essential components of this analysis are imminence and alternatives—the threat posed by the non-state actor must be imminent[46] and there must be no alternatives to the use of force as a means to deter or repel the threat posed by such individual. Thus, most experts assert that, outside of armed conflict,

---

[44] See Blank 2012.

[45] ICJ, *Legality of the Threat or Use of Nuclear Weapons*, Advisory Opinion, (1996) ICJ Rep 226, para 246; ICJ, *Military and Paramilitary Activities in and Against Nicaragua (Nicaragua v. United States)*, (1986) ICJ Rep 14; Eritrea-Ethiopia Claims Commission, Partial Award (*Jus Ad Bellum*), Ethiopia's Claims 1–8 (The Federal Democratic Republic of Ethiopia and the State of Eritrea), 19 December 2005, available at: http://www.pca-cpa.org/upload/files/FINAL%20ET%20JAB.pdf. For an extensive treatment of *jus ad bellum* and the use of force in self-defense, see Dinstein 2005.

[46] See Guiora 2012 ("An imminent threat in the terrorism paradigm is just that—a clear and present danger—that unless mitigated endangers innocent civilians. It is not an amorphous threat, distant in time; quite the opposite for it indicates that unless specific measures are taken with respect to the person posing the threat harm will befall those not in a position to protect themselves").

the targeting of suspected terrorists must be restricted to cases in which there is credible evidence that the targeted persons are actively involved in planning or preparing further terrorist attacks against the victim state and no other operational means of stopping those attacks are available.[47]

Within an armed conflict, military necessity provides the authority for a party to a conflict to use all force—within the bounds of the law—necessary to achieve the complete submission of the enemy.[48] Armed conflict is fundamentally a struggle between organized belligerent forces, not individual operatives. The authority to use all measures not otherwise prohibited by international law to compel the enemy's prompt submission is not based on an individualized assessment of threat, therefore. Instead, all attacks are directed towards the enemy in the collective sense—the law presumes that attacking all enemy operatives, even those not posing an immediate threat at the time of the attack, contributes to this collective objective, thus justifying such attacks by military necessity.[49] This authority extends beyond the neutralization or elimination of immediate threats to the broader purpose of defeating the enemy as an entity itself, rather than the individuals who comprise the enemy force. For this reason, the law envisions a robust and broad power to attack and disable the enemy based on the presumption that, by nature of being part of the enemy, all members of the enemy force pose a threat.[50]

Recently, arguments by some scholars that LOAC imposes an obligation to capture in lieu of using deadly force during armed conflict demonstrate that the individualized threat determination requirement from the law enforcement framework applicable outside of armed conflict (thus in the context of uses of force in self-defense) seems to have bled over into the armed conflict paradigm.[51] This merging

[47] Kretzmer 2005, p. 173. See also Schmitt 2008 ("If law-enforcement measures (or other measures short of self-defense) will assuredly foil a terrorist attack *on their own,* forceful measures in self-defense may not be taken. The issue is not whether law enforcement officials are likely to bring the terrorists to justice, but instead whether, with a reasonable degree of certainty, law enforcement actions alone will protect the target(s) of the terrorism. For instance, if members of a terrorist cell can confidently be arrested, that action must be taken in lieu of a military attack designed to kill its members").

[48] US Department of the Army Field Manual 1956, at app. A-1.

[49] See, e.g., Sassòli and Olson 2008, p. 606 ("Combatants are part of the military potential of the enemy and it is therefore always lawful to attack them for the purpose of weakening that potential").

[50] In an international armed conflict, all members of the military forces of a party to the conflict are legitimate targets of attack at all times; in a non-international armed conflict, all fighters in an organized armed group that is a party to the conflict are similarly targetable at all times. See Gurulé and Corn 2011, pp. 70–76 (discussing the rules governing targeting of enemy forces in international and non-international armed conflict and noting that (1) "a member of an enemy force […] is presumed hostile and therefore presumptively subject to attack" in international armed conflict, and (2) "[s]ubjecting members of organized belligerent groups to status based targeting pursuant to the LOAC as opposed to civilians who periodically lose their protection from attack seems both logical and consistent with the practice of states engaged in non-international armed conflicts"); Melzer 2008, p. 995 (stating that members of organized armed groups are targetable based on their status in non-international armed conflict).

[51] See, e.g., Goodman 2013.

of heretofore wholly separate use of force authorities and concepts of necessity stems at one level from the conflation between the self-defense and armed conflict justifications for targeted strikes. In turn, these conflations have introduced another layer of confusion in the debate over the boundaries of armed conflict, particularly one between a state and one or more terrorist groups. As the hard-to-define parameters of an ongoing armed conflict with terrorist groups raise serious concerns about too many areas being subsumed within an area of armed conflict and the use of lethal force as a first resort, questions of geography paper over more substantive underlying debates about the nature of the authority to use force. In essence, a narrow geographical "battlespace" results in a more narrow set of authorities to use force, because anywhere outside of that narrow geographical area will automatically be subject to the more restrictive use of force paradigm of international human rights law and law enforcement that applies outside of armed conflict.

What proponents of this methodology forget however, is that in armed conflict, the enemy is not targeted solely to eliminate the individual threat that he or she poses. Those who resist set geographical parameters or argue for a flexible and shifting notion of the boundaries of conflict begin from the premise that the purpose of armed conflict is to accomplish the submission of the enemy as a collective entity—whether another state's forces, a non-state armed group or a terrorist organization. The raid in which U.S. forces killed Osama bin Laden in his Pakistan hideout in May 2011 offers a useful example of how these differing presumptions play out. Bin Laden was the acknowledged leader of al Qaeda, the group with whom the U.S. has been engaged in an armed conflict for over a decade. As the commander of the enemy forces, bin Laden was a legitimate target of attack, just like any other member of the enemy forces and, as leader, a particularly high value target.[52] The U.S., and most commentators, viewed the killing of bin Laden as governed by LOAC because it occurred within the armed conflict between the U.S. and al Qaeda—hence the team had "the authority to kill Osama bin Laden unless he offered to surrender; in which case the team was required to accept his surrender if the team could do so safely".[53] Others, however, argued that because the conflict's geographical parameters were territorially limited to Afghanistan, the raid occurred "far from a battle zone" and was therefore governed by human rights law.[54]

By focusing exclusively on where an individual is at the moment of an attack, this approach presumes that an individual not located in the throes of the hostilities is not

---

[52] Although identifying who is a member of a transnational terrorist group for the purposes of targeting analysis is extraordinarily difficult and fraught with uncertainty, some cases, such as that of Bin Laden, are straightforward.

[53] Press Briefing by Press Secretary Jay Carney (4 May 2011), available at: http://www.whitehouse.gov/the-press-office/2011/05/04/press-briefing-press-secretary-jay-carney-542011.

[54] See O'Connell, The Death of Bin Laden as a Turning Point, Opinio Juris blog entry (3 May 2011), available at: http://opiniojuris.org/2011/05/03/the-death-of-bin-laden-as-a-turning-point/; O'Connell, The Bin Laden Aftermath: Abbottabad and International Law, Foreign Policy (4 May 2011), available at: http://afpak.foreignpolicy.com/posts/2011/05/04/the_bin_laden_aftermath_abbottabad_and_international_law ("On May 2, no fighting was going on in Pakistan that would rise to the level of 'armed conflict' as defined under international law").

engaged in the conflict. As such, this approach divorces territory from all other considerations and, more importantly, ignores the idea of the enemy as a collective entity whose members fight on behalf of that collective entity, not as individual actors. Thus, bin Laden was a legitimate target not because he posed an imminent threat at the precise moment of the raid, but because targeting and eliminating or neutralizing the leader of the enemy forces would contribute greatly to the "complete submission of the enemy as soon as possible".[55] The argument that because he was in Pakistan rather than Afghanistan, he was no longer in the conflict zone and therefore not falling within the LOAC paradigm ignores completely the idea of military operations as designed to defeat the enemy as a collective entity. In effect, "the test for [LOAC] applicability does not change; it is a question of determining the existence of an armed conflict between [the] state A and [the armed] group…"[56] and then, of course, whether the individual is a member of that group.

In contrast, U.S. drone strikes in Somalia and Yemen raise the same question from the opposing standpoint. To the extent that the U.S. is targeting individuals in such locations under the rubric of self-defense, the legal justification for targeting someone is that he or she poses an imminent threat and there is no alternative means of deterring that threat. The steady U.S. conflation of armed conflict and self-defense when discussing the justifications for any targeted strike wherever it occurs leaves one to wonder, however, why there do not seem to be attempts to have such individuals apprehended by either local authorities (where possible) or by our own forces. The absence of such efforts could suggest that the U.S. is using the targeted strikes to defeat or neutralize the relevant terrorist group (al-Shabaab or al Qaeda in the Arabian Peninsula, for example) as a whole—a justifiable reason for targeting an individual in an armed conflict, but not in the self-defense context where human rights norms govern. In essence, this methodology presumes that al-Shabaab, al Qaeda in the Arabian Peninsula, or other groups, are part of the broader armed conflict with al Qaeda, which is a controversial and as yet unsupported conglomeration of armed groups into one broad conception of enemy writ large. And yet the fact that the debate over these strikes centers on the geography of the strikes, rather than the targets of the strikes and the group with whom they are associated, demonstrates that the dichotomy between eliminating an individual threat and achieving the submission of the collective enemy has been lost in the shuffle.

Debates about geography and armed conflict—including whether the discussion should be had at all—thus essentially mask these completely opposing conceptions of the purpose of attacks in armed conflict and the strategic imperatives that drive military decision-making. In the end, such debates are not really about the boundaries of the battlefield at all and those engaged in the debate are simply operating on different frequencies. No less, drawing somewhat arbitrary lines between areas where enemy operatives can be targeted as a first resort and areas where they can

---

55 US Department of the Army Field Manual 1956, Article 3 (defining the principle of military necessity).

56 Lubell and Derejko 2013, p. 16.

only be targeted as a last resort after alternatives are exhausted does not comport with the strategic and operational approach to defeating an enemy that drives military operations in all situations. Because the goal of a military operation is to achieve the complete submission of the enemy in a corporate sense, geographical parameters drawn on the basis of each enemy as an individual threat will simply be irrelevant. The result will be a disconnect between law and military operations—always a troubling consequence.

## 11.6 Conclusion: The Interrelationship Between Law and Geography

Woven throughout much of the debate over the boundaries of the battlefield and the presumptions examined in this chapter is the complex relationship between *jus ad bellum* and LOAC, also called *jus in bello*. An armed conflict occurring inside the territory of more than one state—particularly one between a state and a non-state group operating outside its borders—inherently raises questions regarding sovereignty, territory and the authority to use force across state borders. For some, the existence of the armed conflict and the location of the enemy forces inside another state is sufficient to satisfy any *jus ad bellum* considerations regarding the use of force inside the territory of that other state. For others, each use of force across state borders, even if against a non-state group and not against that state, requires an independent *jus ad bellum* justification of consent, United Nations authorization or self-defense. Indeed, it is difficult to discuss geography and military force beyond the territory of a single state without encountering *jus ad bellum*. As a result, isolating debates about the geography of armed conflict from questions regarding the legality of using force inside the territory of another state—while essential to a productive debate—can prove to be a perplexing challenge.

The inherent biases stemming from the dichotomies presented in this chapter build on and reinforce this foundational confusion in the debates about boundaries. When one speaks of geography in terms of formalized legal limits, another speaks of geography in terms of strategic policy for counterterrorism and military operations. Territorial constraints on one side and a threat-driven approach on the other. These dichotomies and the presumptions they engender hobble any effective exploration of whether "the battlefield"—often a rhetorical substitution for conflict in today's discourse—has geographical parameters and, if so, what those parameters are. As a result, before tackling the geography questions, it is first necessary to address the dichotomies and understand the presumptions and how they affect the debate. Traditionally, LOAC balances a variety of interests, such as military necessity and humanity, and over the years has developed to respond to the needs and changes of those in combat and those suffering from the deliberate and incidental effects of combat. In order to maximize the development of the law going forward, debates about application of the law—whether where, when or how—must be stripped down to the central and foundational issues before using those issues as the building blocks for analysis of more complex questions such as geography and battlefield parameters.

## References

Anderson K (2010) Targeted killing and drone warfare: how we came to debate whether there is a 'legal geography of war'. In: Berkowitz P (ed) Future challenges in national security and law. http://media.hoover.org/sites/default/files/documents/FutureChallenges_Anderson.pdf

Blank L (2010) Defining the battlefield in contemporary conflict and counterterrorism: understanding the parameters of the zone of combat. Georgia J Int Comp Law 39:3–38

Blank L (2011) A square peg in a round hole: stretching law of war detention too far. Rutgers Law Rev 64:1169–1193

Blank L (2012) Targeted strikes: the consequences of blurring the armed conflict and self-defense justifications. William Mitchell Law Rev 38:1655–1700

Corn G (2009a) Back to the future: de facto hostilities, transnational terrorism, and the purpose of the law of armed conflict. Univ Pennsylvania J Int Law 30:1345–1354

Corn G (2009b) What law applies to the war on terror. In: Lewis M (ed) The war on terror and the laws of war: a military perspective. Oxford University Press, Oxford, pp 1–36

Corn G (2012) Self-defense targeting: blurring the line between the jus ad bellum and the jus in bello. Int Law Stud 88:57–92

Corn G (2013) Geography of armed conflict: why it is a mistake to fish for the red herring. Int Law Stud 89:77–107

Dinstein Y (2004) The conduct of hostilities under the law of international armed conflict. Cambridge University Press, Cambridge

Dinstein Y (2005) War, aggression and self-defence, 4th edn. Cambridge University Press, Cambridge

Goodman R (2013) The power to kill or capture enemy combatants. Eur J Int Law 24:819–853

Gregory D (2011) The everywhere war. Geogr J 177:238–250

Guiora A (2012) The importance of criteria-based reasoning in targeted killing decisions. In: Finkelstein C et al. (eds) Targeted killings: law and morality in an asymmetrical world. Oxford University Press, Oxford, pp 303–325

Gurulé J, Corn G (2011) Principles of counter-terrorism law. West Law School, St. Paul

Herndon R et al. (2004) Effects-based operations in Afghanistan: the CJTF-180 method of orchestrating effects to achieve objectives. Field artillery Jan–Feb 2004, http://sill-www.army.mil/firesbulletin/archives/2004/JAN_FEB_2004/JAN_FEB_2004_FULL_EDITION.pdf

ICRC (2004) Advisory service on international humanitarian law, What is international humanitarian law. www.icrc.org/eng/assets/files/other/what_is_ihl.pdf. Accessed 26 Sept 2014

Kretzmer D (2005) Targeted killing of suspected terrorists: extra-judicial executions or legitimate means of defence? Eur J Int Law 16:173–212

Lewis M (2012) Drones and the boundaries of the battlefield. Tex Int Law J 47:293–314

Lubell N, Derejko N (2013) A global battlefield? drones and geographical scope of armed conflict. J Int Crim Justice 11:65–88

Melzer N (2008) Interpretive guidance on the notion of direct participation in hostilities under international humanitarian law. Int Rev Red Cross 90:991–1047

O'Connell M (2009) Combatants and the combat zone. Univ Richmond Law Rev 43:845–863

O'Connell M (2010) Unlawful killing with combat drones: a case study of Pakistan 2004–2009. Notre Dame Law School, Legal Studies Research Paper 09–43

Oppenheim L (1952) In: Lauterpacht H (ed) International law: a treatise, 7th edn, vol 2. Longmans, London

Roth K (2004) The law of war in the war on terror. Foreign Affairs 83:2–7

Sassòli M, Olson L (2008) The relationship between international humanitarian and human rights law where it matters: admissible killing and internment of fighters in non-international armed conflicts. Int Rev Red Cross 90:599–627

Schmitt N (2008) Responding to transnational terrorism under the jus ad bellum: a normative framework. Nav Law Rev 56:1–41

The White House (2013) Fact sheet: U.S. policy standards and procedures for the use of force in counterterrorism operations outside the United States and areas of active hostilities. www.whitehouse.gov/the-press-office/2013/05/23/fact-sheet-us-policy-standards-and-procedures-use-force-counterterrorism. Accessed 1 April 2014

Uhler O et al. (1958) Commentary on IV Geneva convention relative to the protection of civilian persons in time of war 20 (Pictet J ed, Griffin R and Dumbleton C trans)

UK Ministry of Defence (2004) JSP 383—The joint service manual on the law of armed conflict. www.gov.uk/government/publications/jsp-383-the-joint-service-manual-of-the-law-of-armed-conflict-2004-edition. Accessed 1 April 2014

UN Human Rights Council and Alston P (2010) Report of the special rapporteur on extrajudicial, summary or arbitrary executions: study on targeted killings (28 May 2010). UN Doc. A/HRC/14/24/Add.6

US Department of the Army (1956) Field manual 27-10—the law of land warfare. www.loc.gov/rr/frd/Military_Law/pdf/law_warfare-1956.pdf. Accessed 1 April 2014

# Chapter 12
# Crossing Borders to Target Al-Qaeda and Its Affiliates: Defining Networks as Organized Armed Groups in Non-International Armed Conflicts

**Peter Margulies and Matthew Sinnot**

**Abstract** Al-Qaeda's dispersal and the rise of regional terrorist groups such as Al-Shabaab in Somalia have raised the stakes for defining an "organized armed group" (OAG). If an entity fails the OAG test, a state may use only traditional law enforcement methods in responding to the entity's violence. Both case law and social science literature support a broadly pragmatic reading of the OAG definition. While the International Criminal Tribunal for the former Yugoslavia (ICTY) has cited factors such as existence of a headquarters and imposition of discipline, ICTY decisions have found organization when evidence was at best equivocal. Moreover, terrorist organizations reveal surprisingly robust indicia of organization. Illustrating this organizational turn, a transnational network like Al-Qaeda operates in a synergistic fashion with regional groups. Moreover, recent news reports have suggested that current Al-Qaeda leader Dr. Ayman al-Zawahiri has attempted to assert operational control over the specific targeting decisions of Al-Qaeda affiliates, although that effort has not been uniformly successful. Furthermore, while Al-Qaeda does not micromanage most individual operations, it exercises strategic influence, e.g., through a focus on targeting Western interests. When such strategic influence can be shown, the definition of OAG is sufficiently flexible to permit targeting across borders. In addition, the doctrine of co-belligerency, borrowed from neutrality law, provides a basis for targeting that is not confined by state boundaries. Even when

---

Peter Margulies professor of Law, Roger Williams University. An earlier version of this piece was published as *Networks in Noninternational Armed Conflicts: Crossing Borders and Defining "Organized Armed Group,"* 89 Int'l L. Stud. 54–76 (Naval War College 2013). Matthew Sinnott J.D 2014, Roger Williams University School of Law; B.B.A. Hofstra University, 2011; 1st Lt. United States Marine Corps. The views expressed are the author's own and do not necessarily represent the views of the U.S. Marine Corps/Naval Service or the U.S. Department of Defense.

---

P. Margulies (✉) · M. Sinnot
Roger Williams University, Bristol RI 02809, UK
e-mail: pmargulies@rwu.edu

M. Sinnot
e-mail: msinnott10@gmail.com



T.D. Gill et al. (eds.), *Yearbook of International Humanitarian Law 2013*,
Yearbook of International Humanitarian Law 16, DOI 10.1007/978-94-6265-038-1_12

these indicia are absent, individuals within non-Al-Qaeda groups may be targetable if they engage in coordinated activity with Al-Qaeda.

**Keywords** Terrorist networks · Law of armed conflict · Organized armed group · Al Qaeda affiliates · Al Qaeda in the Arabian Peninsula · Boko Haram

## Contents



## 12.1 Introduction

As Al-Qaeda has dispersed, the precise definition of an "organized armed group" (OAG) under the law of armed conflict (LOAC) has become increasingly vital. The United States currently targets certain members of Al-Qaeda and affiliated organizations not only in Afghanistan, but also in other countries.[1] However, while the elements of Al-Qaeda that were present in Afghanistan immediately after September 11 presumably constituted an OAG, it is less clear that supposed affiliates outside Afghanistan are part of the *same* OAG. The answer to this question raises the stakes of targeting decisions. If affiliated groups are part of an OAG under the Al-Qaeda "umbrella," then arguably the United States has the right to target them wherever they are.[2] But if groups outside Afghanistan are *not* part of Al-Qaeda, then targeting them requires a separate armed conflict and a separate *jus ad bellum* justification for the use of force.[3] Formulating and applying the OAG criteria is therefore an essential enterprise.

---

[1] Brennan 2011; Koh 2010; Chesney 2013.

[2] If the state in which the group is currently located is willing and able to deal with the threat, the United States should defer to that state's efforts. Deeks 2012, pp. 499–503; Chang 2011, pp. 25–36 (consulting neutrality law to define "enemy" who can be targeted or detained); Ingber 2011 (cautioning that neutrality law does not provide useful guide for detention of non-state actors in NIACs).

[3] Dinstein 2005, pp. 204–211.

This Article responds to this high-stakes challenge with a pragmatic approach[4] along two axes. First, it argues for a broad interpretation of the definition of "organized armed group" framed by the International Criminal Tribunal for the former Yugoslavia (ICTY) in *Prosecutor v. Tadic*.[5] In practice, while the language of the definition appears to be narrow, case law and scholarship have often expanded the concept. Second, the Article shows that terrorist groups generally, and Al-Qaeda in particular, reveal a surprising degree of organization. Some of this organization takes unconventional forms, dictated by the special circumstances of terrorist networks. Yet terrorist groups actually have many of the same needs for organization as state entities, including the pervasive need to control agency costs. Moreover, Al-Qaeda exists in a synergistic relationship with many regional groups, providing training and influencing their choice of targets. Strategic influence of this type is a sufficient justification for targeting affiliates.

The Article proceeds in two sections. Section 12.2 outlines the lessons of case law and commentary regarding the definition of OAG. This section suggests that the language used may seem narrow, but has often been interpreted in more flexible fashion. Section 12.3 discusses the status as OAGs of terrorist groups in general and Al-Qaeda in particular. It concludes that such groups often possess the degree of organization required for recognition under the laws of armed conflict. Furthermore, Al-Qaeda as a network often exercises strategic influence on its affiliates that justifies targeting. Even when Al-Qaeda does not exercise such influence, U.S. forces can legally target individuals within non-Al-Qaeda groups if such persons coordinate lethal operations, planning, or logistics with Al-Qaeda. However, the approach to targeting outlined here has limits. The U.S. cannot legally target certain groups, such as the Islamic State of Iraq and Syria (ISIS) or Nigeria's Boko Haram, that lack concrete ties to Al-Qaeda or a demonstrable intent to attack U.S. interests. Targeting such groups would require a legal basis independent of the United States' non-international armed conflict with Al-Qaeda.

## 12.2 Organizing the Case Law on OAGs

Both case law and evolving trends on the ground have precipitated the problem of transregional conflicts and organized armed groups. State conflicts with organized non-state actors are considered conflicts not of an international character (NIACs).[6] At least at first blush, one would assume that a NIAC can take place only on the territory of a single state; if the territory of more than one state is involved, it seems

---

[4] Glennon 2010, p. 20 (recommending "broader and more flexible interpretive method").

[5] ICTY, *Prosecutor v. Dusko Tadić*, Decision on the Defence Motion for Interlocutory Appeal on Jurisdiction, Appeals Chamber (IT-94-I-AR72), 2 October 1995, para 70.

[6] *Hamdan v. Rumsfeld*, 548 U.S. 557 (2006), pp. 628–632.

incongruous to deny the "international character" of the conflict.[7] Moreover, treaties and case law have required that each party to an armed conflict be an OAG. Additional Protocol II (AP II) defines OAG in a narrow way. According to AP II, OAGs must be "under responsible command, [and] exercise such control over a part of [a state's] territory as to enable them to carry out sustained and concerted military operations and to implement this Protocol."[8] Some groups, like Hamas in Gaza or the now-defunct Liberation Tigers of Tamil Eelam (LTTE) of Sri Lanka, might meet this definition, but, a network such as Al-Qaeda will not. Al-Qaeda's dispersion therefore makes precise definition a priority.

### 12.2.1 The High Stakes of LOAC Definitions

Much hinges on the breadth of the definition of a NIAC. A narrow definition subjects state forces to the more rigorous demands of international human rights law (IHRL), which permits the use of deadly force only when an individual poses a concrete, imminent threat to the life of a law enforcement officer or other individuals.[9] The European Court of Human Rights has defined such threats narrowly, second-guessing the use of lethal force by law enforcement even when the target was a pair of known terrorists whom authorities rightly believed had planted an explosive device that they planned to trigger in the near future.[10] Under IHRL, terrorists have a greater opportunity to operate with impunity. Applying the law of armed conflict (LOAC), in contrast, diminishes the non-state actor's room to maneuver. It allows states to target individuals whom it believes to be performing a

---

[7] ICRC 2011, p. 10 (discussing "multinational NIACs [in which]... multinational armed forces are fighting alongside the armed forces of a 'host' state—in its territory—against one or more organized armed groups" as well as "transnational" conflict between "Al-Qaeda and its 'affiliates' and 'adherents' and the United States"); Watkin 2011, pp. 3–12 (discussing dilemmas in conflicts against non-state actors); Corn and Jensen 2009 (arguing that NIAC concept does not fit well in analyzing conflicts involving global terrorist networks such as Al-Qaeda and suggesting "transnational armed conflict" as a superior alternative).

[8] Article 1(1) of Protocol Additional to the Geneva Conventions of 12 August 1949, and Relating to the Protection of Victims of International Armed Conflicts, opened for signature 12 December 1977, 1125 UNTS 3 (entered into force 7 December 1978) (Additional Protocol I).

[9] ECtHR, *McCann v. The United Kingdom*, Judgment (Appl. No. 18984/91), 27 September 1995; Corn 2011, p. 35 (analyzing relationship between LOAC and law enforcement paradigms); Bellinger and Padmanabhan 2011, pp. 210–213 (same); Criddle 2012 (arguing that IHRL paradigm fits most cases involving violence by a state's nationals within a state's own territory); Luban 2013 (asserting that law of armed conflict shows insufficient regard for welfare of civilians and that human rights law is superior in this respect); Hakimi 2012 (arguing for functional criteria that transcend distinction between LOAC and IHRL).

[10] *McCann* (Ryssdal J, dissenting), supra n 9, paras 7–22; Margulies 2013 (critiquing *McCann*).

continuous combat function (CCF).[11] Even narrow definitions of CCF recognize that an individual who performs this role may spend much time in pursuits other than presenting a concrete, imminent threat to the other side. A typical uniformed soldier, for example, may spend time marching, building an encampment, or even sleeping. The soldier can be targeted by an enemy state's forces in any and all of these activities.[12] Just as a state can target an opposing state's uniformed forces without a showing that an individual soldier faces a specific, imminent threat, LOAC would allow targeting of a member of an organized non-state actor whom the state reasonably believed to be engaged in CCF.

However, the greater latitude allowed states in targeting terrorists makes human rights advocates blanch at the prospect of higher civilian casualties.[13] More latitude in targeting may increase the risk of mistakes, in which a state erroneously targets innocents or causes collateral damage among civilians.[14] Advocates of greater state latitude will argue that states can and should build in systems that minimize mistakes, such as a lawyer's review and approval of targeting decisions. However, state advocates would add, opponents of state latitude have a bad case of hindsight bias[15] regarding state action. State critics regard all civilian casualties as avoidable, a position that the laws of war have never taken. However, proponents of state latitude would argue, critics fail to consider matters from an *ex ante* perspective, involving the incentives for violent non-state actors. When violent non-state actors

[11] Israeli Supreme Court, *Public Committee Against Torture in Israel v. The State of Israel*, Judgment (HCJ 769/02), 13 December 2006, para 39 (asserting that fighters who make themselves regularly available to terrorist groups for acts of violence are directly participating in hostilities for such time as they make themselves available; any interlude between acts of violence is merely "preparation" for further violence). In this analysis, the court lent a flexible reading to concepts that the ICRC has defined more narrowly. International Committee of the Red Cross 2009, p. 54; Rona 2012 (criticizing United States' targeting standards as unduly broad); but see Schmitt 2010, p. 731 (criticizing narrow reading in ICRC Guidance); Watkin 2010, p. 661 (criticizing ICRC's failure to dismantle "revolving door" mechanism for terrorist groups).

[12] Walzer 1977, p. 143; but see Blum 2010, pp. 138–150 (questioning whether use of lethal force should always be permissible against uniformed combatants).

[13] Ohlin 2013. Although the definition of an OAG is relevant to targeting decisions, the targeting debate also raises other issues beyond the scope of this Article. Compare Anderson 2012, pp. 391–396 (rejecting argument that sophisticated technology behind drones that makes targeted killing easier also undermines practical checks on willingness to wage war); Chesney 2011 (suggesting that targeted killing under certain conditions is consistent with LOAC); Margulies 2012b, pp. 1471–1477 (same); Paust 2010 (asserting that targeted killing is legal under international law as long as targeting force observes principles of distinction and proportionality), with Alston 2010 (arguing that targeted killing in state that is not geographic site of armed conflict violates international law); O'Connell 2012 (same); cf. Daskal 2013 (suggesting additional guidelines to regulate targeted killings).

[14] But see Goldsmith 2012, p. 131 (noting involvement of military lawyers in targeting decisions as check on errors); McNeal 2012, pp. 331–342 (discussing process engaged in by U.S. military prior to authorization of drone strike).

[15] Roese 2004, pp. 260–261 (describing hindsight bias as "tendency to believe that an event was predictable before it occurred, even though for the perceiver it was not" and that harm was avoidable even when it was impossible to prevent).

believe they can operate with impunity, risks to civilians increase.[16] Curbing violent non-state actors thus reduces net risks for civilians.

Moreover, state critics often fail to acknowledge that while a broader definition of OAG confers advantages on a state in the arena of targeting, with that advantage comes greater accountability for all parties to the NIAC.[17] A state in a NIAC must observe the strictures of the Geneva Convention's Common Article 3, such as humane treatment of captives.[18] These provisions are generally considered *jus cogens* and therefore non-derogable.[19] OAGs incur the same duties; one purpose of the requirement that a group have a minimum level of organization is that it would be unfair to require a disorganized group to observe IHL because it lacks the structure to do so. Individuals who target civilians can be made to answer for violations of municipal law, such as the prohibition on murder. In contrast, OAGs who target civilians may be prosecuted in international tribunals for crimes against humanity, instead of merely being answerable in the sometimes-dysfunctional justice systems of their countries of origin. The targeting advantages reaped by states are thus paid for by greater accountability elsewhere in the IHL framework.[20]

### 12.2.2 Unpacking the ICTY Formulation

At first blush, state critics may have an edge in the definitional debate regarding OAG. Some passages in case law have propounded a narrow definition of OAG that requires something approaching the attributes of state entities.[21] In *Prosecutor v. Limaj*, the ICTY suggested that to meet its criteria, an OAG should have a headquarters, a unified command, and a military police unit that will arrest malefactors.[22] Without these attributes, a group is considered not an OAG, but a criminal

[16] Margulies 2013, Lewis 2012 (suggesting that geographic restrictions on states' ability to target terrorist groups with global operations would grant these groups asymmetric advantage).

[17] Ohlin 2013.

[18] Article 3 of the Geneva Convention Relative to the Protection of Civilian Persons in Time of War, opened for signature 12 August 1949, 75 UNTS 287 (entered into force 21 October 1950) (Geneva Convention IV).

[19] IHRL provisions are often subject to derogation. Cf. ICRC 2011, p. 15 (describing applicability and scope of IHRL, particularly extraterritorial applicability, as "work in progress").

[20] Human Rights Council 2012, para 134 (noting accountability under IHL of anti-government armed groups in Syria).

[21] ICTY, *Prosecutor v. Limaj*, Judgment Trial Chamber (IT-03-66-T), 30 November 2005, paras 113–117; cf. Pejic 2011, pp. 191–192.

[22] Ibid, paras 113–117; see also ICTR, *Prosecutor v. Akayesu*, Judgment Trial Chamber (ICTR-96-4-T), 2 September 1998, para 626 ("responsible command" entails "degree of organization [that permits the group] […] to plan and carry out concerted military operations, and to impose discipline"; group must also "dominate a sufficient part of territory" and "operations must be continuous and planned").

band or an assemblage of individuals engaged in civil unrest such as a riot.[23] Individuals in such groups cannot be targeted as readily as participants in an armed conflict, but instead are protected by IHRL.

Acts of terrorism sit uneasily within this paradigm. "[I]solated acts of terrorism" probably do not demonstrate the level of organization required for a NIAC.[24] Moreover, some commentators have noted that several major nations have addressed significant acts of terrorism through traditional law enforcement.[25]

If a terrorist entity can elude definition as an OAG within one state, it can even more readily elude such definition in the regional or global context. The United States confronts extremist organizations not merely in one country, but in multiple regions, that feature ties of varying closeness to Al-Qaeda. Some have argued that Al-Qaeda' relationship to such groups involves only "very loose ties" typical of a "confederation of like-minded fellow travelers, many of whom are fighting *separate* armed conflicts in different regions of the globe."[26]

Treaty law and the ICTY jurisprudence actually permit greater flexibility in the definition of OAGs. While AP II applies to some NIACs, other NIACs are governed by Common Article 3, which contains no requirement that a party control territory.[27] The International Committee of the Red Cross (ICRC), a group with special competence regarding LOAC, has also signaled that flexibility is important. In one study, the ICRC observed that to be considered an OAG, an entity should merely have a "minimum of organization."[28] That terminology strongly suggests that a rigid, itemized checklist would be counterproductive.[29]

---

[23] In some cases, a criminal enterprise may be so organized and its violence against state officials so intense that classification as a NIAC is appropriate. See Bergal 2011, pp. 1042–1088.

[24] ICTY, *Prosecutor v. Boskoski and Tarculovski*, Judgment Trial Chamber (IT-04-82-T), 10 July 2008, para 190.

[25] ILA 2010, p. 25; cf. Scheppele 2010, p. 451 (asserting that global counter-terrorism measures permit states to disguise substandard governance as counter-terrorism); Setty 2010, p. 153 (suggesting that counter-terrorism policies in United States, United Kingdom, and India raise human rights concerns).

[26] Ohlin 2012, p. 75 (emphasis added) (noting this view while not necessarily endorsing it); Martin 2012, pp. 245–246 (suggesting that groups with nominal Al-Qaeda ties actually have little in common); Geiß 2009, pp. 134–135 (global Al-Qaeda network structure appears "rather basic" and "rudimentarily organized"); cf. Ohlin 2013 (offering more pragmatic view); Lubell and Derejko 2013, p. 86 ("the applicability of the *ius in bello* is not as geographically bound as may have been assumed").

[27] Ohlin 2013, p. 1279; Schmitt M 2012, pp. 604–606 (discussing relationship between APII and Common Article 3); cf. Paulus and Vashakmadze 2009, p. 117 (discussing importance of flexibility in definition of OAG).

[28] ICRC 2008, p. 5.

[29] However, the ICRC has also indicated that the criteria mentioned in the ICTY jurisprudence are useful guides. See International Committee of the Red Cross 2011, p. 8 (requiring a "certain level of organization," which may include but is not limited to "the existence of a command structure… disciplinary rules…headquarters," and logistical, attack, and negotiating capabilities).

Moreover, the ICTY jurisprudence is far more flexible than it may appear.[30] In *Prosecutor v. Boskoski & Tarculovski*,[31] a case involving the targeting of civilians by a non-state group, the ICTY noted that terrorist acts could form a pattern that would constitute an armed conflict.[32] *Boskoski* can be read as standing for either one or two eminently pragmatic propositions. First, OAG should not be assessed in a vacuum, but on a sliding scale that also includes the other *Tadic* criterion—intensity.[33] Second, the best proof of OAG is in the operational details of violence that members of the group have caused. A group's sheer ability to mount sustained terrorist attacks is evidence of a "high level of planning and a coordinated command structure."[34]

The ICTY's treatment of evidence also suggests substantial flexibility in the definition of OAG. In *Limaj*, for example, the ICTY found that the Kosovo Liberation Army (KLA) was organized even though evidence of discipline was "scant" by the court's own admission.[35] Witnesses differed widely on when the military police cited by the tribunal had been established.[36] If the military police were a salient symbol of organizational discipline, this divergence in recollection seems odd. Moreover, as the ICTY acknowledged, there was no record of any imposition of discipline among KLA members.[37]

The *Limaj* court sought to buttress this decidedly equivocal evidence of discipline with a proxy: other nations and entities dealt with the KLA in a way that suggested that they regarded the group as organized,[38] although evidence for this point was slim. For example, the ICTY acknowledged that representatives of other entities were "sometimes unclear about the KLA's command structure."[39] Indeed, one report described the KLA's structure as "a mystery" and "more a matter of diffuse horizontal command."[40] *Limaj* also noted that the General Staff of the KLA "did not have a consistent…location."[41] While the tribunal made much of the

---

[30] See Ohlin 2013, p. 1284 ("legal support for [requiring] centralization is misplaced"); Sivakumaran 2012, p. 1137 (noting that in many groups appropriately designated as OAGs, structure will be "horizontal," rather than "pyramidal"); Schmitt 2011, p. 129 (arguing that group's structure "need not be strictly hierarchical or implemented in any formalistic manner").

[31] *Prosecutor v. Boskoski and Tarculovski,* supra n 24.

[32] Ibid, para 185 (noting that terrorism may be part of NIAC if it is part of "protracted campaign").

[33] Ibid, paras 182–183; see also Blank and Corn 2013 (discussing flexibility in ICTY approach); HRC 2012, para 134 (asserting that anti-government armed groups in Syria should be considered OAGs that are accountable under IHL).

[34] *Prosecutor v. Boskoski and Tarculovski,* supra n 24, para 204.

[35] *Prosecutor v. Limaj*, supra n 21, para 116.

[36] Ibid, para 113.

[37] Ibid, para 116.

[38] See ibid, paras 128–129.

[39] Ibid, para 131 (citing Austrian Embassy report).

[40] Ibid (also observing that American diplomat Richard Holbrooke seconded this perception).

[41] Ibid, para 104.

KLA's governing regulations, it acknowledged that the authorship and date of the regulations were not apparent on the regulations' face.[42] Yet the ICTY brushed past these apparent failures of organization, explaining pragmatically that the KLA was "effectively an underground operation, operating in conditions of secrecy out of concern to preserve its leadership" and "under constant threat of military action" by Serbian forces.[43] Therefore, it was "no surprise that the organizational structure and the hierarchy of the KLA was confusing."[44] More than any other factor, the court relied on the KLA's knack for recruiting new followers.[45] Based on this one criterion and modest evidence of others, the court was satisfied that the KLA's fluid and contingent structure did not undermine its classification as an OAG.

Precedent from elsewhere also argues against a narrow definition of organization. Consider *Abella v. Argentina (Tablada Case)*,[46] involving an attack on an Argentinean army base by rebels, followed by alleged state mistreatment of the attackers that the plaintiffs characterized as a violation of Common Article 3. The Inter-American Commission on Human Rights (IAHCR) first ruled that AP II did not limit the situations in which armed conflict existed. The tribunal observed that armed conflicts "not of an international character" that trigger Common Article 3 need not be "large-scale and generalized hostilities or a situation comparable to a civil war in which dissident armed groups exercise control over parts of national territory."[47] Suggesting the need for flexibility, the IAHCR noted that NIACs could also involve "confrontations between *relatively* organized armed forces."[48] The tribunal's use of the term, "relatively," to modify the requirement of an OAG suggests that a narrow or rigid definition would be counterproductive. While the tribunal added that an armed conflict must be something more than "riots, mere acts of banditry or an unorganized and short-lived rebellion,"[49] its analysis indicated that requiring a significantly more elaborate showing would merely allow parties to escape accountability. Turning to the specific facts, the IAHCR found it sufficient that the rebels' attack on the base was "carefully planned, coordinated and executed."[50]

---

[42] Ibid, para 110; see also ibid, para 124 (discussing KLA's lack of communications equipment).

[43] Ibid, para 132; cf. Byman and Waxman 2000, p. 25 (finding that KLA failed to show "that it was capable of holding territory against the Serbian Army") and p. 28 (describing KLA as initially "poorly organized" and as gaining strength only with NATO assistance).

[44] *Prosecutor v. Limaj*, supra n 21, para 132.

[45] Ibid, para 118.

[46] IACmHR, *Abella v. Argentina (La Tablada)*, Case No. 11.137, Report No. 55/97, 18 November 1997, para 152.

[47] Ibid.

[48] Ibid (emphasis added).

[49] Ibid.

[50] Ibid, para 155. While the ICTR set out a narrower standard in *Prosecutor v. Akayesu*, that standard has generally not been followed and "is regarded as exceedingly high." See Geiß 2009, p. 136 n 40.

Tribunals have also expansively defined a non-state actor's capacity to comply with IHL. Terrorist groups generally do not comply with IHL; often their standard operating procedure involves fundamental violations such as the targeting of civilians. But tribunals have viewed terrorist groups as *able* to comply with IHL, even if those groups are disinclined to do so.[51] A contrary view would create perverse incentives, allowing a group to free itself from the risk of targeting by increasing its violations of otherwise applicable norms.[52]

Buttressing this flexible approach, the ICTY has also broadly interpreted the *Tadic* requirement that violence be "protracted." Interpreting the term "protracted" narrowly would again create perverse incentives. Violent non-state actors could strike first and then claim that the conflict was not yet a protracted one, thereby precluding a state from utilizing the full range of responses permissible under LOAC. Instead, the state would be limited to the far narrower repertoire of force permissible under a law enforcement paradigm. To avoid creating this perverse incentive, the ICTY has viewed the term "protracted armed violence" in a pragmatic fashion, as referring generally to the intensity of the violence, not its timing per se.[53]

## 12.3 More Than Meets the Eye: The Organization of Terrorist Networks

Just as a deeper look at case law suggests that the definition of OAG is more flexible than it initially appears, terrorist groups are more organized than their historical image suggests. Although some scholars have viewed earlier acts of terror as the product of individual discontent, they actually involved careful planning.[54] Today's terrorist groups, including Al-Qaeda, also display far more organization than is commonly understood.

---

[51] *Prosecutor v. Boskoski and Tarculovski,* supra n 24, paras 204–205 (pattern of IHL violations does not support inference that group is unable to comply).

[52] Cf. ibid, para 205 (explaining that tribunal "cannot merely infer a lack of organization… [because] international humanitarian law was frequently violated by [the group's] members"); Zawacki 2013 (arguing that Muslim insurgent groups in Thailand have sufficient organization and coordination to constitute an OAG).

[53] ICTY, *Prosecutor v. Ramush Haradinaj et al.*, Judgment Trial Chamber (IT-04-84-T), 3 April 2008, para 49 (noting that term, "protracted armed violence" has been "interpreted in practice […] as referring more to the intensity of the armed violence than to its duration"); see also *Abella v. Argentina (La Tablada)*, supra n 46, para 155 (noting that "brief duration" of attack did not preclude classification as NIAC); cf. Paulus and Vashakmadze 2009, pp. 106–107 (arguing that *Tadić* "protracted armed violence" criterion refers to intensity as well as duration).

[54] Hoffman 2008, pp. 135–136 (discussing careful organization behind assassination of Austrian Archduke Franz Ferdinand, which precipitated World War I).

### *12.3.1 Terrorist Groups, Organization, and Agency Costs*

Terrorist groups require organization because they wish to influence actors who are often organized. Terrorist groups play a multi-level game of the kind made famous by Robert Putnam, involving internal and external actors.[55] Internal actors include people within the organization and within the community that the group purports to represent—Al-Qaeda purports to represent a particular religious vision, while a group like Hamas purports to represent Palestinians and the Kurdistan Workers' Party (PKK), Kurds. External actors include states where the terrorist group is principally located, other states where the group wishes to extend its influence, groups of states such as Western nations or states in the Middle East, international organizations, and other terrorist groups.[56]

Terrorist groups use violence for both expressive and instrumental ends. Violence expresses their commitment to a distinctive vision that the mundane corruption of other parties obscures.[57] Certain kinds of violence, such as suicide attacks, express this commitment in an even clearer form—sending messages about the group's commitment to its cause.[58] Instrumentally, violence serves as a spoiler, derailing negotiations between states and moderate members of their own community.[59] On occasion, terrorist groups find it expedient to mitigate violence, to avoid alienating key constituencies or to gain time to regroup from state pressure.[60] Managing violence to maximize both expressive and instrumental goals requires organization. Maintaining fidelity to these goals in the face of state pressure and internal disagreement requires a particular agility in organizational form.

Like any other entity, a terrorist group needs some form of discipline. Without discipline, agency costs proliferate, as undisciplined members pursue their own impulses or agendas to the detriment of the organization's goals.[61] However, discipline requires institutional memory, as leaders monitor, document, and assess the performance of subordinates. Documentation can be exploited by the group's foes, providing information about operatives and planned attacks. Terrorist groups including Al-Qaeda grapple with the conflict between uniform messaging and secrecy.

Al-Qaeda has coped with this dilemma by cultivating a portfolio approach that maximizes versatility in structure and decision-making, as well as in operational plans.[62] Wise investors use portfolio theory to diversify risk. The careful and

---

[55] Putnam 1988.

[56] Abrahms 2008, pp. 85–86; Chenoweth et al. 2009, p. 183.

[57] Hoffman 1998, pp. 168–169.

[58] Abrahms 2008, pp. 85–86.

[59] Kydd and Walter 2006, pp. 72–75.

[60] *Holder v. Humanitarian Law Project*, 561 U.S. 1 (2010), pp. 2729–2730; Margulies 2012a, pp. 486–493.

[61] Gilson and Mnookin 1994 (discussing virtues and risks of working through agents).

[62] Waxman 2010, pp. 433–437 (distinguishing between "top-down" and "bottom-up" threats).

prudent investor never entrusts all of her resources to one company or even one sector. Rather, the investor pursues some measure of risk diversification. If one investment fails to bring returns, others can pick up the slack.

Al-Qaeda employs a portfolio approach to operations. Officials have recognized that Al-Qaeda needs to be right only once to achieve its expressive and instrumental goals, while security officials must be right every time.[63] Running several plots simultaneously keeps state adversaries guessing, lodging the initiative with Al-Qaeda. Even if the vast majority of attacks are prevented, one catastrophic attack sends the message that Al-Qaeda is still on the map. That message encourages further attacks and distorts government policies. Al-Qaeda uses a similar approach to organizational form. It varies its structure, as the need requires, equipping its personnel to leverage "evolving relationships" rather than being wed to a particular organizational structure.[64] Sticking with one organizational form would also give an advantage to Al-Qaeda's adversaries.[65] Al-Qaeda has adopted an approach to structure that minimizes this risk, mixing command decisions with subordinates' operational initiative. While some have argued that most terrorist acts are the product of independent, grassroots efforts,[66] that picture is decidedly incomplete. According to terrorism expert Bruce Hoffman, Al-Qaeda is a "remarkably agile and flexible organization that exercises both top-down and bottom-up planning and operational capabilities."[67]

Accounts of terrorist groups as creatures of chaos are inaccurate. It turns out that terrorist groups breed bureaucracy. Like lawful organizations, terrorist groups wrestle with the ubiquitous problem of agency costs. Al-Qaeda, like a state military unit, uses personnel drawn from a variety of backgrounds it expects to fulfill the group's mission.[68] However, operatives may have agendas of their own. For example, they may have an interest in looting civilian property or skimming money from the group and enriching themselves.[69] Alternatively, terrorist operatives may engage in *more* violence than the group's leaders find optimal, because the operatives have developed habits of violence while leaders sometimes believe that relative restraint enhances the organizational brand.[70] Bureaucratic rules and procedures can help the terrorist group address these problems.

---

[63] Townsend 2006.

[64] Sawyer and Foster 2008, p. 200.

[65] Sinno 2011, p. 318 (noting that networks such as Al-Qaeda are less vulnerable to state retaliation because of the mobile and dispersed nature of their leadership).

[66] Sageman 2008, pp. 23–24.

[67] Hoffman 2008, p. 134.

[68] Shapiro and Siegel 2012, p. 73; Mueller and Stewart 2012, p. 88 (arguing that individual defendants convicted in the United States of terrorism-related crimes were often lacking in competence and judgment); cf. Chellaney 2001–2002, pp. 96–97 (noting, as an example of agency costs in counter-terrorism, that aid to South Asian governments and non-state groups to fight terrorism has been siphoned off for other purposes).

[69] Shapiro and Siegel 2012, pp. 54–55.

[70] Mueller and Stewart 2012, p. 91 (asserting that Muslim population worldwide has been alienated by Al-Qaeda's indiscriminate violence).

Consider the case of Al-Qaeda in Iraq (AQI). AQI was a "cohesive organization with shared personnel across 'official' names, institutional memory, embedded management practices, and permanent salaried employees."[71] Both AQI and its successor organization, the Islamic State of Iraq (ISI) took steps to enforce discipline among members.[72] For example, terrorist groups such as AQI keep copious records of the success and failure of operations, even though maintaining such records greatly enhances the risk that adversaries will obtain custody of this information and use it against these groups.[73] Groups such as AQI clearly believe that committing rules and communications to writing tightens the organization of the group, making defection or shirking more difficult. AQI required signed pledges by fighters who consented to conditions on various activities.[74] For example, AQI threatened to expel members who engaged in ordinary criminal conduct, such as looting, which would distract from the group's ideological agenda.[75] ISI instituted controls that would bring a glow to the most austere of accountants, decreeing that, "[f]or every amount paid out of [organizational] funds, the recipient is required to provide two signatures…one for receiving the money and another one to show how the money was spent."[76] Another ISI pronunciamento declared that, "[a]ll properties, small and large, will be inventoried."[77] The ISI also required operatives to upload information on flash drive, to be "sent every week to the [group's] administrator."[78] The proliferation of flash drives and memory sticks obviously ratchets up the risk that some of the information contained in these devices will end up in the hands of the group's adversaries.[79] However, ISI apparently determined that the benefits of such a structure to group discipline outweighed those risks.

ISI also kept careful track of all of its operatives, cataloguing incoming fighters, ongoing staff, and "exiting brothers."[80] These internal records distinguished between the assignments of new staff, who might be suicide bombers or perform other roles.[81] This record keeping, like the ban on looting, served strategic and ideological purposes. Operatives in Iraq were often foreign nationals who had entered Iraq because ISI's practice of violence resonated with their preconceived beliefs or habits.[82] Left to their own devices, these recruits might engage in violence

---

71 Shapiro and Siegel 2012, p. 48 n 32.
72 Ibid, p. 47.
73 Ibid.
74 Ibid, p. 48.
75 Ibid, pp. 49–50.
76 Ibid, p. 50.
77 Ibid.
78 Ibid, p. 51.
79 Ibid, p. 50.
80 Ibid, p. 51.
81 Ibid.
82 Ibid, p. 52.

"for its own sake."[83] However, indiscriminate violence, like looting, could impair the group's messaging. Record keeping also enhances the propaganda capabilities of terrorist groups. In most groups, claiming credit for an attack is as important as the attack itself.[84] Claiming credit announces to the world and to other terrorist groups that the organization has "arrived." Claiming credit for violence also enhances the group's commitment: a suicide attack, for example, signals the sincerity of the attacker's beliefs and those of the organization.

One can also view a strategy relying on suicide attacks as a decision about the costs of internal monitoring. Suppose that a terrorist leader orders a conventional (non-suicide) attack. For whatever reason, the attack fizzles. The group's leadership then has a difficult time in evaluating the causes for the attack's failure in a "noisy" environment,[85] where many factors can impede optimal execution. An attacker who survives a suboptimal attack will likely have many excuses for why the operation failed to go as planned. The leader will need to weigh those excuses before deciding on the staffing for the next attack. A suicide attack dispenses with the excuse-sifting phase, and also gives the suicide operative no exit strategy apart from outright desertion. Since that path leads to disgrace,[86] a suicide attack is often a good way of ensuring discipline. However, making sure that the operative has sufficient ties to the organization and a "track record" of violence and ideological commitment requires some degree of organization.

### *12.3.2 Terrorist Networks and Global Reach*

Al-Qaeda displays this mix of organizational forms in its relationships with affiliated groups.[87] While Al-Qaeda's core remains in Pakistan, its lack of geographic proximity to other groups is not necessarily a weakness. Network theory teaches us that physical proximity is less important when knowledge and values can be shared in other ways.[88]

Links between Al-Qaeda and regional groups are synergistic along a number of axes. The Taliban/Al-Qaeda link has been durable and effective because it combined the embedded localism of the Afghan Taliban with the extreme Islamist

[83] Ibid.

[84] Abrahms 2008.

[85] Shapiro and Siegel 2012, p. 73.

[86] This is a particularly compelling factor when groups also provide social services and cash benefits to operatives' families. Berman and Laitin 2008, p. 1955; Magouirk 2008, p. 358 (discussing Hamas's provision of social services).

[87] For more on the strengths and weaknesses of networks, see Eilstrup-Sangiovanni and Jones 2008, pp. 11–33; see also Chesney 2013, pp. 183–189 (discussing interaction and entropy in Al-Qaeda's relationships with groups in Yemen and Somalia).

[88] Borgatti and Cross 2003, pp. 432, 436, 439, 441.

network of schools and camps based in Pakistan.[89] In other situations, regional organizations seek out Al-Qaeda when state pressure has weakened the organization.[90] Allied with Al-Qaeda, groups can share information on effective strategies and learn from their mistakes.[91] Al-Qaeda has historically welcomed such overtures, since they assist the global group in extending its brand.[92] More sophisticated technology, including improvement in transportation and communications, has made it far easier to coordinate activities across regions.[93]

Experts have identified a number of characteristics of the relationship between Al-Qaeda and its regional affiliates. According to Thomas Joscelyn, a Senior Fellow at the Foundation for Defense of Democracies, affiliates often swear a loyalty oath or *bayat* to Al-Qaeda's leadership.[94] Affiliates swearing the *bayat* include Jabhat al Nusra in Syria, which is currently one of a number of groups seeking to topple the Assad regime.[95] Joscelyn, speaking to Congress in July, 2013, noted that Al-Qaeda and its affiliates "form an international terrorist network that is focused on both acquiring territory and executing terrorist attacks against the West." According to Joscelyn, "Al-Qaeda's general command guides the overall strategy pursued by the affiliates and even sometimes gets involved in specific tactical matters."

Al-Qaeda often sends key operatives into the field to assist affiliates. For example, Al-Qaeda in the Arabian Peninsula (AQAP) is run by Nasir al Wuhayshi, who was Osama bin Laden's aide-de-camp for several years before 9/11.[96] According to a Defense Department report, "Al-Qaeda in Libya: A Profile" published by LOC in August 2012, core Al-Qaeda sent senior operatives to Libya. There are also credible reports that key Al-Qaeda members have gone to Syria to aid extremist rebels' efforts to topple the Assad regime.[97] Dr. Ayman al-Zawahiri, Al-Qaeda's current leader, has ongoing contacts with extremists among the rebel forces.[98] Most recently, Zawahiri has sought to unify disparate extremist elements in Syria under the core Al-Qaeda banner,[99] although one such group, ISIS, has defied Zawahiri's attempts.[100]

---

89 Staniland 2012, p. 171.

90 Byman 2012, pp. 14–15.

91 Ibid, p. 15.

92 Ibid, p. 13.

93 Pressman 2007, p. 64.

94 Joscelyn 2013.

95 Ibid; cf. Boulos 2013.

96 Joscelyn 2013.

97 Sly 2013 (describing presence of Kuwaiti and Saudi fighters among extremist Syrian rebels).

98 Barnard and Schmitt 2013.

99 Morris and DeYoung 2013 (discussing Zawahiri's efforts to clarify territorial focus of two Al-Qaeda offshoots active in Syria).

100 Boulos and McDonnell 2014 (reporting on ISIS's assassination of Abu Khaled Suri, whom Zawahiri had supposedly designated as an envoy between ISIS and the Al Nusra Front). ISIS as a group represents the evolution of ISIS into an organization that is active predominantly in the Syrian civil war.

Other examples of this sponsor-affiliate relationship abound. For example, AQAP, which operates primarily in Yemen, began as a result of "direct orders" from Osama bin Laden to Al-Qaeda members on the ground in that region.[101] Today, AQAP is both more "professional" in its operations and more linked to the Al-Qaeda "core."[102] Indeed, the U.S. recently closed many embassies around the world because of credible reports that Dr. Zawahiri had sent a letter to AQAP leaders ordering attacks on US diplomatic facilities.[103]

The Al-Qaeda sponsor-affiliate relationship is also alive and well in North and East Africa. In North Africa, Al-Qaeda of the Islamic Maghreb (AQIM) enjoys a partnership with Al-Qaeda.[104] Dr. Zawahiri announced a "blessed union" with AQIM, leading both groups to focus on attacking French interests.[105] In Somalia, the terrorist group Al-Shabaab publicly pledged its loyalty to Al-Qaeda.[106] Operatives trained in Afghanistan camps transferred to Somalia to provide training to Shabab members.[107] The two organizations now cooperate on a host of matters, from ideological instruction to advanced tactics.[108] Zarqawi's AQI "willingly merged" with bin Laden's group, although the latter had been weakened by the erosion of its base in Afghanistan after September 11.[109] Credible evidence indicates that members of Al-Qaeda in Iraq have been assigned to "establish cells in other countries."[110]

Al-Qaeda provides training for operations elsewhere. For example, the perpetrators of the London subway suicide attacks obtained training from Al-Qaeda branches in Pakistan.[111] Indeed, Al-Qaeda provided training in Afghanistan, Pakistan, and Yemen to as many as 3,000 violent extremists from the United Kingdom, who subsequently returned there, "embedding themselves" in communities and developing plans for further attacks.[112] While discrimination and alienation from the mainstream in the United Kingdom and elsewhere may have facilitated additional recruitment, "much of the terrorist threat in the United

---

[101] Farrall 2011, p. 132; cf. Byman 2012, pp. 5–6 (discussing relationship between Al-Qaeda and AQAP); Novak 2009 (same).

[102] Byman 2012, p. 6.

[103] Miller et al. 2013.

[104] Byman 2012, p. 6.

[105] Ibid.

[106] Ibid.

[107] Ibid, p. 7.

[108] Ibid.

[109] Farrall 2011, p. 133; cf. Levitt 2004, pp. 38–39.

[110] Hoffman 2008, p. 135. The pattern of collaboration with Al-Qaeda is not monolithic; members of some groups have broken away. See Byman 2012, pp. 7–8 (discussing Egypt's Gama al-Islamiya, many of whose members renounced violence after influence of Al-Qaeda led to widely criticized 1997 attack on tourists at Luxor).

[111] Hoffman 2008, p. 138; Celso 2012, p. 35; cf. Pressman 2007, p. 65 ("[f]undraising, recruitment… and training may take place in many countries simultaneously for transnational groups").

[112] Hoffman 2008, p. 138.

Kingdom today stems from deliberate, long-standing subversion by Al-Qaeda."[113] Al-Qaeda–linked networks released videotaped martyr's wills by the attackers.[114] Other plots, such as the conspiracy to target trans-Atlantic passenger aircraft in 2006, also have ties to Al-Qaeda networks in Pakistan or Yemen.[115] Groups such as Hezbollah have global networks that attract financing and recruit new members.[116] Moreover, some terrorist groups have strong ties to transnational criminal enterprises that share the proceeds of drug trafficking, kidnapping, and prostitution.[117]

Groups partnering with Al-Qaeda buy into a distinctive operational focus. While many groups have local agendas, groups under the Al-Qaeda umbrella must agree to pursue attacks on Western interests.[118] The attacks on Western interests are a signature element of Al-Qaeda; perpetuating these attacks allows groups under the Al-Qaeda umbrella to "stay on message."[119] Moreover, Al-Qaeda insists on specific approval for attacks outside a subsidiary's regional base.[120] For example, when a Danish newspaper published caricatures of the Prophet Muhammad, Al-Qaeda asked its Iraqi branch to carry out attacks on Danish interests.[121] United States officials believe that Hezbollah operatives played a significant role in the July 2012 attack in Bulgaria on a bus carrying Israeli tourists.[122] In addition, Al-Qaeda requires certain operational modalities for attacks outside a branch's region. Al-Qaeda pushes suicide attacks and patterned attacks on particular kinds of targets, such as public transportation, government structures, and infrastructure.[123] This layer of specific operational control demonstrates Al-Qaeda's organizational contours and confirms its existence and functioning as a "united front."[124] Al-Qaeda

---

113 Ibid.

114 Celso 2012, p. 35.

115 Ibid.

116 Levitt 2004, p. 35. My point here is not that Hezbollah is affiliated with Al-Qaeda, but that Al-Qaeda may emulate Hezbollah's worldwide financial activities. Winer 2008, p. 116 (discussing Al-Qaeda's funding connections in Saudi Arabia).

117 Williams 2008, pp. 138–139 (describing involvement of LTTE in heroin trade, human trafficking, gun-running, and extortion).

118 Farrall 2011, p. 133; cf. Byman 2012, p. 11 (noting that "common consequence of the embrace of an [Al-Qaeda] label is for a group to seek out Western targets within a group's theater of operations"); Pressman 2007, p. 65 (discussing proliferation of Osama bin Laden's strategy of attacks on Western targets). David H. Petraeus, the former director of the Central Intelligence Agency, told congressional committees that AQIM and individuals in Libya with ties to Al-Qaeda may have contributed to the attack on the American diplomatic mission in Benghazi, Libya that resulted in the deaths of Ambassador J. Christopher Stevens and three other Americans. Schmitt E 2012.

119 Farrall 2011, p. 133.

120 Ibid, p. 134.

121 Ibid.

122 Kulish 2012. The European Union recently added Hezbollah's military wing to its list of terrorist organizations, based in part on this incident. Barnard 2013.

123 Farrall 2011, p. 135.

124 Ibid, p. 133.

also has structural mechanisms that ensure communication and guidance. It uses information committees that are tied to senior leadership and operational planners.[125]

A networked approach driven by an anti-Western strategic focus has many advantages for Al-Qaeda. Shared ideology lessens the likelihood of deterring the group through ordinary law enforcement or negotiation. Suicide bombers will not blink at the prospect of arrest and trial. Rather, involvement with the legal system confers another opportunity for the attackers to brand themselves as martyrs.[126] In addition, networks such as Al-Qaeda and its affiliates are far less amenable to negotiation than territory-based groups. Groups that control territory within a single state may on occasion be a party to successful negotiations, as the IRA demonstrated.[127] Such movements may gain a stake in negotiations, as they seek to ease state pressure on their territorial base.[128] In contrast, the disaggregation of territory and operations in transnational networks mean that those groups lack a "return address." Since transnational groups can readily shift their operations,[129] state pressure is not an effective deterrent. The absence of an effective general deterrent only exacerbates the risk of armed conflict from transnational groups, and makes specific deterrence or incapacitation of the group's operatives all the more imperative.[130]

### *12.3.3 Targeting Networks*

Based on this analysis of terrorist and network organization, targeting of members of an Al-Qaeda affiliate is permissible on one of two showings. First, U.S. officials could conclude that Al-Qaeda exerts a strategic influence on the targeted group. To satisfy this test, officials should have a reasonable basis for believing that Al-Qaeda guides some or all of the alleged affiliate's choice of targets. Mere subscription to an ideology is not enough—nor is financing, although financing can be one factor contributing to an inference of strategic influence. Policymakers should have a reasonable belief that Al-Qaeda has leveraged money, recruits, training, or expertise to encourage the affiliate's targeting of Western interests or moderation in the

---

[125] Ibid, p. 135.

[126] Slobogin 2003, pp. 44–46 (noting intransigence yielded by ideological commitments of members of terrorist networks); Newton 2009, p. 32 (noting that terrorist groups are often "undeterred by existing criminal law").

[127] Pressman 2007, pp. 68–70.

[128] Ibid, p. 69.

[129] Ibid, p. 70.

[130] But see Eilstrup-Sangiovanni and Jones 2008, pp. 36–37 (noting that network form can create security problems because of looser control by leadership and reliance on local operatives infiltrated by law enforcement, while acknowledging that security issues have not necessarily impaired groups' abilities to cause massive harm to civilians).

targeting of Muslim civilians. Ongoing correspondence or exchanges of information about targeting or operations should give rise to an inference that such influence is present. Al-Qaeda's role in the training of an affiliate's recruits should also have evidentiary significance.[131] No rigid hierarchy need be shown—indeed, as we have seen, the case law from transnational tribunals has often required less hierarchy than meets the eye.[132]

Even if an Al-Qaeda affiliate is not part of the same OAG, it could still be a co-belligerent of Al-Qaeda in a NIAC with the United States.[133] Under traditional conceptions of co-belligerency, a state that is an ally or coalition partner of a state engaged in an international armed conflict (IAC) will be said to be a "co-belligerent" of its ally or partner. Any state offering aid to a party to the IAC that is inconsistent with neutral status would be considered a co-belligerent. By analogy, co-belligerency should apply to non-state actors. Indeed, U.S. officials made precisely this argument in congressional hearings in May, 2013, as justification for military action against terrorist groups in locations other than Afghanistan and Pakistan.[134]

In addition, an individual who belongs to an organization located beyond the Afghanistan theater could also be directly linked to core Al-Qaeda, even if that individual also belongs to an organization whose overall Al-Qaeda ties are more attenuated. Such an individual might consult with core Al-Qaeda on targeting decisions or might receive logistical or planning support from core Al-Qaeda for particular operations. For example, the U.S. has apparently targeted members of Al-Shabaab because it has concluded that those individuals have *personal* links to Al-Qaeda,[135] even though U.S. officials have not publicly declared that Al-Shabaab *as an organization* has such ties.

Determining that a particular individual is part of Al-Qaeda's network of affiliates, part of a co-belligerent group, or is directly linked to core Al-Qaeda does not end the targeting inquiry. In addition, as the US conceded, an individual must be in

---

[131] See *Prosecutor v. Ramush Haradinaj* et al., supra n 53, para 86 (discussing importance of training).

[132] Of course, targeting suspected terrorists is only one aspect of an effective counter-terrorism strategy. Aid that reaches needy individuals and groups can help good will toward the West and counter the appeal of terrorist groups. Chakravarty 2010, pp. 325–329.

[133] The US adopted this view in congressional testimony in 2013. See US Senate Armed Services Committee 2013 (testimony of Acting Defense General Counsel Robert Taylor and Assistant Secretary of Defense Michael Sheehan); cf. ibid (testimony of Professor Geoffrey Corn) (discussing concept of co-belligerency in terms of "shared ideology, tactics and indicia of connection between high-level group leaders"); cf. Ohlin 2012, pp. 70–72 (noting that co-belligerency is concept drawn from law of neutrality, under which a state that is a party to an international armed conflict can attack another state that has not declared its neutrality in the conflict; also asserting that doctrine may not be apt analogy for situation of non-state actors in NIACs, who lack states' special status under Westphalian system and therefore may not have adequate notice that they are expected to declare their neutrality or face attack).

[134] US Senate Armed Services Committee 2013.

[135] News briefing 27 January 2014, The Chicago Tribune, 13; Preston 2014, p. 3.

a location that is part of a NIAC.[136] While some critics of U.S. policy have asserted that the US asserts the right to target individuals anywhere, U.S. policymakers have not made this sweeping claim. Indeed, John Brennan expressly disclaimed this view in his 2011 Harvard speech.[137] Moreover, the White Paper disclosed in early 2013 suggests that an area has to have attributes of an armed conflict to justify targeting individuals found there. The inquiry here should be functional. In addition to hostilities, this would include activities that are necessary for hostilities, such as planning, training, and transporting firearms, munitions, and supplies. For example, U.S. officials believe that the AQAP and Al-Shabaab cooperate in maintaining supply routes for weapons.[138] That cooperation, along with Al-Shabaab's targeting of Western interests,[139] would be enough to link Al-Shabaab with a NIAC that pits the U.S. against AQAP.

However, the model would counsel caution in targeting the violent Nigerian extremist group, Boko Haram. Loosely translated as "Western Education is a Sin," Boko Haram has for years conducted a bloody campaign of violence against Nigeria's government and its people.[140] Amnesty International has estimated that Boko Haram's attacks in early 2014 alone killed more than 700 people, many of them civilians.[141] Boko Haram's activities drew world attention after its April 2014 abduction from a rural school of two hundred girls whom the group proclaims it will sell off into the human trafficking market.[142] Nevertheless, the brutal bent of the group should not obscure its lack of fit with the model adopted in this chapter.

---

[136] US Department of Justice White Paper 2013, p. 4 (arguing that targeting is appropriate under law of armed conflict in location where a party to an armed conflict "plans and executes operations from a base" and thus projects force to another location, even if actual hostilities at base site are not "intense and protracted"). Even in the absence of a NIAC, a state has the right to use self-defense to address imminent threats. Under customary international law, imminence has been defined narrowly, to encompass only threats that required an immediate response, with no "moment for deliberation." Webster 1841. Recently, distinguished international lawyers and scholars have suggested that the special challenges posed by violent non-state actors who operate clandestinely may require a broadening of the definition of imminence. Koh 2014. This broadening might entail permitting the use of force at the last "window of opportunity" to stop a planned attack. Bethlehem 2012; Schmitt 2013, pp. 89–90; Chesney 2014, pp. 320–323. One can also construe US policy-makers as arguing that even absent imminence, an organization that poses a "continuing threat" can be targeted outside of the armed conflict paradigm. Ibid. That argument is more sweeping than the approach outlined in this Article. A sweeping claim of authority to use lethal force beyond traditional imminence or the scope of armed conflict raises substantial doctrinal problems and poses tensions with international human rights law.

[137] Brennan 2011.

[138] Klaidman 2012, pp. 249–251 (reporting on information provided by Ahmed Warsame, who described himself as a "conduit" between AQAp and Al-Shabaab).

[139] Hubbard 2014 (noting Al-Shabaab's deadly attack on mall in Nairobi, Kenya frequented by Westerners).

[140] Sergie 2014.

[141] Amnesty International 2014, p. 10.

[142] Abubakar and Levs 2014.

Formed by Mohammed Yusuf in Borno, Nigeria in 2002, Boko Haram combines an Islamist focus that is reminiscent of Al-Qaeda with recruitment tactics that tap into northern Nigerian resentment of official corruption and poor economic prospects.[143] Boko Haram originally sought to implement a strict form of sharia law in its area of operations.[144] It had no firm intention of overthrowing the Nigerian government or embracing Al-Qaeda's global agenda. However, after a massive and allegedly brutal crackdown on Boko Haram by the Nigerian government in 2009 that resulted in the death of its leader, the group reoriented itself.[145] Since then, it has stated its intention to topple the Nigerian government and erase all forms of Western influence.[146] To implement more local aspects of its goals, the organization has conducted an increasing number of brutal attacks on government centers, prisons, schools, and towns through both suicide bombings and indiscriminate slaughter.

Given the increasing severity and method of attacks, many experts believe that the group is being counseled and inspired by AQIM and Al-Shabaab.[147] In addition to the growing number of statements from the group praising Al-Qaeda and incorporating the Al-Qaeda philosophy, the 2011 bombing of a U.N. facility in Nigeria indicates that the group may be looking to actively involve itself in Al-Qaeda's global jihad.[148] Evidence about sharing resources such as weaponry and expertise, having its members trained in Somalia, and consistent communications between AQIM and Al-Shabaab members has U.S. officials concerned about another expansion of Al-Qaeda into the lawless regions of Nigeria.[149] These connections and coordination are said to have helped transform Boko Haram from the "machete-wielding mob" it once was into an organization that has matched the capabilities of other Al-Qaeda affiliates such as Al-Shabaab and AQIM.[150]

While these factors may suggest that Boko Haram can be targeted by the U.S., that is not the end of the story. The group has thus far concentrated on attacks within Nigeria directed at Nigerians.[151] Because Boko Haram's affinity for Al-Qaeda seems limited to generalized ideological tenets and it has not clearly pivoted to targeting U.S. interests, U.S. officials cannot legally classify Boko Haram as participating in the United States' NIAC with Al-Qaeda. Therefore, members of Boko Haram would not be targetable by the U.S. under international law, unless some separate basis for targeting existed, such as the Nigerian government's consenting to American help in Nigeria's own NIAC with Boko Haram.

143 Maiangwa et al. 2012, pp. 44–47, 53.

144 Ibid, p. 44.

145 Ibid, pp. 47–48.

146 Karimi and Carter 2014.

147 Zenn 2014.

148 Benson 2011.

149 Ibid.

150 Zenn 2014.

151 Maiangwa et al. 2012, p. 49.

## 12.4 Conclusion

One need not read the modern jurisprudence defining an OAG as being limited to groups with headquarters, fully functioning logistics, or ironclad discipline. While the ICTY decisions include language setting out these criteria, the facts of the cases are actually far more ambiguous. In cases such as *Limaj*, the ICTY found organization when traditional evidence was equivocal. The ICTY jurisprudence and the analysis of many commentators point toward a more pragmatic approach.

That said, terrorist organizations often reveal surprisingly strong elements of organization. Like other entities, terrorist groups devise mechanisms to deal with the problem of agency costs. They monitor, assess, and document performance of their personnel, and make appropriate changes when needed. These measures exist even when they appear to endanger the groups' security.

The versatile approach to organization that marks terrorist groups within a state also holds true for transnational networks such as Al-Qaeda. Al-Qaeda operates in a synergistic fashion with regional groups. Many groups have received training from Al-Qaeda's core feeder sources of schools and camps, and have sworn allegiance to Al-Qaeda to enhance their appeal and access to resources. Direct operational control is rarely present. However, strategic influence, including a focus on targeting Western interests, is common. Indeed, Dr. Ayman Zawahiri, Al-Qaeda's current leader, has recently displayed his influence over a range of groups, including AQAP and the Syrian Nusra Front, although Zawahiri has apparently terminated or indefinitely suspended Al-Qaeda's dealings with ISIS.

When such strategic influence can be shown, the definition of OAG is sufficiently flexible to permit targeting across borders. The venerable doctrine of co-belligerency provides additional authority for targeting, as long as the location where a strike takes place possesses some indicia of an armed conflict, such as planning, training, or logistics. In addition, U.S. officials could target individuals within alleged Al-Qaeda affiliates such as Al-Shabaab, if those individuals have operational, logistical, or planning ties to Al-Qaeda. This would be true even if U.S. officials lacked sufficient evidence to conclude that Al-Shabaab or another group to which an individual belonged had exhibited overall ties to Al-Qaeda. However, the approach outlined here is not infinitely elastic. It would limit targeting of groups such as ISIS, which has resisted Al-Qaeda guidance, or Nigeria's Boko Haram, which lacks sufficiently concrete ties with Al-Qaeda or a demonstrable intent to harm the U.S. To target these groups, U.S. officials would need an independent legal basis, such as Nigeria's consent in the case of Boko Haram. This approach imposes some geographic and functional limits, while denying the initiative to violent non-state actors who are part of Al-Qaeda's network.

## References

Abrahms M (2008) What terrorists really want: terrorist motives and counterterrorism strategy. Int Secur 32(4):78–105

Abubakar A, Levs J (2014) 'I will sell them,' Boko Haram leader says of kidnapped Nigerian girls. www.cnn.com/2014/05/05/world/africa/nigeria-abducted-girls/index.html?hpt=hp_t1. Accessed 28 May 2014

Amnesty International (2014) Nigeria: more than 1,500 killed in armed conflict in North-Eastern Africa in early 2014. http://www.amnesty.org/en/library/asset/AFR44/004/2014/en/543f7ac9-6889-4f02-bf5a-d73832e04229/afr440042014en.pdf. Accessed 28 May 2014

Anderson K (2012) Efficiency in bello and ad bellum: making the use of force too easy? In: Finkelstein C, Ohlin J, Altman A (eds) Targeted killings: law and morality in an asymmetrical world. Oxford University Press, Oxford, pp 374–399

Barnard A (25 July 2013) Lebanon: Hezbollah's leader rails against terrorist designation. New York Times, A11

Barnard A, Schmitt E (2013) Militants flood havens in Syria, posing a threat. New York Times, A1

Bellinger J, Padmanabhan V (2011) Detention operations in contemporary conflicts: four challenges for the Geneva conventions and other existing law. Am J Int Law 105(1):201–243

Benson P (2011) Al Qaeda links to Nigerian terror group. http://security.blogs.cnn.com/2011/09/23/al-qaeda-links-to-nigerian-terror-group. Accessed 26 Sept 2014

Bergal C (2011) The Mexican drug war: the case for a non-international armed conflict classification. Fordham Int Law J 34(4):1042–1088

Berman E, Laitin D (2008) Religion, terrorism, and public goods: testing the club model. www.nber.org/papers/w13725. Accessed 26 May 2014

Bethlehem D (2012) Self-defense against an imminent or actual armed attack by non-state actors. Am J Int Law 106(4):769–777

Blank L, Corn G (2013) Losing the forest for the trees: Syria, law, and the pragmatics of conflict recognition. Vanderbilt J Trans Law 46(3):693–746

Blum G (2010) The dispensable lives of soldiers. J Legal Anal 2:115–170

Borgatti S, Cross R (2003) A relational view of information seeking and learning in social networks. Manag Sci 49:432–445

Boulos N (2013) Rebels confirm Al-Qaeda link; Al Nusra front's Syrian leader also acknowledges ties to a militant Iraqi group. Los Angeles Times, A3

Boulos N, McDonnell P (2014) Syrian rebel leader killed. Los Angeles Times, A3

Brennan J (2011) Strengthening our security by adhering to our values and laws. www.whitehouse.gov/the-press-office/2011/09/16/remarks-john-o-brennan-strengthening-our-security-adhering-our-values-an. Accessed 26 May 2014

Byman D (2012) Breaking the bonds between Al-Qa'ida and its affiliate organizations. www.brookings.edu/~/media/research/files/papers/2012/7/alqaida%20terrorism%20byman/alqaida%20terrorism%20byman.pdf. Accessed 26 May 2014

Byman D, Waxman M (2000) Kosovo and the great air power debate. Int Secur 24(4):5–38

Celso A (2012) Al-Qaeda's post-9/11 organizational strategy: the role of Islamist regional affiliates. Mediterr Q 23(2):30–41

Chakravarty A (2010) Feeding humanity, starving terror: the utility of aid in a comprehensive antiterrorism financing strategy. Western New England Law Rev 32(2):295–338

Chang K (2011) Enemy status and military detention in the war against Al-Qaeda. Texas Int Law J 47(1):1–73

Chellaney B (2001–2002) Fighting terrorism in southern Asia: the lessons of history. Int Secur 26 (3):94–116

Chenoweth E, Miller N, McClellan E (2009) What makes terrorists tick? Int Secur 33(4):180–202

Chesney R (2011) Who may be killed? Anwar Al-Awlaki as a case study in the international legal regulation of lethal force. Yearbook Int Humanit Law 13:3–60

Chesney R (2013) Beyond the battlefield, beyond Al-Qaeda: the destabilizing legal architecture of counterterrorism. Mich Law Rev 112(2):163–224

Chesney R (2014) Postwar. Harvard Natl Secur J 5(1):305–334

Corn G (2011) Extraterritorial law enforcement or transnational counterterrorist operations: the stakes of two models. In: Banks W (ed) New battlefields, old laws: critical debates on asymmetric warfare. Columbia University Press, New York, pp 23–44

Corn G, Jensen E (2009) Transnational armed conflict: a "principled" approach to the regulation of counter-terror combat operations. Israel Law Rev 42(1):46–79

Criddle E (2012) Proportionality in counterinsurgency: a relational theory. Notre Dame Law Rev 87(3):1073–1112

Daskal J (2013) The geography of the battlefield: a framework for detention and targeting outside the "hot" conflict zone. Univ Pennsylvania Law Rev 161(5):1165–1234

Deeks A (2012) "Unwilling or unable": toward a normative framework for extraterritorial self-defense. Virginia J Int Law 52(3):483–548

Dinstein Y (2005) War, aggression and self-defence, 4th edn. Cambridge University Press, Cambridge

Eilstrup-Sangiovanni M, Jones C (2008) Assessing the dangers of Illicit networks: why Al-Qaida may be less threatening than many think. Int Secur 33(2):7–44

Farrall L (2011) How Al-Qaeda works: what the organization's subsidiaries say about its strength. Foreign Aff 90:128–138

Geiß R (2009) Armed violence in fragile states: low-intensity conflicts, spillover conflicts, and sporadic law enforcement operations by third parties. Int Rev Red Cross 91(873):127–142

Gilson R, Mnookin R (1994) Disputing through agents, cooperation and conflict between lawyers in litigation. Columbia Law Rev 94(2):509–566

Glennon M (2010) The fog of law: pragmatism, security, and international law. Woodrow Wilson Center Press, Washington

Goldsmith J (2012) Power and constraint: the accountable presidency after 9/11. Norton and Company, New York

Hakimi M (2012) A functional approach to targeting and detention. Mich Law Rev 110 (8):1365–1420

Hoffman B (1998) Inside terrorism. Columbia University Press, New York

Hoffman B (2008) The myth of grass roots terrorism. Foreign Aff 87(3):133–138

Hubbard B (2014) The franchising of Al-Qaeda. New York Times, Sunday Review, 4

Ingber R (2011) Untangling belligerency from neutrality in the conflict with Al-Qaeda. Texas Int Law J 47:75–114

International Committee of the Red Cross (2008) How is the term "armed conflict" defined in international humanitarian law? www.icrc.org/eng/assets/files/other/opinion-paper-armed-conflict.pdf. Accessed 26 May 2014

International Committee of the Red Cross (2009) Interpretive guidance on the notion of direct participation in hostilities under international humanitarian law. www.aco.nato.int/resources/20/Legal%20Conference/ICRC_002_0990.pdf. Accessed 26 May 2014

International Committee of the Red Cross (2011) International humanitarian law and the challenges of contemporary armed conflicts. www.icrc.org/eng/assets/files/red-cross-crescent-movement/31st-international-conference/31-int-conference-ihl-challenges-report-11-5-1-2-en.pdf. Accessed 26 May 2014

International Law Association (2010) Final report on the meaning of armed conflict in International Law

Joscelyn T (2013) Testimony: Al-Qaeda future challenges. United States House of Representatives, Foreign Affairs Committee, subcommittee on terrorism, nonproliferation, and trade. Congressional Quarterly-Roll Call

Karimi F, Carter C (2014) Boko Haram: a bloody insurgency, a growing challenge. www.cnn.com/2014/04/17/world/africa/boko-haram-explainer/. Accessed 28 May 2014

Klaidman D (2012) Kill or capture: the war on terror and the soul of the Obama presidency. Houghton Mifflin Harcourt, Boston

Koh H (2010) The Obama administration and International Law. www.state.gov/s/l/releases/remarks/139119.htm. Accessed 26 May 2014

Koh H (2014) Testimony: hearing of the senate foreign relations committee, authorization for the use of military force after Iraq and Afghanistan. Federal News Service

Kulish N (2012) Despite U.S. fear Hezbollah moves openly in Europe. New York Times, A1

Kydd A, Walter B (2006) The strategies of terrorism. Int Secur 31(1):49–79

Levitt M (2004) Untangling the terror web: identifying and counteracting the phenomenon of crossover between terrorist groups. Sch Adv Int Stud Rev 24(1):33–48

Lewis M (2012) Drones and the boundaries of the Battlefield. Texas Int Law J 47(2):293–314

Luban D (2013) Military necessity and the cultures of military law. Leiden J Int Law 26 (2):315–349

Lubell N, Derejko N (2013) A global battlefield? Drones and the geographic scope of armed conflict. J Int Crim Justice 11(1):65–88

Magouirk J (2008) The Nefarious helping hand: anti-corruption campaigns, social services provisions, and terrorism. Terrorism Political Violence 20(3):356–375

Maiangwa B, Uzodike U, Whetho A, Onapajo H (2012) "Baptism by Fire": Boko Haram and the reign of terror in Nigeria. Africa Today 59(2):40–57

Margulies P (2012a) Advising terrorism: material support, safe harbors, and freedom of speech. Hastings Law J 63(2):455–519

Margulies P (2012b) The fog of war reform: change and structure in the law of armed conflict after September 11. Marquette Law Rev 95(4):1417–1489

Margulies P (2013) Valor's vices: against a state duty to risk forces in armed conflict. In: Banks W (ed) Counterinsurgency law: new directions in asymmetric warfare. Oxford University Press, Oxford, pp 87–107

Martin C (2012) Going medieval: targeted killing, self-defense and the jus ad bellum regime. In: Finkelstein C, Ohlin JD, Altman A (eds) Targeted killings: law and morality in an asymmetrical world, Oxford University Press, Oxford, pp 223–252

McNeal G (2012) Are targeted killings unlawful: a case study in empirical claims without empirical evidence. In: Finkelstein C, Ohlin J, Altman A (eds) Targeted killings: law and morality in an asymmetrical world. Oxford University Press, Oxford, pp 326–346

Miller G, Gearan A, Raghavan S (2013) U.S. authorized series of drone strikes in Yemen. Washington Post, A1

Morris L, DeYoung K (2013) Rebel leader is killed in Syria. Washington Post, A1

Mueller J, Stewart M (2012) The terrorism delusion: America's overwrought response to September 11. Int Secur 37(1):81–110

Newton M (2009) Exceptional engagement: protocol I and a world united against terrorism. Texas Int Law J 45(2):323–375

Novak J (2009) Arabian peninsula Al-Qaeda groups merge. www.longwarjournal.org/archives/2009/01/arabian_peninsula_al.php. Accessed 26 May 2014

O'Connell M (2012) Unlawful killing with combat drones: a case study of Pakistan, 2004-2009. In: Bronitt S, Gani M, Hufnagel S (eds) Shooting to kill: socio-legal perspectives on the use of lethal force, Oxford University Press, Oxford, pp 263–292

Ohlin J (2012) Targeting co-belligerents. In: Finkelstein C, Ohlin J, Altman A (eds) Targeted killings: law and morality in an asymmetrical world. Oxford University Press, Oxford, pp 60–89

Ohlin J (2013) The duty to capture. Minnesota Law Rev 97(4):1268–1342

Paulus A, Vashakmadze M (2009) Asymmetrical war and the notion of armed conflict—a tentative conceptualization. Int Rev Red Cross 91(873):95–125

Paust J (2010) Self-defense targetings of non-state actors and permissibility of U.S. use of drones in Pakistan. J Trans Law Policy 19(2):237–280

Pejic J (2011) The protective scope of common article 3: more than meets the eye. Int Rev Red Cross 93(881):189–226

Pressman J (2007) Rethinking transnational counterterrorism: beyond a national framework. Washington Q 30(4):63–73

Preston S (2014) The framework under U.S. law for current military operations. United States Senate Committee on Foreign Relations. www.foreign.senate.gov/imo/media/doc/Preston_Testimony.pdf. Accessed 28 May 2014
Putnam R (1988) Diplomacy and domestic politics: the logic of two-level games International Organizations, 42(3):427–460
Roese N (2004) Twisted pair: counterfactual thinking and the hindsight bias. In: Koehler D, Harvey N (eds) Blackwell handbook of judgment and decision making. Blackwell Publishing, Malden, pp 258–273
Rona G (2012) US targeted killing policy unjustified. www.jurist.org/hotline/2012/02/gabor-rona-targeted-killing.php. Accessed 26 May 2014
Sageman M (2008) Leaderless Jihad: terror networks in the twenty-first Century. University of Pennsylvania Press, Philadelphia
Sawyer R, Foster M (2008) The resurgent and persistent threat of Al-Qaeda. Ann Am Acad Polit Soc Sci 618:197–211
Scheppele K (2010) The international standardization of national security law. J Nat Secur Law Policy 437–453
Schmitt E (2012) Petraeus says U.S. tried to avoid tipping off terrorists after Libya attack. New York Times, A10
Schmitt M (2010) Deconstructing direct participation in hostilities: the constitutive elements. New York Univ J Int Law Politics 42(3):697–739
Schmitt M (2011) The status of opposition fighters in a Non-international armed conflict International Law studies 88:119–144
Schmitt M (2012) Unmanned combat aircraft systems and International Humanitarian Law: simplifying the oft benighted debate. Boston Univ Int Law J 30(2):595–619
Schmitt M (2013) Extraterritorial lethal targeting: deconstructing the logic of International Law. Columbia J Trans Law 52(1):77–112
Sergie M (2014) Boko Haram. www.cfr.org/nigeria/boko-haram/p25739. Accessed 28 May 2014
Setty S (2010) Comparative perspectives on specialized trials for terrorism. Maine Law Rev 63 (1):131–174
Shapiro J, Siegel D (2012) Moral hazard, discipline, and the management of terrorist organizations. World Polit 64(1):39–78
Sinno A (2011) Armed groups' organizational structure and their strategic options. Int Rev Red Cross 93(882):311–332
Sivakumaran S (2012) Command responsibility in irregular groups. J Int Crim Just 10 (5):1129–1150
Slobogin C (2003) A jurisprudence of dangerousness. Northwest Univ Law Rev 98(1):1–62
Sly L (2013) Al-Qaeda's Iraq affiliate expands presence in Syria. Washington Post, A1
Staniland P (2012) Organizing insurgency: networks, resources, and rebellion in South Asia. Int Secur 37(1):142–177
Townsend F (2006) 10 Ways to avoid the next 9/11: the President's plan. New York Times, Section 4, 13
UN Human Rights Council (2012) Report of the independent International Commission of Inquiry on the Syrian Arab Republic, 2012. UN Doc. A/HRC/21/50
UN Human Rights Council and Alston P (2010) Report of the special rapporteur on extrajudicial, summary or arbitrary executions: study on targeted killings, 2010. UN Doc. A/HRC/14/24/Add.6
US Department of Justice White Paper (2013) Lawfulness of a lethal operation directed against a U.S. citizen who is a senior operational leader of Al-Qa'ida or an associated force. http://msnbcmedia.msn.com/i/msnbc/sections/news/020413_DOJ_White_Paper.pdf. Accessed 28 May 2014
US Senate Armed Services Committee (2013) The law of armed conflict, the use of military force, and the 2001 authorization for use of military force. Federal News Service
Walzer M (1977) Just and unjust wars: a moral argument with historical illustrations. Basic Books, New York

Watkin K (2010) Opportunity lost: organized armed groups and the ICRC "Direct participation in hostilities" interpretive guidance. New York University J Int Law Polit 42(3):641 (et seq)

Watkin K (2011) "Small wars": the legal challenges. Int Law Stud 88:3–12

Waxman M (2010) The structure of terrorism threats and the laws of war. Duke Comp Int Law 20 (3):429–455

Webster D (1841) Letter to Henry Fox, British minister in Washington. http://avalon.law.yale.edu/19th_century/br-1842d.asp#web1. Accessed 28 May 2014

Williams P (2008) Terrorist financing and organized crime: nexus, appropriation, or transformation? In: Biersteker T, Eckert S (eds) Countering the financing of terrorism. Routledge, Abingdon, pp 126–149

Winer J (2008) Countering terrorist finance: a work, mostly in progress. Ann Am Acad Polit Soc Sci 618:112–132

Zawacki B (2013) Politically inconvenient, legally correct: a non-international armed conflict in southern Thailand. J Conflict Secur Law 18(1):151–179

Zenn J (2014) Boko Haram's international connections. www.ctc.usma.edu/posts/boko-harams-international-connections. Accessed 28 May 2014

# Table of Cases[1]

## International

### Ad Hoc Arbitrations



### ECOWAS Court of Justice



### EULEX Kosovo



### European Court of Human Rights



[1] The table of Cases was compiled by Mrs C.C. Diepeveen, Middelburg, The Netherlands, cdiep@zeelandnet.nl



T.D. Gill et al. (eds.), *Yearbook of International Humanitarian Law 2013*,
Yearbook of International Humanitarian Law 16, DOI 10.1007/978-94-6265-038-1

### International Criminal Tribunal for Rwanda



### Permanent Court of International Justice

*Advisory Opinions*



### Special Court for Sierra Leone



### Special Tribunal for Lebanon



### United Nations Human Rights Committee



## National

### Australia

*High Court*



### Bangladesh

*Supreme Court*



*International Crimes Tribunal*



### Bosnia and Herzegovina

*War Crimes Section of Court of Bosnia and Herzegovina*

# Index[2]



[2] The Index was compiled by Mrs C.C. Diepeveen, Middelburg, The Netherlands, cdiep@zeelandnet.nl



T.D. Gill et al. (eds.), *Yearbook of International Humanitarian Law 2013*,
Yearbook of International Humanitarian Law 16, DOI 10.1007/978-94-6265-038-1

## C

**D**

**J**

The manufacturer's authorised representative in the EU is Springer Nature Customer Service Centre GmbH, Europaplatz 3, 69115 Heidelberg, Germany. If you have any concerns regarding our products, please contact ProductSafety@springernature.com

Printed and bound by CPI Group (UK) Ltd, Croydon, CR0 4YY

30/09/2026

02225447-0013